"[*Grief of My Heart*] is as much a memoir as it is a painful attempt to try to keep the memory of the human rights violations in Chechnya from being buried under shifts in geopolitical realities . . . The book provides a quick primer in the history of Russian-Chechen tensions dating back to the times of Ivan the Terrible and Peter the Great."

—**Sandip Roy,** *San Francisco Chronicle*

"Revealing and fascinating . . . Exceptional . . . The description of Baiev's departure to New York from the Moscow airport, where he was stopped, interrogated, and eventually allowed to board the plane as the doors were being closed, is so suspenseful . . . Baiev's description of the nature of medical and surgical practices in the United States as compared with what he experienced back home is itself a reason to read the book . . . This is an important testimony that belongs in the annals of the history of medicine."

—**Mark Field, Ph.D,** *New England Journal of Medicine*

"Baiev's account of the first two years of the second Chechen conflict . . . makes for some of the most extraordinary passages about war ever written."

—**Thomas de Waal, TheMoscowTimes.com**

"Occasionally a book speaks so directly to our times that it transcends the limitations of the written word. Such a book is [*Grief of My Heart*], a memoir by Chechen doctor Khassan Baiev. A riveting testimony about the savagery of war and how ordinary people do and do not survive it, this book ought to be required reading for all government officials and the citizens who elect them . . . In spite of its tragic subject matter, [*Grief of My Heart*] also offers a glimmer of hope and leaves the reader with a sense of awe at the courage and selflessness of ordinary people under extraordinary circumstances."

—**Pat MacEnulty,** *South Florida Sun-Sentinel*

"A real-life Hawkeye Pierce . . . [Khassan Baiev] has humanized the Chechens, whom others have portrayed as terrorists. Russian president Vladimir Putin has tried to equate Russia's fight against the Chechens with the U.S. battle against al-Qaida. Those who read this stirring memoir will be hard-pressed to see the situation so simply."

—*~~d~~* **review**

"[*Grief of My Heart*] gives Amer~~~~ ~~~~o consider as our government's quest~~~~ ~~~~rains it from condemning atrocities c~~~~ ~~~~ist, one marvels at how a man can con~~~~ ~~~~ath and persevere under the most perverse conditions . . . ~~~~ ~~~~ind the headlines—an eye-opener."

—*Booklist,* **starred review**

more . . .

to the students of Mass Bay.

Baiev 11.14.05.

Grief of My Heart

Memoirs of a Chechen Surgeon

Khassan Baiev

WITH RUTH AND NICHOLAS DANILOFF

WALKER & COMPANY   NEW YORK

Originally published as *The Oath: A Surgeon Under Fire*
in the United States of America in 2003 by
Walker Publishing Company, Inc.
First paperback edition published in 2005
Distributed to the trade by Holtzbrinck Publishers

For information about permission to reproduce selections from this book,
write to Permissions, Walker & Company, 435 Hudson Street,
New York, New York 10014

Library of Congress Cataloging-in-Publication Data available upon request

ISBN 0-8027-7709-0 (paperback)
ISBN-13 978-8027-7709-6

Book design by Chris Welch
Book composition by Coghill Composition Company

Visit Walker & Company's Web site at www.walkerbooks.com

Printed in the United States of America

2   4   6   8   10   9   7   5   3   1

Dedication

For my parents—Dada and Nana—who lived through the repressions of 1937, the Deportation of 1944, the Second World War, and now the first and second Chechen wars.

For my nephew Adam Tepsurkaev, a journalist, murdered in cold blood for revealing the evils of war through his video reports to the British news agency Reuters.

For those doctors who lost their lives bringing help to others, among them: Ibragim Taramov, Aslanbek Shidaev, Amadi Ismailov, Israil Ukaev, Musa Tazurkaev, Rashid Dadaev, Said Umarov, Satsita Gairbekova, Sultan Ibragimov, Ruslan Baimurzaev, Mairbek Tovsultanov, Lecha Zagalaev, Albert Dakaev, Lom-Ali Rasuev, Nasruddin Ekubov, Anatolii Zdor, Arbi Edelgiriyev, and Lolita Aidomirova.

For the nurses who perished along with them: Marina Khamitova, Natalya Rifaryeva, Enisa Asieva, Lina Abubakarova, Toita Kutaeva, Madina Dadaeva, and Shovda Zagalaeva.

And for the members of the International Committee of the Red Cross who were murdered by persons unknown at Noviye Atagi in 1996: head nurse Fernanda Calado (Spain), nurse Gunnhild Mylebust (Norway), nurse Ingebjorg Foss (Norway), nurse Sheryl Thayer (New Zealand), construction technician Johan Joost Elderbout (Netherlands), and medical administrator Nancy Malloy (Canada).

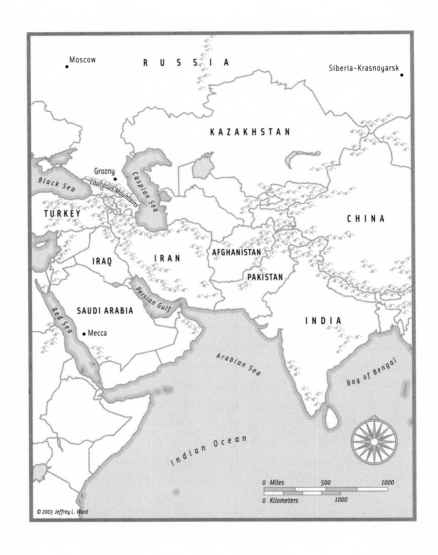

Moscow

R U S S I A

Siberia-Krasnoyarsk

KAZAKHSTAN

Grozny

Black Sea

Caucasus Mountains

Caspian Sea

CHINA

TURKEY

IRAQ

IRAN

AFGHANISTAN

PAKISTAN

Persian Gulf

Red Sea

SAUDI ARABIA

Mecca

INDIA

Arabian Sea

Bay of Bengal

Indian Ocean

0 Miles   500   1000

0 Kilometers   1000

© 2003 Jeffrey L. Ward

Contents

Acknowledgments   ix

Preface   xiii

Prologue   xv

Introduction   1

Part 1   Before the War

Chapter 1   Dada and Nana   11

Chapter 2   Ancestors   28

Chapter 3   Becoming a Doctor   43

Chapter 4   Finding a Wife   67

Chapter 5   The Eve of the First War   89

Part 2   The First War

Chapter 6   The Hospital Opens   105

Chapter 7   Heaven and Hell   117

Chapter 8   Young Soldiers   130

Chapter 9   Raduyev and Sasha   142

Chapter 10   Saving Alkhan Kala   160

Chapter 11   Escape from Grozny   167

Part 3   A Fragile Peace

Chapter 12   Rebuilding   187

Chapter 13   An Eclipse of the Soul   201

Chapter 14   Mecca   211

Chapter 15   Rising Crime   223

Part 4   The Second War

Chapter 16   War Again   241

Chapter 17   Reaching a Climax   256

Chapter 18   Double Jeopardy   277

Chapter 19   Descent into Hell   289

Part 5   Refuge in America

Chapter 20   My Escape   313

Chapter 21   Hard Choices   327

Chapter 22   Heartbreak   337

Chapter 23   Hope and Despair   343

Epilogue   359

Appendix: Where Are They Now?   363

Index   367

Acknowledgments

Many people in many places helped me survive my country's tragedy. If I could, I would like to thank them all by name because the smallest gesture of goodwill is a gift of generosity my family and I shall never forget. In writing these acknowledgments, I fear that I will forget to mention someone, and if this happens, I hope those who have been inadvertently overlooked will forgive me.

I want to express my gratitude to those who assisted my family's resettlement and to those who helped me bear witness to a conflagration that I hope no one else will ever live through. Let me start with those good people in New York City who helped me find sanctuary in the United States: Rachel Denber, Peter Bouckaert, Veronica Matushaj, and their colleagues at Human Rights Watch; my friends Viktor Tatarkin and Svetlana Moskvitina; Ed Kline; and Muhammad Rahman and Majida Hilmi.

In New Jersey: Hamid Ozbek-Umarov, his daughter, Handan, and their family; Musa Shamsadov; Maret Tsarnaeva; Ruslan Tsarni; Hamid Batash; Salavdi Gudaev; and Kemal and Aynur Catto.

In Washington, D.C.: Larry Ellis and Chris Reichel; George and Tanya Renko; Dr. James C. Cobey; Dr. Judy B. Okawa; Dr. Paul Levine; Maureen Greenwood and her colleagues at Amnesty International; Irene Lasota of the Institute for Democracy in Eastern Europe; Dr. Zbigniew Brzezinski, Glen Howard, and their colleagues at the American Committee for Peace in Chechnya; Senator Paul Sarbanes and the late Senator Paul Wellstone; Steven H. Schulman and Wendy Atrokhov of the law firm of Latham and Watkins; Len Rubenstein, executive director of Physicians for Human Rights; Stephanie Robinson of the Lawyers Committee for Human Rights; Fiona Hill of the Eurasia Foundation; Barbara Haig of the National Endowment for Democracy; and Sibila and Victor Ananev and Inna Dubinskaya of the Voice of America.

In Boston and Massachusetts: Suzanne Serkin, Douglas Ford, and their colleagues at the Boston office of Physicians for Human Rights; Joshua Rubenstein of Amnesty International; Liuba Vartikovsky and her husband, Win; Bill Stevens, Dale Swett, Vittorio Recupero, Harold Oshima, and Clark Edson of the Tohoku Judo Club of Somerville; Olympic athlete Jimmy Pedro; Allen and Pam Berger; Tanya and Andrei Gorlin; Gwendolyn Whittaker; Galina Khatutsky; Miranda Daniloff Mancusi and Peter Mancusi; Natividad "Natty" Morrissey; former Governor Michael Dukakis; Anwar H. Kazmi of DAA Enterprises; Shahin M. Shahin of Alpha Auto Sales; Mary Giles of the Davis Center for Russian Studies; the teachers of the Needham Elementary School; Sue Morgan and Lauren Lele of Newton-Wellesley Hospital; Yael Cohn and Robert Kennedy of the Needham Housing Authority; Dr. Natasha Kandror, Dr. Karina Tsatourian, and Dr. Alla Tandetnik; Ksenya and Gregory Khinchuk of Boston University; English teachers Terri Horton and Maureen Davidson; Dmitrii and Lena Zaitsev, Usman Dombaev, and Howard and Mameve Medwed; and Stephen Welch and Evelyn and Mac Musser of Nantucket.

In Portland: Ruslan Yusupov and Ramzan Magomedov.

In Los Angeles: Pam Bruns; actor Noah Wyle and his wife, Tracy; Jane Olson of Landmine Survivors Network; Victoria Riskin and David Rintels; Oleg Takhtarov and his wife, Masha; and Sultan Zubaraev.

In Vermont: Charlene and Peter Huyler; Dick Andrews and his wife, Stephanie; Dr. John Sinclair and his wife, Nancy; Pam and Ed LeFay; Jill Pond; Caleb Daniloff and his wife, Chris Vielmetti; Terry and Tom Wilhelm; Bob Tucker; the teachers at the Andover-Chester Elementary School; and Carole Gilbert, Director of Green Mountain Union High School.

In Florida: Khalid Khamza and his wife, Naveen Yassen; Abdulalim Abdurahman; Mirsad and Lenka Krijestorac; The Islamic Center of Boca Raton; and the Islamic community of south Florida.

For their help in Moscow: Arbi Abubakarov; Anne Nivat, correspondent for the French newspaper *Liberation*; Musa Muradov, editor of *Groznenskii Rabochii*; Dima Belovetsky, correspondent for *Literaturnaya Gazeta*; Tatiana Batinyeva of *Izvestiya*; Vasilii Shchurov of *Trud*; Karina Melikyan of Reuters; and General Director Dr. Vladimir Visarionov and Dr. Ilya Frishberg of the Institute of Plastic Surgery and Cosmetology.

In Krasnoyarsk: Rector Viktor Prokhorenkov of the Medical Institute; Dr. Albert Karger, Dr. Anatoly Levinets, Dr. Sergei Vladimtsev, Dr. Boris Igumnov, Dr. Yuri Vinnik, and Dr. Kireyak Mukhsiyev; senior coach Alexei Krivkov; and Svetlana Lechieva and Dr. Svetlana Prakhina.

In Chechnya: Issa Muradov, Muslim Zhantaev, Khamzat Yesaev, Ramzan Tsakaev; and my teachers Anatoliy Barishev, Ludmilla Zhdanova, and Khava Khuseinova.

In Jedda: Zakiya, Salakh, and Raghad Mutabbakani.

My thanks also go to the following in England: Helen Gummer and Cassandra Campbell of Simon and Schuster; literary agent Andrew Nurnberg; Paul and Alex Wheeler; Sir Adam Roberts and his wife, Prinky; and Bulat Betalgiry.

In the United States: George Gibson, president and publisher of Walker & Company, and his wife, Linda; editor Jackie Johnson and her colleagues at Walker; Nina Kovalenko; Dr. Jerry Draven; Dr. Charles and Polly Keck; literary agents Ike Williams and Brettne Bloom; and Ruth and Nicholas Daniloff.

Preface

I WROTE *Grief of My Heart* for two reasons. First, I wanted the world to know that war is a hellish thing which victimizes the innocent. In war there are no winners. Second, and equally important, I wanted to introduce my readers to the Chechen people.

During the second war with Russia, when there was a lull in the bombing or I found shelter in the cellar against a bombardment, I wrote a diary of everything that happened that day, often hour by hour. I wrote sometimes in the dark, with code words and abbreviations, for fear of my notes falling into the hands of Russian soldiers. When possible, my nephew Adam videotaped the conditions in my hospital and interviewed patients. We wanted the world to know the horrors of war and how ordinary people suffer. My diary is the basis for this book, along with my memories of my boyhood in Chechnya.

Before the recent wars with Russia, most people in the West had never heard of Chechnya. Few people could find it on the map. They didn't know that our history goes back thousands of years. They knew nothing about our traditions, our struggle to be free, or our spirit, born high in the mountains of the Caucasus.

The Russian government always hung labels on us. In the nineteenth century, during the twenty-five-year-long Russian-Caucasian wars, the czars called us "savages" and "cutthroats." In 1944, when the whole Chechen population was deported to Kazakhstan, the Soviets called us "traitors" and "Nazi sympathizers." Fifty years later, in 1994,

when the first Russian-Chechen war broke out, the Russian government referred to us as "bandits." After the terrible tragedy in New
York on September 11, 2001, the Russians told the world we were
"international terrorists."

I wanted this account of my work as a surgeon in Chechnya during
the wars with Russia to transcend politics and stereotypes. I wanted to
tell the truth, and the truth consists of the good and the bad, the serious and the not so serious. Often the truth is painful. Writing this book
forced me to remember things I would rather forget. It also forced me
to write about personal things which in Chechen tradition we don't reveal. The threat of annihilation and years of warfare have conditioned
us to hide our emotions lest they weaken us in the eyes of our enemies.

Maybe because we are such a private people, the outside world
doesn't know who we are. I ask my fellow Chechens to forgive me if
I have been indiscreet or if I have violated some of our traditions. For
example, it is considered improper for a man to talk about his wife
and children. We do not keep photographs of them in our wallets or
on the wall. However, I wanted to show Chechens as human beings.
I have introduced my readers to my family. I have talked about my
wife and children, about my friends. I have also talked about individuals who have brought honor to our nation, as well as those who have
brought shame.★ Good and bad people exist in all societies, in Chechnya, in Russia and the United States, and in every other country. I
wanted my readers to see us as human beings with a capacity for love,
anger, and sorrow. In this, we are no different from other people. We
have families we love. We want our children to be educated and contribute to our society. We want to breathe fresh air and do productive
work. And like everyone else, we want to live in freedom.

★To protect the safety of some people, I have changed their names.

Prologue

ONE NIGHT IN the fall of 2000, I woke up from a bad dream that had often plagued me during the Russian-Chechen wars. In this nightmare I saw the injured lying on the ground, blood gushing out of their wounds like water from a dam; they looked up, imploring me to save them.

"Put on the tourniquets!" I yelled. "Tighter! Tighter!" And still the blood flowed. "Tighter! Tighter!" And the blood kept coming. In desperation, I cried out, "They'll die if we can't stop the bleeding!" And then, in this dream, I saw snakes slithering toward me, tongues flicking, trying to bite me. I ran. They gained on me. I jumped over them, but they kept coming, winding themselves around my ankles. What did they want from me? I swore I had done all I could.

When I woke up that morning in New York, I felt physically sick.

"You look like hell," said Viktor, a friend whom I was visiting. We had known each other almost twenty years earlier in medical school in Russia.

I stared at my face in the bathroom mirror. I had seen the same bloodless complexion on the wounded while working as a surgeon during Chechnya's wars with Russia. I felt cold and clammy and suspected a bleeding ulcer. Once or twice it had flared up in recent months, but nothing like this. Or maybe my old stomach wound had reopened. My friends from New Jersey drove to New York to pick me up and took me to their house. All day I tried to walk off the pain, but finally around 6 P.M. my friends called an ambulance and I was rushed to the nearby hospital in Summit.

During the wars in Chechnya, I knew I could die at any moment, so I used to keep a piece of paper in my pocket with my name and address written on it. I always prayed that whoever found my body would take it to my hometown for burial because the Koran commands us to bury the dead within twenty-four hours.

What worried me now was not so much dying, but dying in the United States. Who would pay to return my body to Chechnya? Even if someone were willing to make the arrangements, I doubted the Russians would allow my corpse to be transported to Chechnya through Moscow. I wanted to be buried in the town where I was born—beside my grandparents, my uncles, and my cousins in the small cemetery in Alkhan Kala near Grozny, the capital. I wanted to know that whenever people passed the burial ground, they would say a prayer for me.

As I lay on the gurney in the emergency room, I grew more and more agitated because there seemed to be no urgency in this hospital. All the staff did was ask questions. No painkillers, no blood pressure check, nothing to stop the bleeding. Maret Tsarnaeva, a Chechen friend, had volunteered to interpret for me. I overheard her talking to the nurses. Had I spoken English then, I might have felt more in control of the situation. But without the language, I was as helpless as a child even though I was a doctor.

Maret kept telling me to relax, but I had forgotten how. During the past years while running a hospital in wartime, I had lived on overdrive. Life or death hung on a single minute. At the start of the first war, it took me two hours to amputate a leg. By the time I escaped to the neighboring republic of Ingushetia six years later, I had it down to thirty minutes. A prayer to Allah, a tourniquet to cut off the blood to the leg, a shot of painkiller to the mangled foot, a drip of Polyglukin★ to raise the blood pressure. Then the vertical incision, some seven inches above the line of amputation. Peel back the flesh and muscles to create flaps to cover the stump. Then down to the bone with the knife; through the soft tissue, through the muscles, tying off arteries, veins, and nerves as you go; finally, the hand saw, through the long bone of the tibia, through its companion bone, the fibula, then suturing the skin and muscle flaps over the stump. By the end, I could almost have performed the operation with my eyes closed. Sometimes the lighting was so poor, I might just as well have been blind.

"BAIEV. His name is Baiev, Khassan," Maret said to the nurse who wrote it on a clipboard. "B . . . A . . . I . . . E . . . V. Born April 4, 1963, in Chechnya . . . just put Russia."

The pain felt like burning coals in my stomach, and I imagined the blood oozing into my intestinal tract. I made a fist with my hand and pressed it against the spot below my ribs. A nurse arrived and drew some blood. "What's the blood for?" I asked.

"They are testing you for AIDS and syphilis," Maret whispered.

"AIDS and syphilis! That's not the first thing to worry about when someone is hemorrhaging," I said. "Can't they at least give me something for the pain?"

"The nurses can't prescribe anything without permission from the doctor," Maret said.

I thought of my nurses—especially Rumani, who was the only one I trusted to transport seriously wounded patients through Russian fire. At the start of the war, her husband wanted her to join him and their children in the neighboring province of Ingushetia. But she refused.

★Polyglukin is a solution manufactured in the former Soviet Union used to raise arterial blood pressure in cases of major blood loss and shock. It carries the Latin name *polyglucinum* and is similar to solutions available in other countries under the names of Dextravan, Expandex, Macrodex. It is described in M.D. Mashkovskii, *Lekarstvennyye Sredstva*, Moscow: Meditsina Publishing House, 1977, pp. 62–63.

"My place is helping Khassan," she had insisted. Her courage made me ashamed. She was a woman, and I should have been protecting her, not asking her to dodge Russian snipers. Several times during a bombing attack, she and another nurse pushed me to the floor or up against the wall, shielding me with their bodies.

"What are you doing?" I had asked, embarrassed, the first time it happened.

"We've got to protect you!" Rumani said. "There are several of us, but you are our only doctor."

THE CLOCK OVER the nurses' station in the emergency room of the New Jersey hospital read 1 A.M. I had been lying in the corridor for four hours. Maret said it was a busy night, which explained why the service was so slow. All the examining rooms were curtained off. To me, the place seemed very quiet, only an old woman and a man in the waiting room. The man waved his arms in the air and shouted for a nurse. The place was spotless and smelled of antiseptic. No blood on the linoleum floors here, only polish. No bucket of severed limbs in the corner; only a pot of yellow and white flowers stood on the table next to the magazines and a box of tissues.

"They want to know about your insurance," Maret said.

"Insurance?"

"Health insurance," she repeated.

"I don't have any."

I never asked my patients about insurance. In Chechnya, doctors and nurses at my hospital worked without pay after the outbreak of the war with Russia in 1994, when salaries had dried up. We all worked for nothing. That was our understanding of the Hippocratic Oath. We treated whoever needed help, whether they could pay or not; whether they belonged to the Chechen or Russian side.

The nurse's endless questioning made my heart pound. I wanted to jump off the gurney and escape. The whole thing reminded me too much of interrogations by Russian soldiers at military checkpoints in Chechnya. I closed my eyes again and took a deep breath, remembering a Russian soldier who leaned into my car at a check-point, unshaven, with red-rimmed eyes. I could smell vodka on his breath. I handed him my documents.

"Baiev, Khassan?" he said.

I nodded.

"So you have been treating bandits?" he said.

"I have been treating the wounded."

At checkpoints, the Russian guards would start cross-examinations, hoping for a bribe or threatening with a rifle butt. When I was driving to the hospital with an emergency patient, every minute counted. If we were delayed the wounded might die on the way. And sometimes the guards wouldn't let us through at all.

I OPENED MY eyes and looked down at my hands, wondering if I would ever use them again for surgery. I ran my thumbs over the palms. The muscles were enlarged from all the sawing. Recently, a friend asked me how I could reach inside a wound with such large hands to tie off the veins. By the time I was forced to leave Chechnya, my hands were so blistered and swollen I couldn't have done another operation even if I had wanted to. Now the swelling had gone down, and the skin was smooth. Unfortunately, my head has not recovered as quickly as my hands.

A man in a white coat, carrying a clipboard, approached. He leaned over the gurney and spoke in a loud voice, apparently believing he could make me understand that way. Maret translated for me. He asked how I felt, when I first noticed the pain—the same questions the nurse had asked. He looked so young. I told Maret to ask him to do an endoscopy. At least, if the doctor put a tube down my throat into my stomach, we would know what was going on. He shook his head. "The gastroenterologist won't be in until tomorrow," he said and ordered the nurses to start me on a saline drip.

I felt exhausted. It was now close to 3 A.M. I closed my eyes, and the troubling images returned. I could see my close friend Khamzat Azhiev, lying in the corridor of my little hospital in Alkhan Kala, his pants dark with blood. When I saw him lying there, I couldn't believe it. Only a few nights earlier he and I had sat at his kitchen table drinking tea. We had known each other since childhood, but after I finished medical school in Siberia and returned home to Alkhan Kala we became close friends. He had attended the police academy and worked in the local police department.

He must have seen the horror in my face. He smiled and gave me a wink as if to say, "Easy there, I'm just another one of your patients now." I stepped around the other wounded lying in the corridor and knelt down beside Khamzat. Shrapnel had shredded his blue and white sports outfit, and blood flowed from under his hip, turning the mattress red.

"Nothing terrible." I took his hand. "Your lungs may be slightly affected."

That was a lie; the volume of blood told me that the wound was massive, probably fatal. But I could not tell Khamzat he was dying. To tell a patient the truth often means he loses hope, and without hope there is nothing to fight for. I needed his hope. I refused to accept he was dying. He seemed so calm, so still, not imploring me to save him as did another friend when he was gunned down in his car.

I fought for Khamzat's life as though he had every chance. "Put him on the operating table immediately," I ordered Rumani. I always prayed before an operation, but this time I asked Allah for forgiveness, too, for putting my friend above the others.

I cut off what remained of Khamzat's jacket and pants and threw them on the pile of blood-soaked clothes in the corner of the operating room. I eased him onto his side and saw the blood pulsating out of a large wound in his back over the left lung. I took his blood pressure reading, which was dangerously low. I gave him a shot of morphine, then inserted my index finger into the gash. The wound was deep, and I felt the warmth of the blood against my finger as it rushed into the stomach cavity.

I concluded that a fairly large piece of shrapnel had severed the pulmonary artery and the middle lobe of the left lung. I slid my finger out and packed gauze into the wound to stem the flow of blood. If only I had the proper instruments and medication for general anesthetic, I would cut through his ribs, separate them, and locate the source of the hemorrhaging. At that time Khamzat was breathing easily enough, which meant the blood hadn't penetrated the pleura membranes covering the lungs and the lungs had not collapsed.

I managed to stabilize Khamzat. Although I knew he didn't have a chance, I ordered Rumani to transport him to a better-equipped hospital in Atagi. We waited until nightfall. Only after dark was there any chance of avoiding Russian fire, and only then if you drove without lights. Rumani made it to Atagi all right. But when the doctors opened up the wound, they found the shrapnel had damaged the spine, paralyzing him. Khamzat survived the operation but died the next day.

STARING UP AT the ceiling, waiting for treatment, I longed to be home. Since my arrival in the United States in April 2000, not a day had gone by that I didn't ask myself why was I here, that I didn't think of my relatives back home, of my wife, Zara, or my children. I felt my place was in my own emergency room, not in the pristine surroundings of the hospital in Summit.

I pressed my hand against my stomach again and closed my eyes. I had been hooked up to a saline drip for a while, and the pain subsided slightly. At 5 A.M., I asked Maret to inform the nurses I was leaving. The nurses signed me out with an appointment to visit an expensive gastroenterologist in his office at 10 A.M. I skipped the appointment. Instead, the next day I called an American doctor friend, who arranged for me to be treated on a pro bono basis for what turned out to be an ulcer.

As for so many of my countrymen—they are still to be treated. The war goes on in Chechnya. Civilians die every day. If not killed by Russian gunfire, they die from dysentery, heart attacks, strokes, hypertension, a virulent form of tuberculosis that doesn't respond to antibiotics, and malignant tumors caused by smoke and chemicals in the air. Many of the survivors have physical and emotional wounds that probably will never fully heal. My country is a medical disaster area, and I cannot rest until I return. But I know I can't go home again—at least not yet—not while Russian troops and a few Chechen extremists are pursuing me. The Kremlin called me a terrorist doctor because I treated Chechen freedom fighters. The extremists called me a traitor because I treated wounded Russian soldiers. In truth, it was the civilians I treated most, and they still need my help.

The Oath

About Chechnya

NICHOLAS DANILOFF

O THE WESTERN world, the name Chechnya is synony-
mous with international terrorism. This rebellious juris-
diction of Russia is widely believed to be a province of
lawlessness and a target for Middle East radicals who want to turn it
into an Islamic republic. The seizure of the Nord-Ost Theater in
Moscow in October 2002 by Chechen hostage takers only heightened this belligerent image. The truth behind the headlines, however,
is quite different. Insiders know that the vast majority of Chechens
are hardworking people, anxious for home rule, loyal to ancient customs, and at odds with Islamic fundamentalists.

Although Chechnya at war has been described by journalists, including some who have disguised themselves to evade official con-
trols, no foreign observer has been able to give the world a picture of
what it means to be a Chechen today. That picture, at last, emerges in
this courageous memoir by Dr. Khassan* Baiev, a Chechen surgeon
who treated all in need at great risk to himself.

The Republic of Ichkeriya, as its leaders like to call it, lies in a valley
on the north slopes of the Caucasian Mountains, which divide Russia
from the Middle East and Christianity from Islam. About the size of

---

*Khassan is more accurately pronounced Hassan than Kassan. In Russian,
his name begins with the Latin *X*. The Russian (Cyrillic) alphabet is derived
from Greek, Latin, and Hebrew. Transliteration from Russian to Latin may
represent *X* as *H* or *KH*.

Connecticut, Chechnya is bounded on the west by Ingushetia, a small republic of related peoples, and on the east by Dagestan, a multiethnic Russian province on the Caspian Sea. To the south lie Georgia, Armenia, and Azerbaijan, which became independent with the collapse of the Soviet Union in 1991.

Chechnya's struggle for independence goes back hundreds of years—the Chechens rebuffed Russian forces in the sixteenth century when Ivan the Terrible tried to conquer the territory. The determination to defend their unique, non-Russian culture has focused generations of Chechen males on fighting skills and physical strength. In sports, they gravitate to martial arts, particularly judo, tae kwon do, and a self-defense sport called sombo. Even today, mothers rock little boys to sleep with lullabies urging them to be brave warriors.

The most serious Russian efforts to dominate Chechnya and Dagestan began with Peter the Great when he sought a route over the Caspian Sea to Persia and India. In 1732, Russian troops were forced back from the village of Chechen, but the next 200 years were marked by further attempts to pacify the Chechens or force them into exile. When Alexander I dispatched General Alexei Yermolov in 1816 to conquer the region, Yermolov declared: "I desire that the terror of my name should guard our frontiers more potently than chains or fortresses, that my word should be for the natives a law more inevitable than death. Moderation in the eyes of the Asiatics is a sign of weakness, and out of pure humanity I am inexorably severe."*

Yermolov built a series of fortresses in Chechnya and unleashed a policy of annihilation. His actions were so ferocious that Nicholas I (who succeeded Alexander in 1825) recalled him in 1827 for excessive cruelty. To this day, the name Yermolov is brandished by Russian troops as a warning to the Chechens to submit.

---

*Cited in Yo'av Karny, *Highlanders: A Journey to the Caucasus in Quest of Memory,* New York: Farrar, Straus and Giroux, 2000, p. 48. General Alexei P. Yermolov's writings have been published in Moscow at various times in the nineteenth and twentieth centuries. One notable edition is: N. V. Yermolov, *Zapiski Alekseia Petrovicha Yermolova,* 2 vols. Moscow: 1865–1868.

In the 1830s, Nicholas I renewed the attempts to dominate the North Caucasus and vie with England for control of India in what Rudyard Kipling called "the Great Game." But his forces came up against another great fighter, Imam Shamil. Under his leadership, the clans of Chechnya and Dagestan fought the Russians for thirty years until Shamil's surrender in 1859.

The efforts to control the North Caucasus did not stop with Shamil's demise. Although St. Petersburg decreed that religious and cultural freedoms should be respected, Russian military officers regularly ignored instructions as they continued to fight Chechen resisters. Between 1860 and the turn of the twentieth century, the St. Petersburg czars encouraged the Chechens to resettle among the Muslims of Turkey, but the Turks repelled them by force to Jordan and Syria.

At the end of the nineteenth century, a period of uneasy peace developed between Russia and Chechnya. Britain, France, and Holland began to invest in the area, and engineers arrived to drill for oil, create refineries, and build railroads. Following the Russian Revolution, a new surge of resistance erupted when the North Caucasus declared itself independent in 1918. During the civil war that followed the revolution, the Red Army moved in and imposed Soviet rule. By 1929, Stalin began the brutal collectivization of agriculture throughout Russia, redrawing the boundaries of the ministates in the Caucasus according to the principle of "divide and conquer."

Toward the end of the Second World War, Stalin accused the Chechens of collaborating with the Nazis in hopes of gaining postwar independence, and ordered their deportation to Kazakhstan, Kirghizia, and Siberia. On February 23, 1944, the NKVD secret police appeared without warning, executing the infirm and shipping off 1 million Chechens in cattle cars. During the six-week journey, according to popular memory, half the population perished. Russian police archives, however, indicate that the total number deported was 600,000, with 200,000 dying en route. In exile or in prison, the surviving Chechens continued to resist as witnessed by Aleksandr Solzhenitsyn in *The Gulag Archipelago*:

The Chechens never sought to please, to ingratiate themselves with the bosses. As far as they were concerned, the local inhabitants and those exiles who submitted so readily belong more or less to the same breed as the bosses. They respected only rebels.

And here is an extraordinary thing—everyone was afraid of them. No one could stop them from living as they did. The regime which had ruled the land for thirty years could not force them to respect its laws.*

In 1957, Nikita Khrushchev pardoned but declined to rehabilitate the Chechens. When they returned home, they found their houses taken over by Russians, Ukrainians, Armenians, and others. They were forced to start over from scratch. Throughout the Brezhnev era, 1964–82, they lived and worked with the Russians under the stern tutelage of the Communist Party leaders and the police.

When Mikhail Gorbachev came to power in 1985, he set about ending "the era of stagnation" that had marked the seventeen-year rule of his predecessor. Gorbachev was concerned that the slow pace of innovation in industry and the poor quality of Soviet products would cause the Soviet Union to enter the twenty-first century as a backward industrial nation. His approach was to lower the profile of the police, promote a policy of *glasnost* (transparency), and ease the penalties for speaking out.

Gorbachev, however, failed to think through the implications of freer speech. Shortly, the three Baltic republics of the Soviet Union— Estonia, Latvia, and Lithuania, forcibly annexed at the start of World War II—began pressing for independence. The Soviet Union started falling apart, and hard-line conservatives attempted a coup in August 1991. When the putsch failed, the constituent republics of the Soviet Union began declaring independence, and Chechnya announced on

*Aleksandr Solzhenitsyn, *Arikhipelag Gulag, 1918–1956,* vol. V–VII, (Russian edition), Paris: YMCA Press, 1975, pp. 420–421. See also: Sebastian Smith, *Allah's Mountains, Politics and War in the Russian Caucasus,* London-New York: I. B. Tauris Publishers, 1998, p. 121.

September 6 that it was henceforth "sovereign." Dzhokhar Dudayev, a Chechen and former Soviet air force general, was elected president and declared on November 1 that Chechnya had seceded and should be considered independent—the achievement of a centuries-old dream.

When Gorbachev stepped down at the end of December 1991 and Boris Yeltsin emerged as the new leader of the successor state—the Russian Federation—Dudayev was one of the first to declare his support for him. But in the following years, Chechen relations with Moscow deteriorated. Surrounded by self-seeking advisers, Dudayev turned Chechnya into a free-trade zone in which adventurers, carpetbaggers, mafia operatives, and criminals flourished. By 1994, the Kremlin leaders were deeply concerned that lawlessness was taking over, weakening Russia's southern flank and hindering access to the rich deposits of oil in the Caspian Sea. Moscow leaders worried, too, that an independent Chechnya would encourage other ethnic jurisdictions to secede, leading to the disintegration of the Russian Federation. Still another misgiving was the spreading Western influence in Russia's own backyard: American, British, French, and German companies were moving into the region to exploit its natural riches and lessening Moscow's influence.

Yeltsin and Dudayev talked about negotiated solutions but never achieved one. In December 1994, Yeltsin ordered the Russian army to invade, setting off the first Russian-Chechen war. A critical turn of events occurred the following year when Russian troops massacred villagers at Samashki and Bamut. In retaliation, a Chechen field commander named Shamil Basayev moved into southern Russia and seized a hospital in the city of Budyonnovsk, taking hostage some 2,000 patients, doctors, and visitors. When Russian attempts to free the hospital failed, Prime Minister Viktor Chernomyrdin agreed to talk to Basayev in a nationally broadcast conversation on June 18, 1995. This exchange ended the immediate crisis and led to a ceasefire, an exchange of prisoners, and an agreement to negotiate further on Chechnya's political status.

In the ensuing year, political talks bogged down. Frustrated with the slow progress, President Yeltsin and Defense Minister Pavel Grachev began to accuse the Chechens of being part of an international conspiracy to turn the entire Caucasus region into an Islamic state. Then another dramatic event happened on the night of April 21, 1996, when President Dudayev was mortally wounded by an explosion and Vice President Zemlikhan Yandarbiyev, a hard-liner, succeeded him. The talk-and-fight period continued until August, when Russian general Aleksandr Lebed concluded a truce with Colonel Aslan Maskhadov, the Chechen chief of staff, on August 25, 1996, calling for the political status of Chechnya to be finally resolved by December 31, 2001.

As the first war came to an end, Chechnya set about the job of recovery. But on December 16, 1996, six workers of the International Committee of the Red Cross were murdered by masked men, believed to be Chechen collaborators in the pay of the Russian secret services. The killings appeared designed to discourage international aid for Chechnya and to disrupt the presidential elections of January 27, 1997. Nevertheless, Colonel Maskhadov won 64.8 percent of the vote in balloting that the Organization for Security and Cooperation in Europe termed "free and fair."

Rebuilding proceeded with difficulty, however, over the next two years. Moscow sought to bring Chechnya to its knees by blockading its borders with Russia. A new crisis erupted on August 2, 1999, when Basayev invaded Dagestan with a force of about 2,000 men, hoping Dagestan would join Chechnya in forcing Russia to withdraw. The maneuver failed, and Basayev was forced to retreat.

Four months later, Boris Yeltsin issued the surprise announcement that he was resigning, and named Vladimir Putin acting president with national elections to follow within ninety days. Putin was elected president of Russia on March 26, 2000. His efforts to bring Chechnya to heel again faced stiff resistance from some 5,000 loosely organized fighters. This time, Moscow ordered overwhelming power, leveling the capital of Grozny, setting up checkpoints all over Chechnya, and creating "filtration camps" to weed out fighters from peaceful civilians by fair means and foul.

When suicide bombers demolished the World Trade Center towers and attacked the Pentagon on September 11, 2001, President Putin was among the first foreign leaders to rally to President George W. Bush's call for a war against global terrorism. The Russian president was quick to denounce these violent acts in the United States as international terrorism and took advantage of the moment to charge that this evil had invaded his country too. Putin and his aides asserted that Osama bin Laden had sent operatives into Chechnya with untold volunteers, weapons, and financing.

The truth of these allegations has never been convincingly demonstrated. But, at last, an unusual eyewitness has shed new light on what is a complex historical, political, and humanitarian situation. A decade before the first war broke out, Khassan Baiev went to Russia to get a medical education, where, along with his classmates, he pledged himself to the Hippocratic Oath, promising help to all in need. During the war, he lived by that oath, treating peaceful civilians, Chechen fighters, and Russian soldiers without discrimination. For this devotion, he was targeted for assassination by Chechen extremists and the Russian military, who both considered him a traitor to their cause. Through a fluke of good luck—which he attributes to the Almighty—Dr. Baiev barely escaped from Chechnya in February 2000 and made his way to the United States, where he now lives with his wife and six children.

Ruth and I met Khassan Baiev in May of 2000 when he came to Boston at the invitation of Physicians for Human Rights. As he spoke about the plight of the civilians and the horrors he had witnessed, his voice was flat but his hands trembled with emotion.

That afternoon, Ruth and I took Khassan to Concord; as an eyewitness to Chechnya's struggle for independence, he stood on the bridge where the first shots in the American Revolution were fired. Over tea, Khassan told us he dreamed of writing a book about everything that had happened to him. Struck by his honesty and courage, and given the interest Ruth and I developed for the Caucasus region as Moscow correspondents, we felt compelled and honored to help him share his story with the world.

Part 1

Before the War

Chapter 1

Dada and Nana

I WAS BORN in Alkhan Kala in 1963, some four years after my family returned from exile in Kazakhstan and thirty minutes be fore my twin brother, Hussein. "I was making bread one day and rolled you out of the dough," my mother said when I asked where I came from.

Our town, Alkhan Kala, is a settlement of 16,000 inhabitants located six miles southwest of the Chechen capital, Grozny, near the Moscow-Baku railroad line and highway. It lies in a fertile valley looking out on the snowcapped mountains of the great Caucasian range. If you go south and turn left toward Dagestan, the highway and railroad will take you to Baku, capital of Azerbaijan. If you turn right and keep going, you will cross into the neighboring republic of Ingushetia and then into Russia. The edge of town drops down to the Sunzha⋆ River, which rises in the Caucasian foothills and empties into the Caspian Sea.

The settlement developed in the eighteenth century after Peter the Great dispatched Cossacks to the Caucasus region to extend and secure the southern borders of the Russian Empire. Several old stone houses remained next to a fort until a Russian missile destroyed them in the recent war. Dada—that's what we call fathers in Chechnya— said a famous Cossack colonel lived in the largest house and that many

⋆*ZH* has a soft *J* sound, as in the French word *jour* or the English word *azure*.

educated people gathered there. Today the colonel's once beautiful wooden fence is riddled with bullet holes. In Soviet times, his house served as a post office and as the offices of the local council. Few Chechens lived in Alkhan Kala before the Russian Revolution of 1917. The endless conflicts with Russia in the nineteenth century forced them into the mountains, where they lived off the land and raised livestock.

A large Russian cemetery is located on the outskirts of the town, along with two Chechen cemeteries and a common burial ground for soldiers killed in the Second World War. In 1991, after the Soviet authorities lifted the ban on religious worship, people collected money for the mosque, which we constructed on a side street off the central square. The town boasts two bazaars, one near the railroad station and the other adjacent to the square. A café, a cinema, and several benches where the elders sit and talk complete the square. Until 1991, when the economy collapsed, Alkhan Kala had a large poultry farm, a grain elevator, and a large wood-processing plant that exported furniture and wood products all over the Soviet Union.

Exiled in the Deportation to Kazakhstan during the Second World War, my family returned to Alkhan Kala in 1959. Dada managed to buy an unfinished house on one of the main streets. One of my earliest memories is of a *belkhi*, a community get-together, to finish the house. I was only four, but I remember sitting on the ground and sifting sand through a wire sieve. We mixed the sand with a fine yellow clay and sawdust. Then the women stood on sawhorses and slapped this adobe mixture on the walls. That first house had four small rooms. The main room was the kitchen, where Nana (my mother) cooked, we all ate and bathed, and where Hussein and I shared a narrow bed.

Dada slaughtered a sheep for the volunteers, and during breaks we ate *zhizhik-galnish*, the Chechen national dish of dumplings and boiled mutton dipped in garlic sauce. The women sat at one table, the men at the other. A *belkhi* provided the opportunity for the young women to dance, the older women to gossip, and the men to show off their accordion playing. It also gave the boys a chance to eye the girls.

Me (right) and my twin,
Hussein.

If a boy was taken with a girl, he would first have to approach an older
woman and get her to introduce him.

I look back on those early childhood days as happy times. Nana
baked our bread. We milked the cows and grew our own food. Waking in the morning, I watched the peaks of Mount Kazbek and Elbrus
emerge out of the mist. Mount Elbrus, it was said, was where the
Greek gods chained Prometheus for stealing their fire. Nana told us
that the dark squiggle, resembling a figure 2, on the eastern slope of
Mount Elbrus was the lair of a sleeping dragon of Chechen legend. In
1991, when I flew over Elbrus from Grozny to Odessa, I saw that the
"lair" was actually a deep volcanic gorge.

Generation upon generation of our ancestors had gazed on the same
snowy peaks, navigated the same precipitous paths, and looked down
into the same gorges. During the recent wars with Russia, when I felt
my sanity slipping, just looking at those peaks gave me a sense of calm.

Dada dominates my childhood memories. Whenever I see our national dance, the *lesghinka*, performed, I remember the fast-paced notes
of his accordion and how he would wake Hussein and me in the middle of the night to dance for him. Hussein and I jumped up, almost simultaneously, from the narrow bed in the kitchen. Not to obey Dada

meant risking a beating, so we threw on our clothes and scurried into the next room. There Dada sat with the accordion on his lap, the electric lamp lighting up the tiny room, reflecting off the glass jars on the windowsill where he had planted his onion bulbs and medicinal herbs. He wore a suit, reserved for special occasions, his lamb's-wool *papakha* hat, and the soft, black leather boots that elderly men in Chechnya wear.

"Time to dance!" he called out, directing his voice toward the adjoining room where my sisters slept. Then he placed his accordion on the floor, limped over to the old gramophone on the table under the window, and dropped a record on the turntable. Nana and my sisters came out. The familiar beat of the Chechen national dance filled the room. Nana sat on a chair. Her long, curly, black hair, which crowned her head in a braid during the day, hung down on her back under her scarf. Even when I was only nine years old, I sensed she didn't like Dada waking us up to dance, but to protest would have put him in a bad mood.

Dada liked Hussein to dance with Malika because he was taller than I and put more energy into his movements. Malika, our senior by ten years, was my favorite sister. I danced with Razyat, who was three years older than Hussein and I were. Razyat was Dada's favorite, because she was the youngest daughter. My other two sisters, Tamara and Raya, were married and living in the households of their husbands nearby in town.

Malika glided around the small room in a perfect circle, her arms rising and falling like branches of a tree in the breeze. She had taken dancing lessons and knew the finer points of the Chechen national dance—shuffling her feet in such a way that she appeared to float, avoiding eye contact with her partner.

"Faster, faster!" Dada shouted. "Arms and legs, more energy!" He made a fist with his left hand and snapped out the rhythm with the fingers of his right, keeping time like a metronome. Hussein guided Malika with thrusts of his fists: first to the left, then to the right, straight ahead, falling back, turning, his feet striking the floor.

"No touching!" Dada yelled if Hussein brushed Malika.

My sister Razyat.

Some nights we danced until the sun rose over the mountains, and it was time for my sisters and my mother to milk our three cows.

Though my childhood memories are happy, Dada and Nana and other adults encountered terrible difficulties after they returned from exile and found themselves third-class citizens in their own country. Their houses had been taken over by Cossacks, Russians, Ukrainians, Armenians, and citizens of other national groups, who accused them of being "traitors" and refused them jobs.

As I grew older, I came to understand what my parents had endured, and vowed I would do everything in my power to make their lives easier. Dada has lived through the Russian Revolution of 1917, the purges of the late 1930s, the Second World War, the 1944 Deportation, the chaos following the collapse of the Soviet Union, and now the brutal wars with Russia. Taking Dada to the mineral baths when he was an old man always reminded me of his suffering. Scars marked his body, and under his skin were pieces of shrapnel the doctors couldn't remove. During the Second World War, when the Soviet Union attempted to annex Finland, he fought on that icy front and was wounded twice. Later he was transferred to Murmansk in the far north, where he fought until the end of the war. An injury to his right leg left him with a limp.

In 1944, after a brief stay at home following his release from the military hospital, the Soviet authorities deported him to Kazakhstan. Thirty five years later, some Young Pioneers—a kind of Communist equivalent of the Boy Scouts—in Murmansk discovered photographs and notes Dada and his wartime friends had stuffed in a bottle and buried in the trenches. Only then did the local military authorities recognize Dada as a veteran and award him a pension and medals. Whenever I looked at Dada decked out in his war medals on Soviet holidays, I felt pride mixed with bitterness at the unfairness of things. All those medals—the Order of Victory over Nazi Germany, the Order of the October Revolution, the Order of Glory, the Order of Labor, and the Order of the Red Banner—and yet Chechens indiscriminately had been accused of being Nazi collaborators! The Soviet authorities sent Chechens to fight in the worst places because they were good fighters, but when Chechens distinguished themselves in battle, Moscow refused to recognize their valor.

It turned out that my father was the sole survivor of his unit in that northern hell during the war. The museum in Murmansk invited him to open a special exhibit on the war during the Gorbachev era, but by that time he was too lame to travel. What has always amazed me about Dada is that he never complained or said anything negative about Russians. He had many Russian friends. In Kazakhstan he even adopted Larissa, a little Russian girl whose parents had died and who was about to be placed in an orphanage. Larissa lived with us until she married a Chechen man and moved to his home in the town.

Nana's life was as harsh as my father's. One spring day in 1936, when she was thirteen years old, the secret police arrived at her house and arrested her parents as kulaks—that is, small landowners whom Stalin eliminated in his efforts to collectivize Soviet agriculture. They were never seen again, leaving my mother to raise her four siblings with help from distant relatives. Throughout my childhood, Nana worked as a porter at the grain elevator to supplement the family income. For many years Dada had been denied a war veteran's pension, and as he aged, his war injuries made work difficult for him. Even so,

Dada showing off his
World War II decorations.

he was always occupied with herbs and giving medical advice to anyone who asked for it. Whenever I went by the grain elevator to see
Nana, I was always upset to see her there covered in chaff. The work
was backbreaking. I know that for Nana, life with Dada was not always easy. He was always off socializing with his friends and would
hand out money and help to anyone who asked for it.

DESPITE MY THIRTY-MINUTE head start in this world, which des-
tined me to be the eventual head of our family, Hussein was taller and
weighed more. Hussein was robust, while I suffered a caved-in chest
and bowed legs. He was rarely sick. I was always plagued by one illness
or another. I imagined I was a disappointment to Dada.

At five, I contracted a chronic ear infection, which damaged the
auditory nerve and landed me in the hospital for months. Then in
second grade, the condition reoccurred, this time making me practi-
cally deaf. At night, I bit into my pillow to smother the pain. I didn't
dare tell Dada because I had disobeyed Nana and had gone outside
without a hat. If he found out, it would be: "Into the kitchen!" for a
beating.

I relied on Hussein to fill me in on what Dada and Nana talked about
at the dinner table. In class, I didn't understand a thing the teacher said,

My sister Malika (left) and
Nana.

so Hussein repeated the lessons to me during breaks. Finally, my teacher
realized I was hard-of-hearing, and she told my parents. I was taken back
to the hospital for more painful and ineffective ear irrigations. Whenever
I heard the doctor's footsteps in the corridor, I hid under the bed because the pain was excruciating. "Take me home! Take me home!" I
screamed when my parents came to visit. In the end the doctor told my
parents not to come to the hospital. But when they did, they viewed me
from around a corner so I wouldn't see them. My hearing improved, but
for months after I was released, I felt weak.

"You shouldn't bother with sports," Dada said, "leave that to Hussein." Nana tried to comfort me. "Maybe Allah doesn't mean for you
to be a good sportsman," she said.

Being a weakling filled me with shame. How could I defend the fatherland, women, children, and the elderly—all the things that Dada
and the family elders said were important? A man must know how to
defend himself, otherwise he won't survive, everyone said. Chechens
need to be strong. Our people had learned that from all those years of
resisting the Russians. And here I was a weakling. I was determined to
do something about it.

One summer when I was thirteen, my life began to turn around with the help of a judo coach named Vakha Chapaev.

After school and during holidays, my job was to mind the cows in the pastures on the other side of the Sunzha River. Hussein preferred to work in the courtyard, so he could slip off and play soccer with his friends. The pastures belonged to the town, and all my friends—Khizir, Khamzat, Bislan, Bayali, Lyoma—brought their cows there to graze. We swam, fished for carp, trapped grass snakes, and hunted turtles in the bogs. Dada ordered me to remove any leeches from my legs after wading in the water and place them in a jar so he could use them on a woman to treat varicose veins.

We also played games to make us strong warriors. My favorite game was *urse lovzar,* in which you balance a knife on different parts of your body, then flip it so that it falls and sticks in the ground. Then there was *lyanga*: You fix a piece of lead inside a round ball of sheepskin, then try to keep it in the air by bouncing it off your foot. If the local collective farm had turned out its horses, we would sometimes catch them and practice riding tricks popular with horsemen in the Caucasus.

When I wasn't playing, I liked to sit on the bank, dangle my feet in the cold water, and watch the boys play soccer with Vakha Chapaev in the field across the river. After the game, Vakha, a small squat man, taught the boys martial arts such as judo and sombo. Sombo is a self-defense sport invented in Russia in the 1930s after Stalin dispatched envoys to various countries to research hand-to-hand combat.

I was fascinated by martial arts. Most men in Chechnya go in for judo, sombo, boxing, or wrestling. One afternoon I asked my cousin Alman to look out for my cows while I threw off my clothes and swam across the river. The water was cold, the current strong, and it took all my strength to reach the other side. Once there, I sat down to watch the martial arts class. After I had been swimming the river every afternoon for a week, Vakha beckoned to me. He looked me up and down as I stood there dripping in my knee-length, black underpants—we called these "family pants" because one size was supposed to fit all in a good Soviet family.

"How would you like to have a go at fighting him?" he asked, pointing toward a young man who had broad shoulders and bulging biceps.

I nodded almost without thinking. Although I didn't win the fight, I know I didn't disgrace myself because afterward Vakha asked me if I wanted to join the group on a regular basis. From then on I swam across the river every day. I took with me an old jacket without buttons which substituted for a kimono, a thick rope for a belt, and worn-out sweatpants, all of which I hid under a rock for use the next day. Sometimes my lessons with Vakha were interrupted when a cow took it into her head to wander off. Then I jumped in the water, swam to the other side and herded her back. In November, when the weather turned cold, Vakha invited me to train with him and some of the other boys in Grozny. Hussein joined us.

We hid this activity from Dada because he would have forbidden it. He felt we should concentrate on our studies and viewed athletes as lazy people who wanted an excuse not to work. I could hide things from him but never from my sisters—especially Malika—who looked after us boys when Nana was working at the grain elevator. Malika and Razyat must have felt sorry for us because they slipped us a few kopeks for the bus ride into Grozny. When we didn't have money, we rode freight trains. Hussein and I were more familiar with the train timetables than with our arithmetic tables. As the Moscow–Baku train was about to pull out, we would jump on the last car and clamber up the ladder onto the roof. Once, by mistake, we mounted the train to Nazran instead of Grozny. We didn't make it home until after 1 A.M., and our angry parents and worried neighbors "greeted" us in the street. "Into the kitchen!" Dada ordered.

We stole to pay for the expenses when we traveled to another town for a competition. Naturally, we never called it stealing because lifting government property in Soviet times was never considered theft, just enterprise. Had we stolen from an individual, Dada would have whipped us. We mounted raids on the cornfields of the collective farm on the opposite bank of the Sunzha. This required a careful strategy with one of us distracting the mounted guard, while the other filled the bags with corn. Following a successful raid, I rose at 5 A.M. the next day, lit the stove in the courtyard where my mother baked bread, and boiled the corn. Then I stacked the ears in a bucket, covered them with plastic to retain the steam, and rushed down to the station. I sold ears for ten kopeks apiece to passengers on the waiting train.

Building up my strength took time. At competitions, Hussein usually took first prize, while I always lost. The more I lost, the more determined I became to overcome my weakness. I constructed a chinning bar in the inner courtyard of our house. I did pull-ups, lifted weights, and ran. Gradually, my spine and hands strengthened, and in my next-to-last grade at school I could do leg-lifts with 110 pounds yoked to my ankles. Neighbors, even people from other towns, came by to watch.

A few weeks before my fourteenth birthday, I took first prize in judo at the Grozny All-Russian Junior Championship. Held on February 23 to commemorate Soviet Army Day, this was my first important fight. Elated, I now was qualified to enter other major national competitions. For me, it was as though I had won the Olympics. I felt as if I had gained control over my life, and at last, I could confess to Dada about my secret training. He would forgive me when he saw the certificate. When I entered the room, he was sitting in front of the television listening to a concert of popular Chechen folk songs. I handed him my winner's certificate.

"What's this?" he said.

"I won the championship in judo."

"So you have been sneaking off to Grozny without my permission?" he said. I nodded. "You deceived me! You snuck off when you were supposed to be in the pastures with the cows!"

Unbuckling his belt, he rose from the chair. "Into the kitchen!"

"Please don't beat me!" I shouted. "I'll never deceive you again."

I braced myself for the thrashing. One, two, three . . . ! The belt whipped across my back. I cringed each time but managed to hold back my tears.

"You will stay at home and attend to your schoolwork!" Dada roared. For a month after this, I was not allowed to leave the town under any circumstances.

Malika and Razyat tried to intercede without success. Finally, my chief coach, Felix Kutsel, paid Dada a visit. I think he won Dada over when he suggested that boys who go in for sports don't have time to drink or smoke.

Chechen etiquette was on my side, too. "You are a guest in my house, Felix Petrovich," Dada said. "I cannot refuse your request." Tradition holds that a guest's request must be fulfilled, however much you dislike it.

Hospitality was all important to Chechens, especially Dada. One time he left Hussein, Razyat, and me alone in a cornfield all night because he was with guests. That morning Dada had handed us five sacks. "Here, fill these, and I will come back to pick you up later in the day," he said. We waited for him all day and through the bitterly cold night. The next morning he arrived just as the sun was coming up over the mountains. He said he had been celebrating with friends and couldn't leave before the last guest departed.

Dada's disapproval over my winning the championship disappointed me. "Life does not end with a single victory," he said. "There are troubles and obstacles enough ahead."

Like most Chechen fathers, Dada never displayed affection or paid me compliments. Strange as that may seem to westerners, we believe that praise weakens you and education is designed to make you resilient to hardship. All of this probably relates to our history of always being under attack. We rarely express our feelings openly. We never use the word *love,* though that doesn't mean we don't have those feelings. On the contrary, our families and friends are the most precious things in our lives. If I received caresses, it was from Nana or my sisters, and then only until I was ten. By that age, a boy is supposed to be man enough not to be coddled. We believe love is demonstrated by action, not words. I have always understood love as loyalty and support of family, friends; love is education of children; love is helping the elderly.

I always knew Dada loved me—even when he beat me—but the way he expressed it was by preparing us for the difficulties ahead. He did this by forcing us to work hard, endure frequent beatings and numerous lectures on how Chechens should conduct themselves.

As I approached adolescence, my relationship with Dada began to change. We say that until the age of seven a boy is an angel. For the next seven years he learns to become an adult. At fifteen, he is a man. By the time I had reached eleven, my father's drinking had begun to embarrass me. Sometimes he disappeared for weeks on end. Knowing how this distressed my mother and sisters, I went to the family elders, asking them to talk to Dada. For him, as for everyone all over Chechnya, the opinion of the elders was very important, and for a while he stopped drinking. But then one summer he went off to the Caspian Sea for a month without my mother.

One morning, I heard the approach of his old Pobeda car with its broken muffler.

"Dada's come! Dada is back!" We all rushed out onto the street, but instead of stopping at the house, he continued on to the café in the square. I don't know what came over me. Malika and Nana were so upset. I rushed down to the café, where my father and his friends sat before a spread of barbecued mutton, rice, greens, and vodka. Furious, I ran over to the table, grabbed the edge, and tipped it over, sending the glasses and plates crashing to the floor.

Silence. Shock. Then my father's friends began laughing. "What a brave boy!" one of them said, turning to my father. Another friend reached over, hugged me, dipped his hand into his pocket, and handed me a ruble. After that, Dada's friends left the café, and he came home. I expected him to beat me, but he did not. Not long after, he stopped drinking for good, and I sensed he looked on me with new respect.

Two years later, another crisis occurred in our family, and I think the way I coped with it increased my father's respect for me. Razyat was kidnapped by a would-be suitor. She was seventeen at the time and had just completed a three-year nursing program at a vocational school. Bride stealing is one of those traditions we Chechens have tolerated, though not necessarily approved of, for hundreds of years. A girl may be abducted either against her will or with her consent (if she really wants to marry the man, but her parents oppose the marriage). The Soviet authorities had tried to stamp out bride stealing, passing a law that any kidnapping must be reported to the police. The law was ignored. We had our own way of dealing with the situation, especially if the abductor had made sexual advances to the girl during the kidnapping. This meant she was no longer pure and no man would marry her. The punishment for inappropriate "touching" is having your pants removed in public. Such terrible humiliation brings shame, not only to your family but to your whole clan.

Razyat's kidnapper was a young man, called Aslanbek, from a neighboring town. With the help of three friends, Aslanbek grabbed her as she was leaving the hospital where she worked, threw her in a car, and took her to the house where he lived with his parents.

We learned of the kidnapping when a delegation of elders from Aslanbek's town arrived to negotiate a resolution and a marriage contract. My father had checked out his family and didn't think they were good enough for her. Besides, he didn't want Razyat living in another town.

"Go get her back!" he ordered me. Lecha Tepsurkaev, my sister Raya's husband, drove me to Aslanbek's house, where I found Razyat surrounded by six or seven women of various ages. They tried to convince Razyat that Aslanbek would make a wonderful husband, that he was a member of a large and respected family with a house. I looked at Razyat. She was sobbing.

Now the women turned their pressure on me. "You are too young; you don't understand the situation," one aunt said. I felt very uncomfortable, but I managed to withstand the pressure. I asked the women to leave the room so I could talk to Razyat alone.

"Do you want to stay in this house?" I asked.

"No," she said, sobbing.

"If you don't want to stay, just come home with me," I said, moving toward the door. She followed me.

Out on the street a crowd of people had assembled, including Aslanbek's four brothers. "You won't get away with this!" one of them called out. "We will come and steal her again."

"Fine," I said, "you know where we live. Just because I am young, don't think you'll get away with this. If any of you—or your relatives—comes to our house and tries to touch my sister, I will shoot you." All the elders were there, listening. I admit I was scared. Then Lecha drove us home.

The next day at lunchtime, several cars drove up to our house and parked in the street. Aslanbek's brothers and their friends spilled out of the vehicles. Razyat was in the house. I grabbed the gun off the wall and ran outside. At school we took military training, and I knew how to disassemble, clean, and reassemble a gun. But this was the first time I was prepared to use one.

"Look," I said to the group assembled in the street. "If Razyat doesn't want to marry your brother, it's not going to happen by force!"

I was ready to kill before I would let them take Razyat. I raised the gun, my finger on the trigger, and pointed it toward the brothers. There was no way I could stop now. My honor and that of my family were at stake. At that moment our neighbor, realizing the situation was turning dangerous, rushed over and grabbed my arm. The gun went off in the air. Aslanbek's brothers and friends jumped in the cars and drove off. That was the last we saw of them.

Aslanbek's family felt humiliated that Razyat had rejected their son, so we sent a delegation of family elders to smooth things over.

I was involved in another bride stealing years later, this time when my friend Bekhan fell in love with a girl called Asyat. The trouble was that Asyat's father and brothers wanted her to marry another boy in the town. One evening when we were all over at Bekhan's house, his mother threw down a challenge to us. She wanted Bekhan married, and she liked Asyat.

"If you boys were men, you would go steal her and bring her back here tonight," she taunted. That was all we needed. We jumped in the car, drove to Grozny. We found her in the store where she worked, and grabbed her. One of her brothers, who worked for the police, saw us and gave chase. In the end we abandoned the car, took a taxi, and deposited her in the house of Bekhan's aunt. By the time the family elders arrived to negotiate, Asyat was hysterical. She wanted to stay with Bekhan, but her brothers wanted her back. After the family forced us to swear on the Koran we hadn't "touched" her, she returned to her family and married another man. Bekhan was heartbroken.

Having proved to be a man in my father's eyes by bringing Razyat home, my role in the family shifted. Until then Hussein seemed to be the dominant one, perhaps because he was so outgoing and full of good humor, whereas I tended to be shy and more serious. I was easily embarrassed. Winning athletic competitions gave me confidence, and I came to understand that one day I would be the head of the family and I had better be prepared for the responsibility. Hussein, meanwhile, seemed increasingly willing for me to take the lead. As the younger son, his role was to stay with our parents until they died and make sure they were buried properly. Needless to say, as long as Dada is alive, he will be the titular head of the family.

I straddled two cultures while growing up. The Alkhan Kala Middle School No. 1, which I attended, was one of the best Russian-language schools, with pupils winning medals at all sorts of national scholastic competitions. One of my schoolmates was Shamil Basayev, who grew up to become Chechnya's notorious field commander. (Little did I suspect that this quiet boy, several classes below me, would one day come to the attention of General Gennadi Troshev, commander of the North Caucasian Military District. This officer would announce a $1-million price on Basayev's head.) My teachers were both Chechens and Russians. Two in particular I remember to this day. Khava Zhaparovna was a Chechen who spoke Russian perfectly. She taught history with such enthusiasm that you could hear a pin drop whenever she lectured, and she had a way of making students behave. Tamara Mikhailovna was a Russian math teacher who had been born in Chechnya and spent all her life there until the collapse of the Soviet Union. She took an interest in each of us. She would sometimes say,

"When some of you grow up, and you occupy an important post, you will carry within you our contribution. That is our good fortune."

In the classroom I learned about the czars, studied Russian grammar, and recited the poems of Pushkin and Lermontov. Moscow never thought Chechnya possessed a culture of its own. If you spoke Chechen at school, the teachers punished you, which meant that many children, especially in urban areas, didn't know their native tongue. At home, we always spoke in Chechen. Dada and Nana introduced us to Islam as well as to our traditions.

When I was in high school, sports was my first love. The time spent training and earning money to travel to competitions meant that I shortchanged my studies. The grading system ran from 5 to 1, equivalent to the American A down to F. I got 3s and 4s, which would get me into a technical institute but nothing higher. Not that I didn't understand the importance of learning. Dada drummed this into me, telling me that a whole generation had missed getting an education during the Deportation and we had to make up for it now. "How come your sisters always got 5s," he shouted when he saw my grades, "and you only get 3s?" One freezing November morning, when Hussein and I overslept, Dada whipped us out of bed and forced us to go to school dressed only in our underpants. He chased us down the street and shoved us through the classroom door. "Here they are!" he exclaimed. "Two slackers!"

After graduation, everyone was expected to go on to some technical school or to the university for further training. There was always a lot of medical talk in our house. Both Malika and Razyat had graduated from the three-year program at the Grozny Nursing School. Dada was obsessed with herbal medicine. He subscribed to the magazine *Soviet Health* and was forever trying out new diets. Old men were always coming by for his rose hip tea to relieve their urinary problems. Occasionally, I fantasized about becoming a doctor. However, I never talked out loud about it because of my school grades. I was sure people would laugh and think me arrogant if I suggested it.

Chapter 2

Ancestors

EVERY SUMMER DURING my childhood, Dada moved the family to the mountains, to his ancestral village of Makazhoi, located seventy-five miles southeast of Alkhan Kala. Driving up the twisting dirt road with the snowy peaks in the distance, I felt as though I was traveling back in time. Each summer we learned something new about Chechen history from Dada or the elders.

No one knew the age of Makazhoi, one of several hamlets perched on the side of the mountain, but it must have been very old because stones in the cemetery bore Arabic inscriptions which Dada said went back to the eighteenth century. The houses of hewn stone blocks looked like cards stacked against the flanks of the mountain, the roof of one house forming the courtyard of the one above it. The entrance to our ancient family dwelling was through an archway leading into a corridor about sixty feet into the mountain. To the right of the passage were the family rooms where my grandmother, grandfather, aunts, uncles, and cousins lived—about thirty people in all. The left-hand side of the passage facing out over the mountains opened into a courtyard, where the family kept chickens and cows.

People call the region "Little Switzerland" for its lakes and water-falls. A short drive along a narrow track takes you to the famous Blue Lake with water so cold and deep that people disappear when they try to swim in it—or so the stories go. Looking out across the valley on a clear day, you can see the ruins of an abandoned village and the remains of a stone combat tower.

Dada loved Makazhoi. He would have lived there all year if the road wasn't impassable in the winter. He had a large fruit and vegetable garden and his own cattle, which his relatives living year round in the village minded in the winter. When we were there, Dada made us work long hours. We planted potatoes, wheat, sunflowers, and corn. All summer we mowed hay. We tended cattle and guarded the fields from wild animals. We envied the boys whose parents sent them off to Young Pioneer camps in the summer.

"I want you boys to understand that the soil is your friend and to know what it can produce," Dada said.

Despite the hard work, I looked forward to the summers. I loved watching the weather come in over the mountains. One minute the sun shone, the next the clouds dropped down, shrouding the peaks in fog. Climbing the twisting paths through the long grass and flowers

A view of "Little Switzerland" looking north from the Caucasus Mountains. (Ruth Daniloff)

Czar Peter the Great confronts Caucasian leaders as he seeks a passage to
India. (Painting by A. F. Rubo, 1856–1928)

toward the summit was like entering a magical realm. You might
glimpse a mountain goat poised atop a crag like a statue of glistening
white marble. The elders forbid anyone to shoot the goats. They dec-
orate the mountains, they say. At night, I listened to the wolves calling to one another. The howls of the wolf, our national symbol, never
frightened me. Our greatest excitement was to be wakened by the
clang of the cans we had strung around the potato patch. "A wild
boar! A boar!" The cry would go up. We jumped out of bed, grabbed
our rifles, and rushed out into the night to shoot at it.

Some of the elders who spent their days on benches in the square
were so old they couldn't remember what year they were born. They
had lived so long under the mountain sun their skins had taken on a
purplish hue. I loved to hear their stories, especially about the heroes of
the Chechen resistance against the Russians, like Sheikh Mansur in the
eighteenth century and Imam Shamil in the nineteenth. The way they

talked, it was as though these events happened yesterday, as though they were there and knew these people.

I will never forget the day one old man invited me to his house. He was the oldest person in the village, probably a centenarian, with a long white beard and a face netted with wrinkles. He said he wanted to show me the sword given to one of his ancestors by the great Shamil.

"Shamil and his followers used to prepare for battle in the tower of one of those villages," he said, waving his arm across the valley. Imam Shamil was a taboo subject I didn't learn about in school. The Soviet authorities claimed he was a spy in the pay of the British in the 1850s, but to everyone in the Caucasus, Shamil was a hero.

The old man kept the precious weapon in a special room in his house with carpets decorating the walls. Standing on tiptoes, he lifted the sword off the pegs and placed it in my hands. It was so heavy I could hardly hold it. Then he helped me pull the blade from the scabbard. The blade itself was blunt, but the handle was beautiful with gold filigree and Arabic writing. If only the sword could speak, I thought as I ran my fingers over the delicate inlays. It would tell me about the *naibs* who fought alongside Shamil, like the famous Baysangur, who lost an arm, a leg, and an eye in the war against Russia. Dada had told me that when Shamil surrendered to the Russians on the mountaintop at Gunib in 1859 to save the women and children from slaughter, Baysangur refused to give up. The Russians finally caught him and tried to hang him. "A reward for anyone who will kick the stool out from under him," they said. But Baysangur managed to kick the stool out from under himself with his one leg before anyone could claim the prize. "Chechens don't surrender," the old man said, taking the sword and replacing it in its sheath. "It's not in our nature."

Touching the cold steel of the blade brought to mind so many stories I'd been told: how the czar had tried to bring Shamil to his knees by kidnapping his son and raising him as his own in the court at St. Petersburg; how Shamil had retaliated by capturing two Georgian princesses and their Belgian governess. Walking home from the old man's house that day, I looked out across the valley. I could almost swear I saw Shamil galloping down from the mountains, his black banner held aloft, the silver powder casings on his tunic glistening in the sun.

LOOKING BACK ON it, I think Dada staggered his stories over the summers, waiting until he thought Hussein and I were old enough to absorb the information. Hussein and I often asked to visit the abandoned village we could see from our house, but Dada always claimed he was too busy. Then one morning when we were thirteen, Dada told us to hurry with our breakfast—he was taking us to the ghost village. We set off down the path from our house, crossed the dirt road, and descended the mountain for about half a mile. It was one of those days in the mountains when the colors jump out at you. The long grass along the path brushed against our legs, and the buttercups, daisies, irises, and edelweiss blossomed at our feet.

Once we reached the village, we pushed our way through shoulder-high grass and beds of nettles; we reached the central square. The nettles stung through my pants, but I didn't dare complain. The architecture of the houses resembled our own, but most of the walls had collapsed. Trees and long grass choked the courtyards.

"You think this is the only dead village in Chechnya?" Dada stopped and swept his arm down the valley. "Look down there!" he said. "What do you see?"

At first, I only saw a flock of sheep. He grew impatient. "Look carefully! Don't you see the clusters of houses, along that ridge?" Now I saw what looked like dwellings perched on the ledge against an outcropping of rock.

"The whole of Chechnya is full of abandoned villages," Dada said. "After the Deportation, the only things left in the villages were animals. Makazhoi was abandoned. People came in and took everything after we left."

Dada fell silent, staring off across the valley. When he spoke again, his voice cracked. It was the first time I had ever heard him like that. "The whole valley echoed with the sound of wailing: dogs howling and the mooing cows because they needed to be milked. Their udders filled to bursting, and they died." Listening to the fate of the animals terrified me, and I thought of our cows at home suffering like that.

Dada led us to the main cemetery. In the far corner were several stones with mysterious symbols, disks, and sticklike figures. He said they went way back to pagan times when people worshiped the sun and the moon, long before Islam reached Chechnya. Next to the main cemetery was a small enclosure, surrounded by a wire net fence with a large obelisk in the middle. "People from the ravine are buried here," he said.

We asked about the ravine, and he said that Stalin's police threw the unwilling and the infirm over the edge of a cliff to die during the Deportation of 1944. Later that summer, Dada took us to the cliff, an outing that is embedded in my memory as if it had just happened. The snow glittered on the distant peaks; the valley was bathed in soft sunlight. I gazed up and saw two eagles wheeling in circles against a sky so blue it hurt my eyes.

"Look down, but don't get too near the edge. And don't stand up! You'll get dizzy," Dada instructed when we arrived at the precipice. Hussein and I crawled through the grass to the edge of the ravine. Hussein held me by the ankles as I leaned forward and craned my head to take in the abyss. About 600 feet below, the river snaked along the valley floor, its roar reverberating off the rocks so I had to strain to hear Dada tell about what happened on February 23, 1944.

"They shoved the old and crippled over the edge, just to get rid of them quickly!" he said. "Some were our cousins—Karim and Uzum. A number of distant relatives, too. The able-bodied were forced to walk to Vedeno about twenty miles to the east to be shipped like cattle to Kazakhstan. We called it 'the Road to Death.'"

As he spoke, I imagined living bodies hurtling into the void, twisting and turning, clothes billowing in the wind as they plunged, faster and faster. I wondered if their bodies were recognizable as they smashed against the rocks. Did a shrub break their fall? Who survived to tell about this atrocity?

Holding on to tufts of grass, I inched forward again, stretched my neck, but saw no bushes. Nothing but darkness and the silver thread of the river glinting in the sun. My head spun, and I edged backward to safety, feeling nauseous, and waited for Dada to continue.

"From Vedeno, they packed people into trucks." Dada paused, then spoke loudly to be heard above the roar of the river. "They took us to the nearest railroad station. Like animals, they herded us into cattle cars. We were stacked like cigarettes in a pack, men and women standing on the straw together. We held up the babes and children so they wouldn't get crushed.

"After days, the stench of excrement and vomit clogged our lungs. We could barely breathe. Then one by one, people started dying. You'd turn to say something, and the person next to you was dead. The men would carry the corpses over to the corner of the car and lay them like cordwood. The corpses rotted until the train made a stop and they could be thrown out. The moans of the dying and the cries of women grieving for their children rose above the thumping of the wheels." Dada sighed. "By the time we reached Kazakhstan, after a month on the road, the railroad cars were half empty. Half a million died en route."

Dada explained how everything was so well organized by the Soviet authorities that the operation must have been planned way in advance. At each stop along the way, Russian demonstrators met the cattle cars. " 'Traitors! traitors!' they yelled, 'we should kill you!' and heaved stones against the train. 'Traitors! traitors!' " I heard the anger in my father's voice. "They called us traitors!" He fell silent.

Of course, I had heard stories about the Deportation growing up. It was impossible not to hear them. Everyone had lost a relative. Everyone had stories. But during Soviet times you dared talk about the Deportation only behind closed doors and only in a low voice. It was another one of those cover-ups in Soviet history. Most of what I knew about that terrible event was from old women who gathered around our kitchen table. Once, when they thought I wasn't listening, I heard Nana tell my oldest sisters, Raya and Tamara, how women were too ashamed to relieve themselves in the railroad cars in front of men, so held on until their bladders ruptured and they died. Again and again, the old women talked about how they couldn't bury the dead, how they heaved the corpses out of the train for the dogs and jackals to devour. Not being able to bury the dead within twenty-four hours is a sacrilege for us.

"How did they get the bodies up from the ravine to bury them?" I asked.

Dada's face took on a faraway expression. "There were about 200 corpses in all," he said. "The *abrekhs*—these were people who lived as outlaws in the mountains ever since the Soviets came to power—hauled them up. They lashed the bodies to horses. It took them four days."

"Start from the beginning," I said. "What happened to you?"

After being wounded on the northeastern front during the Second World War, Dada said, he was released from the hospital and sent back to Chechnya. His wounds still festered, and he was in severe pain from the shrapnel in his legs and thigh. One day he noticed tents in the field on the mountainside behind Makazhoi. First one tent, then another, all manned by soldiers wearing the uniforms of the Ministry of Internal (Police) Affairs. The uniforms made him uneasy. In his travels he had heard rumors about purges, how people disappeared at night never to be seen again.

"I went to the head of the local council and asked him why all those soldiers were gathered there. He said that the Soviet army needed to rest. I mentioned the word *deportation,* and he laughed as if I had said something crazy."

The councilman added, "I am sure that the troops are being garrisoned in our republic so they can breathe fresh air and rest for the final assault on Berlin."

"What he and I didn't know was that similar tents were going up all over the mountain areas of Chechnya. And not only in Chechnya but in neighboring republics like Ingushetia, Kabardino-Balkaria, Karachayevo-Cherkess, Kalmyk, and farther afield, too. Stalin had already deported the residents of the German colonies who lived along the Volga River and the Tartars from the Crimea."

On the morning of February 23, 1944, the NKVD secret police, which commanded the interior troops, summoned all the men to the square. At first, people thought the soldiers wanted help with food supplies, but when they saw the guards posted and machine guns at strategic places near the administrative buildings, they figured it was to celebrate Soviet Army Day, which falls on February 23.

After all the men assembled, a drunken NKVD officer staggered up the steps of a platform in the square, raised his megaphone, and addressed the crowd. People fell silent. He announced that the Checheno-Ingush Republic was being disbanded! All its people were being deported beyond the Caspian Sea for collaborating with the Nazis. For a moment the crowd fell silent, stunned; then the roars of protests began. Why? Why? The questions ricocheted around the square.

"You are bandits and traitors and have been helping the Germans!" the officer repeated over the loudspeaker.

Anger rippled through the crowd. To call a Chechen a traitor is like calling him a coward. Fighting words. Accusing the people of helping the Germans was crazy. Many of them had no idea a war was going on. They were illiterate. They had no electricity, no newspapers, and they almost never came down from the mountains.

A Chechen lieutenant with medals draped on his chest and a red star on his cap pushed his way through the crowd and onto the platform. "What are you saying?" he shouted, pounding the medals on his chest, his face flushed with fury. "Me, a traitor? I am a veteran. I fought at Stalingrad! I rallied to the call: For Homeland and Stalin!" Then he punched the NKVD man in the face.

"Me, a traitor?" His voice choked, and he wiped tears from his eyes with his fist.

Two guards rushed onto the platform, twisted his arm, and dragged him off. "I wouldn't care even if you were a general!" one of them yelled. "If you are a Chechen you are a traitor!"

"They called us traitors!" Dada fell silent. I sensed the pain behind his words. "They must have shot that lieutenant on the spot," he said when he finally spoke. "I heard shots almost immediately."

Dada said the soldiers moved from house to house, pulling women out by their hair and throwing belongings into the street. They tore apart pillowcases and mattresses, sending feathers flying, hoping to find money or jewelry. The sound of gunfire echoed around the village. Throughout the highlands of Chechnya, the NKVD troops shot the inhabitants of hamlets in out-of-the-way places in cold blood, so as not to be bothered with transporting people to the valley. Dada told us that, up in the mountains at a place called Hybakh, the troops herded 600 men, women, and children into a barn, doused it with gasoline, and set it ablaze, the oldest victim being a 104-year-old man, the youngest, a day-old infant. Another massacre took place on the other side of Chechnya at Galanchozh, when bad weather held up trucks carrying about 500 deportees. Impatient, the guards shot the able-bodied, then pushed invalids, children, and the elderly off a high bank into Lake Galanchozh.

Even villagers in the valley did not escape the fate of their mountain relatives. On the day of the Deportation, the NKVD troops broke into the district hospital at Urus-Martan and shot several hundred sick and wounded patients, including small children. The corpses were then se-

Deportation of Chechens in 1944. (Painting by Sultan Yushaev, 1989)

cretly buried in a common grave hurriedly prepared by the soldiers in the hospital courtyard. For several decades the local population knew nothing of this burial ground. It was only at the beginning of the 1990s that the Chechens discovered this grave as a result of a letter sent to a Grozny newspaper by a Russian woman who had worked as a nurse in the hospital. The remains were then dug up and reburied according to Muslim traditions.

Dada described how in Makazhoi a great column of people more than a mile long—women carrying children, some people riding in horse-drawn carts—started down the mountain. People's faces turned blue from the icy wind sweeping off the snow-covered peaks. The old men chanted and prayed; the women wept. Anyone who tried to escape was shot, as were the infirm who couldn't keep up. "Several men rushed the soldiers," Dada said. "They were bayoneted and shoved into the ravine."

Dada said that at the railroad station, he remembered the troops beat their drums to drown out the cries of the women and children and the chanting of the men. Then Dada told a horrible story about a woman giving birth in the railroad car. She was so ashamed; she didn't want the men to know what was going on so she pulled a blanket up over herself. She died in childbirth, and so did the baby. When the women uncovered her, they saw she had bitten through her bottom lip to stop from crying out.

"And don't think the dying stopped when the people left the cars," Dada said. "People were already sick when they arrived in Kazakhstan, and the authorities ordered local doctors not to treat us 'traitors.' You name it, and we died from it: starvation, cold, dysentery, inflammation of the lungs. 'No jobs for Chechens,' the authorities said, so we starved."

Dada told how he ended up in the little settlement of Vasilevka in Kazakhstan on the windswept steppes, where the temperature fell to minus 60° (Fahrenheit) in winter and rose to 120° in summer. At first, the reception was hostile, but he finally landed a job on a state farm and managed to build a small house. There he met and married Nana. She gave birth to Tamara and Raya. Later, Razyat and Malika were also born in Kazakhstan. In between, Nana gave birth to triplets. For four months she struggled to keep the three babies alive, but the cold penetrated their lungs and they developed trouble breathing. Taking them to the hospital in the neighboring town would have meant arrest. To travel without authorization, even to the next village, even to see relatives, was prohibited and punished by ten years in prison. First one baby girl died, followed by her baby sister an hour later. All that night Dada and his friends fed a fire in the corner of the Chechen cemetery, so that by morning the ground would be melted enough to dig a grave. The baby boy held on for another month before he died, too.

"So why, when you had made a life for yourself in Kazakhstan and had a job and a house, did you decide to return home?" I asked Dada.

"How could you ask such a question?" He looked angry. "*Daimokhk!* Our fatherland! Every day for fifteen years I dreamed of going home and of seeing Makazhoi again."

That morning when we sat in the long grass with the sun on our backs listening to Dada's stories, nothing made sense. How could such horrible things have taken place? "Why, if so many Chechens like you had fought in the war," I asked, "why did they say you were traitors? Why did they pick on us?"

"It was Stalin and his secret police chief," Dada replied. His answer didn't satisfy me, but I didn't dare question him further because I heard the emotion in his voice.

Many years later in the United States, I got my first chance to read the secret order disbanding the Checheno-Ingush Republic. I knew of the existence of this *ukaz* but had never seen it. It and other documents were reprinted in a book, published in Moscow after the Soviet Union collapsed, which I found in the house of an American who had traveled widely in the Caucasus. Although I was prepared, the words shook me.

In connection with the fact that during the period of the Great Patriotic War, especially during the period of the German Fascist invasion in the Caucasus, many Chechens and Ingushis betrayed the

Homeland, defected to the German occupation forces, became saboteurs and spies, infiltrated the rear of the Red Army, carried out orders from the Germans to form armed bands to fight the Soviet authorities over a long period of time, were engaged in dishonest work, carried out bandit raids on surrounding regions, robbed and killed Soviet peoples, the Presidium of the Supreme Soviet announces:

1. All Chechens and Ingushi living on the territory of the Chechen-Ingush Republic, and in adjacent regions, are to be resettled in other areas of the U.S.S.R. and the Chechen-Ingush Autonomous Soviet Socialist Republic is to be liquidated.

The Council of People's Commissars is to relocate the Chechens and Ingushi in new areas of settlement and render them the necessary employment assistance.

2. To create the District of Grozny, with administrative center in the city of Grozny, within the Stavropol Region of the R.S.F.S.R.

3. To transfer to the Dagestan Autonomous Soviet Socialist Republic the following sections of the former Chechen-Ingush Autonomous Soviet Socialist Republic . . .*

The order was signed on March 7, 1944, two weeks after the Deportation by Soviet president Mikhail Kalinin, second only to Stalin.

As I read those words, I recalled the day when Hussein and I crawled to the edge of the cliff and looked into the void.

The depth of the Deportation's imprint on the soul of our nation came home to me again one June day in my last year at school when I saw the skeleton of our neighbor's grandfather lying on a table in a courtyard. That morning I had seen a large crowd of men outside the house next door. Curious, I went over to see what was going on. Our neighbor, Said-Akhmad Magomadov, was unpacking a cardboard box and spreading the contents on a long table made of

---

*Tak Eto Bylo, Natsional'nyye repressii v SSSR, 1919–1952, 3 vols., Moscow: Insan Publishers, 1993, vol. 2, p. 87.

planks and covered with a white sheet. At first I was confused; then I shrank back in horror. Very gently he was removing human bones—dark brown in color—from the box; first the skull, then the ribs, the arms, the legs, until the complete skeleton lay there. I eased forward; it was the first time I had ever seen a human skeleton. As Said-Akhmad arranged the bones on the sheet, his hand moved over them as if in a caress. "It's his grandfather. He brought him home from Kazakhstan," someone whispered. I saw several elders wipe their eyes. Once the skeleton was complete, Said-Akhmad donned linen gloves and with the help of several elders started to wash the bones with soap and water in preparation for the ritual burial. The return of Said-Akhmad's grandfather caused a sensation in Alkhan Kala. It was the first time anyone had brought remains home for burial. Everyone attended the funeral, and people, including Dada, began dreaming of going to Kazakhstan to bring back the remains of others who had died there.

SUMMERS IN MAKAZHOI were an opportunity for Hussein and me to learn more about our Makazhoi clan, which consisted of some 100 families. Dada wanted us to understand the network of family connections that make up a *teip,* or clan. It was hard to remember all the names, there were so many. My father's cousin Nozhu Yesayev was the senior elder of our *teip.* His role was to oversee the welfare of the clan, which included everything from negotiating disputes to nudging young men into marriage and starting a family so the clan would remain vital and Chechnya's traditions wouldn't die.

The summer of 1979 following our sixteenth birthday, it was time for Hussein and me to learn about the *ch'ira,* the blood feud between our neighbor's family and our great-great-grandfather.

"You have reached manhood and are no longer exempt from revenge," Dada said. He explained how our great-great-grandfather and our neighbor's ancestors had fought with a *kinjal, a* dagger, over a piece of land. He knew the details as if the fight had happened yesterday, although the vendetta itself had been resolved years ago after the elders and relatives on both sides assembled and agreed to end the dispute. Our great-great-grandfather was wounded in the hand, he said. Our neighbor's ancestor was wounded in the stomach and died. Even though our families were now on very good terms with our neighbors, Dada warned us to be extra courteous with them.

"You must tell your children about the feud as I have told you," he said. "When you depart this life, you must never leave problems for the next generation to deal with. Be careful so that you don't leave a trace of sorrow."

Little did I realize during those summers in Makazhoi with Dada how the memories would sustain me during the most difficult periods of my life. I remember the beauty of the mountains, but also I remember the day when Hussein and I looked down into the ravine. I still see those two black eagles soaring in the sky, and a shiver runs down my spine.

Chapter 3

Becoming a Doctor

OST PEOPLE EXPECTED I would go in for sports after I graduated from school. Thanks to my performances in the All-Russian Junior Championship and the All-Union Junior Championships in judo, I was gaining a national reputation, so that eighteen cities around the Soviet Union invited me to attend their institutes. In addition, I had letters from twelve teacher-training colleges, as well as proposals from departments of law, economics, and even from the Moscow Institute of International Relations. They saw me as someone who could bring prestige to their institution by coaching or winning competitions for them. The Soviet system placed a huge emphasis on sports as a way to demonstrate the superiority of communism. I was flattered by their solicitations and I loved athletics, but I didn't want to become a coach. In the tenth grade—the last year of school—I decided to try for law school, which would require intensive studying after graduation to prepare for the entrance exams.

The day after graduating from high school in June 1979, I took a train to Kustanai, a city in northeast Kazakhstan, to join Dada, who had taken a job as a foreman of a construction team of seven Chechens working on a huge collective farm. I was accompanied by my friend Khassan Taimaskhanov. Dada usually went to Makazhoi in the summers, but after our neighbor Said-Akhmad brought his grandfather's remains home for burial, Dada saw a job in Kazakhstan as an opportunity to find the remains of the triplets and other relatives.

43

My friend Khassan was a straight-A student and said he would re-view chemistry and physics with me after work to give me a better chance of getting into an institute. We also reviewed biology. For the next five months, Khassan tutored me. We worked seven days a week, although Sunday was a short day so we could do our laundry and go to the public baths.

Dada, a Communist Party member, was a very demanding con-struction foreman, which often irritated me. "It's not good enough," he would say, "you must do everything honestly. After we leave, you can't have everything fall apart and have them blame us."

One day Dada left to make the 360-mile train trip to Vasilevka, where the family had lived during the Deportation. When he re-turned, he was very upset. He had found the Chechen burial ground, but there was nothing left. "I looked for the graves of my grandfather and the three babies who died, but I couldn't find them. Everything was overgrown and the ground flattened," he said. "I said a prayer over the ground."

In November, we returned home to Alkhan Kala, where I worked ten hours a day at the wood-processing plant, pushing heavy logs into the circular saw. At the end of my shift, I would study another two or three hours with the help of a Russian woman who lived next door and taught at the elementary school across from our house. By June 1980, my tutors thought I was ready to enter an institute of higher learning. I wondered if I was good enough to get into law school and become a public prosecutor or a criminal investigator; I wanted to get into a pro-fession that would contribute to society and eventually would allow me to support Dada and Nana.

That summer of 1980, I traveled to the city of Krasnoyarsk in Siberia with my school friend Musa Salekhov to apply to the Institute of Law. Musa was also a judoist and member of the Soviet national team. It wasn't the first time I had been to the Siberian city. In the ninth and tenth grades, I had made the 2,000-mile trip by train to compete in several competitions, and I had attended the Burevestnik judo training camp located ten miles outside the city on the Yenisei River. My old

Musa Salekhov (front row, left) and I (front row, right) open the
new stadium at Krasnoyarsk in 1983.

coach from the camp, Alexei Alexeyevich Krivkov, met us when we
landed at the airport.

I liked everything about Krasnoyarsk: its history, the way the snow
crackled under your feet in winter, and the summer evenings when
the sun didn't set until 1 A.M. and you could stroll along the Yenisei
River. In the seventeenth century, Krasnoyarsk was little more than a
fortress that protected Russian explorers and fur trappers from local
tribesmen. By the beginning of the twentieth century, it had become
a hotbed of worker unrest. Today it is a city of 1 million with twelve
institutes of higher learning, more than 100 factories, lots of parks,
and avenues lined with silver birch trees.

Alexei hailed a taxi to take us to the bus to the Burevestnik camp. As
we drove down the main streets of the city, I noticed an impressive
looking four-story building of yellow brick, with steps leading up to an
entrance surmounted by four columns. At the peak of the roof was a
six-foot-high symbol of a chalice with a white snake coiled around it.

"Stop!" I yelled to the driver, "what's that building?" The driver
slowed down, then explained the building was the home of the Kras-

noyarsk Medical Institute, which had moved from Leningrad during the Second World War to escape the Nazi blockade. "What's that emblem of a snake up there on the roof?" I asked. A symbol on a building was common enough, but it was usually the head of Lenin or the Soviet hammer and sickle, not a snake. The driver didn't know anything about the serpent. But that's when I heard an inner voice: Why couldn't I be a doctor? Only later did I learn that a coiled snake has a special meaning in medicine: Since the snake sheds its skin every year, it represents renewal and healing.

I turned to Musa, excited. "You know, that's where I really want to go. Let's forget the law school and apply to the Medical Institute tomorrow."

"Sounds all right to me," Musa said. "If you think that's the right place, let's apply . . . just as long as we get in somewhere."

Alexei Krivkov frowned. "It's unrealistic," he said. "I used to work at the physical education department of the Medical Institute, and it's very difficult to get in. Besides, they don't like athletes, and they'll do everything to stop you." Originally, Alexei had encouraged us to come to Krasnoyarsk, but now he had turned negative on the medical school. "I'm afraid I won't be able to help you there," he said.

I remained silent. That's still where I want to go, I thought.

AFTER SUPPER AT the Burevestnik camp, I sat on a bench overlooking the Yenisei River. It was a beautiful spot in the forest on the grounds of a large state farm. I let my eyes wander over to the far bank, where the forests disappeared into the distance. The sun sparkled off the water, and I felt excitement in my stomach. The building with the emblem of the snake had ignited my childhood fantasy of becoming a doctor. The decision was already made. I believe God predetermines your fate; the great challenge of life is to discover your destiny early. Becoming a doctor was what I really wanted to do.

"You'll have to study too hard, and a sportsman can't afford to do that." Alexei's voice broke into my reverie. "How can you train for competitions at a professional level and undertake all those studies?"

I let his voice float out over the fast-flowing water. He wanted me in his stable of athletes. It was early in his career, and he thought I would help make his reputation as a coach. He held me up as an example to his Russian sportsmen. "Why can't you be like Khassan and not drink or smoke?" he would tell them. I knew that studying to be a doctor would be hard, but I wanted that more than anything else. Hard work did not scare me; Dada had seen to that.

The next day Musa and I ascended the stone staircase, entered the great hall, walked across the white marble floor, and climbed to the second floor of the Medical Institute to submit our applications. Halfway up, I stopped to look at the mural of a physician dressed in a white coat. He gazed into a microscope while his students looked at him with admiring eyes. As we reached the second floor, I noticed a text in Cyrillic letters covering one of the walls. I read it twice. It was the Hippocratic Oath. Several sentences particularly impressed me: "I will use my power to help the sick to the best of my ability and judgment; I will abstain from harming or wronging any man by it. I will not give a fatal draught to anyone if I am asked, nor will I suggest any such thing. Neither will I give a woman means to procure an abortion. . . . If, therefore, I observe this Oath and do not violate it, may I prosper both in my life and in my profession, earning good repute among all men for all time. If I transgress and forswear this Oath, may my lot be otherwise."

"WHERE ARE YOU from?" A tall, middle-aged woman greeted us. She was the chair of the admissions committee. "Where are you from?" she asked again.

"From the Checheno-Ingush Republic," I replied.

"We only take applicants from Siberia and the Far East," she said. "You should apply to medical schools in your region." A half smile flitted across her face as she delivered the news. Something told me she was putting me off. I was aware of the unwritten, illegal rules designed to keep non-Russian nationalities out of certain professions.

"Show me where it is written that I cannot be admitted," I said.

"I am, after all, from the Russian Federation—Chechnya is part of Russia—it is not a Union Republic."

I was betting that rules discriminating against certain nationalities would not be the kind you wrote down. After all, the Soviet Union claimed all people were equal. The woman fell silent, then picked up my papers and shuffled through them.

"Of course, you will have to pass the four entrance examinations," she said. I knew that if the admissions committee didn't want a Chechen in the Medical Institute, they would make sure I flunked, but I was determined to try. I was right. Musa and I were the only two applicants who failed. At this point Musa decided to drop out, saying he would concentrate on judo and reapply the following year. After the results were announced, I went back to the admissions committee to complain.

"The only reason I failed is because I am from the North Caucasus," I said, "and I intend to submit an official complaint."

The admissions chairwoman shrugged. "If you feel that way, you can retake the examination but with two more questions," she said. As I expected, the two new questions were impossible to answer, and I flunked again.

This time, the examiners wanted me to sign a document, accepting the results. But I refused.

"The material doesn't even appear in the school curriculum, and I intend to write to the rector and ask for a special committee to look into this," I said. The woman looked blank. "I am also going to send a letter to the Soviet Sports Committee in Moscow and to the newspapers." That threat had a definite effect. The Soviet Sports Committee was a powerful organization in charge of sports all over the Soviet Union, and I was well known to them.

The examiners told me I could take exams in biology and anatomy; thanks to my friend Khassan's tutoring over the previous summer, I scored two 5s. This brought my overall score to 18.5 points. But to enter the Medical Institute I needed at least 19 points.

I was half a point short because I had a weak high school record, and I didn't know where to go from there. A few days later when I went to work out at the local gym in Krasnoyarsk, I ran into my coach, Alexei Krivkov. "Does the Medical Institute know that you are already a Master of Sport and that you have won all those competitions?" he asked. Master of Sport was one of the steps up the honor hierarchy of athletics in the Soviet Union, and it was not often that a schoolboy could attain it.

"I didn't tell them because I know they think all athletes are stupid."

"You should tell them now," he said.

"I won't humiliate myself any more. They are determined to keep me out, and I am not going to go begging."

Alexei said he knew Yuri Ivanovich Yakovlev, the head of the physical education department at the institute. He would go himself to tell Yakovlev that I was an accomplished athlete at seventeen who could win competitions for the institute. Krivkov and Yakovlev then approached the rector of the medical school, who, as it turned out, didn't consider athletes to be morons. He had been an athlete himself, a competitive skier. He said he would give me another shot at entering the school if I could prove myself with two victories: a match at the local club and one at the regional championships. Both were in the self-defense sport of sombo.

My future depended on winning those matches. I won the first easily, but the regional tournament was more difficult. For the next three weeks, I practiced three or four hours every day to improve my speed, which is an essential ingredient of judo and sombo. I was better at sombo than judo, and I preferred it. The moves, some 300 in all, are the same in the two sports, but the rules are stricter in judo. On the morning of the competition, all the contestants lined up for a lottery to determine who their opponent would be and what weapon they had to defend against: a wooden pistol, knife, club, stick, or rope.

We stood back-to-back to our opponents. Mine turned out to be a man weighing about 260 pounds to my 150. When the signal sounded, I whirled around rapidly and assessed the situation. His size was actually to my advantage because I could move much faster than he. I made an upward thrust with my right fist, engaged his right arm, then hooked in my left, twisted hard, forcing him to drop the knife. It took just a few seconds, and I had won!

Winning the two competitions still did not automatically guarantee me a permanent place at the Medical Institute. I was classified a "candidate student." I could attend classes in the fall but had no official status until January, and then only if another student dropped out. Probationary students received no housing, and at the beginning of the academic year there were no rooms to rent in all of Krasnoyarsk.

For the next two months, Musa, who had signed up for a medical preparatory course, and I slept in the downtown airport lounge. We would arrive late in the afternoon after training, grab a cup of tea and a sandwich, and study on the hardwood benches till about midnight. Then we curled up in our blue wool sweatsuits with the homeless and slept to the sound of a female voice announcing arrivals and departures. When the police chased us out of the lounge, we decamped to the railroad station.

Many of the homeless became our friends. Some were highly educated and had been thrown out of their families because of drinking. It made me realize you can't condemn someone simply because of hard times. One day, after we had been living with the down-and-outs for about two months, a policeman approached me in the airport lounge. Time to move again, I thought, stuffing my books into my bag.

"I see you're reading lots of books. Who are you?" he said.

He appeared shocked when I said I was a student at the Medical Institute as well as an athlete. "Follow me," he said. He took us to an office on the other side of the airport to meet the police chief, who appeared equally taken aback by our homelessness. "It's a disgrace for students to live like that," he said. "I'm a sportsman too, and I will go and talk to the head of the phys-ed department at the institute."

He must have gone to the rector because within a month, the institute offered me a room on the first floor of one of the student dorms adjacent to the institute. This was one of the rooms used by in-

stitute support staff; all students lived on the higher floors. I was delighted and invited Musa to share it with me.

In January, I became an official student. A year later, in 1981, Musa
was accepted and entered the Medical Institute. That same year, my
twin, Hussein, joined me in Krasnoyarsk and entered the Agricultural
Institute. My parents expected me to look out for him because he was
the younger, if only by a few minutes.

The program at the Medical Institute began with lectures and sem-
inars every morning in physics, organic chemistry, biochemistry,
higher math, biology, anatomy, Latin, and the history of the Communist Party. Classes began at 8 A.M. and went on until 5 or 6 P.M. In the
third year, the students selected a specialty, and I chose dentistry. I figured if I became a dentist, I could later go on to be a facial surgeon.
The idea of being a surgeon had lain dormant in my head since I saw
a certain American film in the 1970s. I don't remember the title, but
the plot was about a famous actress whose face was ruined by a plastic
surgeon who had allowed an infection to develop. She was about to receive an Oscar, but when the nurse removed the bandages, her face
was such a mess she couldn't attend the ceremony. I remember feeling
so sorry for her and thinking how great it would be to be able to repair her face so she could get the award.

Gynecology and obstetrics were required courses, even for students
who planned to go into dentistry. "You are all going to be doctors,"
the professor of gynecology explained to our class. "Who knows? You
may end up on some state farm far away from anywhere and be the
only one around who can deliver a baby."

Male doctors in Chechnya do not do deliveries; that's the province
of women physicians. So I never took the course very seriously until
it came time for us to move from simulating births with dummies to
the real thing. When I was assigned to a delivery room, I thought all
I would have to do was show up, observe a few births, and leave.

"How long do you expect me to stay?" I asked the doctor in charge.

"All night, young man." She looked surprised, handed me a list of
four patients in Ward No. 8, and told me to take their histories, then

take their vital signs. I was just about to enter the ward when I over-heard a woman's voice inside utter the word *Caucasian*. That term covers all the different national groups living north and south of the Caucasus Mountains. I stopped and listened.

"Some Georgian is on duty today," the voice continued. "I won't let him near me."

"Me neither," another voice chimed in.

"No Georgian will examine me," added another woman. "You know what they are like."

They thought I was a Georgian. Imagine if they had known I was Chechen! Terrified, I knocked at the door and entered. All conversa-tion stopped.

"I've been told to take your histories and examine you," I said. Si-lence. Then the woman nearest the door spoke up. "We don't want to be checked by you," she said. "We've already been checked."

"If that's how you feel, I won't insist." What a relief, I thought. I would tell the obstetrician in charge that the women refused to be touched by me, and then I could go home.

The obstetrician took one look at me, her face turning red. Furi-ous, she threw her sheaf of papers on the table. "You follow me!" she said, drawing herself up and striding out. I had difficulty keeping up with her. Like a ship in full sail, she marched toward Ward No. 8 and threw open the door.

"So who is refusing to have him check her?" she shouted. "Quick, I want an answer."

No one spoke up. "All right then, pack your bags, go home, and have your husbands take over your deliveries," she said.

"It's not that we are against him," one of the women said and nod-ded in my direction. "We are embarrassed. We just want to know if there is another student doctor."

The obstetrician grunted and turned on her heel, indicating for me to get on with taking the histories, checking their pulse and blood pressure.

With great embarrassment all around, I managed to examine the four women. Then we moved to the delivery room. The screams of the women scared me. Everything I had learned on the dummy models during the course flew out my head. At the four birthing tables in the room, each woman was at a different stage of labor, all of them in pain, moaning and screaming that this was the last baby they would ever have. After I helped deliver the first baby, a boy, easing his wet little body out of the birth canal and cutting the umbilical cord, I lost some of my terror. Three babies later, I gained control and was even able to reflect on the marvel of a new life.

Later, Musa Salekhov was horrified when I told him about my experience. He said that if he had to go through that, he would quit the institute.

MY SCHEDULE DURING my five years at medical school was grueling, but looking back, I don't think I would have survived the recent Russian-Chechen wars without my dual training as athlete and doctor. It was as though Krasnoyarsk was preparing me for this future ordeal, which required enormous physical stamina and mental fortitude. Each day, I rose at 6 A.M. and went running. After class, I worked out at the gym for two or three hours, then went to the study hall where I stayed until well after midnight. Whenever I went to an athletic competition, I carried two bags, one for clothes and one for books. I studied on planes, in trains, in buses and hotels. Taking time out for a competition meant I had to make up the classes.

In the fall of 1980, I traveled abroad for the first time as a member of the Soviet team, to Poland for the International Junior Tournament. This opened my eyes to KGB control over sports in the Soviet Union, a degrading process. KGB representatives of the Soviet Sports Committee lectured us on how to conduct ourselves as upright Soviet citizens and accompanied us abroad. Prior to leaving, the team was required to visit the Lenin Mausoleum in Moscow. We would wind silently through the mausoleum and were supposed to pledge to uphold the honor of the Soviet Union and the Communist Party as we walked around Lenin's corpse. Fraternization with

The Soviet National Sombo team in Sukhumi, U.S.S.R., 1983. I am in the
third row, third from left.

colleagues from other countries was forbidden. Talk to a "foreigner,"
and you were summoned for interrogation.

Despite the difficulties, I found my medical studies and sports com-
plemented each other. Knowing anatomy helped me gauge my opponent's moves and countermoves. Muscles react in different ways. I
knew from the evident tension in my opponent's muscles what moves
to expect and how to respond. During the years I represented the institute, we rose from twelfth to first place in Krasnoyarsk. The Krasnoyarsk Sports Committee was pleased at my success and awarded me
monthly payments of 340 rubles (510 dollars), about three times the
amount that a Soviet laborer made at the time. (Nana was making 120
rubles, about 156 dollars, a month.) I was now able to send money
home to my family.

AT THE MEDICAL Institute I had no time for socializing, which
made the other students think me strange. When I wasn't studying, I
was training. I learned later that the girls thought I was abnormal and

called me Fanatik behind my back. This was the first time I had met Russians of my age, and I was shocked. The boys sometimes drank beer behind the lids of their briefcases during lectures, smoked, cursed, told dirty jokes in front of the girls, even hugged them in public. The girls would use foul language, too. When a girl told an off-color joke in front of me, I blushed. I suspected they did it on purpose to see my face go red. In the end, I plucked up enough courage to ask them to refrain from telling dirty jokes in my presence. They laughed and from then on would tease me and say, "Khassik, we want to tell a good one—please leave the room!"

At first, the other students avoided me; the girls, especially, sat as far away as possible. Many Russian women think that men from the North Caucasus are too brash with Russian women. Little did they realize my shyness with girls. In Chechnya I had never been alone with an unmarried woman—other than my sisters—unless in the presence of a chaperone. I knew how to behave with Chechen women, who were shy around men, but I had no idea how to treat Russian girls, who smoked, drank vodka, went to cafés alone, and held hands with their boyfriends in public.

The attitude of the other students changed toward me after Professor Vagram Surenovich Emiksiuzyan summoned me to the floor of the auditorium one day before his lecture on the history of the Communist Party. Professor Emiksiuzyan was from the South Caucasus—from the Armenian Soviet Socialist Republic—and he must have been sympathetic because I was from the same region.

"You," he said, pointing to me in the back row, "where are you from?"

"Chechnya," I said, standing up.

"Come down to the well of the auditorium," he said. "I want to shake your hand!"

I felt all eyes on me as I made my way down from my seat at the back of the amphitheater.

"Comrades, do you know who is studying with you?" Professor Emiksiuzyan addressed the class. The students came to attention, and the auditorium fell silent as I fidgeted beside the professor.

"Baiev, Khassan!" Professor Emiksiuzyan announced with a flourish. "It is always a pleasure for me, a Caucasian myself, to hear in the Academic Council that our student, Khassan, is winning all these athletic awards. TV and newspapers are often reporting on his achievements."

He paused for his words to take effect. "And to think that *you* don't even know who he is!"

I felt embarrassed. I had kept my extracurricular activities secret. After this incident, I noticed that the girls began to move to my side of the classroom.

By the end of the second year, the other students had started to accept me. Although the girls wouldn't admit it and still joked about my old-fashioned ways, I think they secretly liked how I treated them. They invited me to their birthday parties and pressed me to join them at cafés. They knew I would never get drunk, and were glad I was there to protect them from anyone who did.

Then I got to know Marina. At first, when she learned that I came from Chechnya, she made it clear that she didn't want anything to do with me. She was a Russian, and if we passed on the stairs, she greeted me coldly. Her aloofness didn't worry me. On the contrary, I found it attractive. She reminded me of Chechen women who behaved modestly in front of men. I had noticed her before because she was so pretty, with dark hair, which fell over her shoulders. She didn't use a lot of makeup and wore bright-colored clothes. In the third year, I found myself sitting next to her at a surgery lecture.

"Where do you come from?" I asked.

"From Shakhty," she said. Shakhty is a town in southern Russia that is near the border of the North Caucasus.

"So you are one of my countrywomen," I quipped. She frowned at me as if I had said something insulting.

By a strange coincidence, Marina lived with her grandmother in an apartment on the second floor of a building near the gym where I worked out. It turned out that I had met Marina's grandmother long before as she worked as an attendant at this sports complex. Whenever I saw her, I greeted her and inquired about her health, as is the custom in Chechnya when you talk to your elders. I learned later from Marina that her grandmother had commented on my manners. "Why don't you come by for tea?" her grandmother urged one afternoon when she met me outside the gym. I gladly accepted.

Their apartment consisted of two small rooms, a tiny kitchen, bathroom, and separate toilet. A balcony off the main room looked out over the gym. On that first visit, we sat around a small table in the kitchen. Marina served tea with an assortment of homemade jams, which she laid out on the table in small saucers to spoon into the tea. Her grandmother did most of the talking. Marina tried to warn me not to ask about her health, but my earlier inquiries about her health gave her an excuse to list all her maladies, aching joints, bunions, heart palpitations. Then she brought out an old album and showed me photographs of herself during the Second World War. "I was part of a women's battalion," she said with pride. I told her that my father had also fought in the war on the Finnish front and later at Murmansk. That pleased her.

From then on, I often dropped by for tea after training. I loved sitting in the cozy kitchen and eating the jams. Marina helped me with lectures I had missed because of training, and we discussed what we had learned in class that day. Marina, who wanted to become a dentist, was a good pianist and would often play for me.

For the next two years, my chaste relationship with Marina exhilarated and tormented me. She was so easy to talk to and had a good sense of humor. In her company I felt relaxed. Yet I knew I could never marry her. She was a Russian, and my family wanted me to marry a Chechen girl. That was expected of me. I wanted a Chechen bride, too, and it had nothing to do with feelings against Russians or Chechnya's endless tension with Russia. I wanted a woman who would speak my language to our children, who would understand the suffering of our people, support my relatives, and observe our customs, such as being ready to receive guests at any hour of the day or night. I knew that when the time came, my family would help arrange a marriage for me. I trusted them to select a wife who would make a good mother. We believe marriage is a permanent relationship which encompasses the whole extended family. You may not be in love when you marry, but love and commitment to family develop later.

Sometimes I weakened and imagined Marina and I had a future together. Then I would remember my parents and how upset they would be if we married. I recalled the stories of Chechen men marrying Russian women: the quarrels, the divorces, the suffering children. I knew that Marina would find living under the same roof with Dada and Nana and my sisters too hard. She wouldn't understand our traditions.

What I had observed of Russian traditions, I didn't like. They talk about equality, but from everything I observed, the men drink, leaving the women with a double burden at home and no support for the children. Some Chechen men drink too much, but it is not an epidemic as it is in Russia, where the average life span of a male is about fifty-eight years. We believe it is shameful for a man not to support his children. Actually, we believe women are more valuable than men, as reflected in the proverb that the life of a woman is worth two men. We also believe that men and women have different roles to play. Women look after the children and the home; men provide for them, although some of our women have careers and want more independence.

Of course, some Chechen men do marry Russian women. After arriving in Krasnoyarsk, Hussein started courting Rita, a Russian woman. I tried to discourage this relationship—not that I had anything against Rita—because I worried that marriage to a Russian would separate him from his cultural roots and could result in his staying in Krasnoyarsk, which would upset our parents. In the end Hussein married Rita but kept the marriage secret from our parents. Later, when Hussein visited home, he never brought Rita or his children. He only brought his family home after the start of the second Chechen war in 1999.

My friend Shahid's marriage to a Russian fell apart after his father died and his younger brother was killed in a car crash. At that point Shahid wanted to return to Chechnya. His wife accompanied him with the children. In the beginning she appeared to adjust, but with time she became increasingly unhappy and wanted to return to Kras-noyarsk. Shahid's family refused to let her go, so one day she fabri-cated a letter saying a member of her family was dying and she had to leave. She left without the children and didn't return. She wrote ask-ing for the children, but they said they wanted to stay in Chechnya, and Shahid's family refused to let them join their mother.

IN OUR FOURTH year, male students were required to do several months of military training at a base outside Krasnoyarsk. We were as-signed medical-related exercises, like donning antichemical warfare suits and running five miles. I lost a lot of weight on the poor military rations, which made it difficult because, at the time, I was training for the All-Union Judo Cup. I admit it; I had become single-minded—a driven man with no time for emotional entanglements. I wanted to become a doctor and an athlete. I had to study hard and train so that I could continue winning athletic competitions for the medical school.

In 1983, however, I encountered an obstacle that almost caused me to drop medicine and sports altogether. That year, as a result of win-ning several top national competitions in judo and sombo, my coach said I was ready for the World Youth Championship in Spain that fall. The institute gave me three months off to train on condition I made up my medical courses in the summer. I traveled to a special sports camp run by the Soviet Sports Committee in the town of Vladimir, some 120 miles from Moscow.

Before I left for Vladimir, an official of the Krasnoyarsk KGB summoned me and asked that I report on the other team members, something I could never do. Being an informant was counter to all Chechen traditions. I explained that if I accepted his offer, I would dis-honor myself, my family, and my whole clan. "My father would shoot me if he found out that I had done such a thing," I said.

"If you don't work for us, you will not go to the world champi-onship," the KGB man replied.

I felt my future closing in. The KGB would concoct any phony rea-son to throw me off the team. I braced myself for what might happen at the training camp in Vladimir. One morning, I discovered I had been locked into my own room. Being late for morning lineup was a serious infraction which could result in expulsion from the program. I went out onto the balcony, walked over to the next room, pushed open the balcony door, walked back into the hotel corridor, and found an open staircase leading downstairs.

Another time, the soccer coach forced me to play goalie. I protested because I had never played that position. Near the end of the game, I fell trying to stop the ball. At that moment, I felt a savage kick to my lower ribs from a player I had never seen before. The pain was so great I couldn't stand up. The coaches assumed I would drop out, but I was determined to prove them wrong. Four times a day for the next month I massaged the huge swelling above my hip with grease I got at a pharmacy. Finally, the swelling went down.

After I beat the fighter who was chosen to take my place, the Soviet Sports Committee agreed that I should join the team. Reporters came from the newspaper *Soviet Sport* to interview me. In Krasnoyarsk, articles appeared in the media about me. We were scheduled to fly from Moscow's Sheremetyevo airport to Madrid. Once seated in the plane, I heaved a sigh of relief. At long last, my dream was coming true.

Then I felt a tap on my shoulder. I turned around and saw three men in plain clothes standing next to my seat. Two I recognized as coaches from the Soviet Sports Committee; the third I hadn't seen before. "Take your bag and get out of the plane," one of the coaches said.

"What is this about?" I rose to my feet. It didn't take long to figure it out.

"Follow us, and we will explain." They led me from the plane and across the tarmac to the waiting room. They didn't invite me to sit down.

"The Soviet Sports Committee has decided to withdraw your name from the team," one of them said.

"But I beat Sidorov!" I exclaimed. I knew the real reason I wasn't going. My anger welled, and it was all I could do not to hit them, but I would not give them the excuse to arrest me.

"That's their decision. We can't do anything about it," the KGB stooge said. He shrugged and turned away.

After the men left, I flopped down on the bench in the waiting room, deflated. All that training, for nothing. Being a Master of Sports, having a black belt, and winning all those medals counted for nothing if you were a Chechen and if you refused to report on your teammates for the KGB. I had been naive to think that winning medals for the Soviet Union was more important than keeping Chechen athletes down. During that pre-Gorbachev time, a ceiling existed beyond which we Chechens couldn't rise. We could compete in national championships, in European championships, but not in a world championship or the Olympics.

Finally, after three hours, I managed to get up and find a bus going to Moscow. I stayed in Moscow a couple of nights with a friend who was studying there. I was overcome by a feeling of complete emptiness. It seemed like the end of everything. I was convinced I would have to go home and forget Krasnoyarsk; go back to helping my parents, working in the fields, and attending the livestock.

WHEN I OPENED the gate to our house, I found my family sitting around the kitchen table. They were shocked to see me. "I was forced off the plane," I told them. "I'm going to give up medical school, too!"

Dada frowned. After a few minutes of silence he said, "This sort of thing happens all the time to Chechens. Get used to it!"

"I've lost all interest in studying," I protested.

"Get back there!" he barked. "Life does not end with this. Sports are a temporary thing; your profession is for your whole life!"

Four days later, I flew back to Krasnoyarsk. My enthusiasm for international competition was gone. There was no point when the Soviet Sports Committee decided who would win and who would lose. I stopped going to the gym and began spending more time on my studies.

★ ★ ★

AS GRADUATION APPROACHED at the end of the fifth year in 1985, everyone started getting nervous about the coming *rasprede-leniye*—distribution of job assignments. In the Soviet Union, you owed three years to the state after your free education. The government dispatched students to different parts of the country. Often the places were at the ends of the Earth—in the wilds of Siberia, in the far north, or on the border with China. During those years, they completed their residency and worked as doctors in rural areas.

One evening before the announcements were made, Marina and I took a walk along the banks of the Yenisei River. The night was balmy, and the Northern Lights streaked the sky purple. Marina was on edge. I knew she was waiting for me to tell her my plans and hoped they would include her. She had told me earlier that she had broken off her engagement to a local boy and that her parents were pressuring her to marry after graduation. I was also nervous, believing that if Marina and I were sent to the same place, we would end up married. I felt my life spinning out of control. I prayed to Allah that my good grades and athletic victories would keep me in Krasnoyarsk.

Classmates and teacher at the Medical Institute. I am in the second row, far left.

Suddenly, Marina started sobbing. "I love you. I can't imagine life without you."

I begged her to stop crying. "You know what kind of conditions we are brought up in, in Chechnya," I said. "To live there, you have to be born there. You would not survive it."

"If you love someone enough, you will adjust," she said.

"I don't want to ruin your life. It's for your own good."

She fell silent. I felt terrible.

Finally, Job Assignment Day arrived. We gathered in the rector's large office. Everyone was tense, waiting with great anticipation. An unknown official began reading out the placements. Marina's number came up before mine. The professor announced, "Blagoveshchensk— one year of dental residency followed by two years of work."

I took a deep breath. "Please, Allah, don't let me go there too." I muttered a prayer under my breath as I waited for my number to come up.

"Number twenty-two, Baiev, Khassan." The professor said, his voice echoing off the walls. I felt it coming, but I gasped when he said, "One year of residency in Blagoveshchensk and two years' service in Tynda."

Everything I had fought for began to crumble. Blagoveshchensk was

Me and my medals.

on the border with China; Tynda, a tiny settlement on the newly constructed Baikal–Amur railway.

What happened next is hard to explain. I lost control of myself. I
looked around the room and saw the rector sitting in the front row.
Over the years he had taken a liking to me. Often he stopped me in
the corridor to shake my hand, inviting me to come to him with
any problems. I went down to him and addressed him directly, asking if this was the way I was being repaid for bringing honor to the
institute.

He was taken aback. Then he rose to his feet and turned to face the
audience. "I must have been distracted by too much work," he said.
"This young man should not be sent to Blagoveshchensk. He is still
young and still has many more competitions to go to."

He pointed to all the silver cups I had won, which were displayed
on his shelves, and said he would revise the order. I was allowed to
stay in Krasnoyarsk for my residency.

The relief that swept over me also carried sadness and guilt. At last
I plucked up the courage to look at Marina. Her face dissolved in despair, and I knew she was fighting back tears.

Our graduation ceremony was held on June 22, 1985, at the metal-
lurgical factory, in a huge hall with marble columns and red plush curtains. Dignitaries made speeches, including the chairman of the local
Communist Party, who emphasized our responsibility to the state.
Special awards followed the speeches. I was recognized for studying
well and for my sports achievements. Then we all stood up, and one of
the professors read the Hippocratic Oath, which we recited together,
word for word. I knew that I had committed to myself always to place
the lives of my patients above my own. My hand shook when I received the diploma, and afterward I rushed outside to the park overlooking the Yenisei River so I could look at it without anyone
observing me. I had done it.

Seeing Marina off to Blagoveshchensk was painful. In the airport
departure lounge in Krasnoyarsk, we took last place in the check-in
line, waiting to postpone the good-byes for as long as possible. The

line grew shorter, and we both fell silent. I didn't know what to say or what to do.

As she passed her ticket to the clerk, she gave me a strange look. Her expression was a mixture of love and contempt. "Oh you! . . . *Akh ty!*" She didn't finish the sentence. I sensed her bitterness. Then she shook her head and turned away to hide her tears. She picked up her luggage and walked toward the gate. I waited for the gate to close; then I turned and started back through the crowd to the bus to take me back into the city.

At the institute, I headed for my room, closed the door, and threw myself down on the bed. I refused all contacts. I needed time to recover, to convince myself that what I had done was right. Friends banged on the door, but I refused to open it. I wasn't hungry. The only thing I consumed was water. I lay on my bed trying to read medical books and the local newspapers. "Oh you! . . . *Akh ty!*" Marina's words rang in my ears. I kept telling myself we Chechens were different. I kept hearing Dada's voice: "Chechens must be strong. We must always expect the worst. To succumb to emotions is weakness." Finally, after ten days, I shaved and reentered the world.

I DID MY medical residency working in the maxillofacial department. At the same time, I tutored students on oral and facial carcinoma. Oncology taught me a great deal about anatomy and about the human organism's will to live. A patient may be in agony and dream of release, but the body doesn't permit it, as though life is orchestrated by some outside force.

After completing my residency and an internship in plastic surgery of the face and jaws, I decided it was time to go home. I had lived in Russia for nine years, and I needed to become reacquainted with Chechnya. But the rector of the Medical Institute offered me various incentives to stay on. I could do further graduate work, hold a position in one of the departments, or even head the physical education department. He tried to persuade me with offers of an apartment and other benefits. But I refused all the blandishments because I did not want to be tied down to Siberia. In the end, I was assigned to Partizansk, some 120 miles from Krasnoyarsk, where I worked as a dentist in a local clinic attached to a state farm. It was obviously punishment, but it wasn't the far ends of the Earth, where Marina and some of the other students ended up.

I stayed in Partizansk only four months because my sister Raya became ill with what we thought was ovarian cancer and I was urgently needed at home. Since I had already completed my residency, the Medical Institute gave me its blessing. At the beginning of May 1988, I returned to Grozny to start a new life as a doctor in my own country.

Chapter 4

Finding a Wife

A FTER NINE YEARS away, it was wonderful to be back with my family. As I entered my childhood home, memories from the past flooded over me: the raids on the cornfield; waking to the smell of bread from Nana's stove in the courtyard; Hussein and I jumping up from our little bed in the kitchen and rushing outside to grab some freshly made bread and milk warm from the cow; Dada marching us to school in our "family underpants." When I went down into the empty cellar, I could still smell the hundreds of watermelons Dada used to store there.

While I was away in Krasnoyarsk, Dada had built a new four-room brick house next to the original house he acquired after returning from Kazakhstan. He and Nana had moved there, leaving the old house for Malika and Razyat, though they still all lived as one family, eating their meals together. When I came home, Malika and Razyat moved into the brick house with Dada and Nana and left the old house for me. I have never slept so well as I did those first nights back home.

Fortunately, it turned out that Raya had an ovarian cyst, not cancer, and she recovered fully. Once I knew that she was all right, I drove into Grozny. I couldn't wait to walk the streets again. With its shade trees, parks, fountains, and alleys lined with flowers, it was the most attractive city in the North Caucasus. Like Alkhan Kala, Grozny was founded as a fort by the much hated nineteenth-century general Alexei Yermolov. On the western outskirts of the city were the factories and oil refineries which, after Baku, had made Grozny the oil capital of the Soviet Union and produced the wealth to construct several fine buildings. I hadn't fully realized the importance of oil in Grozny's history until a friend drove me to see the six-foot brick marker standing among the rusting oil tanks and derricks with the iron plaque in the center reading, "Here the English first drilled for oil in 1893." Farther down the road was Grozny's so-called English District, with its brick, semidetached cottages with brown tile roofs. The Tudor-style houses stood out from those constructed by Russian, Armenian, and Dutch businessmen in Grozny before the Russian Revolution of 1917.

During the time I had been away, the atmosphere in Grozny had changed. *Glasnost* and *perestroika* had created chaos after Mikhail Gorbachev came to power in 1985. The Baltic states were in revolt. Independence movements mushroomed in the Caucasian republics of Georgia, Armenia, and Azerbaijan. Chechnya, which had been struggling for independence for hundreds of years, saw an opportunity to shake off the Russian yoke. Russians still held the top posts in the Communist Party and the oil industry. The KGB police acted like Big Brother, watching our every step.

Grozny before the war—the most beautiful city of the North Caucasus.

Now that I was home, I couldn't wait to start treating patients. The authorities in Krasnoyarsk had excused me from any further obligations in Partizansk. I accepted a job in the trauma department of the First City Emergency Hospital in Grozny, which treated people from all over the republic. The hospital was in the center of the city next to Grozny's famous Petroleum Institute, which attracted students from all over the Soviet Union, and not far from the university. If I took the fast route from Alkhan Kala along the Moscow–Baku highway, it took less than twenty minutes to reach work. But I preferred the slower route over the back roads because accidents happened almost every day on the highway.

It was said that the 700-bed Emergency Hospital was originally built to treat the workers of the Red Hammer Factory, which produced military equipment and ammunition during the Second World War. These Stalin-era buildings were solid, not like the flimsy ones constructed under Nikita Khrushchev. On the other hand, the medical equipment was either out-of-date or nonexistent, and the doctors had little idea what was going on in major medical centers in the rest of the Soviet Union, let alone the outside world. The specialty of reconstructive surgery was primitive, and cosmetic surgery was considered an exotic practice performed only in Moscow or capitalist nations.

Mostly, I treated victims of car accidents, burns, malignant tumors, and congenital defects like cleft palates and harelips. I felt such satisfaction after treating patients—especially children with deformities—and returning them whole to the world. I thanked fate for taking me to Krasnoyarsk and giving me such wonderful teachers. My salary was now about $140 per month, one of the highest for doctors in the Soviet Union.

One Sunday morning at 1 A.M. a few weeks after I had started working, I was urgently summoned to the hospital. Zura, a twenty-two-year-old bride, had been rushed to the emergency room with multiple skull fractures on her wedding day after the vehicle in which she was riding had spun out of control and collided head-on with a truck. I flung on my clothes and headed for the hospital. Running down the corridor, toward the emergency room, I heard her screams.

One look at the elongation of her features beneath the bloody pulp that was once her face, and I knew that the bones beneath her face were seriously fractured. The x-rays confirmed the damage. Her blood pressure was low, her skin pale and clammy. Besides the breaks in the jaws, she had a broken nose, fractured eye sockets, and fractures of the sinus walls. She could not talk and had difficulty swallowing. Stabilizing her was my top priority.

First, I had to stop the bleeding, then drain off liquid from her spinal column to alleviate pressure in her head, and, finally, stabilize her jaws. I affixed metal "Tigershted" splints to her upper and lower jaws, threading fine titanium wire around each tooth and the corresponding "toothlets" in the splints. I removed one broken tooth on the fracture line to make a gap for a feeding tube, which would be used after the operation for small infusions of bouillon, juices, and sour cream. Then I inserted an oxygen tube in one nostril, prescribed painkillers, sedatives, and antibiotics.

"Let me operate on her," I begged the chief surgeon. I wanted to show what I had learned at Krasnoyarsk. Although I was only twenty-five, I was the only doctor in the republic with a specialty in maxillo-facial and oral surgery. I had already done similar operations. I was sure I could put Zura's face back together. "You have golden hands. You were meant to be a jeweler," a Moscow clairvoyant called Juna had once told me. Instead of gold and precious stones, I worked with slivers of bone, muscle, and skin.

The chief surgeon frowned. "You're only a dentist; you can't operate on her," he snapped. "We will send her to Dagestan to the hospital in Makhachkala," he added.

"My training is as a dental surgeon," I insisted, emphasizing the word *surgeon*. "And I have performed similar operations. She could die on that hundred-mile trip. We can do the operation here." The chief surgeon remained silent. "You can create a committee; have the most experienced surgeons stand next to me during the operation," I continued.

Zura's relatives were even less enthusiastic about me doing the

operation than the chief surgeon. "What! That man do the operation?" I overheard Zura's sister tell one of the relatives. "He looks
more like a prizefighter than a surgeon."

Finally, the chief surgeon relented because of my experience in reconstructive surgery. "You can do the operation, but I am going to invite a team of experienced doctors to observe and assist you."

Before I donned my scrubs and mask, I excused myself and withdrew to an empty office next to the operating room. There I turned
to the wall, took a deep breath, closed my eyes as our judo and sombo
coaches had taught us, and let the tension drain from my body. In my
head, I heard the words they would have us recite: "I am not afraid. I
am strong. I must be an example to others." I said a quick prayer, asking Allah to help me, entered the operating room, and prepared for
the surgery.

My assistant passed me a scalpel. The distinguished observers took
their positions at my back, including Chechnya's leading traumatologist, as well as the chief of the hospital's emergency department. I felt
perfectly calm.

After administering a local anesthetic, I made an elliptical incision
in Zura's lower neck to introduce a breathing tube into the trachea.
Once that was done, we administered general anesthesia through the
tube and then made two cuts along the eyebrow line at the outer edge
of the eye sockets. Once the bone was exposed, I drilled small holes
through the ridge of her eye sockets, on both right and left sides.

Finally, I inserted a hollow needle through the right eyebrow incision and worked it down through the flesh under her right cheek, ex-
iting through the gums above the splint on the upper jaw. Through the
needle, I threaded a fine titanium wire, looped it around the end of the
upper splint, and pushed the free end of the wire back up the hollow
needle. When I could grasp both ends of the wire, I slid the needle back
out of the flesh, free of the ends of the wire. I repeated this maneuver
on the left side. The only thing left to do was to pull up on the wires
on both sides of her face, easing the dislocated bones back into their
original positions. Then I passed one free end of the wire on both sides

of the face through the holes in the supraorbital ridges, twisted the two wires together, corkscrew-like, so they would create and maintain pressure on the dislocated bones, thereby immobilizing the skull. Over the next six weeks, the bones and fractures would gradually knit together. The whole operation took six hours.

After the operation, the chief traumatologist congratulated me in the surgeon's lounge. My techniques had given him new ideas for his own work, he said.

A few days later, Zura was able to breathe through her nose, and I removed the tracheal tube and sewed up the incision. Six weeks later, I checked Zura's x-rays and saw the bones had knitted. She recovered fully, and several months later, her family invited me to their home and also took me to the place where the accident had happened.

I wanted to continue in cosmetic surgery. Over the next couple of years the hospital allowed me to operate on private patients at the end of my official workday, starting with young women who disliked the shape of their noses. The face-lift I performed for one woman named Raya established my reputation as a cosmetic surgeon. The day she came to my office, she was distraught. "I am twenty-seven years old and I used to be very fat; then my husband died, and I lost all this weight," she sobbed. "Now everything sags. I work in a beauty shop, so how can I sell beauty products when I look so awful?"

Women who wanted cosmetic surgery often took me into their confidence. They knew I wouldn't reveal their secrets: hopes that a face-lift would bring back a wandering husband, or a new nose would attract a suitor. At times I felt more like a psychologist than a surgeon.

"I can guarantee to make you look prettier," I would tell them, "but surgery can't control the minds of suitors or husbands. All I can promise is to do my best."

Raya's new face thrilled her. Without informing me, she slipped her before-and-after pictures to the local television station, along with a letter telling them how I had changed her life. I hadn't charged her for the face-lift, so I think she wanted to repay me with publicity. That was the last thing I wanted. I didn't need the interruption of reporters and cameras outside the operating room. After the program aired, over 100 women and girls arrived at the hospital armed with pictures from magazines showing how they wanted to look. One administrator of the hospital ordered them out on the street. This attention embarrassed me and undoubtedly annoyed the hospital administrators.

A strict Muslim may question the practice of cosmetic surgery, because the Koran says you shouldn't alter what Allah gave you. That may be true, but I saw myself as a sculptor who could repair birth defects. My reward was seeing the expression on a woman's face when she looked in the mirror after a successful operation, watching how she carried herself with greater confidence as she left my office; how she smiled and thanked me.

My reputation spread. At first, I didn't charge my private patients; then I began asking money from people who could afford to pay—the nouveaux riches, film stars, singers, and actresses. Mikhail Gorbachev's *perestroika* was gaining ground, and private enterprise was no longer illegal. I used my earnings to improve my office, dividing the space with a curtain to create a consulting room and a small operating room. The hospital administrators did not object to my after-hours work. In Moscow, a face-lift cost the equivalent of $3,000. In Grozny, I did the procedure for $300, the price of a round-trip plane ticket to Moscow. The waiting period for my services grew from weeks to months.

I began saving a lot of money. I went to Moscow to buy the latest equipment, including American supplies from Johnson & Johnson because I dreamed of opening my own clinic one day. I began stockpiling equipment and supplies. I bought a new car. I purchased a three-room apartment for Malika next to First City Emergency Hospital where she worked and a five-room apartment for myself in an old building not far from the sports stadium, so I could work out after hours. I wanted to build a new house for my parents and began accumulating building materials.

ALTHOUGH I IMMERSED myself in work, it was impossible to ignore the storm clouds on the horizon. Walking to and from the hospital through the square next to the presidential palace, I saw gatherings of middle-aged and elderly people. Sometimes I stopped to talk to them, and they reminded me of the Deportation and expressed fear that Russia still wanted to wipe out the Chechens. It was clear that our people desired political and religious freedom. Islam had always played an important role in our lives. Government workers and schoolteachers wanted to worship without losing their jobs, as had been the case under communism. Village elders were busy collecting money to build mosques or restore old ones. Talk of independence was everywhere.

Prior to the 1991 referendum on Chechnya's independence, I attended a public meeting to hear General Dzhokhar Dudayev speak. It was standing room only. Dudayev was the only Chechen to have risen to the rank of general in the Soviet military, before resigning his commission and returning to Chechnya to become a political leader in March 1991. Delegates had come from all over the region to hear him and voice their opinion on the political future of Chechnya. General Dudayev, a slightly built, charismatic figure with a black belt in karate, stepped up to the podium. He was immaculately dressed in a dark business suit and tie, and had a pencil-thin mustache.

"Because of our oil, we can live like the Kuwaitis," he said to the crowd. He went on to talk about Chechnya's resources such as oil and mineral water. (The latter sold for a dollar a bottle in the West.) There was no need for Russia anymore. "We will live in mansions with golden faucets like they have in Kuwait," he promised.

After he spoke, delegate after delegate called for the end of repression, recalling the Deportation and the era of Imam Shamil when the North Caucasus united under the flag of Islam to drive the Russians out.

I didn't know what to make of Dudayev's vision. I wasn't an economist, but I had the feeling that things were moving too fast. I wasn't against independence but against confrontation with Russia. Chechnya is a small country. How could it survive economically if not on friendly terms with Russia? No one knew how much oil Chechnya possessed or how we would go about developing and exporting it.

Selling mineral water to the West was also a novel idea. Still, I felt that if such an experienced leader as Dudayev was talking this way, there must be something to it.

Friends asked me why I didn't become involved with the fight for independence. My answer was simple: "Medicine—not politics—is my passion."

On November 1, 1991, Chechnya declared its independence and announced it had seceded from the Russian Federation. Dada was skeptical. "Independence will never work out in practice," he said. "The Russians are calm now, but get them riled up and you'll have trouble. There will be too many victims."

N O W   T H A T   I had a job and was making money, my family started pressuring me to get married. I knew I would have to find a wife sooner or later; I wanted a big family, but at the time I was so immersed in my work that I didn't want to think about it.

"The family elders think it is time for you to get married," my sister Malika said one day as she chopped cabbage on the kitchen table to make soup. Over the sound of Malika's chopping, I heard horns, gunshots, and loud music because somewhere on the other side of town a wedding was taking place. Weddings inevitably gave my sisters the opportunity to raise the issue of finding a wife for me.

The wedding procession raced through the streets to pick up the bride and deliver her to the house of her husband-to-be. The hullabaloo grew louder as the cars approached. First the lead car with the elders and relatives roared past our house, followed by a column of other vehicles with the groom's male relatives and friends. The men wore white shirts under dark suits; the women silk dresses and head scarves. Ribbons and balloons festooned the cars. After the procession passed, I turned to Malika and grinned. She gathered up the bits of cabbage, dropped them into a saucepan of boiling water on the stove, and looked at me with a knowing smile as if to say, "Isn't it about time for you, too?" She was so predictable.

I sighed. "I'm too busy, but I'll think about it."

"Dada says that if you can't find a wife, then the family will do it for you." Malika approached the stove, removed the lid on the saucepan, and stirred the *borscht* with a wooden spoon. "The elders are beginning to ask if you have a family in Krasnoyarsk, and if you secretly married a Russian woman there," she said.

Dada operated behind the scenes, posing any question on this subject through my sisters or my mother. The rumors about having a wife in Krasnoyarsk bothered me. When Nana and Dada found out that Hussein had married Rita, they were devastated, although they never talked about it.

"I will try," I told Malika. Rumors like that dishonor our family.

IN MY FIRST attempt at finding a wife, I was helped by a Russian gynecologist at the hospital whose name was Natasha. We had become friends after I treated one of her patients injured in a car crash. "How would you like to meet this very pretty Chechen girl?" Natasha said one day as we drank tea in the surgeon's lounge between operations. "Zina is a graduate of the Medical Institute in Makhachkala and is doing her residency in gynecology."

I agreed, although without much enthusiasm. It seemed everyone was working on getting me married.

Zina joined us for tea a few days later. She was very pretty with blond hair and blue eyes. After that, I bumped into her a couple of times in the hospital and walked her to the bus stop. Her parents and grandparents were respected in their village, her siblings upstanding. Everyone said she was industrious and would make a good wife.

The next time I met Zina in the street outside the hospital, I asked if I could visit her at home. Of course, she understood what that meant. You don't ask a girl for a visit unless you have marriage in mind. She agreed.

Zina lived in Shali, a town some five miles south of Grozny. I decided against taking my cousin Musa Saponov with me, though taking a male witness is the custom. Musa, the son of my adopted sister Larissa, was a jokester. The friend's role is "to sell" you to the girl by telling her what a wonderful husband you would make. Such compliments would embarrass me, and I knew Musa would never stop joking about it. As tradition requires, I requested Zina's neighbor to announce my arrival to her. Zina's sister greeted me at the door and led me into a large room with ornate moldings around the ceiling and heavy lace curtains over the windows. After Zina entered, she and her sister served me tea. I made the usual inquiries about the health of her parents, then introduced the subject of marriage.

"I guess you know why I am here," I said. Zina looked at the floor and nodded. "You know everything about me, and I know everything about you. You must understand I am very busy at the hospital, so I don't have time to pay you a lot of visits." I waited for Zina to respond, but she remained silent. "So you must think about my proposal and consult with your parents." I paused and got ready to leave. "I will return in three days for the answer."

As she saw me to the door, I noticed that her face had turned white. I had been a bit brusque, I thought.

Several days later, I returned to Zina's house and asked if she had made up her mind. She didn't answer. I waited, but she only stared at the floor. "I assume your answer is no," I said. She still didn't react. "I understand," I said, rising to my feet. "I thank you for your time," I added, trying to be polite, and walked out the door.

I made two more awkward efforts to find a wife, and each time the woman turned me down. My fourth try was with Zara. I remembered seeing her as a small girl on the bus or when her family came to visit ours. When I returned from Krasnoyarsk, I hardly recognized her. She had grown into an attractive young woman with dark curly hair, pale skin, and a mischievous smile. She worked in a jewelry store. My older sister Raya and Zara's mother were good friends. Our family elders approached her family to learn if they would welcome me as a suitor. They agreed. So I visited her, as I had visited Zina and the other two women. The result was the same: She turned me down. I felt terrible.

"That's it!" I said to my sisters Malika and Razyat, not wanting them to know how humiliated I felt. "Look, I've tried. There must be something wrong with me. I keep getting rejected."

Malika and Razyat, who were drinking tea at the kitchen table, looked up, shocked. Then they scolded me. Zara must have reported my behavior to Raya, who told Razyat and Malika. "You have lived in Russia too long," Razyat said. "You are ignoring our traditions! How can you expect any woman to accept you when you treat them like that, giving out those ultimatums, and refusing to court them properly. You must go back to Zara."

The whole episode embarrassed me, and I didn't want to admit I was wrong. But I met with Zara again. My sisters had persuaded her to overlook my impolite behavior. She and her relatives agreed to accept me as a suitable husband, which made my family very happy. According to our traditions, there must always be witnesses to such important arrangements as setting the date for a wedding. Zara was accompanied by the wife of her brother, and I was joined by my close school friend Khassan Taimaskhanov. The wedding date was set for September 19, 1992.

I went ahead with plans I had already made to go to Moscow in June of 1992 to see if I could arrange a three-month internship at the Institute of Cosmetology on plastic and reconstructive surgery. My techniques were out of date. Science is always moving forward, and I wanted to further my training, particularly with Professor Ilya Frishberg, the famous Russian cosmetic surgeon. Although I was a little apprehensive about leaving Chechnya in such uncertain times, I felt if I didn't grab the chance to do the specialization, I might never have another opportunity to improve my skills.

My cousin Musa Saponov met me when I got off the plane in Moscow, and found me a room in the Rossiya Hotel, from where he operated an import-export business. After a few weeks, I moved out of the hotel and in with friends because of harassment from the hotel doorman or the police in the street. Either they demanded to see my documents, or they threatened to take me to the police station if I didn't give them money. There was much more blatant hostility toward

My cousin Musa Saponov (left) who helped me so much in my early
professional years.

Chechens than I had encountered during my years in Krasnoyarsk, and
it was easy to distinguish Chechens from Russians or from other nationalities on the street by our strong features and by the way we dressed
and moved.

   Soon after I arrived, Musa offered to drive me to the Institute of
Cosmetology, where I hoped to persuade the director to offer me an
internship. At 9:30 A.M. the heat was scorching, and the asphalt
steamed. Sidewalk vendors had already set up their stands, and people
stood in long lines for *kvas* (a refreshing drink made from rye flour and
malt) to quench their thirst near the Mayakovskii metro stop. At the
entrance, a small girl in a torn dress held out a grubby hand for money.
The rich were becoming richer and the poor, poorer in the Russian
capital. Wherever you went, you ran into beggars. Musa guided his
new Ford through the traffic, weaving in and out of the lanes on the
Ring Road. That morning, he wore one of those cherry-colored
jackets so fashionable in Moscow in 1992.

   I got out of the car and walked up to the Institute of Cosmetology, which like most buildings in Moscow was under repair. The entrance hall was empty, but I could hear voices from the second floor, so I climbed the stairs and asked a couple of workmen where I could find the director.

They pointed out a half-open door through which I could see a secretary. "The institute is closed, and we are not receiving anyone," she said when I asked for the director.

"Please ask him to see me for a few minutes," I said.

She shook her head and turned back to the magazine on her desk.

"I've come a long way," I insisted.

"Where have you come from?" She looked up.

"From Grozny."

"All right, I'll tell him, but I don't know if he will receive you." She rose from her desk and disappeared, returning a few minutes later. "Follow me," she said abruptly.

Professor Mikhail Pisarenko, a balding man in a white coat, looked up from his papers when I entered his office, his eyes lighting on my cauliflower ear. (I was used to Russians looking at that ear.) He motioned me to sit down. I glanced around the office. On the wall to my left hung three large icons. One was of the Virgin Mary. I did not recognize the others, which I assumed were Christian saints. A religious man, I thought, as my nervousness receded. He must be a decent person.

I explained to Pisarenko that I wanted to improve my surgical technique by specializing at his institute. The professor listened to me, nodding his head while drumming his fingers on his blotter. He asked me about my medical training, followed by questions unrelated to medicine: Where was I living in Moscow? How long had I been here?

"Come back tomorrow between nine and ten," he said. "I'm not certain about the fees. You'll have to see the bookkeeper."

I left and walked back to the car. Musa laughed when I told him we had to return the next day. "That gives them time to check you out with the KGB," he said. "He probably thinks you are some crime boss who is going to take over his institute. But don't worry. If you are paying, then he will probably let you in."

When I returned the next morning, the bookkeeper announced

that the tuition for an advanced course was 150,000 rubles (about 5,000 dollars). She shoved an application form across the desk. The price seemed high. Now that the authorities had given the green light to capitalism, the Institute of Cosmetology, like every other private enterprise, was struggling to survive. The Russian government was bankrupt. Government salaries and subsidies were things of the past. It was everyone for himself, with the weak and elderly falling between the cracks.

I learned later that all the other students were charged 100,000 rubles (about 3,300 dollars), but the institute demanded 150,000 rubles from two women doctors from the Baltic states and from me. People assumed Chechens were criminals, so we had to be rich. I also discovered later that I had made Professor Pisarenko so nervous that he had asked the KGB to place a bug under the table for my second visit.

Just how hostile Moscow had become to Chechens came home to me one evening when Musa and I were drinking tea in my room. The television was on, with the volume turned down, and we were discussing the latest news from Chechnya. Suddenly, Musa interrupted me in midsentence. He leaped from the sofa, raced across the room to the TV, and turned up the volume. The words *Chechen Billions* flashed across the screen, followed by a voice-over of the lines from Lermontov's famous "Cossack Lullaby":

O'er the stones the Terek bubbles	*Po kamnyan struitsya Terek*
Muddy ripples jump to life	*Pleshchet mutnyi val*
Evil Chechen crawls the bankside	*Zloi Chechen polzet na bereg*
Carefully sharpening his knife.	*Tochit svoi kinzhal*

The program talked about Chechens accumulating vast wealth through corruption and theft; then it showed a police sting operation against what they claimed was a Chechen crime ring.

"Russian propaganda depicts us all as mafiosi," Musa said angrily. "There are Dagestani gangs, Georgian gangs. There are Russian gangs like the 'Solnechnaya,' 'Podolskaya,' 'Ryazanskaya' gangs, but they never mention them. It's always the Chechens."

After the program ended, Musa and I sat in silence. We each knew what the other was thinking. The Kremlin propaganda machine was preparing the Russian population for eventual use of force in Chechnya.

That night, I couldn't sleep, kept awake by my thoughts and the floor attendant shouting at some drunks outside my room. Why did Russians fear us so much? I wondered. *Chornie zhopy* (black asses) they called us behind our backs and sometimes even to our faces. Maybe since we have big families, the Kremlin imagines Muslims overrunning Russia from the south as the Mongols did in the Middle Ages.

As I tossed on my narrow bed, listening to the traffic below the window, I heard my father's voice: "They said we collaborated with the Nazis. That was their excuse to deport us." But I didn't want to think about it, not about deportation or genocide. I had Russian friends. I was grateful to Russia for teaching me everything I knew about medicine. Right then, all I wanted was to perfect my skills and help people. The Institute of Cosmetology accepted me for a three-month internship, which would not begin until late fall.

When trouble flared up in Ingushetia that summer, I realized that the North Caucasus was a tinderbox waiting to ignite. The conflict was over a strip of disputed territory, in this case the Prigorodny district located in North Ossetia and claimed by the Ingush. The Prigorodny conflagration was another legacy of Stalin's divide-and-conquer policy. As happened with the Chechens, when Nikita Khrushchev amnestied the small nations of the North Caucasus in 1957, the exiles returned home to find other peoples had occupied their lands.

The Kremlin dispatched troops to the area, and large-scale fighting broke out. Seeing pictures of the wounded on the evening news, I had a strong desire to go there. Chechens view the Ingush as cousins. We belong to the same ethnic group and were, in fact, one province, called the Checheno-Ingush Republic until Chechen declared its independence. Ingushetia opted to remain within the Russian Federation. When a group of wealthy Chechen and Ingush businessmen in Moscow chartered a plane to carry medical supplies to Ingushetia, I accompanied them.

Working in Ingushetia for several weeks was my introduction to war and to the realization that the principal victims were the innocent civilians. Mostly, I reconstructed bones, jaws, and skulls which had fractured into many pieces. I wasn't prepared for the crimes of war—like the corpse of a young girl I saw who had been raped and burned with cigarettes all over her body. I returned to Moscow deeply troubled that if this could happen in Ingushetia, it could happen in Chechnya.

IN SEPTEMBER 1992, I flew back to Grozny with all sorts of supplies for my wedding to Zara. We didn't send out wedding invitations, because in Chechnya anyone who wants to attend a wedding comes, which usually means the whole village. My friends arrived from as far away as Krasnoyarsk and Moscow. Our family slaughtered two cows and several sheep for the occasion. We consider marriage, along with birth and death, to be one of life's most important transitions. The wedding day itself and the days of celebration following it belong to the bride, though it is the groom's family that organizes the event.

Chechen weddings are different from Western ones. We do not have a ceremony in which the couple come together before a religious or civil authority figure, nor do we exchange rings publicly. Rather, a mullah explains to both parties separately, in front of witnesses, what their obligations will be. The wedding celebration itself usually starts about noon and goes on throughout the day and into the night, often for as long as a week. The bride is considered "the queen" of the celebration. At our wedding, all attention was on Zara, while I, the bridegroom, kept a very low profile. In fact, I spent the first day of the festivities at the hospital in Grozny operating on a boy with a broken jaw. That evening, our mullah called on me and Zara separately to bless our union and outline my marital duties. He read me a passage from the Koran, in front of my witnesses, saying that the marriage should be consummated on that first night and that I should take care to be gentle with Zara.

For a few days after the wedding, Dada went out of his way to avoid contact with me, so I shouldn't feel embarrassed. When a son brings his new bride home to live in the house with his parents—which is our custom—a kind of awkwardness arises. The parents know that the young couple are soon to be initiated into the mysteries of conjugal life. That awkwardness can last for a few days or even weeks.

Although I hardly appeared during the week of celebrations, I saw it all later on videotape shot by a friend. There on the screen were my closest male friends—my cousin Musa Saponov, Vakha Isayev, and Adlan Vitayev—loading the contents of Zara's dowry into the black Lincoln limousine, which transported her like a princess to our house. On the hood of the Lincoln, tied down by yellow ribbons, was a red and yellow prayer rug, and a propped-up baby doll dressed in a miniature white wedding dress—a symbol of fertility and happiness. The cars slowly wound through the potholed streets of Alkhan Kala, honking their horns, young men fired off Kalashnikov rifles, and boys strung ropes across the road, stopping the cars until passengers coughed up coins.

There stood Zara in her magnificent white dress of embroidered silk and tulle, her eyes downcast behind her veil, while the mullah read her prayers from the Koran before two male witnesses. We consider this moment far more binding than the Russian law, which requires a marriage to be recorded at the Registry Office. Our house overflowed with women dressed in their best clothes, adjusting Zara's veil, placing dishes on the table, taking them off, laughing. There was my mother in a gray dress, smiling. There was a neighbor dancing the *lesghinka* in the square; my classmate Musa Salekhov goading the accordion player to increase the tempo; everyone clapping rhythmically and whooping.

I believe that fate determines the woman you marry. Married life is not just two people; it is a network of relatives. For me, it was more important how Zara treated Nana and Dada than how she cared for me. Once she adjusted to becoming a full member of our extended family, I knew we would have a happy life together.

Some westerners may assume that all Muslim countries are the same, and that women in Chechnya are oppressed, as they were by the Taliban in Afghanistan. That is not true. Chechen women are educated and have professions. Education was a positive legacy from Soviet times. Often women stay at home because we have large families without such modern conveniences as washing machines and dishwashers. Women usually cover their heads with scarves outside on the street—such traditions help preserve our culture. Without them, we will disappear as a nation; our traditions are the glue that hold us together, especially in chaotic times when everything is falling apart.

AFTER THE WEDDING, suppressing my premonitions about approaching war, I returned to Moscow to prepare for the November start of my three-month specialization at the Institute of Cosmetology. There I found a small apartment in the center of Moscow. Zara would join me in a couple of months.

Although there was growing hostility toward Chechens in Moscow—Chechnya had declared its independence from Russia in November a year earlier—my colleagues at the Institute of Cosmetology treated me with respect. The institute had so many patients that Professor Frishberg had expanded his department into a small church on Solyanka Street that had been shut down by the government. Entering the building felt strange. On the outside, it looked like a Russian Orthodox church, a place where people once worshiped. But inside, it had been reconfigured into a scientific center with an operating room on the second floor and several wards.

By the time I began studying with Professor Frishberg, he was in his seventies. A tall, thin man with glasses, he always wore a dark suit and tie and had a good sense of humor if you didn't rub him the wrong way. The day I observed him tighten the eyelids of a patient, I knew I was in the presence of a master. The pieces of skin he manipulated were no bigger than a millimeter (.04 inches). He had written many books and given demonstrations in foreign countries, which included his technique for reducing blood seepage during operations. How to identify troublesome patients was a favorite topic of his. "A mentally unstable person can make your life hell," he used to say, "especially if something goes wrong." There was no malpractice insurance in Russia.

While I enjoyed my three-month internship, Zara and I settled into married life. When Zara announced that she was pregnant, I was very happy to hear this news. After the internship ended, we stayed on in Moscow for me to do a four-week surgical practicum during the month of February. Then the Institute of Cosmetology offered me a steady job, which I accepted. I would have preferred working in Chechnya, but Russia's economic blockade had cut off medical salaries there. Many doctors, like my friend Issa, had been forced to leave the hospital. Before I left for Moscow, I saw him on a street corner in Grozny trading in foreign currency. "What can I do? I have a family of seven to support," he said with a shrug. To survive, people began trading, especially after Dudayev declared Chechnya a free-trade zone. Those with initiative started making money. They traveled regularly to Turkey, the United Arab Emirates, and Pakistan to buy basket loads of goods and resell them in Chechnya.

The Institute of Cosmetology also operated along capitalist lines, with a brochure advertising services and a price list. The prices were so cheap compared to those in the West that people booked months in advance, coming from as far away as Scandinavia. I received a regular monthly salary in addition to bonuses from satisfied patients. Seventy-five percent of our patients wanted cosmetic surgery; the other 25 percent had serious deformities or burns.

Some people, like a famous Soviet actress who came in for her third face-lift at age 80, balked at the fees. Under communism, medicine had been free. I don't know whether it was true, but people said she was once Stalin's mistress. She certainly acted like it, throwing a fit when she saw the price list.

THAT AUGUST, ZARA returned home to be with her family while she awaited the baby. In September, I flew back to be with her. I didn't attend the birth itself on October 31, 1993. Birth in our country is a private matter between women. Our firstborn was a beautiful healthy girl. Nana named her Maryam. (Usually, the naming of a child falls to someone from the older generation.) It took me a while to get used to the idea of being a father and to take her in my arms. When I finally did, the feeling of pride that swept over me was tempered by fears for her future. After Maryam's birth I returned to Moscow. As is our custom, Zara stayed at home for three months while the women in the family taught her how to look after her first child. After that period, she and Maryam joined me in Moscow.

One day, my cousin Musa Saponov took me aside. "You should start making money on the side like everyone else," he said. He assured me there wasn't anything illegal about it. "All you need is good organization. You could act as a middle man with all your contacts in the sports world. A businessman buys a truckload of cigarettes. Your job is to find buyers, that's all. And you get one percent of the profits."

At first I was reluctant to get into this kind of business. I was a surgeon, and I felt uncomfortable about all this buying and selling. For so many years, trading had been a crime. People were sent to prison for selling a pair of jeans. Then it was called "speculation," and now it was called "free enterprise" and was encouraged. "Everyone is doing it," Musa repeated. He finally convinced me.

My first business deal was a truckload of cigarettes imported from England. I never saw the truck or the cigarettes. My only role was to make telephone calls to line up buyers. Within a short time, I had a list of clients who trusted me. During the day, I worked at the institute. I would finish about 4 P.M., go home, and start making phone calls. My first deal, on which I spent an hour or two, netted me some $4,000. I earned money every evening. You couldn't trust the banks, so I hid the money in the shelf behind my shirts, hoping that no one would break into the apartment and find it.

Before long, Zara, Maryam, and I moved out of the apartment to a fancy house off the highway where high government officials had their dachas. The two-story house was luxurious, with four bedrooms, a maid's room, a bathroom on each floor. A high wooden fence surrounded the compound, along with a security checkpoint just inside the huge metal swinging gates.

At first, having all that money went to my head. At thirty, I felt liberated and started spending extravagantly. I bought a Lincoln town car for $25,000 and hired a chauffeur. I wore designer suits and Italian shoes. I purchased French and Italian dresses for Zara. She and I both liked to be well dressed. We could hold our heads high on the streets of Moscow, where most people viewed Chechens as little better than vermin. I realized soon enough that people who saw me being driven by a chauffeur assumed I had made money illegally because I was Chechen.

I never thought of myself as nouveau riche. I disliked the way the "new Russians" behaved, throwing money away at casinos, showing off, and driving their Mercedes through Moscow at breakneck speed. Eventually, I became embarrassed by my Lincoln, so I would ask the driver to drop me a few blocks from the institute, and I walked the rest of the way. One night, my car was stolen. Oddly enough, I felt as if a burden had fallen from my shoulders. Suddenly, I could breathe easier. No longer did I have to worry about being robbed all the time. I didn't even bother about informing the police, not that they would have helped me. Auto theft was one of their sidelines.

Chapter 5

The Eve of the First War

T THE BEGINNING of August 1994, I gave up my house and left Moscow to go home. Zara was five months pregnant with our second child, and I had sent her and Maryam home a month earlier. Although my family tried not to alarm me when they telephoned me in Moscow, it was becoming clear that the situation in Chechnya was deteriorating rapidly. In addition to the hijacking of buses in neighboring North Ossetia for which Chechens were blamed, there were numerous armed skirmishes, and from everything I heard and read in the Moscow media, which were invariably biased against the Chechens, it was clear that talks with the Kremlin to avoid war were going nowhere. I feared the worst. Boarding the plane for Grozny, I had a premonition that I would not be returning to Moscow soon.

When I stepped from the plane at Grozny airport, I was startled to see how militarized the city had become. Chechen militia in camouflage fatigues cradled rifles at the bottom of steps. Army jeeps lined the edge of the airfield, and soldiers guarded the route into Grozny. On our way to Alkhan Kala, the taxi driver recounted the latest shootings in the city. Listening to him, I had the feeling that Chechnya was on the brink of civil war.

"There are gunshots going off all the time," the driver said. "Everyone who can is leaving, but they say they are closing the borders."

I looked out the taxi window. Vendors were selling sacks of flour and vegetables out of the back of trucks. Everywhere, women lined up for food. I reminded myself to check our storeroom at home to make sure we had supplies of flour, sugar, and dried meat. Given the tense atmosphere, I was sure prices would be going up. When I reached home, everyone seemed well, though I saw the worry on the faces of Zara, Malika, and Nana; I tried to crack a few jokes to cheer them up. Everyone worried about the kind of world our children would grow up in.

The next day, a visit to the First City Emergency Hospital in Grozny, where Malika still worked as a nurse, confirmed how bad things were. Plastic bags, cigarette packets, newspapers, and discarded food were scattered all over the courtyard. Dogs hunted for scraps in the piles of garbage and around the periphery. Vendors peddled medical supplies in the hospital corridors because hospital supplies were running out. Inside the building everyone wore street clothes, and you couldn't tell the staff from patients or relatives. Doctors now asked patients to supply everything: medicines, painkillers, bandages, food, bedding, nursing care, even fuel for the emergency generators and heating. Meanwhile, the armed skirmishes between political opposition groups kept the wounded coming in.

A few days after my arrival, I walked past the Presidential Palace and saw a burned-out Russian tank. The Russians, in an attempt to intimidate the population, had rolled several tanks into Grozny, parking them outside the Presidential Palace. It was a show of force guaranteed to create a reaction. A bystander said someone had thrown a grenade down the turret of one of them, igniting ammunition and fuel. The explosion had hurled the turret across the street and revealed a gaping hole under the tank. Nearby lay three incinerated corpses. Looking at the charred bodies of the young Russian soldiers, I felt sickened. It was the first time I had seen bodies reduced to roasted hunks. So this was what awaited our country, I thought.

By now I realized that returning to Moscow was out of the question. When I had recited the Hippocratic Oath with my graduating class, I had sworn to treat anyone in need, and Chechnya was going to need help. I couldn't in good conscience be in Moscow doing face-lifts for wealthy patients. I decided to take a job at the hospital, although it meant working without pay.

Lots of doctors were leaving Chechnya. "If I had a profession like yours," my cousin Musa said, "I'd get out of Chechnya and find work somewhere else. This situation is going to go on for a long time." My parents, my sisters, and Zara feared for me. "War is a terrible thing," Dada said, advising me to leave the country. "Doctors are always in the line of fire."

I found it hard to ignore the wishes of my family and friends, but I knew that before long the wounded would flood the hospital and doctors and nurses would be needed. I had to stay. Thanks to my work at the clinic and my business deals in Moscow, I had saved a fair amount of money, which I had brought home and given to my mother to hide in the special place that only she knew about. I also had a cache of medical instruments and some supplies, which I had stored in my house for the clinic I dreamed of starting. Compared to so many, I was very lucky.

So began my new life as a war surgeon at the First City Emergency Hospital. I expected to face danger, but I believed that a talisman given to me by a Muslim sage in Krasnoyarsk would protect me. Inside the tiny pouch, which I always wore around my neck, was a piece of folded paper. The old man had told me that my whole life was written there in Arabic. "You will have a long and interesting life," he had predicted.

Going from being a cosmetic surgeon who worked with small pieces of flesh and bone to practicing emergency medicine took some getting used to. In the next months, I learned that gangrene was my enemy because it attacks a human body like a rabid animal, devouring the flesh. Dirt enters wounds so easily; bacteria flourishes; yellowish pus bubbles up from under the skin; the flesh decays. The only course is to remove the dead tissue surgically; otherwise, the advance may be so rapid that amputation is the only way to save the patient's life.

At the hospital I found a major problem was how to deal with the poor, who couldn't afford to buy supplies from the vendors. I devised a scheme whereby people who had money helped those who didn't. I handed a well-off patient a list of hospital supplies for his or her treatment, followed by a request to triple the amount.

"What you don't use I will give to someone who can't afford it, in your name," I said.

Persuading patients to accept free help was difficult sometimes. Debts based on friendship are debts to be repaid. If you are not in a position to return a favor, you are reluctant to accept it—like the old man who entered my office with a fast-growing tumor on his palate. The moment I saw him in his sheepskin hat, leather boots, and buttoned tunic with circular collar, my heart went out to him. The way he held himself with such pride reminded me of the old men of Makazhoi.

"I have this thing in my mouth," he complained. "Recently, I haven't been able to eat, and it bleeds a lot. The dentist said I should come to you."

He had a tumor that would block his throat within a week or two. "We need to operate immediately," I told him.

He remained silent.

"I don't take money for my operations," I said, sensing his embarrassment. "If you don't believe me, go ask the people waiting outside in the corridor. If you can't afford the medicines, I have some in reserve."

He said nothing.

"We are all in this terrible situation," I continued. "All I need is your consent; then I can schedule an appointment."

He rose to his feet, smoothed down his tunic, and prepared to leave. "It's too much of a bother for you."

"It's no bother," I pressed him, knowing the urgency. "I'll do it tomorrow. Who knows? I may be needing your help one day."

"You won't need me." He gave me a toothless grin.

"We always need your help," I insisted, "because you are older and wiser. Young people need your help." He seemed to appreciate my words of respect and finally agreed to the operation.

WHILE IT WAS still summer, I managed a quick trip to Makazhoi, where I fell in love with a Caucasian sheepdog puppy, a ball of white fluff with black nose and eyes and a long feathery tail. The owner of the litter gave him to me and wouldn't accept any money. For over six centuries sheep herders have bred these powerful mountain dogs to guard against wolves and thieves. I named the puppy Tarzan and took him back to Alkhan Kala to train as a guard dog.

At the end of August, sporadic bombing began over Grozny. It started at 5:30 one afternoon, just as the light was fading; thunderous explosions from the direction of the military airport at Khankala, some ten miles east of the city. The windows of the operating room shook, doors rattled, and the floor under my feet shuddered. I rushed into the street with the other nurses and doctors and looked up. Two planes appeared through the twilight, low on the horizon—first one, then the other, the noise of their engines growing louder as they approached. They streaked across the sky before us, then turned south, circling the city and making another high-speed dive in the direction of the airport. As they passed, I looked for the markings on the wings; there were none. Then I saw their rockets streak earthward, trailing white plumes. I closed my eyes, said a few words of prayer, and waited for the explosion. My thoughts went to my family, hoping they were all right.

Within an hour the wounded started pouring in. This was my initiation into the effect of bombing. Bullets, rockets, mortars, shrapnel—each produces its own kind of wound. A small piece of hot metal makes only a small wound, but a bomb can pulverize the body.

A few weeks after the first attacks, as Malika and I were driving home after work, we experienced a bomb explosion firsthand. Approaching Grozny's oil district, we heard the screech of a plane going into a dive above us. I stepped on the gas to get as far away as possible. An explosion, a street away, rocked the car and almost overturned it as we came to a stop. We jumped out and ran back to see if we could help. "What have they done? What have they done?" Malika screamed.

It was a frightful scene. The bomb had plowed into a street full of people, leaving a hole about fifteen feet across and six feet deep. Asphalt, bricks, telephone poles, trees lay everywhere, as if a large excavator had dug up the area. The first thing I saw were three burned-out cars with drivers and passengers cremated in their seats. Next to the car lay a man who had been decapitated; nearby was a human arm attached to a blood-soaked sleeve, a child's foot in a sneaker. Wounded people, corpses, body parts, and bloody items of clothing littered the street like pieces of refuse. Women screamed and beat their breasts, appealing to the *vird* of their clan for help. (Most clans have a *vird*, a disciple of Muhammad, to whom people in crisis appeal for help.) "*Va Ustaz, va Ustaz! Gede tkhum!*" they shouted. "Oh, Master, help us!"

I approached what looked like an elderly woman, only to find her dead, her stomach split open, her colon and small intestines splattered in the dirt. I was used to operating on intestines, but that was nothing like this. The evening was chilly, and a steamy vapor rose from the woman's entrails, along with an indescribable smell which lingered in my nostrils for several weeks, making it almost impossible for me to eat.

Soon passing cars began stopping, and we immediately started loading the twelve or thirteen survivors for a dash to the hospital. We managed to ship them off in about twenty minutes. Many of the rescuers were returning from the market, and they emptied out their shopping bags for the gruesome task of gathering body parts. It was a sickening job, which took us the next hour. Shreds of clothing were often the main means of identification. My knowledge of anatomy was helpful when it came to identifying which piece of bone or flesh belonged where, and to whom. But often recognizing the human scraps was impossible. The unidentified body parts were buried in a mass grave within the traditional twenty-four hours.

Driving home that night, Malika and I were deep in thought, thankful for our escape but stunned by what we had seen. Once home, Malika went to her room and cried. Dada and Nana listened to my account of what happened in shocked silence. "You must give up your work," Nana said. "You must stay at home. Don't risk it."

HISTORY HAD TAUGHT us to expect attacks from Russia, but now that one actually had happened, we found it hard to accept. For more than seventy years, we had lived under Soviet rule. We were all supposed to be Soviet people, living in harmony, and many of us had good Russian friends. How could Russia bomb its own citizens? How could it bomb Grozny, where half the inhabitants were Russians?

At first, the Kremlin denied the planes were Russian. Azeri planes were responsible for the bombing, Russian officials said, although they couldn't explain why Azerbaijan would bomb us. Three days later, when the planes returned, our artillery shot one down and took the pilot prisoner. That night, the pilot confessed on local television to being Russian, and the newscasters showed how the Russian markings on the plane had been painted over.

Following that first bombing, people rolled up to the hospital in any vehicle they could find to remove their ambulatory relatives and friends to their homes or to a hospital outside the city. In their place came new batches of wounded. I wondered how long it would be before the bombs started hitting the center of Grozny. The first ones had been directed at strategic targets on the outskirts of the city such as factories, bridges, and oil refineries.

At first, it was difficult to work through the sound of falling bombs, but gradually, thanks to my athletic training, I was able to focus my concentration. Between operations I did push-ups and, when possible, withdrew to a quiet place to recall the inspirational words of our coaches before an athletic competition, admonishing us to be strong. We piled sandbags in the hospital windows; eventually, the thud of bombs became like the buzz of an annoying fly in the background. I was conscious of it but trained myself to ignore it. I was so focused on my work in the operating room that I forgot everything else.

On the afternoon of December 11, 1994, I was operating on a young boy who had taken a blast of shrapnel in the face, shattering his jaw and reducing his right eye to liquid. I scraped what remained of the eyeball from the socket, cauterized the blood vessels, and prepared the muscles to hold a glass eye. After I had placed gauze wadding in the socket and bandaged his head, I instructed the nurse to remove him to the ward. Walking back to the doctors' lounge, I heard a thunderous explosion, followed by the sound of artillery. The building shook. The attack was clearly moving closer to the center of the city.

Zara was due to deliver our second child by C-section in two weeks. That explosion convinced me that she should have the operation immediately, before the Russians launched an all-out attack and it would be impossible to get her to the maternity hospital. Troops were already massing on the other side of the border. I took off my scrubs, put on my street clothes, and rushed out to my car. I looked at my watch. It was 3:15 P.M.; in another hour it would be getting dark.

I drove to Alkhan Kala at great speed. "Get Zara ready!" I shouted to Malika as I ran into the house. "We are leaving immediately for the hospital." I could tell by Zara's face that she was frightened, but she didn't say a word. Nana started crying.

"Don't worry." I tried to calm her.

"People say the Russians have crossed the border," she said.

I packed my instruments, some sterile gauze, and sheets, in case we didn't reach the hospital in time. By custom, my brother Hussein—not I—should have accompanied Zara to the hospital to have a baby, but he and Rita were still living in Krasnoyarsk. As I was to discover, war forces people to ignore traditions.

By the time we reached Grozny, the streets were empty, the bazaar was closed, and shops and kiosks were boarded up. Everyone had retreated into their cellars. I pulled the car up in front of the Central Maternity Hospital and jumped out, leaving Malika and Zara in the backseat. The building was dark; the reception desk empty. I ran upstairs. Not a patient, doctor, or nurse was in sight. I ran back downstairs and jumped in the car. "We need an anesthesiologist. We have to get Ruslan Yusupov!" I shouted, putting the car in gear. Ruslan Yusupov was a doctor who worked at the Fourth City Hospital.

We drove full speed through the empty streets to the apartment building on the other side of the river where Ruslan lived. I found everyone in his apartment building huddled in the basement. "Is Ruslan there? I need a doctor!" I shouted down from the top of the stairs. I saw a faint light and heard voices; in the darkness I made out a group of figures below. "My wife needs an urgent cesarean!" I called. Conversation stopped. Then to my relief, Ruslan rose from the floor and came up the steps. "Do we have an operating gynecologist?" he asked.

"Aminat! We have to go and find her," I said.

Ruslan got in the car with Zara and Malika, and I drove to Aminat's apartment. She didn't hesitate when I told her about Zara, although her relatives protested, saying it was too dangerous.

I held my breath. She and I had worked together, and I had often helped her out. "He is a colleague," she replied. "He would do the same thing for us."

Back at Central Maternity Hospital No. 1, we rushed Zara up to the operating room. My help was no longer needed. I walked down to the courtyard to wait in the car. No lights illuminated the streets; the sky was black. Without people, there was an eerie feeling about Grozny; it was like a ghost town. In the distance I could hear explosions and the sound of gunfire. Out there people were dying, yet on the fifth floor of the hospital a new little individual was about to come into the world. Worried about Zara and the baby, I tried to calm my nervousness with prayer. Allah would decide the outcome: Would the child be all right?

After what seemed liked ages, Aminat emerged from the hospital, holding a bundle wrapped in blankets. "Congratulations! You have a boy!" Thrilled as I was to have a son, I hardly had time to look at the baby. I pulled 500 rubles (about $150 dollars) out of my wallet and gave it to her. It's our custom to reward the doctor who delivers a boy.

"Get Zara out here," I shouted. "We have to leave here immediately!"

Ruslan and Malika carried an unconscious Zara from the hospital. I lowered the back of the front seat till it touched the rear seat and placed Zara, wrapped in sheets and a blanket, on this makeshift bed. After Malika got in the backseat, Aminat passed her the baby. Ruslan and Aminat squeezed in next to them. After we dropped the doctors off at their apartments, we started for Alkhan Kala, driving slowly without lights over the potholed streets, fearing that the slightest bump would burst Zara's stitches. In the distance, the thud of bombs and the flash of red in the sky from the burning buildings told us the shelling was getting nearer. "Pray," I said over my shoulder to Malika.

After we arrived home, Nana came up with a name for our son: Islam. Most Chechens have both a religious name and a secular one. Islam had the two rolled into one: in Chechen the word *is* means "nine," and *lam* means "mountain"; but in Arabic, *islam* means "submission." Three days later, we slaughtered a sheep and invited the elders and other guests to celebrate the birth. The mullah read from the Koran. I marveled at how life goes on even when surrounded by death.

THROUGHOUT DECEMBER, THE bombing increased; sometimes as many as twenty-five air raids a day. The air filled with dust and the acrid smell of ash. People flooded from the city, some to refugee camps in Ingushetia, some to their mountain villages, leaving mostly ethnic Russians, who made up the majority of the population of Grozny, in the city. I felt sorry for these Russians, who looked on Grozny as their home. They didn't have relatives to give them shelter and were vulnerable to the worst horrors of war.

Throughout the republic women called for a peace march to stop the Russian tanks from advancing. Whenever Chechnya has been under attack, women have joined the battle, even taking up arms in the nineteenth century when Shamil's mountain hideout was bombarded by the Russian army. Many of the women from Alkhan Kala, including several of our neighbors, joined the march. On one day in mid-

December, I could hardly get through the column of women on the Moscow-Baku highway. Women of all ages blocked the road: old women who could hardly walk, young girls, and mothers. The column stretched for forty miles from Grozny to the border of Ingushetia, where the Russian tanks waited.

I got out of my car and pushed through the crowd. Five old women, weighed down in bulky coats, separated themselves from the others and formed a circle, their feet picking up the hypnotic beat of the *zikr.* The *zikr* is not another traditional dance like the *lesghinka* but an ancient ritual rooted in the Muslim philosophy of Sufism. On-lookers joined the rhythm, clapping and chanting words of the Muslim Declaration of Faith in Arabic: *"La ilaha illallah. La ilaha illallah!"* (There is no God but Allah!)

These women were expressing the spirit of Chechnya, a spirit that struggles against terrible odds and helps the individual find peace with God. The *zikr* is danced at any occasion: at weddings, funerals, before an act of a blood revenge, before going into battle. Villages have their own versions of the *zikr,* but they all have the same purpose: to lift the soul onto a higher plane. During a *zikr* I have heard old men with rusty voices sing like opera singers, and the voices of old women soar with the angels. The ritual confounded the Soviet authorities, who couldn't make up their minds if it was an illegal religious ceremony or a dangerous war dance. Whichever, they tried to ban it. Still, the secret police couldn't prevent people from performing the *zikr* at funerals. Russia has never understood us, I thought as I made my way back to my car to return to the hospital.

That evening on the TV news, we saw an incredible scene: Row upon row of Soviet tanks lined up at Achkoi-Martan, a village on the border between Ingushetia and Chechnya. Then the TV showed the Russian commander, General Ivan Babichev, a hulking figure dressed in a sheepskin coat and fur hat, surrounded by a group of pleading women, who told him his tanks would advance into Chechnya over their dead bodies.

"We have not come here to kill innocent civilians," he told them.

"My tanks will not advance." Then the general embraced the women. "We will find some kind of settlement to solve this problem," he said.

Some people believe that General Babichev told the women he wouldn't attack just to get rid of them. But I believe that he was a decent man who didn't want to mow down civilians. A few days later, General Pavel Grachev, the Russian minister of defense, relieved Babichev of his command, and the tanks advanced anyway.

Every night, through the sound of explosions, we listened to the Russian military spokesman on TV tell the world that no bombing sorties had occurred over Grozny that day. The number of doctors and nurses in the hospitals dwindled, and administrators walked off the job. By the end of December, only 15 doctors out of the original 500 remained at the First City Emergency Hospital.

On December 31 a bomb hit the Kavkaz Hotel next to the Presidential Palace not far from the hospital. Already Russian troops had crossed the borders and were massing outside Grozny. Inside the city Chechen fighters, under the command of Colonel Aslan Maskhadov, a former Soviet officer, waited to repulse the attack. We suspected that the hospital could be the next target, but no one wanted to suggest leaving.

Our small team of remaining medical personnel gathered in the doctors' lounge. We were all frightened, but we didn't want to show it. I looked at my friend Movsar Idalov, a trauma specialist. He looked calm, but I knew that like me, he was trembling inside. We all turned to our elder, Khamzat Elmurzayev, a fifty-five-year-old surgeon; he would be the one to make any decision. Khamzat hesitated, then told us that everyone was leaving Grozny and that we should too.

"We can't stay here any longer," he said. "We all need to go home to our villages and set up medical centers. That's where help will be needed."

Six of the doctors volunteered to stay with the remaining patients, mostly elderly Russians, in the basement shelter where we had transported them when the windows blew out. Their relatives either had abandoned them or had left Chechnya. I packed my operating table and instruments into the car and headed home to Alkhan Kala just in time. Hours later, in the first minutes of New Year's Day 1995, the Russian army launched a massive tank assault on Grozny. The first Russian-Chechen War had begun in earnest.

Part 2

The First War

Chapter 6

The Hospital Opens

I TOLD MY friend Ruslan Ezirkhanov that I wanted to open a hospital. He was deputy director of the DOK wood-processing plant in Alkhan Kala and had recently been elected by townspeople to be the chairman of the local council. He and I spoke as soon as I returned from Grozny. He was a striking-looking man of forty with dark brown hair and gray eyes and had graduated from the Institute of Forestry at Krasnodar. Married with four children, he was one of the most trusted figures in Alkhan Kala. He said he would meet with the elders and inform them of my plans.

The day after I arrived home, January 1, 1995, six of the ten town elders called on me, including an agronomist named Hasilbek Kurbanov. He was a distant relative of my father and from the same clan in Makazhoi. While Nana served us tea and jam, the town elders told me they wanted to place the town's medical services in my hands.

I set a deadline of three days to have the hospital up and running. Once the elders publicly announced the need for help, volunteers poured in. Before long, I had a workforce of more than 100 people under me. I had to turn some away. Suddenly, people who were idle, depressed, or fearful had something useful to do. Many believed that if I was going to open a hospital—if I was going to stay—I somehow knew that the war would bypass Alkhan Kala. They believed I had inside information. I remained silent. I had no such certainty.

Early January 1995, we opened the hospital in Alkhan Kala in a two-story building that had once served as an infirmary. Hard times had forced it to close. What remained of the infirmary now stood in a tumbledown state with no windows or doors and a leaky roof that let in rain and snow.

The call went out from the mosque for beds and bedding. I had managed to bring some medical supplies from Grozny; the rest came from my personal reserves. We also had supplies, such as glucose packets, antibiotics, anesthetics, and suture kits donated by the Red Cross, Doctors Without Borders, and Doctors of the World.

I told Zulai, a seamstress, to sew a red cross onto a large white sheet. "Why do we need that?" she asked. I explained to her and others that under international law no one had the right to attack a hospital. We flew the flag from a ten-foot pole above the hospital so that it was visible from the air. No doubt that added to the false belief of the townspeople that a hospital in Alkhan Kala would protect them. I never carried a gun and refused to have anyone working with me carry a weapon. If you carry a gun, you end up using it. Killing wasn't the business of doctors. The military training I got in Krasnoyarsk was elementary—to kill, you have to be specially trained. My only weapon was a scalpel.

Keeping the hospital clean was a constant battle. The temperature hovered around freezing, melting the snow during the day and creating mud underfoot. I placed two troughs of water at the entrance and appointed a guard to make sure everyone washed their feet before entering.

The committee of elders performed invaluable services. They kept lists of the dead and contacted relatives as to the whereabouts of the wounded. They also selected a person from each street to solicit donations for the hospital. At least twice a week, I went to them with a list of supplies we needed.

The first two weeks, I mainly treated outpatients suffering from influenza, bronchitis, intestinal problems, high blood pressure, or asthma. Then the wounded began coming in from Grozny, along with a flood of refugees, including a large number of Russians. Locals took them into their houses, sometimes as many as twenty people to a room. Rumors flew back and forth. Refugees said that during the first few hours of the tank assault on Grozny, Chechen fighters killed several hundred Russian soldiers. No one understood how Russian commanders could send young, inexperienced recruits into Grozny in tanks, without maps and without air cover. I thought of the six Chechen doctors left behind in the basement of the First City Emergency Hospital in Grozny and prayed for their safety. I learned later that after the Russians moved into the city, they held these doctors in the hospital for two weeks to treat their wounded soldiers.

Each morning, I climbed to the third-floor attic of our house and looked over the valley through the old military binoculars given to my father by a Russian soldier during the Second World War. On a clear day, I could see to the edge of town and, in the distance, the smoke billowing over Grozny six miles to the northeast. Through the lenses I saw the tanks, sitting on the horizon like predatory animals, their barrels pointed in our direction. Part of me still couldn't believe they would shoot at innocent civilians.

The Russians considered Alkhan Kala a strategic objective because the Moscow–Baku railroad and highway ran just south of it. Inevitably, the Russians moved against us. Starting in January, the shelling of Alkhan Kala was intermittent. By the end of the month, it had become fierce, with daily attacks. Helicopter gunships terrified the population, flying in low, with large-caliber machine guns mounted on their noses. They flew so close you could see the gunners feeding in the ammunition belts. The elders told the people not to shoot at the helicopters and posted guards to see that they didn't. At night the Russians used night-vision binoculars from the air and from the ground to spot moving objects. "They are trying to provoke us so they have an excuse to unleash fire on the town," the elders said. Since the start of the war, electricity in town was sporadic. One day we would have a few hours of light; then it would go dark for several days. Increasingly, we lit the house with kerosene lamps and candles; we ran the televison off a small generator.

Many people left for Urus-Martan, a town located fifteen miles down the valley to the south; the rest took shelter in their cellars. People hated the cold, damp, cramped cellars. The stairs were hard for Dada with his lame leg, and, like many others with physical handicaps, he usually refused to take shelter. Some nights, I returned home so exhausted I couldn't move an inch from my bed, and I would refuse to go down to the cellar too. My workload had increased, and I soon realized that if I didn't teach the public some first aid, I would be overwhelmed.

"Do not wrap the wounded in blankets, because that won't stop the bleeding. The patient can die from loss of blood," I told the people gathered outside the mosque to hear me speak. "Don't panic. Try and find out where the wound is and apply a tourniquet. If possible, remove clothes before coming into the hospital; otherwise I have to spend time cutting them off."

Blood was always in short supply. Everyone working in the hospital—the nurses, the twelve security guards, and myself—gave blood regularly. I consulted my medical encyclopedia to find out how much blood an individual can safely give, the recommended recovery time, and the diet to maintain strength. Once we got used to it, we could give blood once every two weeks, even once a week in emergencies.

One evening after a week of particularly heavy bombardment, Ruslan visited me. "The elders have told the young men who had taken up arms to leave town. Now we have to go to the Russian headquarters and tell them that all our fighters have left and for them to stop shelling," he said. He wanted me to accompany him. At first, I was reluctant. I didn't think I could contribute anything useful. But in the end I relented.

The next day, accompanied by three of the elders, Ruslan and I walked the two miles to the Russian garrison. I carried a white flag. The camp guards at the entrance looked at our papers and waved us through. A Russian general with a florid face and a well-pressed uniform lounged against a troop carrier. When he saw us, he straightened up and greeted us cordially. After a few pleasantries, Ruslan got down to business.

"There are no fighters in our town. Your men are shooting at innocent civilians," Ruslan explained.

"The soldiers get drunk," the general said. "I'll try to stop it."

On our way home we had to dodge sniper fire. Despite the general's promises, the shelling didn't stop in the following days either. In fact it got so bad, I decided to take Malika, Razyat, Zara, and the children to Zara's relatives in Urus-Martan. I wanted my parents to accompany them, but they refused. Persuading the elderly to leave home was almost impossible. If they were to die, they wanted to be on home territory and be buried with their relatives in the cemetery.

"I have had my life. It's you young people who have to go," Dada said.

Nana refused to leave our livestock: 3 cows, 2 calves, 2 bullocks, and 100 chickens. During a Russian attack she kept popping up from the cellar to feed them. "Someone has to milk the cows and feed the chickens," she said. When a shell killed Malyutka, a cow who obeyed Nana like a dog, she wept as if for a child. We transported Malyutka to the animal graveyard outside the village and threw her on top of the other fallen animals, mostly goats and horses.

Nana was convinced her chickens were psychic. True, before an attack, they started running and clucking in an agitated way along the fence. I felt sorry for the animals. They were so terrified, some even died of fright. At the first sign of shelling, the cattle pressed themselves against the walls of the barn. A dog or cat would invariably poke its head through the opening I left for air under the hurricane door when we piled into the cellar, its head stuck in the hole, its hindquarters quivering outside, desperate for human contact.

A lot of meat went to waste because animals killed in war hadn't been slaughtered correctly. When I was a child, I had learned the usual rituals from Dada during Bayram, the holiest day in the Islamic calendar. On that day we kill a sheep to commemorate Abraham's willingness to sacrifice his son; we thank Allah for giving us the animal, then thank the sheep for offering its life. According to tradition, the animal must face toward Mecca. Dada would take his knife and expertly slit the sheep's throat. After the cut, he poured water down the sheep's mouth to ease the dryness of the throat that develops in moments of stress. After the sheep had been bled for about five minutes, Dada would dab blood on our foreheads, so that all would know we had made the sacrifice and thanked the Almighty.

One afternoon, the Russians sent a helicopter gunship to destroy the mosque around the corner from us. Earlier a shell had toppled the minaret. I was home when the air assault began. Nana and Dada wouldn't budge from the kitchen. I heard the roar of the gunship's rotors overhead. Outside, Tarzan was barking and straining against his rope. Usually, he began barking before the bombing started; then I would unleash him so he could hide under the planks in the courtyard, but now I didn't have time.

"To the cellar!" I yelled to Dada and Nana, who were in the kitchen, but they ignored me. Dada sat in his chair wearing his sheepskin *papakha,* and my mother stood over the stove as though nothing was happening. I knew from the way the helicopter gunship hovered above the mosque, like a giant bird of prey, that it was poised to strike. I ran down to the cellar. Then a thunderous missile explosion shattered the heavy white walls of the mosque like eggshells. The blast blew out the windows of our house, scattering debris everywhere. When I emerged from the cellar, Dada stood in the middle of the room, my mother and a next-door neighbor beside him.

"I've seen it all before," he said, straightening his shoulders as if he wouldn't dignify a Russian attack by moving a single inch.

ON JANUARY 17, 1995, a missile struck the roof of the hospital at 9:30 A.M. I was in the operating room on the first floor along with another doctor, a refugee from Grozny who arrived a week earlier, and two nurses. We were bandaging the leg of a local Chechen fighter. The detonation was terrifying, shattering windows, shaking the walls, and bringing down half the roof. We all threw ourselves facedown on the floor. I cradled my head in my hands. I couldn't breathe. Plaster dust clogged my throat, and debris rained down on my back. Another explosion; a woman screamed, followed by the thud of falling beams. I may have passed out—I was not sure. I pressed my body to the floor until the explosions subsided, then staggered to my feet. Stars flashed before my eyes, or maybe it was dust, and I felt dizzy. The door of the operating room lay on the floor. An icy wind whipped through the open windows, flapping the shreds of curtains Zulai had made for us.

I looked around for the nurses and the doctor. I saw one nurse lying unconscious in the corner. I struggled to stand up and hurried over to her, my feet crunching the broken glass. I placed my thumbs in the cavity behind her ears and pressed down. Her eyes flashed open. Then I placed my thumb and forefinger on either side of her brows just above the nose and applied pressure. I had learned about the acupuncture pressure points from a book on Chinese medicine and often used them when a person passed out on the operating table. After she came to, I pulled her to her feet, and together we went out into the corridor, holding on to the wall for balance. The other nurse and doctor had escaped to safety and left for Urus-Martan.

"Anyone there?" I shouted. On the other side of the building, more screams. "Is anyone there?" I repeated. No reply, only the sound of falling plaster and the thud of distant guns. I felt disoriented as if in a nightmare, feeling I would soon wake up. I stumbled to the window overlooking the courtyard and looked out. Below I saw two men unloading someone from a car and carrying the person into the hospital.

"Where's Khassan?" a voice shouted.

I felt my way along the corridor, stepping over the piles of plaster and broken glass. I rounded the corner, and there on the floor not far from the entrance lay wounded men, their blood trickling onto the broken glass and plaster on the floor.

"Doctor, can you help?" a woman called out.

I looked over at the wounded men. There must have been seven or eight of them. I had treated hundreds of emergency cases but always with help and never all at once like this. Fear gripped me. My chest tightened, and I had trouble breathing. I had no idea what to do. It was as though I had forgotten everything I had learned in medical school, as though I had never seen a wounded person before. I was so confused, I didn't know where to start, whom to treat first. At any moment the hospital could take another hit, I thought. I wanted to clap my hands over my ears to muffle the groans of pain and run from the hospital.

"Khassan, you are losing control," I told myself. I took a deep breath. I had to pull myself together. I couldn't leave. The wounded were waiting for me to do something. I stumbled over to the box in the corner and rifled through the bits of broken plaster to pull out the rubber tourniquet straps. *First, identify the seriously wounded, then stop the bleeding.* Gradually, I regained control.

For the next seven hours, I amputated several limbs, removed shrapnel, and sewed up gashes. It turned out I was the only person with medical training left in the hospital. Everyone else had fled. The hospital was out of commission—the work of the townspeople destroyed in seconds. The building had operated for only three weeks, and Zulai's white flag with the red cross lay in tatters under the rubble. So much for the protection of the Geneva Convention. All that the flag had done was to signal to the Russians where to bomb. And about all I could do now was stabilize the wounded so that their relatives or friends could transport them to the hospital in Urus-Martan. The remaining patients I took to my house.

ALKHAN KALA WAS now under constant attack. I managed to persuade my parents to join the rest of the family in Urus-Martan by promising I would look after the livestock. A mass of cars, carts, tractors, buses, and trucks choked the road out of town. Women and children screamed in panic as long-range Russian artillery shelled them; dead and wounded lay at the side of the road. At the entrance to Urus-Martan, the locals met the refugees and took them to their houses. That night, I made another six trips to Urus-Martan, transporting children and the wounded. By the next day, the only people left in Alkhan

Kala were old men, a couple of old women, and 100 volunteer fighters who stayed to defend the town.

After the damage to the hospital, I relocated all medical services to my house. I received the wounded in the courtyard and performed operations in the wood-paneled entrance hall on the ground floor. In May 1993 when I began building the house, neighbors made fun of the eighteen truckloads of soil I had removed to build a large root cellar and storeroom. The house was completed in 1994. Two iron doors in the cement floor of the summer kitchen led down into the cellar. I placed triple-decker bunk beds against the basement wall and laid planks in the middle of the concrete floor for mattresses. With Nana, Malika, and the other women gone, I needed someone to prepare food for my patients, whom I sheltered in the basement. Addi, a forty-year-old cameraman for the local television station, volunteered.

Addi was an enormous help. He prepared meat soups for the wounded men in a large aluminum cauldron outside in the courtyard. He also baked bread in my mother's tandoor-like, earthen oven. In addition to Addi, three young boys from the neighboring village changed dressings, passed around the bedpans, cans of water, and soap, and helped turn the patients so they wouldn't develop bedsores. Several patients had to be turned two or three times a day.

The heavy artillery fire continued nonstop. Snipers strafed the town from nearby hills. At night, I put on a white camouflage uniform and went out into the snow with the old men, including our family friend Hasilbek, to bring in the wounded. We also collected the dead and gave them temporary burials until their relatives could give them a proper funeral.

And it wasn't only the Chechens we buried. One day, as I stood in the attic of my house, I observed something, which if I hadn't seen it with my own eyes, I would never have believed. Through the binoculars I saw men scattering in all directions, a helicopter gunship firing on them. At first I thought they were Chechens, but as I looked closer I saw that they wore Russian boots and soldiers' tunics. Russian officers were shooting their own men, probably because these recruits were terrified to enter Grozny, where our fighters waited for them!

A few days later on the outskirts of town, near a bombed-out house, we found dogs devouring several of the corpses. The smell made me gag, and I felt my stomach rise up. If not for the dog tags, we wouldn't have known they were Russian soldiers because the bodies were so mutilated. We wrapped the remains in sheets and buried them. Hasilbek shook his head in disgust. "What kind of people are the Russians?" he said as we shoveled earth over the remains. "They don't even bother to collect and bury their dead."

Later, we sent word to the Committee of Soldiers' Mothers, a grassroots organization in Moscow, about these dead and urged them to send someone to pick up the remains. Eventually, these courageous mothers journeyed to Chechnya, crossed the front lines with the help of Chechen mothers, to search for their sons or what remained of them.

ON JANUARY 30 my house was struck by a missile at about 3 P.M. I was standing outside talking to neighbors when I heard the distant sound of the Russian helicopter. The Russians had apparently found out that I was treating Chechen fighters at home. I had frequently warned people not to enter my house in groups—because the Russians could spot them through binoculars or night-vision scopes—but often they ignored me. At that time, I had thirty-two wounded men in my cellar and another eight lying outside, all wrapped up, on cots in the summer terrace of the house.

Something told me that the helicopter was targeting my house. Over the last weeks, I had developed a sixth sense, almost as if I could read the intentions of the pilot. I had noticed that people's survival instinct, like that of animals, becomes acute in extreme conditions. I called it *perestroika* of the organism. It was similar to participating in a judo competition. I could tell instinctively which move my opponent would make.

The engine was faint at first but grew louder. Now the helicopter came into view. A few seconds later, I saw its tail lift upward, signaling the start of an attack dive.

"Into the cellar!" I yelled. The neighbors rushed in. I always kept one of the two iron doors leading to the cellar open, and I literally dove headfirst down the ten steps. The missile hitting the house was like an enormous thunderclap overhead. The blast threw everyone against the walls. I felt my head hit the concrete. For several minutes I lay unconscious. The reinforced concrete ceiling above us cracked as the house collapsed upon it, showering us with brick dust, which seeped into our hair, nostrils, and between our teeth. The ceiling held, thanks to the reinforced steel rods, but now we were trapped inside. The place was totally dark; we were entombed in a giant coffin. We knew that as long as it was still light outside, no one could dig us out for fear of the helicopter returning. There was no doubt that the direct hit had killed the patients on the summer terrace.

Many hours later—well into the night—some forty volunteer fighters started to dig us out. At 2 A.M., we surfaced like miners from the pit, our faces covered in red dust. Everyone looked at me to see my reaction to the destruction of the house. My belongings were scattered across the street as if lying in a landfill. I managed to control myself. I said that the important thing was that we were alive and that you could always rebuild a house; but inside I burned with anger. I had only just finished the house. The wrought iron gate with its beautiful scrolling, which I had ordered specially made, now straddled the roof of the little house next door where my parents lived; the medical books I had collected over the years lay in the rubble.

Friends and neighbors, including my sister Raya's fifteen-year-old son, Ali, helped me go through what was left of the house. I rescued some books and covered them with a plastic sheet. Then, while it was still dark, we packed the wounded into cars with the help of volunteers and drove them to Urus-Martan. Before leaving, I untied Tarzan. With me gone, he would have to fend for himself like all the other stray dogs wandering the streets. As I drove out of Alkhan Kala in pitch darkness, swerving to avoid the bomb craters in the road and the sound of ex-

Twice during the fighting my house was hit, and ultimately destroyed,
by rockets.

plosions in the background, I wondered how to break the news about
the house to the rest of the family. Dada would take it philosophically—
he hadn't wanted me to build the house in the first place, saying it would
only get destroyed. Nana, on the other hand, would be horrified.

It seemed we Chechens spend our energies building our houses and
our lives, only to have them devastated and to start rebuilding them
again.

Chapter 7

Heaven and Hell

I DID NOT stay in Urus-Martan very long. At the beginning of February, I went to Atagi, a district about fifteen miles southeast of Alkhan Kala, and started working in the regional hospital. Several doctors and nurses with whom I had worked in Grozny were already there. At night, I stayed with a friend or went to visit my family in Urus-Martan, which was not far away to the west.

Although the Russians had occupied most of Grozny, Chechen fighters continued to penetrate the Russians' lines, mounting attacks, then melting away. The Russians replied with their big guns and bombs. I heard it said that there were 100 explosions in a single hour in Grozny, the heaviest bombardment that anyone had seen since the Second World War. At least 100,000 civilians remained there, trapped in bunkers or dying in the rubble of their apartments. Every day, dozens of wounded were transported to Atagi. I had never seen anything like the terrible internal wounds—shredded intestines, livers, kidneys, and sexual organs reduced to ground meat—caused by the lethal fragmentation bombs. Slowed by parachutes, the bombs exploded before hitting the ground, then split into dozens of small bomblets, which dropped further and exploded, spraying shards of metal. Designed to cause maximum infantry casualties in open spaces, this inhuman weapon ended up shredding the bodies of hundreds of civilians.

At the start of the war, I used to wear a flak jacket. However, if you wore any kind of protection, the Russian guards at the military check-points assumed you were a fighter. One night, I crept out to the Sun-zha River and heaved the jacket into the water. Watching it sink, I remembered how it had saved my life on one occasion. A blast had thrown me against a wall. I was unconscious for three or four minutes. In the evening when I undressed, I noticed the flak jacket was riddled with shards of metal.

Among the casualties brought to the hospital in Atagi were Russian soldiers. Chechen fighters brought some of them in. Others were brought by the Russians themselves when they couldn't reach their own field hospital. It never occurred to any of us not to treat them because they were our "enemies." We treated whoever needed help, regardless of circumstances.

I remember the first Russian soldier I treated: a tall skinny boy with blond hair, wearing filthy clothes, smelling horrible, and infested with bugs. It was hard to tell if he was moaning because he was afraid of us or because he was in pain from the shrapnel wounds near his spine. After I shot him full of painkiller, extracted the shrapnel, bandaged him, and sent him to the ward, he calmed down. Later, when I passed through the ward, I heard him and the Chechen fighter in the next cot discussing their wounds. They were laughing. There is nothing worse than this kind of war—where people who have lived with each other for so long in the same society, who have grown to know each other, often to like each other as individuals, who speak the same language, end up on different sides trying to kill each other.

The Chechen fighter's mother, there to look after her own son, also fed the young Russian soldier and gave him clean clothes. She then passed his name on to the council of elders, who tried to contact his family in Russia to come and collect him. A few days later, there was a report on Russian television about the cruel way Chechens supposedly treat Russian prisoners.

I found it hard to think of these pathetic young soldiers as enemies. Our women said these boys shouldn't be away from their mothers. Before they fought in Chechnya, most of them had never even held a gun. They were badly fed and begged for food from the villagers. The elders said it was all right to feed them so long as they were not *kontraktniki,* special forces who signed contracts to serve for a specified number of years and many of whom were convicts released from prison to fight in Chechnya. Wearing their black sleeveless T-shirts and showing off their tattoos, the *kontraktniki* lacked all vestiges of humanity. For them, Chechnya was an opportunity to loot and rape. I didn't see many of them in the hospital because our fighters usually killed them when they got the chance.

Whenever I treated Russian soldiers—at Atagi, at Urus-Martan, or in any other town—I knew their presence put the hospital at risk, so I would discharge them as soon as possible. Families in town who had lost relatives were often very angry and wanted revenge against the Russians. If the wounded soldiers were brought to the hospital by Chechen fighters, we would ask them to take them away and hold them at home as prisoners. When Russians brought their wounded to the hospital and the wounds were not too serious, we told them to wait on the street. Then we dispatched the hospital's guards outside to make sure that no one fired on them while they waited. At times, to guarantee the safety of the Russian soldier-patients, I would sit in my white coat on top of a personnel carrier and escort them out of town. Some people, seeing me sitting on the Russian vehicle, concluded that I was a traitor working for the federal forces.

Nine days after I started working in Atagi, the hospital was hit by a deep-penetration missile. We were operating in the basement, where we had transferred all the patients when the bombing began a few days earlier. At the time, I was removing shrapnel from a young boy's back. My recollections of the attack are vague. I remember worrying that a metal shard was dangerously close to his spinal column, that it could dislodge, hit a nerve, and paralyze him. Then the huge explosion hit, and everything went black. When I came to, I managed to drag out four patients and lay them outside on mattresses in the snow. I believe they were still alive, but I don't remember. Then I heard a voice shouting that I, myself, was injured.

"No, that's blood from the wounded," I said. I felt nothing. Then I looked down and saw the blood dripping out of the bottom of my sweatpants, forming a puddle on the ground. After that, I lost consciousness. I learned later that I was transported to a hospital in Khasavyurt, just over the border in Dagestan, where I lay in a coma for four days. Eight of the hospital staff died in that attack, including three doctors and a nurse.

While in the coma I had a strange and wonderful experience. Weightless, I seemed to float above my own body. This disembodied sensation was a relief. I felt euphoric. I looked down, and there was my body lying on a stretcher in the snow near a building. A hospital, I thought. I had no idea where I was, and I didn't care. Why does everyone have to carry around such a heavy body? I thought. Below me the nurses and doctors pulled back my shirt and began examining the gash where the shrapnel grazed my side. Suddenly, I felt myself whooshing down a tunnel at a very fast speed. It was pitch-black. Then a beautiful landscape opened up. People came to meet me. I didn't know them. They seemed to be from different nationalities, all communicating in a friendly way. Lions and tigers with benign expressions on their faces wandered among the people. I have no words to describe the beauty of the gardens, so many fruits and flowers. I had arrived in heaven.

Then I heard voices, not human voices, and I felt my body being drawn back. I didn't want to go. I tried to resist, but I was powerless. When I opened my eyes, I saw nurses and doctors leaning over patients lying on cots. I was in an intensive-care unit. One of the doctors examined me and said, "This is not a man; this is a machine." I heard a voice say, "Anyone else would have died by now."

I realized that I had almost died, but that knowledge didn't seem to affect me. The strange thing was that I was no longer frightened of death. I knew what paradise was like. I sent word to Malika that I was safe; she was the only person in the family who knew I had been wounded and was in the hospital. I made her promise not to tell my parents or Zara. The doctors wanted to keep me in the hospital, but as soon as I was able to walk, I left without telling them. I knew that it takes time to recover from a concussion, but I had to get back to work. In the beginning, I had trouble with my memory. In the past I memorized telephone numbers with ease and recited poetry while I operated. Now I sometimes struggled to retrieve the right word. Still, I was convinced that Allah had saved me to continue treating my people and that my memory would return with time.

On leaving Khasavyurt, I made a brief visit to our house in Alkhan Kala. I found Tarzan out of control. He had even killed some of our neighbor's chickens and littered our courtyard with feathers and bones. I took him reluctantly to a market on the outskirts of town and asked if anyone wanted him. Immediately, I found a taker. I felt sorry to leave Tarzan with a stranger, but I didn't have time to train him now and the neighbors were complaining. The man promised to look after him and cure his bad habits.

Now that many of the hospitals in Chechnya were out of commission, I went from village to village treating patients in their homes. I performed operations on kitchen tables, on beds, on the floor, and in cellars. After a bombardment, people would seek me out, entreating me to come and save their relatives, like the fifteen-year-old girl who had been struck in her back by shrapnel. She lay on a cot in her kitchen, her clothes glued to her body with blood.

"Hurry! Remove her dress!" I ordered her mother.

"No! No!" The girl cried, her hand clutching the front of her dress.

"He's a doctor," her mother said, as she peeled off her daughter's blood-soaked garments. I rolled the girl on her side. Then I saw the gash in her back, blood pumping out in rhythmic spurts, and I knew if we didn't get to a hospital and give her some blood she would die. Later at the hospital in Urus-Martan, the surgeon removed part of her lung, which had been destroyed by the shrapnel.

Often I traveled to small villages in the mountains where roads didn't reach. I would leave my car and continue on foot to the patient's house. One such patient was a youth who had been hit in the head by a sniper. For twenty-four hours he had lain unconscious in his parents' house.

"Please help him," his uncle begged me. (He had tracked me down to a house in a nearby village, where I was changing the dressing on the amputated leg of one of my patients.) "He is the only son."

That night, I trudged five miles along a narrow mountain path with my instruments. The sky was dark, and the boy's uncle walked ahead with a flashlight. The boy lay on a wooden bunk in the main room of the house, a portion of his brain oozing like gray jelly from the wound on the left side of his head. His breath rattled. One look, and I concluded that blood had accumulated inside the dural membrane, causing a serious swelling inside the cranium. I turned to the parents, who stood next to the bunk with expressions of such agony on their faces— I couldn't meet his mother's eyes. "Only the Almighty can save your son, but if you want me to try, I will," I said. They nodded.

I gave the boy a shot of painkiller in the crown of the head, made an incision, and peeled back a small flap of skin. A relative held his head while I drilled an inch-wide hole through the skull some ways from the injury, and slowly widened the gap with a pair of clippers. I flushed out the incision. I used an ordinary carpenter's drill, so had to pay great attention not to drill too deeply. Then we heard a sudden gurgling sound, like water descending a drain. A spurt of liquid mixed with blood shot out, relieving the pressure to the skull. As I probed in the wound for the pieces of shrapnel, the brain began to pulsate, the blood surging back and forth.

It was hopeless. The boy had lain there for more than a day with his brain pressing against the inside of his skull, damaging vital nerves. I lifted his lids and saw his pupils were dilated, which meant death was near. At 4 A.M., I determined that he had died. After his death, the parents washed and prepared the body for the Muslim burial. I said good-bye and walked back down the mountain. As I got into my car, the sun was coming up, turning the sky orange. Another day, I thought.

I DON'T KNOW what made me go into Grozny one morning in March. Stupidity probably. But I had heard such terrible stories about the capital from the wounded civilians that I wanted to see for myself. That morning, spring was in the air. Maybe the clear blue sky after so many cold, dank days, along with the sun sparkling on the snow, made me feel protected. I didn't tell anyone I was going because I knew how dangerous it was. Although I had a document from the Russian military headquarters stating that I was a doctor and should be allowed safe passage throughout Chechnya, I knew no papers could protect me from some out-of-control Russian soldier whose best friend had been blown up by a Chechen grenade.

Driving into Grozny, I steered my car around the craters left by the bombs and treads of Russian tanks. With the thaw, the ruts filled up with muddy water. On either side of the road, mounds of freshly dug earth marked new graves. At each burial, someone had placed a makeshift marker: a piece of wood for a Chechen burial, a cross for a Russian. Scribbled on every marker was the victim's name, if known, and a description of the clothes on the body— navy blue sports pants, brown boots, a black coat, or a floral dress, anything to identify the body. The Russian broadcasters claimed that people killed along the highway were Chechen guerrillas, although most were civilians trying to escape the city. That morning, an old Russian woman knelt in front of two sticks stuck in the ground in the form of a cross. Who was she searching for? I wondered. A son, a husband, a daughter? Whenever a body was identified, relatives would be contacted, the body dug up and given a proper burial. If you dug up the body and it wasn't your relative, you circulated the description. So many people disappeared without a trace.

Around 10 A.M., I reached the first military post set up by the Russians at the Chernorechye settlement. The posts stood at half-mile intervals along the main roads. Cement blocks and sandbags fortified the bunkers, which were manned by about thirty men. Empty cartridges and unexploded shells lay everywhere. When I made my medical rounds by car, I usually had no trouble with ordinary Russian recruits. They recognized I was a doctor, and if I gave them a few cigarettes, which I carried for that purpose, they would wave me on. It was the *kontraktniki* I had to be careful of.

I passed through the first four checkpoints without a problem. At the fifth, a mile away from Minutka Square in central Grozny, several soldiers stripped to the waist lounged on a couch outside the bunker basking in the warm sun. I assumed the couch had been looted from a Chechen family; it was upholstered in fine leather. When I stopped the car, a soldier, a huge man of about forty, sauntered toward me. He wore the uniform of the *spetsnaz*, the Russian special forces, and carried an automatic rifle. Grenades and ammunition festooned his chest. I rolled down the window. A dangerous individual, I thought; whatever you do, don't antagonize him.

"Get out," he barked.

I got out of the car and handed him my papers.

"So why are you going to Grozny?"

"They are calling for doctors on the radio."

His eyes fell on my key ring, which held a token displaying a Japanese figure dressed in white pants and jacket. "So you do tae kwon do?" he asked.

"No, judo."

"I am a tae kwon do fighter. We could fight each other," he quipped.

I smelled liquor on his breath, and I knew he was trying to provoke me. "I'd like to, but the problem is that your friends would pull the trigger." I tried to humor him.

"No, no. I'll tell them not to shoot you." He laughed.

"Another time," I said.

"So you have been up in the mountains operating on *dukhi*," he said. It was the first time I had heard that Russian word used to mean Chechen fighters. During the Russian-Afghan war, the Russian soldiers called the mujahideen *dukhi*—spirits or phantoms—because they crept in, attacked, and disappeared.

"I operate on the wounded," I said.

"So . . . on *cheki* [Chechen fighters]?"

Two of the *kontraktniki* who had been lying on the couch placed their vodka bottles on the ground and sauntered over with ugly grins on their faces. "Why are you taking so long with that guy?" one of them asked. "Come with us!"

The three of them grabbed my arm and propelled me in the direction of a large house surrounded by an eight-foot-high brick fence. One look at the house, and I knew there was a good chance that if I went in, I would never come out. Most military checkpoints had such a house or deep pits where they held prisoners until they transported them to one of the "filtration camps" in Chechnya. The filtration camps were supposed to be places for weeding out fighters from peaceful civilians, but, in fact, they became houses of torture.

"Let go of me. I am a doctor! I have not been fighting." I tried to pull myself from their grip.

"You been treating *dukhi*!" the *spetsnaz* soldier shouted, hitting me in the back with the butt of his rifle. "Faster! Forward!"

The three of them dragged me into the house, which was partially bombed out. The entrance of the building was dark. Sunbeams came in through gaps in the walls and ceiling. I saw the wall on the opposite side of the room was pockmarked with bullet holes and stained with blood and dried hair. The familiar smell of death hung in the air. This room was where the *kontraktniki* brought people they wanted to torture or kill; maybe as revenge for a buddy killed by the Chechens, or maybe because they were just plain drunk and wanted some fun.

"We'll teach you to operate on *dukhi*," a *kontraktnik* with a vodka-flushed face shouted, shoving me against the wall.

"I operate on the injured," I repeated. "I'm a doctor. Under international law I have the right to treat the injured."

"International law! Who cares about your international law?" A *kontraktnik* sneered and spat on the ground. "We'll show you about international law."

"I have a request," I said.

"Bandits always have a request."

"Give me a piece of paper so I can write down my name and address and put it in my pocket. That's my only request."

"Don't worry, you will have your place in the sewer." They turned to each other and laughed.

"We'll teach you!" They shouted obscenities; then one of them said, "Cover the bandit's eyes, so we can shoot him!"

"Get rid of him good!" A *kontraktnik* tried to tie a band over my eyes, but I managed to push him away.

"You can shoot me, but I will not close my eyes!" I guessed they were superstitious and would hesitate to execute a man who would stare them down with open eyes.

"Close your eyes, bandit!"

"You're not human beings," I shouted. "You will be punished for your evil. You'll see, my brothers will come after you to take revenge for my death. And I won't close my eyes!"

"Shoot the bastard!" Now they started to argue and shout among themselves. "Cover his eyes! Shoot the bastard!"

"Cover his eyes, or he will come back to haunt us."

Suddenly, a door leading into the room burst open, and a Russian major emerged. "What the hell is going on here?" he shouted, his face flushed with anger.

I seized the moment. "I'm a doctor! Where's the law that says that you have the right to shoot me for being a surgeon and treating the wounded?"

The major looked me up and down, then snapped at the others, "Leave him alone!" He turned to me and came straight to the point: "My wife is a surgeon, and out of respect for the profession, I will let you go. But be more careful at the checkpoints. Turn around now and go home. Get the hell out of here! You escaped this time, but next time you'll be executed."

When I got back to my car, I don't know what came over me. I was like a zombie. It was as if I hadn't understood what had happened to me five minutes before. For some reason, I ignored the major's warning and drove straight on to Grozny. I was so euphoric at having escaped death that I thought I was immortal; that I could take risks; that nothing could happen to me now. Ever since that strange experience of entering paradise when I was in the hospital in Dagestan, death no longer frightened me. Although I worried about leaving Maryam and Islam as orphans, I knew my extended family would help Zara take care of them. During the war, complete strangers took children in. Chechens will do everything to prevent children from entering orphanages.

If what I experienced in Dagestan was the entrance to paradise, what I saw in Grozny was an introduction to hell. Before my eyes lay the realm of evil. At one checkpoint I noticed a path across the mud to a latrine made of old gravestones stolen from a Chechen cemetery, the Arabic words still visible. Smoke billowed over the city. Houses were heaps of rubble, flames leaping from their roofs. Twisted metal, beams, and lumps of plaster smoldered in the streets. So many corpses lay decomposing on the streets that the checkpoint soldiers wore handkerchiefs over their faces to block the smell. An old woman dragged a cart filled with plastic bags and boxes. A rat scuttled across her path.

I stood before the gutted Presidential Palace, gagging on the stench, unable to move. Scores of burned-out tanks, army personnel carriers, and jeeps belonging to the Russians littered the street. Under them lay rotting bodies. This once beautiful city with its tree-lined streets was now a carcass, the buildings gutted, entire floors gone, with staircases leading nowhere, the trunks of trees shredded, cars and trams reduced to metal skeletons. Packs of stray dogs roamed the street, scratching in the rubble for human flesh.

I saw one body that had been picked clean by dogs. All that remained was the back of the head, which was protected by a helmet; another body had been devoured to the bone, except for a foot covered by a boot. A military truck rumbled by piled with human bones: legs, arms, spinal columns, ribs, skulls. As the truck hit a rut, a spinal column and collarbone fell onto the street, to be crushed into the mud by an armored personnel carrier. I saw old women with shell-shocked faces, poking through the rubble for something, anything, that once belonged to them. Most of the old people in the city were Russians with no place to go. I saw a dog leap into the air, yelping in pain, as a soldier emptied his rifle into it.

At the checkpoint on the bridge, I glimpsed a placard on the ground. I picked it up. It read: "We are going back to the mountains, but we'll be back! Allah Akhbar!" I put it back. I saw a Russian sniper raise his rifle in my direction. I made no attempt to get out of his sights. He could have killed me like a game bird, but for some reason, he didn't pull the trigger.

The light was fading, and I knew that I had to get back out through the five checkpoints before dark. As I approached checkpoint five—the one where the mercenaries wanted to kill me—I saw some twenty cars lined up ahead of me. They were driven by old men. Young men avoided the open street. I assumed the old men were ferrying women who were looking for a lost relative or wanting to see if their homes were still standing. Then suddenly, my heart skipped a beat: The monster who wanted to execute me was on duty, checking documents. He was walking my way now. I wondered what he would do when he spied me behind the wheel. I froze; it was too late to turn around.

A few more steps . . . and he recognized me. He did a double take, then, full of hatred, waved the butt of his rifle in my direction and yelled at me to break out of line. Somehow, I remained calm, pretending I hadn't seen him. He waved at me again, this time more insistently. My heart raced, but still I did not respond. I suspected he would not shoot me in front of all those cars but would try to provoke me to give himself an excuse for firing.

"Get going, you black ass!" he growled at me a third time right at my window. "Out! Get going!"

I turned the wheel to the left and inched forward, slowly, slowly, past this *kontraktnik*. As I headed down the road, I kept looking more in the rearview and side mirrors than at the road. Was he going to raise that rifle? If I saw the barrel go up, I would dive over into the right-hand passenger seat to try to cheat the shot.

He gave me a last glance; then he turned away and went back to checking documents. I stepped on the gas and raced homeward. Four more checkpoints. But my fears evaporated. I knew that on this day Allah was with me. I was not going to die.

When I got back to my family in Urus-Martan, I told people about the horrors I had seen. They were shocked. Raya's husband, Lecha, was so nervous that he twisted his hat out of shape.

"You fool! You absolute fool!" he kept saying. "You never told anyone where you were going. You could have just disappeared, and no one would ever have known!"

Chapter 8

Young Soldiers

I N EARLY APRIL 1995 enormous explosions could be heard in the west, sounding like the crack of thunder over the mountains. I guessed that villages were being shelled, and I jumped into my car and started toward Samashki to treat the wounded. At the entrance of the village, the Russians turned everyone back. What happened in those three terrible days between April 7 and April 9 I only learned later when the Russian military lifted the blockade and let medical personnel enter the village.

It was a bloodbath. Russian attacks on Chechen villages usually started in the same way, with the military accusing villagers of harboring fighters. However, in most cases—and Samashki was no exception—the village elders had already negotiated with the Chechen field commander to depart from the village with his troops. In Samashki, the Russians then demanded the elders hand over sixty-four rifles. The elders explained they didn't have the rifles. This became the excuse the Russians needed to start a punishment raid, moving their armor and shooting everyone in their path, including elders, women, and children. If the townspeople had rifles, they would have opened fire, but there was no resistance and the soldiers reached the center of town quickly.

People hid in their basements, and the soldiers lobbed grenades in after them, then torched the houses. Bombs rained down. The rampage lasted several days. The soldiers then loaded their trucks with video recorders, television sets, carpets, and furniture looted from the houses left standing.

When the Russian military authorities opened up the village two days later, I went in with Red Cross workers. I hesitate to write about the atrocities we saw because I fear that people will think I am exaggerating. Dozens of charred corpses of women and children lay in the courtyard of the mosque, which had been destroyed. The first thing my eye fell on was the burned body of a baby, lying in fetal position. The flesh had burned off the arms, and you could see the white of the finger bones. I couldn't tell if it was a girl or a boy. A wild-eyed woman emerged from a burned-out house holding a dead baby. Trucks with bodies piled in the back rolled through the streets on the way to the cemetery.

While treating the wounded, I heard stories of young men—gagged and trussed up—dragged with chains behind personnel carriers. I heard of Russian aviators who threw Chechen prisoners, screaming, out their helicopters. There were rapes, but it was hard to know how many because women were too ashamed to report them. One girl was raped in front of her father. I heard of one case in which the mercenaries grabbed a newborn baby, threw it among each other like a ball, then shot it dead in the air. The accounts were hard to believe, as though the soldiers had taken leave of their senses and become rabid dogs. More than 200 people died, and many more were wounded.

Leaving the village for the hospital in Grozny, I passed a Russian armored personnel carrier with the word *SAMASHKI* written on its side in bold, black letters. I looked in my rearview mirror and to my horror saw a human skull mounted on the front of the vehicle. The bones were white; someone must have boiled the skull to remove the flesh. At the first checkpoint, the troop carrier overtook me, and I saw painted on its other side the words *GENERAL YERMOLOV,* a reminder of the cruelty that this nineteenth-century Russian general visited on the North Caucasus.

★ ★ ★

THROUGHOUT THAT SPRING of 1995—March, April, and May—
the Russians pressed southward towards the foothills of the Caucasus.
The carnage was terrible as the Russian tanks and helicopters turned
their guns on roads, bridges, schools, and villages across the republic.
With Grozny already in Russian hands, there was a lull in the fighting
around Alkhan Kala, and in May, I decided to bring Dada, Nana, Malika, Razyat, Zara, Maryam, and Islam back home from Urus-Martan.
They were longing to return. Nana worried about the livestock, and
we feared vandals. Since my house had been leveled, everyone lived in
my parents' little house, which was still standing across our common
courtyard. We hastily rebuilt the roof, which had been blown off.

I started working again in Grozny, this time at the Ninth City Hospital because the First City Emergency Hospital had been heavily
damaged. The Russian military authorities issued me a pass stating I
was a doctor, though there was no guarantee that some drunken
guard at a checkpoint wouldn't harass me. When I was needed for a
particular operation, I traveled to other hospitals around the republic.
In the evenings I did medical rounds in Alkhan Kala. Nana continued
to give me a bad time about going out at night, worrying about
snipers. My life was in Allah's hands, I told her. My medical workload
had become so heavy that I had begun teaching ordinary women how
to change dressings or clean up shrapnel wounds. When I wasn't too
exhausted, I visited my patients. On my way home from the hospital,
I sometimes would stop by for tea and talk with my old school pals,
Adlan and Vakha.

One day when I stopped at a checkpoint just north of Alkhan Kala,
a stocky soldier with blond hair and blue eyes held out his hand for my
documents. As he flipped through my domestic passport, he stopped at
the last page. " Krasnoyarsk?" he asked. His face broke into a grin as he
read my old Krasnoyarsk residence registration.

I explained I had studied medicine there.

"*Nash*! [Ours!]" he yelled out to two soldiers lounging on an army
personnel carrier parked across the road. "This guy's one of ours! *On
nash*!"

The young recruits jumped down from the APC. The one who had checked my passport said his name was Seriozha. He introduced me to his two friends, Kostya and Ivan. They were a sorry-looking trio, wearing split army boots and camouflage fatigues caked with mud and tank grease. They couldn't have been more than eighteen or nineteen years old. Seriozha said he came from a small village in the vast Krasnoyarsk region, not far from the city. We chatted for about half an hour, reminiscing about Siberia. I had warm feelings for people from that part of the world; they were so much more friendly and hospitable than the people of Moscow. The soldiers even knew some of the athletes I had trained with.

From then on, Seriozha, Kostya, and Ivan always greeted me with a smile, a change from the scare tactics encountered at many checkpoints, where humiliating civilians was a pastime. Whenever I passed through their checkpoint, I would bring the odd packet of cigarettes, bottles of soft drinks, or a newspaper. Once they asked for potatoes, which I was happy to bring them. The first time they asked for vodka, I gave it to them. "But don't ask me again," I said. "If you ever need medical help, let me know." I took care not to give them anything in front of any officers or the *kontraktniki*, who mostly were too busy sunning themselves behind the sandbags to notice.

The Russians had set up a puppet government in Grozny. During the day the Russians controlled the city. At night the Chechen fighters mounted hit-and-run attacks. The sound of gunfire was constant.

That May, Boris Yeltsin urged his generals to wind down the war in Chechnya. He had invited many of the world's leaders to Moscow on May 9, 1995, to celebrate the fiftieth anniversary of the Allied victory over Nazi Germany and wanted to demonstrate that his Chechen problems had been resolved. He publicly declared a week's cease-fire, which was ignored by the generals on the ground. Bombs continued to fall, and the wounded poured into the hospitals

A month later, on June 14, 1995, Shamil Basayev and his men crossed from Chechnya into Russia. Motivated by the massacres at Samashki, Bamut, and other villages, they wanted to take action that they hoped would bring the war to an end. Basayev and his men headed for Stavropol or even farther into the interior, but they did not get very far. They were stopped near the Russian-Chechen border and turned back. Russian military forces pursued them to the town of Budyonnovsk, where Basayev seized a hospital. The Russians, trying to flush him out, opened fire on the building. We all watched the Russian attack on a television set hooked up to the Japanese generator. The camera showed patients and doctors hanging white sheets out the windows, appealing to the Russians to back off. But inside the hospital, Basayev's men executed five Russian pilots they had taken prisoner, and threatened to kill more.

Finally, Basayev agreed to negotiate with Prime Minister Viktor Chernomyrdin. And then a most unusual thing happened. Basayev and the Russian premier had a telephone conversation that was broadcast live over national radio. Basayev agreed to leave if the Russian government would guarantee safe passage for himself and his men back to Chechnya. Even more important, both sides decided on a cease-fire, leading to talks to end the war.

Basayev and his men did return to Chechnya, but the fighting continued while peace talks proceeded. By July, the Russians were taking such heavy casualties that the Russian colonel who headed up their military hospital in the old airport hotel came to the Ninth City Hospital in Grozny to ask for help. He said they didn't have a surgeon who could do reconstructive surgery, and he asked me to operate on one of their officers whose face had been very seriously damaged. I agreed to come. The Russian military hospital consisted of about 100 beds. I was met at the entrance by the Russian colonel. As he led me through the courtyard, I saw the wounded lying on the ground, waiting. Inside, men lined the corridor on stretchers. The wards were filled to overflowing, too, with men lying on four-decker bunks. As we walked past them, the Russian colonel shook his head and raised his hand to the back of his neck in a gesture of despair. In the course of a couple of hours, I managed to reconstruct the bones of the Russian officer with the help of their dentist.

Afterward the colonel invited me to his office, where we discussed the number of wounded and dead from both sides. Speaking to the Russian doctor felt perfectly normal, yet there was something strange about it because we were supposed to be on opposing sides. However, we were really both on the side of the wounded. Later, we concluded an agreement with the Russian military hospital whereby each of us would treat the other's wounded along with any of the wounded local citizens. I was happy about this gesture of civility amid all the barbarity.

The next month or two passed without major incident, although the bombing continued. My workload remained heavy at the Ninth City Hospital. It was good to be with my family again. We even had managed to plant a vegetable garden; tomatoes and cucumbers hung on the vines; and peppers were waiting to be picked. Other families who had fled the bombing were beginning to return home.

One September evening about 10 P.M., we heard a knock at the door. We were all drinking tea around the kitchen table. Throughout that day, Zara, Malika, and Razyat had been busy salting and putting vegetables up for the winter. The jars were lined up on the floor waiting to go down into the cellar. There was a chill in the air, and each day the sun set earlier, signaling that winter was on its way. Nana and Zara had already checked the animals for the night.

At first, I thought the knocking meant someone was seeking medical assistance. However, when I opened the gate, I saw the ten-year-old son of our neighbor. "Soldiers are asking for you," he said.

"Russian?" I asked. He nodded.

I tensed, my mind making a quick inventory of anything that might link me to the Chechen fighters . . . but there were no rifles, pistols, or guns of any type in the house. I put on my shoes and went out into the street. At first, I didn't see the three young soldiers huddled against the fence. When they came forward, I recognized them as the young recruits from Krasnoyarsk—Seriozha, Kostya, and Ivan—who always greeted me at the military post north of Alkhan Kala. Fear was written all over their faces. They carried no weapons or other possessions. Judging by the smell of stale sweat wafting in my direction, they hadn't bathed in months. I guessed why they had come, and I didn't like it. They started talking at once.

"We can't take it any longer."

"We want out!"

"The *kontraktniki* beat us up all the time."

"They send us out for vodka any time of day or night. They say, 'Kill for it!' "

"We have nothing against you Chechens. . . . We don't know why we are here . . . We just—"

"Stop!" I interrupted. "Just one of you talk; tell me what you want."

"We are at the end of our rope," Seriozha said, wringing his hands nervously. "Please help us. If you contact our parents—our mothers—they will come for us."

What he said about mothers coming to the rescue was true. I knew of many cases where Chechen families had helped Russian deserters and returned them to their mothers. Moreover, Russian prisoners of war were often billeted with Chechen families because we didn't have detention facilities. For the most part, our tradition of hospitality required Chechen families to treat prisoners as guests. They ate and slept with the families and did odd chores such as chopping wood or mending broken machinery.

Desertions infuriated the Russian military authorities, who tried to brainwash young soldiers into thinking the Chechens would either enslave them or castrate them. A deserter discovered in a Chechen house might be executed by his own officers for desertion, while the owners of the house might be shot, too, for holding "prisoners." Even a Russian civilian could be executed, as happened when a neighbor of my sister Raya gave shelter to a Russian friend whose house had been destroyed and family killed. Several Russian soldiers rolled up in an army personnel carrier, accused him of treason, beat him up, and took him away. He was never seen again.

"Harboring deserters is dangerous," I said to Seriozha. "Tomorrow you'll be missed, and the search will begin. If they think you are in Alkhan Kala, they will seal off the town and shell it."

"They'll think we've gone in the direction of the nearest settlement, the First State Milk Farm, toward Grozny," Seriozha said, with desperation in his voice. "They won't think we came to Alkhan Kala because it's so much farther. We're here because we thought you would help us."

I didn't want them standing in the street where they were visible, so I invited them into our courtyard and told them to wait. I found Dada stretched out on his cot with his crutches propped up beside him.

"It's risky," he said after I explained the situation. "Where would they sleep?" Malika, Razyat, Zara, the children, my parents, and I were all living in my parents' four-room house.

"We can put mattresses down in the hall; they can sleep there," I said. Dada didn't argue. We all knew if the soldiers took to the street again, they would probably be found by the Russian military authorities, who would either send them to prison or shoot them as deserters. Besides, turning someone away from your house was a violation of Chechen hospitality. Even if your worst enemy seeks refuge in your house, you must offer him hospitality. We couldn't in good conscience risk these boys being shot. They were war victims too.

"You can stay here, but you must never show yourselves on the street," I said to the soldiers when I returned. "My family lives in this house, and you must observe our rules: no smoking inside the house, no drinking, no bad language, no dirty jokes, and no going around without a shirt in front of the women." They looked so relieved when I told them they could stay.

Zara cooked up a huge frying pan of potatoes. Malika laid out homemade bread, salted tomatoes, and cucumbers. We invited the young men to the table in the kitchen. From the way they shoveled down their food and held out their empty plates, it was clear they hadn't eaten in days.

We hurried to find them clean clothes. We found sweatpants and sweaters for all of them. The women boiled water on the stove for the metal tub off the kitchen, and we provided them with disinfectant soap to kill their lice. They spent much of the night bathing, while we got rid of their uniforms.

Over the next few days, as they gradually relaxed, their personalities emerged. Seriozha was the quieter of the three. He spent most of the day studying Dada's health magazines. The other two, Kostya and Ivan, played cards or chess, talked, and joked.

At the end of my day at the hospital, I brought them cigarettes, which they smoked in the courtyard. Seriozha assumed the leadership role. One delicate matter concerned the toilet. We Chechens are very modest when it comes to toilet needs. When we have to go, we do so as discreetly as possible. Men and women avoid meeting each other at the outhouse, located outside the house in a distant part of the courtyard. Ours had a cement path leading up to it, with tiles on the floor.

"This is a Muslim household," I told Seriozha. "Cleanliness is very important to us. Tell the boys not to throw cigarette butts or dirty toilet paper on the floor. We've provided everything you need, including a bucket of water you can use to wash yourself with."

"I'm sorry," Seriozha said, looking embarrassed, "it won't happen again." It was touching how they tried to adapt to our ways. Instead of lounging on their mattresses as they did on the first day or two, they rose to their feet when Dada or I entered the room, and they kept their shirts on.

"If this goes on, you'll all turn into Chechens," I joked one day when they stood waiting at the kitchen table for Dada to sit down first.

Seriozha laughed. "I like the way you respect your parents," he said.

He said he and his friends wanted to pay us something, but when I refused, he realized his gesture might be considered an insult. He said he was sorry he even raised the issue.

In the evening we all ate together and chatted around the kitchen table. Dada talked to the young soldiers about herbs and eating a healthy diet. In recent years he had become a vegetarian. He also did his best to cheer them up with his war stories.

"You boys haven't seen anything," he would say. "When we fought in the Great Patriotic, there would be four thousand or five thousand facedown on the battlefield in the morning."

The recruits soon sought out Dada's company, and a friendship developed. They told him about life at the military checkpoint, how the mercenaries and special forces beat them with army boots, seized their food, and swapped it for vodka in the village; how the special troops shot Seriozha's friend and blamed it on the Chechens. They said they were never told that they were coming to Chechnya and that they had no basic training.

"They lied to us; they lied to our parents. They lied to the Russian people!" Ivan said. I knew I had to get rid of the soldiers as soon as possible. We needed to contact their families and supply them with false documents.

Organizing the escape of Russian deserters fell to the women, who during the war carried a heavy burden as important as that of any fighter. We contacted Markha, a woman who lived in Alkhan Kala and who maintained contact with the Committee of Soldiers' Mothers in Moscow. After collecting the names and addresses for the families of Seriozha, Kostya, and Ivan, she took a taxi to neighboring Ingushetia, a two-hour drive. The families of the three young recruits had telephones, so she called them from the post office in the town of Nazran. They were tricky calls to make on an open telephone line. Later, Markha described the conversations.

"Is this the so-and-so family?" she would ask.

"Yes."

"Do you have a son in Chechnya?"

"Yes."

At this point the person on the other end of the line would become tense, fear creeping into the voice.

"Don't worry. Your son is all right. He is with us."

Then she explained that if the mother came to Ingushetia, arrangements would be made to reunite her with her son.

One by one, the Russian mothers started arriving. Markha disguised them as Chechen women, covering their hair with the traditional head scarf and removing all makeup. Then she brought them by car to our house. In those days of the first war, the soldiers at checkpoints only verified the driver's documents and left the women alone. Meanwhile, in the backseat, Markha chatted to the Russian woman in Chechen—the Russian women could not understand Chechen—to avoid suspicion.

A friend of mine at the Russian passport office in Urus-Martan supplied them with a certificate giving each soldier a Tartar name, stating he resided in the region and had lost his documents in a fire. I offered to pay the friend, but she refused.

Seriozha, Kostya, and Ivan stayed with us for more than a week. Everyone was nervous, all praying their mothers would arrive and that none would be left behind. Ivan's mother arrived at 11 A.M. one day. When I returned from the hospital that evening, Zara recounted how Ivan and his mother had wept when they saw each other. I was amazed by the courage of the Russian mothers who traveled to a war zone with no idea of what awaited them. They must have been terrified, for the Russian media had painted us as such barbarians, enslaving hundreds of Russian soldiers. Ivan's mother said she had had to borrow money from relatives for the journey.

Once Ivan's mother had eaten and rested, Markha accompanied the two back to Ingushetia by taxi within a couple of hours. From Nazran, Ivan and his mother traveled to the North Caucasus resort town of Mineral'nyye Vody, where they caught the train back to Krasnoyarsk.

Two days later, while I was at work, Kostya's mother arrived.

Seriozha was the last to leave. I arrived home to find his mother sitting on the old divan in the kitchen between Malika, Razyat, and Nana. She wore a long gray dress and a scarf tied Chechen style. Nana's Russian wasn't all that good, and Malika and Razyat were translating. The conversation was animated. After I greeted Seriozha's mother, she thanked me over and over again.

"I never dreamed Chechens were like this," she said. "I will go back and tell everyone about the Chechen mothers and what they are doing to help us, and what is happening here," she said.

I knew that if she ever tried to write to us, or inform the newspapers about what she had experienced, the FSB would stop the letters. The FSB, or Federal Security Bureau, replaced the KGB secret police after the fall of the Soviet Union.

"Don't ever talk about what happened, and don't try to contact us," I said. "Maybe some day in the future, when quiet times return . . ."

When it was time to say good-bye, Seriozha's mother wept, and the boy had tears in his eyes. I gave him a hug and patted him on the back. "Come back as our guest . . . only don't bring your gun."

After they left, Malika and Zara gathered up the mattresses and replaced them in the corner of the hallway. "The place is so quiet," Dada said.

I was happy to see the last of them. Still, the house felt empty. Over the years since then I have often wondered about the fate of Seriozha and the other young soldiers. Seriozha once told me that when he got out of the army, he wanted to become an engineer. Somehow I doubted he would fulfill his dreams. In this civil war, he had betrayed Mother Russia. From her point of view, he was a traitor. She was unlikely to forgive.

Chapter 9

Raduyev and Sasha

FIGHTING CONTINUED THROUGH the end of the year and into 1996. I rotated between a number of hospitals, at Urus-Martan, Atagi, and the Ninth City Hospital in Grozny. The casualties mounted. When I wasn't operating, I visited patients at home. I preferred to change the dressings myself to check for gangrene. A hint of graying skin meant I needed to drain off the pus and cut away the dead flesh. Some of the bandages, I changed twice a day. Even when I wore clean scrubs, the smell of rotting flesh—like meat hanging too long in the sun—stayed with me. Although emergency medicine is far removed from plastic surgery, I found my former experience at preparing a patient for plastic surgery helpful. It taught me the right moment to intervene in a wound, when to cut away the flesh, when to leave it open, how long to drain it, whether to bandage it.

Sometimes I felt as though I was the little Dutch boy with his hand in the dyke, only I was holding back blood. When I closed my eyes, I saw blood dripping, spurting, oozing, soaking the mattresses, caking my scrubs, collecting in pools on the floor. I became an expert at reading blood: Dark or thinning blood told me my patient was dying; blood changing in color indicated internal hemorrhaging, or that it wouldn't coagulate. You needed to be alert to these indications because we were getting short on supplies and had little donor blood or plasma.

Treating burns in children was the hardest, especially when I didn't have enough sterile solution or painkiller. The children's cries of agony when I removed the dressing tore at my heart, as did telling a mother I had to amputate her baby's leg or arm. Some of the burns were so bad the muscle and bones showed through the charred flesh. I took to bringing the children candy and small toys. I always left my white coat in the doctors' room because as soon as the children saw someone in white, they started to cry. I will always remember one little three-year-old boy with burns over half his body. He had large gray eyes and a lot of dark matted hair. Most children cried when I came into the room, because they knew that pain or discomfort was approaching, but not this little fellow. For reasons I never could fathom, he would smile and call me Papa.

ON ONE NIGHT in March 1996, I had the opportunity to use all my skills as a plastic surgeon. I remember that night so well; it was the night I met a Russian doctor named Sasha. As I drove home, the sun dropped behind the mountains, and darkness was rapidly falling. To the north over Grozny, smoke from the bombed oil tanks spread an orange glow over the sky.

After getting out of my car, I took care not to slip or fall into the potholes left by the Russian bombs. I stepped around the pile of rubble that used to be my house, trying not to think about the effort I had put into building it. We were all alive, and that was what was important. Two days of sun had melted the snow, forming puddles of sludge. The air smelled of soot and rotting vegetation.

Climbing over charred bricks and fallen beams, I let my mind drift over the various matters to be addressed the next morning. Another mine had claimed the leg of a boy tending the cows, and I needed to remind the elders to tell the townspeople once again not to graze their animals in the pasture above the town. I also needed to remind the young men not to gather in the street. The shelling had subsided, but there were still Russian snipers.

As I was about to open the front gate to my parents' house, I noticed several jeeps parked opposite the house where a school once stood. Suddenly, engines roared to life, and headlights switched on, illuminating the whole street. I couldn't believe my eyes: men everywhere. From their khaki fatigues and green bandanas, I knew they were Chechen fighters. They were heavily armed.

A fighter stepped out of the group and walked toward me, holding out his hand in the traditional Arabic greeting: "*Asalaam aleikum*" (Peace be with you). I answered with the standard reply, "*Va aleikum salaam*" (Peace unto you). The man introduced himself as Vakha Dzhafarev, saying he was an envoy from one of the field commanders. He motioned for me to get into one of the jeeps, which had suddenly pulled up beside me. I was used to people intercepting me, rushing me off to treat relatives who had been wounded, but I had never been approached by so many fighters at once.

"What's wrong?" I was intrigued. "Who is wounded?"

"Please come with us," he said. "You'll see when we get there."

Someone important, no doubt. I went into the house and gathered a few standard supplies—instruments, bandages, a hand saw, vials of anesthetics, and surgical wire—from my stockpile in the corner of the bedroom. I noted that we were running short on anesthetics. Then I went back outside, got into the jeep, and we headed off in the direction of the mountains some thirty miles away.

The driver negotiated the precariously narrow mountain road at breakneck speed, and without headlights, so we wouldn't draw Russian fire. He made no attempt to slow down as we passed burned-out armored personnel carriers and abandoned villages. Not much remained after weeks of heavy bombing—only piles of debris, a few stray animals, and a handful of elderly people who refused to leave their homes or the graves of their ancestors. I turned to watch an old man trying to get his dead cow into a wooden cart.

Finally, we arrived at one of the rebel hideouts, which turned out to be an underground chamber camouflaged with heavy branches. I got out of the jeep and followed Vakha down five makeshift steps into a surprisingly large room, which had been hollowed out of the ground. The air reeked of sweat, gunpowder, and cigarette smoke. The clouds had cleared, and a shaft of moonlight fell through an aperture in the earthen ceiling, illuminating a rusty stove. Threadbare rugs hung from the dirt walls—a vain attempt at domesticity—and wooden cots were neatly arrayed around the sides of this makeshift hospital.

On one of the cots lay a heavily bearded figure, his face swathed in bloody bandages, his breathing heavy and labored. The amount of blood oozing through the gauze told me his condition was critical. His skin had taken on that familiar ashen pallor—the color of approaching death—I'd seen so many times before. I walked over to him and lifted his wrist. His pulse was almost too weak to detect.

"Move him to the center of the room," I ordered. I removed the blood-soaked bandages. His face was a bloody pulp mixed with dirt. After swabbing it down as best I could with sterile gauze, I palpated his face and head. A bullet had penetrated the area of the right cheekbone, shattering both right and left sinuses, plowed through the nasal bones, and exited beneath the left eye. The upper jaw was broken in three places, and its fragments hung loosely in the oral cavity. Also as a result of the bullet wound, the soft facial tissues were torn apart and created a big hole in the area between the right cheek and the ridge of the nose.

I turned to Vakha, who was hovering over the figure on the cot. "You'll have to shave his beard," I said, pointing to the scraggly mass of long hair, matted with blood and bits of tissue, which covered his lower face and spread down to his chest.

Vakha looked at me incredulously, then beckoned his men off to the side of the room, where they conferred in low, agitated voices.

"We're running out of time," I called out.

"We can't shave him," Vakha said, leaving the other fighters and coming toward me.

"If you want me to help him, you need to clean his face off," I replied. "I can't work through that mess."

"Don't you know who this is?" he asked in amazement.

I shook my head. His face was so mangled, he was unrecognizable.

"This is Salman Raduyev. He's our leader, and we can't remove his beard."

So that's what this was all about. Salman Raduyev was not just any wounded rebel. He was one of the most famous Chechen field commanders, known for his intemperate outbursts. He became a legend after he raided the Dagestani village of Kizlyar when the Russian-Chechen peace talks started breaking down in January 1996. He seized a busload of hostages and a detachment of Russian special police. Even most Chechens thought he was insane, because of the way he made outrageous threats. I learned later that before transporting Raduyev to the mountain hideout, his followers had literally grabbed him out of the emergency room at the hospital in Urus-Martan, pulled a sheet over him, and declared him dead. They even enacted a burial at the cemetery and erected a stone with his name on it—all to fool the Russians who were looking for him.

In my opinion, Raduyev only helped legitimize Russian propaganda, which portrayed the Chechens as a nation of cold-blooded terrorists. Now the Federals, or Federaly, as we called the Russian troops, were hunting him down. In 1995, after Raduyev had threatened to blow up a major Russian railroad station, the Russian police arrested every Chechen-looking man on the street and took them in for questioning. I looked down at the man who had been the cause of so much suffering for our people. His breathing was shallow. We had to hurry.

"I don't care if this man is Allah himself," I addressed the men on the other side of the room. "If you don't shave him, I can't work on him, and if I can't work on him, he will die. He might die anyway. And, by the way, I'm going to need an assistant."

Heaving a sigh, Vakha disappeared up the steps. One of the men found a pair of scissors and, with the help of two other fighters, began gingerly removing Raduyev's matted beard. Tufts of hair fell in knotted clumps onto the dirt floor. A fighter stepped forward with a twig broom and began sweeping it up. Then someone connected a lamp to a small generator and shone the beam on the patient while I rummaged around in my bag for instruments and various bits of surgical hardware I would need.

A few minutes later, Vakha reappeared with a tall man, flanked by two heavily armed guards. His blond hair and high cheekbones told me he was a Russian. He wore a padded jacket and military boots. I realized that he and I were the only two men in the dugout who were not armed. The man nodded at me and smiled.

"My name is Sasha," he said, holding out his hand. "I'm a doctor."

At that moment, I didn't have time to find out what a Russian doctor was doing in a rebel hideout; I was just relieved to have a competent assistant. I asked everyone to leave, but four of Raduyev's main lieutenants, including Vakha, refused to budge. They had misgivings about the Russian doctor, and evidently they didn't trust me either. So many attempts had been made on Raduyev's life—even by Chechens—I suppose they suspected I might assassinate him on the operating table.

I didn't have time for such worries. Raduyev was in a critical state; he could die at any moment. His left eye was pulverized, and the left half of his skull fractured. Shards of splintered bone barely clung to the mangled flesh. His right eye remained intact, as well as a small portion of his nostrils. Later, I wrote down this description: "Contra-coup injury to the head (critical form), penetrating gunshot wound to the face with extensive damage of the sinuses and nasal bones, damage to the lateral wall and floor of the left orbit; fragmentation of the left zygoma; multiple fractures of the maxilla; defect of soft facial tissue."

First, I inserted into a vein a drip of Polyglukin to increase the volume of blood and raise his blood pressure. Then I injected him with a local anesthetic. Together Sasha and I cleared the operative field, stemmed the bleeding, and watched hopefully as some color seeped back into Raduyev's skin. Next, we immobilized the upper jaw with semicircular splints, which we bolted down with titanium screws. To make sure the jaws would remain perfectly secure, I wrapped each tooth with inter-dental wiring and looped each wire around notches in the brace. I removed one lower front tooth so we could thread a feeding tube into his throat. Then we washed the viable slivers of both sinuses and the left cheekbone and began reassembling them like a jigsaw puzzle with the help of screw-down titanium strips. Finally, we repaired the defect in his face by rotating a skin flap from his forehead over the gap.

Throughout the eight hours we spent operating, Raduyev's men badgered Sasha and me relentlessly. "What are his chances?" they kept asking. "Will you guarantee he'll recover? You know your life will be in danger if he dies."

"Only Allah can guarantee someone's survival," I said each time they asked, but I had a feeling that Raduyev would make it. This man was fueled by his single-minded mission to drive the Russians out of Chechnya at any cost. He was lean but still very wiry; he was not ready to give up, not yet.

During the operation, Sasha and I hardly spoke, but I could tell he was a good doctor from the way he deftly separated the tissue while I fished for the torn blood vessels and tied them off. Very shortly, we developed a natural rhythm, as if we'd worked together for years. When it was all over, Sasha congratulated me on a job well done.

"Sixty percent of an operation's success depends on the assistant," I told him, enjoying that sense of comradery which develops over the operating table even under such extreme circumstances. I wished I could sit down and talk to this Russian doctor, but Vakha insisted on driving me back to Alkhan Kala immediately.

Riding back down the mountain, I was preoccupied. There was something about Sasha I couldn't get out of my mind. I kept seeing his blond head bent over Raduyev, a look of total concentration in his eyes. Not once did he hesitate, even though the patient on the table was Russia's number one enemy.

I soon learned that Sasha was a captain in the Russian Medical Corps and had been captured a few months earlier. The Chechen rebels apparently planned to use him as a bargaining chip and exchange him for the brother of a high-ranking Chechen field commander who had been captured by the Russians and placed in a filtration camp. In the meantime, I hatched my own plans for Sasha. Civilian casualties at the hospital in Urus-Martan where I was working at that time increased every day, and it was getting to be too much for me to handle even with my small brigade of faithful nurses, who had remained with me throughout the fighting. I could use a skilled doctor like Sasha.

I presented my case to the Chechen field commander in charge of prisoners, and he agreed to let Sasha help me until it was time for a prisoner exchange. The next day, Sasha arrived, accompanied by two armed guards. I cordially welcomed him, glad to have a colleague with whom I could work and discuss cases.

Between operations, Sasha chain-smoked in the kitchen while the nurses fussed over him, bringing him tea and whatever soup they could scoop up from the contributions of the townspeople. He was a handsome fellow, and his appeal was heightened by his easy laugh and his respectful way with women. If he saw a woman carrying a heavy sack or box, he would immediately take it from her. He said he lived in St. Petersburg. It had been many months since he had seen his wife and children.

"You are our 'Prisoner in the Caucasus,'" I used to joke, referring to the Pushkin poem of the same name. Each evening, the guards arrived to take him back to the building where they held him.

One day, after Sasha and I had been working together for a month, he told me excitedly that the exchange was set. Then a few days before the exchange, I bumped into him outside the hospital kitchen. I was exhausted; I'd just finished operating on a seventeen-year-old boy who had been wounded when he dashed into the street to help his mother, who was torn apart by a shell before his eyes during a Russian attack.

I noticed that Sasha's face was drained of color. "What's the matter?" I said. "Has someone upset you?"

Sasha took my arm and led me into the kitchen, where we sat down at the table. He reached into the pocket of his scrubs for a packet of cigarettes, his hands shaking.

"The brother of the field commander was murdered in the filtration camp," he said. "Now the commander's family is demanding I be shot in revenge."

This was a disastrous blow. Blood vendettas are a way of life in Chechnya, a time-honored method of justice practiced for centuries, although during Soviet times the KGB tried to put a stop to them. Vendettas were the community's way of dealing with crime. For example, if a drunk driver kills someone, it is considered murder. The relatives and clan members of the accused bring him before a large assembly of relatives and people from the clan of the deceased. He wears a black felt cloak, and his head is covered in a white veil, symbolizing his readiness to die for what he did. The family may kill him or forgive him, in which case the veil is removed and he is set free. However, with forgiveness comes the obligation of the acquitted to offer compensation to the victim's family. There are even cases where the accused is taken into the family as their surrogate son.

"I have not lost my son; I have found him again," the mother says.

Women play an important role in keeping the peace. Men must stop fighting if a woman removes her scarf and throws it on the ground between the antagonists. This gesture can take place at a specially convened group of the family and elders involved, or spontaneously in the street to break up a brawl.

All these rituals and ceremonies helped maintain peace pretty well. However, the economic chaos and the outbreak of the war disrupted everything, including Chechen traditions. Participating in ceremonies and rituals becomes secondary to day-to-day survival. The Russians had killed so many people that Chechens just wanted revenge on any Russian, even if he wasn't directly involved in a family member's death. That was the case with Sasha. I was shocked. I didn't know how to respond.

"Khassan, I have a wife and three kids. Please help me," he begged. "They can't do this to me. I am a doctor, just like you."

I wanted to help Sasha. But I knew that if I did, the field commander could extend his revenge to me and my family.

"How can I help you?" I said, surprised to hear the anger rising in my voice. "If I help you escape, they will come after me. Don't you understand? They will kill me."

Sasha was silent. He didn't try to argue.

That night, I couldn't get Sasha's plight out of my mind. The whole thing was so unreasonable. Sasha was totally innocent; he hadn't killed anyone. On the contrary, he had helped save lives—many Chechen lives, in fact.

I decided I would appeal to the field commander, and through an intermediary I argued that Sasha was a doctor, far more useful to us alive than dead because I used him in the hospital. But I was not very hopeful. From the field commander's perspective, the Russians had broken their agreement, and Sasha's death would even the score.

The next day, while I was making my rounds, I received a message from the field commander. My request had been denied. I didn't know what to do.

I lied and told Sasha I thought everything would be fine. He didn't believe me, of course, and asked me to call his wife in St. Petersburg. I stood in line for several hours at the telephone station to obtain the connection, and when it came through, the static was so bad I could barely hear the voice on the other end of the line.

My call must have been the first news Sasha's wife had received of her husband because when I told her that I was calling on Sasha's behalf, she became hysterical. I could not tell her that Sasha was going to be executed in a few days, but she sensed he was in danger.

"Please, doctor, you can save him," she pleaded. "He's just a doctor. Please, I have three children. I don't know how I will survive without him."

Once more, I was at a loss for words, so I promised I would do what I could.

Ultimately, I had to admit to Sasha that there was nothing I could do. The execution was set. He continued to work with me in the hospital, but now he had trouble concentrating. I would ask him a question or request that he pass me an instrument, and it was as if he didn't hear me at all.

A couple of days after I learned Sasha had been condemned to death, a refugee woman from Grozny lay on the operating table with a broken nose and jaw. I could see she was in pain, but she didn't make a sound. I watched as Sasha gave her a shot of lidocaine. What has he done that he has to die? I thought, as he passed the empty syringe to the nurse. "He's just a doctor." His wife's words echoed in my head.

Suddenly, I made the decision—a decision which to this day I have never admitted to anyone, not even my relatives—which I am disclosing here for the first time. At that moment, I knew I couldn't live with my conscience if I didn't do what I could to save Sasha.

I met Sasha's gaze. "Tomorrow morning at ten o'clock, my car will be at the back of the hospital," I whispered. "Get in and wait for me."

Sasha didn't say anything; he just reached over and shook my hand.

The next morning, the sun was shining. A layer of frost glazed over the rubble of the bombed-out building next to the hospital. I'd parked my car at the back of the hospital, leaving it unlocked, and went inside for a few minutes to give Sasha time to get in without being seen. When I returned to my car, I couldn't see if Sasha was in the back, because the windows were tinted. After closing the door, I turned around, half hoping that he wouldn't be there at all. But he was lying on the makeshift mattress I had placed in the back of the car for transporting my patients. He nodded. We did not speak. I glanced nervously in the mirror as I put the car in gear. The only person in sight was an old woman carrying two full buckets of water—a sight Chechen travelers consider a good omen. "Thank God," I said to myself, "the buckets are full, not empty."

The night before, I had carefully weighed my options and finally decided I would take Sasha to the main Russian military headquarters on the outskirts of Alkhan Kala. Though I knew the plan was insane, I figured leaving in the morning would arouse less suspicion than at night. At the first military checkpoint, a young Russian soldier flagged me down. I pulled over, and when he saw it was me, he grinned. I handed him the usual pack of cigarettes, and he waved me through. The guards at the other checkpoints also recognized me and received a pack of cigarettes to let us pass. I stopped the car some 550 yards from the guard post in front of the main Russian headquarters.

"Never, never tell them how you escaped," I said, looking straight ahead.

"I will never betray you." Sasha reached over to shake my hand. Then he got out and walked toward the guardhouse. As I pulled away, I felt a strange mix of panic and relief. I said a silent prayer that Sasha would keep his promise.

Three days later, in the middle of the night, I heard a knock at my gate. It was pitch-black outside. "The field commander sent us," a voice boomed out of the darkness when I opened the door. A bearded man dressed in camouflage emerged out of the dark. He was flanked by two other men. I was groggy and hadn't realized who they were at first. Then he asked, "Is the number of your car M 0009 NM?" I did not answer.

"You helped the Russian doctor escape," he said.

"Of course, I didn't."

"There are witnesses."

The men ordered me to accompany them. I did not argue. I did not want my family to know what was happening, so I told Dada I had to attend to some wounded and would probably be away for a few days. Once they had shoved me into the jeep, they covered my eyes with a bandana. From the turns in the road made by the jeep, I knew we were traveling in the direction of Urus-Martan. When the vehicle began to buck and veer on a dirt road, I sensed we were heading into the mountains. The jeep came to a stop. The men opened the door, ordered me out, removed my blindfold, and led me to the edge of a large opening in the ground.

"Maybe you will remember helping the Russian doctor after a few nights down there." The man pointed the barrel of his rifle down into the dense blackness; then he bent over, eased a ladder over the edge, and ordered me down. "When you confess, we will let you out," he said.

I counted seventeen rungs before I reached the bottom. Then I heard the scraping of the ladder being hauled up over the sides, followed by a thump of planks dropping over the hole. For a moment, I had trouble breathing; my chest felt constricted.

I felt the darkness envelop me, damp and thick like fog. I was finally able to take a deep breath and gradually came back to my senses. I reached out with my hand to touch the side of the pit. Slowly, my fingers traced its contours. The earth felt rough and uneven; no handholds that I could feel; no escape possible. I sank onto my heels, feeling the damp penetrate my bones. Why hadn't I grabbed a warmer jacket before I left? I chided myself.

The muffled sound of a car starting up broke the silence. I heard voices shouting. They must have left some men behind to guard me. "Tell us where Sasha is!" someone shouted down to me through the planks.

"I don't know," I yelled.

"We don't believe you. Confess, and we will release you."

Telling the truth was out of the question; if I confessed, I would be shot. The only thing I could do was to keep on denying that I had helped Sasha escape. I felt a sense of anger mixed with shame; after all, these were Chechen men who were holding me in a pit. My own people!

The voices stopped, and I lost all sense of time. After a while, I learned to distinguish night from day by the distant voices of the young boys taking the cows up to the pastures in the morning and returning with them in the evening.

Three times a day the guards lowered a canteen of water, a piece of bread, and a lump of meat. When they raised the boards over the entrance, the light blinded me, sending sharp pain through my temples. My toilet was a bucket in the corner, which the guards would haul to the surface when full.

I knew my survival depended on keeping my mind and body occupied. I had seen Chechen prisoners after their release from the Russian filtration camps, with muscles so atrophied they couldn't stand up.

To pass the time, I did physical exercises and prayed. As the days passed, I started to lose hope.

What worried me most was who would look after Nana and Dada now that they were getting old. Hussein was still in Krasnoyarsk. If the war ever ended, I would be the one in the position to earn money. My responsibility as a son was to look after my parents until they died. I thought of Zara and Islam and Maryam, regretting that I had been away so long that the children didn't even know me, that I wouldn't be able to say a last good-bye.

I thought about Sasha too, wondering if he had betrayed me, telling myself that if I hadn't helped him, I couldn't have lived with my conscience. I hoped that if my family ever learned about it, they would understand.

Once in my childhood I had encountered darkness similar to this when I went up into the high pastures with a great-uncle. A lot of people didn't believe me when I told them what had happened that night on my way down from the mountains. I was thirteen years old at the time, and Vosha—I called him by the Chechen word for uncle— was about ninety and more agile than a mountain goat. We had started out from Makazhoi midmorning to take salt licks up to the cows and sheep in the mountain pastures. The sun was high in the sky, and wisps of cloud drifted between the peaks. Vosha strode up the mountain trail ahead of me with the sack of salt on his back. On his head he wore a shepherd's lamb's-wool hat. I was in good physical shape but had nothing like the stamina of Vosha. The salt I was carrying in woolen saddlebags slung over my shoulder became heavier and heavier on my chest and back. I became tired and couldn't keep up with him. Finally, around 3 P.M., we reached the upper pastures, which were guarded by a shepherd and several large, white sheepdogs like Tarzan, so fierce looking they would terrify any wolf. The sides of the mountains were in shadow, and it was beginning to get cold. I dropped my sack of salt next to Vosha's.

"I have just enough time to get down before dark," I said.

He raised his eyes and scanned the mountains. "Why don't you stay here with me for the night and then go down in the morning?"

"My friends are waiting for me. I promised to be there. It's only ten kilometers [about six miles] down, so I have plenty of time."

"Hurry," he said, "before it gets dark. Don't stray off the path and get lost. Once it is dark, you will see nothing."

I started off. I had no flashlight, only a box of matches. The path was narrow, and the stones were hard under my feet. Three quarters of a mile down the path, I saw the entrance to a cave in the side of the mountain. I had heard about the cave from people in the village, who said that a tunnel went fifteen kilometers [about nine miles] down the mountain and came out in the ravine. I was curious to see inside. I looked at my watch. Not even 4 P.M., plenty of time.

I entered the cave and struck one of my matches. I saw the tunnel on the far side and followed it down several hundred feet until it began to narrow and I had to turn around. I had explored caves before, so felt no fear, just curiosity. By the time I emerged, the sun had fallen behind the peaks and the sides of the mountains were dark. I had better hurry, I thought. As I started down the path, I fell and hit my knee on a rock. Then the darkness dropped over me—a darkness found only in the mountains, one so inky you can't see your feet. I lit my last match and held it up. I was still on a path.

"Khassan, where are you?" A voice called out. I stopped and listened. The voice seemed familiar, but I couldn't place it. "Khassan, where are you? Come this way."

Maybe it was Dada or Hussein, who had come up the mountain to meet me, I thought. "I am here. Where are you?" I called back.

"Over here," the voice replied. I started down the path. "Khassan, over here," the voice repeated.

"Where?" I shouted.

"Over here."

I became scared. The voice was so eerie. Then I remembered the elders talking about voices in the mountains. "Whatever you do, don't follow the voices," they had warned. "Stay in one place; wait until dawn." The old men had said evil spirits reside in the mountains, spirits who imitate familiar voices and lure men to their deaths. When I had heard those stories about these mountain *shaitany* (satans)—as the elders call these spirits—I had never believed them.

Pray! That's what the elders had said to do. I dropped down on the path and began to recite a prayer. After that, the voice disappeared. The cold was bitter. I drew my knees up to my chest to try to keep warm. All night I crouched there, listening to the howls of the wolves and the whimperings of the rabbits.

Around 5 A.M., the sun rose over the mountain. I stood up, stiff with cold. When I looked to the left, I saw I was within a few feet of an enormous drop. Another few feet, and I would have gone over the edge.

BEING IN THE pit felt like being at the bottom of a ravine. Based on the thickness of my beard, I guessed I had been there at least a week when a guard lowered the ladder and ordered me to the surface. When I reached the top, I clamped my fists over my eyes to protect them from the blinding light, but still I felt excruciating pain. I couldn't see anything. I only heard men's voices.

"The Russians murdered my brother," a voice boomed.

"I didn't help the Russian doctor escape," I said automatically.

"Why are you doing this?" The same voice continued, ignoring my reply. "Why are you risking your life for a Russian? He's not your relative. He would never understand what you are doing for him."

"I didn't help him escape," I repeated, gathering my strength. My vision came into focus.

"Then why did you make an appeal for his life?" Now the rebel field commander stood right over me, and I could smell the smoke from his cigarette.

"I asked for him to be spared because I needed help in the hospital." I removed my hands from my eyes.

"I would understand if you were doing it to save a Chechen," he said, shaking his head. "Say your prayers, and get ready to die."

I descended the ladder into the pit again. They lowered a jug of water for the ritual ablutions before prayer, then replaced the planks across the opening.

After splashing myself with the water, I knelt in the darkness, and I prayed for my family, for my parents and sisters, for Zara and our children. I forgave the men preparing to execute me. As a Chechen, I understood why they had to do it. If my brother had been killed by the Russians in a filtration camp, I would want the same thing.

What seemed like hours later, I was ordered to the surface again. I heard the sound of men talking. When my eyes adjusted to the light, I made out figures standing against the rock face. The sky was bright blue, and in the distance I glimpsed the mountains. The men's voices were agitated. I knew blood revenge was a complex business, requiring the blessing of the family and the clan elders. Sometimes even a religious leader. Could it be that there was some disagreement about my execution? The evidence must be strong enough to satisfy everyone; perhaps a few of the men had some doubts.

"Maybe you should confess," the field commander said to me.

I barely heard the words. I shook my head.

"Do you have a last wish?" He slipped the rifle from his shoulder and cradled it in his hands.

"Take my body to the outskirts of my village and leave it there," I said, knowing that someone would recognize me and give me a proper burial.

The men stopped talking among themselves and began to intone prayers from the Koran. I was being prepared for death. I closed my eyes. I was conscious of the warmth of the sun on my back. I was ready. Then, in the distance, I heard an automobile horn sounding. Maybe I am dead already, I thought. But the sound of the horn became more strident, more agitated. I opened my eyes. Everyone had turned to look at an approaching cloud of dust. A military vehicle careened around the corner, and a man in khaki fatigues leaned out the window, waving his arm wildly.

"Stop!" he yelled. "Stop! Don't kill him! He's not the one!"

Inexplicably, I had been spared. Minutes later, my captors pushed me into a car and drove me to the outskirts of Alkhan Kala. When I finally got home, I thanked Allah—and I thank him again today—for letting me go on.

Chapter 10

Saving Alkhan Kala

INEVER TOLD my family about Sasha or even how close I had come to execution. Throughout the war, I tried to protect them by downplaying the dangers. Chechens believe that to survive, not only as an individual but as a people, one must overcome fear. For this reason, I find it hard to write about the war and to admit that after being confined in that dark pit, I couldn't sleep without a night-light—just like a child. In the dark, I relived the earth closing in on me and my feelings of helplessness. Whenever I heard a noise at night, my heart raced. I broke out into a sweat and had difficulty breathing. I couldn't stay in bed. I'd fling back the covers and go to the kitchen to escape the voices . . . the voices of my captors.

The only thing that lifted my mood was my patients. In addition to working in the hospital, I did my rounds in the village to change dressings. I saw an increasing number of refugees from Grozny, whom the local people took in and fed. I also treated Chechen fighters in the homes of people who had given them shelter.

Around the beginning of April 1996, not long after Sasha's escape and my time in the pit, we noticed an increase in troops and military equipment around Alkhan Kala, watching, waiting, and ready to strike. The buildup reminded me of what happened to Samashki the year before. There were rumors that Alkhan Kala would soon be attacked. People verged on hysteria. Yet they made little effort to leave. Many had fled once already, then returned; they were too exhausted.

Meetings took place every day. The women gathered in the street, demanding the elders take action, any action. But no one knew what to do. The situation came to a head at 5 A.M. on April 20 when people awoke to discover that the Federals had cordoned off Alkhan Kala, along with two other neighboring villages.

That evening, Ruslan, the chairman of the local council, came to my house, looking exhausted and disheveled. Nana sat him down at the table and served tea. "The Federals are demanding fifty rifles from each of the three surrounding villages," Ruslan said. "They say if we don't produce them, we'll get the same treatment as Samashki." He drained his cup, shaking his head. "Where are we going to get that many weapons? The fighters have all left. The elders have already been to talk to the Federals," Ruslan continued, "but we are thinking of going again tomorrow. We want you to go with us."

"If you think it would help, I'll come," I said.

"Maybe if we have a surgeon with us, it will give us a bit more authority," Ruslan said.

The next morning, I shaved, put on a clean shirt and tie, and joined Ruslan and two elders to walk to the Russian military camp two miles away. We carried a white flag on a long stick, which Ruslan and I took turns flying above our heads. A photographer accompanied us to document the meeting in case the Russians wanted to deny that it ever happened. It was a beautiful, sunny day. We were nervous and didn't talk as we navigated the craters.

The Russian military camp was spread over a large field on the side of the hill. Why do they need this great force? I thought as I looked at the tanks, personnel carriers, and other military vehicles.

The Russians had spotted us coming and were waiting. They had assembled a delegation of six people: a general, two colonels, two majors, and a lieutenant. The general was a heavily built man, about fifty, with a potbelly and florid complexion, a sure signal he liked his vodka.

"This is Khassan, our doctor," Ruslan said, presenting me, in turn, to the general.

The general held out his hand to us. He scrutinized me as if trying to read my thoughts. "Not the Khassan who saved Sasha?" he said, looking at Ruslan.

"I don't know any Sasha," I said.

"You worked in Urus-Martan?" The general continued.

I nodded.

"And you live in Alkhan Kala?"

"Yes."

"So it was you who saved Sasha?" he repeated.

I started to deny it again, but he interrupted me and pulled me aside. "All right, all right," he said. "It will remain between us. . . . What you did for Sasha, I will not forget. You did a good turn by saving him, and I will do everything I can to save Alkhan Kala," he said. The general was evidently a man who understood our Chechen mentality. He sensed there was no way I could admit to anything concerning Sasha.

"You are a general," I said calmly. "Everything depends on you. Not much depends on me."

"Much depends on all of us," he snapped.

"We'll do what depends on us, but please don't let your men create any provocations."

"Don't provoke us, and your village will be safe." He paused. "Understood!"

I nodded. Then the general and I rejoined the others. We talked a few more minutes about a peaceful passport check in the village, assuring each other there would be no incidents. At last, the five of us headed back to Alkhan Kala.

When we arrived in the village, we found, to our surprise, 300 resistance fighters from Samashki and several other villages waiting for us in an abandoned warehouse of the wood-finishing plant. They had heard that the Russians were threatening the village and wanted to defend us. "We won't allow them to do what they did in Samashki!" the Chechen commander had told the townspeople. "We will hide at strategic places around the village and fire on them as soon as they enter."

Allah preserve us! If the Russians had any inkling of this, they would pulverize us. With all that equipment I'd seen on the surrounding heights, we wouldn't have a chance. Maybe the Chechen fighters would defeat the Russian soldiers as they entered the village, but then the Russians would call in air strikes and reinforcements. There would be hundreds of civilian casualties—Samashki all over again.

"We have to persuade them to hold their fire," Ruslan said to me privately, "and pray that the general keeps his word."

That afternoon, we went to talk to the commander and his fighters in the warehouse at the edge of town. When we entered, the men—many of them mere boys—rose to their feet. The commander, a man of about thirty-five in fatigues and a green bandana, separated himself from the others and approached us. Ruslan told him about our meeting with the Russian general. He looked skeptical. Several of the others laughed and shook their heads.

"How can you trust them?" the commander said. "They could create a provocation at any time against a civilian and open fire."

"The general promised me it won't happen." I felt stupid saying this, because they had no reason to trust the Russians. Many of them had become fighters because sisters, brothers, wives, or children had been killed by the Russians.

"Can you guarantee it?" the commander asked.

I shook my head. "How can I guarantee it? But if they start marauding and harassing the women, you should feel free to fire."

The following morning, I went back to visit the general, this time alone. I wanted to look him in the eye again and hear him repeat his promise.

"Do you give your word as general that when your men enter the village, there will be no incidents?" I asked.

He nodded. "You have my word of honor—that is, if there are no incidents from your side," he replied. "We will check passports, and then we will leave the village."

We shook hands on that. Something told me I could trust this man. The Russian military, like many of the world's armies, has a long and proud tradition. A general's word means something, although it would be hard to persuade the Chechen field commanders to believe that.

That night, I tossed and turned, unable to sleep. By not attacking, our fighters would lose the strategic advantage. What it boiled down to was that Ruslan, the elders, and I had become the guarantors of peace for our town. If anything went wrong—and it could very easily—we would be to blame for trusting the word of a Russian general; we would lose all the respect of the townspeople and our families would be disgraced because we had believed the general's word. In our country anything one member of a family does—good or bad—reflects on the family.

I recalled the skepticism in the eyes of the fighters in the warehouse. Maybe I shouldn't have become involved, I thought. Then I remembered Samashki, all the charred bodies outside the mosque, and the mother running through the streets holding her dead baby. So many times the Russians had deceived us. On the other hand, I had many Russian friends who, when the war started, called with offers of help. Doubts churned in my head all night. Even if the general had given his word, I had no faith that the soldiers wouldn't cause trouble. Half the time the officers couldn't control their men. I thought about Sasha and all the trouble he had brought me. Would saving his life guarantee the life of my village, or the exact opposite?

The fighters remained inside the warehouse in case the Russians attacked. But Ruslan and I decided to tell the villagers that all the fighters had left during the night. Otherwise someone might inadvertently raise suspicion if questioned. We arranged for elders to greet the Russian soldiers at the street intersections and along the road leading to the warehouse. Any move the Russian soldiers made toward the warehouse, the elders would try to divert them. Last, but not least, we instructed the villagers about how to behave toward the Russians. The most important thing was politeness, Ruslan said. "If they ask for water, give them water. If they're hungry, feed them."

At 11:00 A.M., the Russian military tightened the noose around the three villages and ordered the troops to move in. The soldiers jumped from their personnel carriers and started going from house to house to check documents. The women greeted them with food and water. I saw one woman run from her house holding out her passport. "Hey, Synok (Sonny)," she cried, "don't you want to see this?" The soldiers' nervousness eased, and their mood lightened. Several even offered their rifles for small boys to hold.

There was a tense moment near the bridge, when a drunken Russian warrant officer demanded vodka and threatened a young man with arrest if he didn't get it. I didn't see this incident myself, but Ruslan told me that a villager informed a Russian officer, who radioed the general, who immediately apologized and ordered the warrant officer arrested.

After the Russian troops withdrew from the town, Ruslan and I slaughtered a sheep for the Russians, scrounged up twelve rifles and a case of twenty bottles of vodka. Before delivering the gift, we cooked the meat over an outside fire. Finding the vodka was almost as difficult as finding the rifles. When we delivered our gift in a huge communal cauldron, the Russian officers slapped us on the back like long-lost friends from the old days and invited us to drink with them. We refused, thanking them politely.

As we trudged the two miles back to Alkhan Kala, Ruslan and I fell silent. I thought about Sasha and the twist of fate that had brought us together. I wondered if he would even learn about what had happened—or, more important, what had not happened—on this day, and what he would say if he knew. That night, for the first time in days, I slept well, reassured that fate has a strange way of repaying good deeds. Alkhan Kala was safe—at least for the time being.

A few days later, the Russians struck a new blow at Chechnya. In recent months, they had been seeking President Dzhokhar Dudayev, who evaded them by hiding out in the mountains, never staying more than one night in the same place. Dudayev would often use his satellite telephone to communicate from his hiding place. Around midnight on April 21, 1996, as he talked by sat-phone with Duma member Konstantin Borovoi in Moscow from an isolated spot in the highlands, Dudayev was mortally wounded by an explosion. Word spread that a Russian jet fighter had detected the telephone beam, locked on the signal, and fired a missile, which flew directly at him standing near his car. The next day, Vice President Zemlikhan Yandarbiyev, who favored an even harder line than Dudayev, took over as acting president.

Chapter 11

Escape from Grozny

ALTHOUGH ALKHAN KALA was saved from the same fate as Samashki, the shelling didn't let up. The townspeople of Alkhan Kala did some repairs to my hospital, and we decided to keep the doors open although the place was not fully operational. I left a set of medical instruments in the operating room in case of emergencies and kept a junior nurse on duty. Meanwhile, I continued working in Grozny, sometimes sleeping at my apartment to avoid driving home late at night during a shelling or after the curfews. I also traveled to different hospitals where I was needed. Each morning when I arrived at the hospital in Grozny, I found crowds outside my office. There was never enough room on the benches for them. I placed four cots in a small room off my office for the people who weren't ambulatory, but mostly the stretchers lay on the floor.

Almost every day I performed amputations. We gave the severed limbs to the relatives to bury in the cemeteries, as is our custom. If no relatives claimed them right away, we buried these body parts in the corner of the hospital courtyard. Despite warnings about the mines, people continued to tread on them, especially when they went out to collect firewood. It was heartbreaking when a child stepped on a mine.

That June of 1996, I lost my best friend, Vakha Isayev. We had been close since school. He worked for the local police as an investigator. It was June 26, a quiet evening with a clear sky. On his way back from work, Vakha had stopped by my house for tea, then left to go home. Nana, Dada, Malika, Razyat, and Zara had already gone to bed. About an hour after he left, I heard a pounding on the gate and the frenzied shouts of my friend Adlan.

"Vakha's been gunned down!" he shouted. "There were guys waiting for him when he got home."

I threw on my clothes, grabbed my medical case, and rushed outside. Vakha lay in a fetal position on the backseat of Adlan's car; blood was everywhere. It was hard to believe the blood-soaked figure was my friend because only a short time earlier we had been drinking tea.

"Khassan, help me, help me," Vakha said when he saw me. "I have two children. I don't know why they shot me."

His voice was filled with fear. Darkness prevented me from seeing the extent of his wounds, only the gaping hole in his thigh. I could see that his hip was fractured, the white nob of the femur bone protruding. I slapped on the tourniquet. Then I lifted his shirt and saw the wound in his stomach with the intestines ballooning out.

"To the hospital, quick," I yelled to Adlan. Since the Russian forces shot at everything that moved in the dark, we would never get through the military checkpoints to the hospital in Urus-Martan; my jerry-rigged hospital was the only place to take him. The operating room was still more or less usable, but the instruments that I had donated had disappeared. Adlan drove the car, and I sat in the back with Vakha.

"Don't worry, Vakha, you'll be all right." I placed my hands on his shoulder and squeezed it.

"Go home and tell Malika we need Polyglukin," I yelled to Adlan as we carried Vakha into the hospital. "We need syringes, drips, bandages. And we need to set up a generator for light!"

A young nurse was on duty at the hospital, and I asked her to help me to clear up the mess in the operating room. We wiped off the table and laid Vakha down. When I shone a kerosene lamp on the wound, I saw his right kidney and liver were exposed, along with the intestines, and I knew there was no hope. But he was still conscious.

If I could stop the bleeding and keep him stabilized until 6 A.M., we might be able to transport him to Urus-Martan. In my heart, I knew it was useless, but as long as Vakha was conscious and breathing, I had to do something. I couldn't just stand there.

"We've got to raise his blood pressure." I said. "Attach two drips!" The nurse was inexperienced, and her hands shook uncontrollably as she searched for the vein in the dim light of the lamp. I grabbed the needle from her. Vakha had lost so much blood, the vein had disappeared. I took his arm, massaged it until I felt the vein bulge under my fingers, then slid in the needle. His system didn't respond. The only hope now was donor blood. Since my blood was O-positive, it was compatible with all blood types.

I tightened the rubber band around my upper arm, raised a vein, and inserted the needle. I hooked it up to the line and started draining my blood directly into Vakha. My nurses and I regularly gave blood, usually about 400 to 500 cubic centimeters, but this time I didn't count. I didn't take my eyes off him. He had stopped talking. His pulse was almost nonexistent, but he kept breathing. The light from the kerosene lamp was poor, and I was so distressed I didn't notice that the needle had slipped out of my arm. I looked down and saw a pool of blood on the floor. I seized the needle, reinserted it, and placed a piece of tape over it this time to hold it in place. From the expression in his eyes, Vakha still knew who I was. I sensed he was trying to convey to me that he knew he was dying.

I placed my hand over his. Then the light went out of his expression, and he was unconscious. I felt dizzy. I was losing him. I removed the needle from my arm.

At 5 A.M., when it was light enough, Vakha's relatives drove him to Urus-Martan. I wanted to accompany him, but I felt terribly weak and could hardly stand up. The surgeons at Urus-Martan operated on him immediately, but he died on the operating table about 7 A.M.

The following day, after drinking lots of sweet tea to regain my strength, I went to Vakha's funeral. The elders rose to their feet when I arrived, an unusual homage to a younger man. I was pleased that everyone knew how I had fought to save Vakha's life, but it will never make up for losing him. I still hear Vakha's plea: "Khassan, help me, help me."

DURING THIS PERIOD, some new family concerns began to trouble me. My fifteen-year-old nephew Ali began slipping away to help the fighters, causing all of us enormous worry, especially his parents, Raya and Lecha. We all understood why he was doing that. Many of his friends were fighting, and he wanted to be with them. His school, like all the other schools in Alkhan Kala, no longer operated, and he felt useless sitting at home. Still, we worried that something would happen to him.

Throughout July rumors circulated that a Chechen counterassault was about to take place on Grozny. I hadn't paid much attention because so many rumors flew about in times of war. We all dreamed of Grozny's liberation from Russian occupation, but at that time the Russians had 300,000 troops deployed throughout the republic. At most, we had only 3,000 organized fighters and an untold number of young men who entered the fray, fired a few shots, then went home to boast to their fellow villagers. Russian tanks patrolled the streets, and their soldiers manned hundreds of heavily fortified military checkpoints in and around the city.

It is impossible for me to remember the exact order of events during those August days of 1996 when the Chechen fighters finally drove the Russian army out of Grozny. "Operation Jihad," they called it. My memory of it begins on the afternoon of August 5. Malika, Razyat, and I were working at the Ninth City Hospital when Malika came to my office; she said everyone was talking about an immediate assault, and she wanted me to get Razyat and go back to Alkhan Kala. I was busy. Since I didn't take the rumors of an impending assault very seriously, I told her to go with Razyat to my apartment across town on the other side of the river. I said I would pick them up later in the evening after paying a call on my friend Magomed Idigov, who was pressing me to visit him.

Magomed, a surgeon colleague, had sent his wife and children to Achkoi-Martan, which he considered safer than Grozny. On this evening, he wanted company, and I couldn't refuse a friend's request. I grabbed my medical case, which I always carried with me, and went to his apartment. In the course of the evening, he persuaded me to stay the night. There was no way I could contact Malika and Razyat about the change of plans, but I assumed they would be safe in my apartment, in the same building as the security police, as long as they didn't go out on the streets.

At 5 A.M., an explosion catapulted me off Magomed's couch. I lay stunned on the floor, then staggered to my feet. Another explosion was followed by mortar fire . . . this was more than just *muzikanty* (musicians), as we called the syncopated gunfire that erupted almost every night. I crawled on all fours to the balcony and looked down through the railings. Dozens of Chechen fighters with rifles and grenade launchers milled in the street. Operation Jihad had begun.

There were screams from the streets. Men were shouting. Women's voices filled with panic as Russian artillery bombarded the city and the Chechen fighters pressed their attack. There was so much fighting on the streets, I couldn't move from the apartment. I was sick with worry about Razyat and Malika. People said that the fighters were attacking government buildings, which included the police department, where my apartment was located. Every time I wanted to leave, Magomed cautioned me to stay. To go out was suicidal, he said. Getting killed wouldn't help anyone. I stood at the window and watched helplessly as helicopter gunships launched rockets at the Fourth City Hospital, killing doctors and nurses who were my friends.

Satsita Gairbekova, chief of the intensive care unit at the Ninth City Hospital, told me later how the *kontraktniki* had taken her and her colleagues hostage. Chechen fighters had attacked the Russian military checkpoint near the hospital, Satsita said. The *kontraktniki* thought if they abandoned the checkpoint and seized the hospital, they would be safe. They put two surgeons against the wall and threatened to kill them, then ordered everyone to wave sheets out of the window as Russian hostages had done when Shamil Basayev had seized the hospital in Budyonnovsk in June 1995.

"We refused, telling them that if they killed any doctors, they would have to kill us all, and that no one would get out alive because the Chechen fighters had the hospital surrounded," Satsita recalled. The *kontraktniki* radioed for air support.

"You guys are insane!" Satsita remembered telling them. "You call for an air attack of the hospital, and you'll be killed."

That panicked the *kontraktniki,* who then ordered Satsita to go out and negotiate for their safe passage from the hospital with the Chechen commander. At great risk Satsita went out into the street and found the commander.

"If you attack the hospital, you will kill twenty or thirty *kontraktniki,*" she told him, "but you will also probably kill five hundred Chechen patients along the way."

At first, the commander wouldn't listen to her. "They'll trick you," he said. "You can't trust them." Finally, he agreed to allow the *kontraktniki* to leave. Back in the hospital, Satsita and the other doctors and nurses put on white coats, formed a protective shield around the *kontraktniki,* and escorted them to the Russian checkpoint.

"The Russian officer thanked us and said we doctors were the only people who behaved in a human way." Satsita gave a bitter laugh. "When we turned to go back, some of the soldiers started firing on us. One nurse was killed, and a surgeon was hit in the leg."

Listening to Satsita, I could hardly control my anger. There were times during this war when I was tempted to exchange my scalpel for a gun.

BY AUGUST 10, I couldn't stand it any longer and decided to leave despite all of Magomed's warnings. I ran down the stairs, my shoes crunching broken glass, and pushed past the people in the entrance-way out onto the street.

"You're dead!" shouted a small boy in a torn green anorak to his friend who crouched behind a burned-out car on the street.

"No! I killed you first. Fall down!"

I stopped in my tracks. I counted fifteen kids of all ages, including girls, playing "war," oblivious to the danger all around them.

"You're dead! I shot you in the back! Fall down!" They held sticks in their hands for guns. In the background you could hear the firing of real guns. I couldn't believe what I was seeing. They had lived with war so long, that was all they knew.

"Parents can't keep them in the cellars all day," a woman in the doorway volunteered. "Either that, or the parents are dead and the kids now live on the streets."

I couldn't get those kids out of my mind. If someone didn't get them off the streets, they could grow into little animals with no knowledge of right or wrong; no traditions to guide them. Bang! Bang! You're dead! That is all they would know.

"Look, there's the doctor!" a Chechen fighter with a green bandana around his head yelled out. A group of five fighters emerged from the bombed-out building next door and pulled me inside.

"Allah Akhbar!" one dark-haired fighter said, raising his fist in the air. He introduced himself as Sultan. Although he was only twenty-four years old—before the war he had been a student in St. Petersburg—he was older than the other volunteers, which made him commander of the small group of some dozen men. Whatever Sultan told his men to do, they did. Sultan said his father was against his joining the volunteer fighters, but after his brother and cousin were killed, he had done it anyway.

"We need you to treat our wounded," he said.

Sultan suggested I use a small room on the first floor of the building next door. The first three floors had been mostly destroyed. This room was a mess but intact. A layer of plaster dust covered everything. Broken glass lay on the floor. A large table, left behind when the owners fled, would serve for operating. As I stood there wondering where to start, a woman entered and introduced herself as Leila. She was around fifty, with dark rings under her eyes, and was wearing a shapeless dress and a head scarf. At first I didn't recognize her, but then I remembered she did cleanup in the operating room at the First City Emergency Hospital.

"I am not a nurse," she said, fighting back tears, then straightened her shoulders and gave me a smile. "But I can help you if you let me. My back is strong. I have some lidocaine and some gauze at home."

"I need all the help I can get," I replied. "Canvas everyone for clean linen and anything that will do as bandages and dressings. We need local anesthetics, anything."

Over the next days until I escaped from Grozny, Leila and I labored together. Without her I couldn't have managed. Our conditions, like those of everyone else trapped in Grozny at that time, were primitive. No electricity, no gas, no water. I lugged my car battery into the apartment to supply power for light by which to operate. Everything was communal. People cooked and shared what little food they had in the streets or in the courtyards over open fires, using any wood available, including household furniture. They scooped up wastewater, which had accumulated on basement floors, filtered it through newspapers, and boiled it. As a result, most patients I saw suffered diarrhea and other intestinal ailments. At night, I returned to sleep on Magomed's couch under blankets that, like everything else, smelled of smoke from the smoldering ruins.

I guess it must have been late on the night of August 11 when I left with Sultan and six fighters to find Razyat and Malika. I simply had to know their fate. I blamed myself for not taking them home the night before the assault. At first, the fighters tried to prevent me from leaving the "hospital," as they called my street-side operating room. They said it was too dangerous; besides, I was their only doctor. But I was determined, and in the end, they agreed provided they escorted me. "Then we know you will return," Sultan said. "To get to your sisters, we'll have to swim across the river. The snipers have the bridge covered."

Skirting the buildings, past the carcass of Grozny's old Russian Orthodox church, we reached the river and crawled to the water's edge, breathing in the stench of oil, mud, and decaying vegetation. Broken bottles, cans, cardboard boxes, and paper littered the bank. As I slipped into the water, I prayed that I wouldn't cut my feet and get an infection like so many of my patients.

Once on the other side, we rounded the bombed-out buildings, dodging in and out of doorways. Sultan and the others knew every back alley, path, and sewer in the city, which gave them an advantage over the Russian soldiers. My throat tickled from the smoke and dust. Everywhere, fires burned in the rubble, and the smell of scorched human flesh filled the air. At the checkpoint near the bridge, a Russian soldier spotted us. He opened fire but missed.

Finally, around 5 A.M. on August 12, crawling on our bellies, we reached the square in front of the apartment building where Razyat and Malika should have been. It had taken us more than three hours to make a journey that would normally have taken thirty minutes on foot. The corpses of Russian soldiers, Chechen fighters, and civilians lay everywhere. Spent cartridges littered the street. "Are you crazy?" a fighter yelled when he saw that I was about to set out across the square. "Don't you see how many have been killed? If you go out there, a Russian sniper will get you!"

I was responsible for protecting my sisters. How could I look Dada and Nana in the eye if something happened to them? Ignoring the fighter's warning, I stepped over the body of an old woman and started across the open space. I heard the sharp crack of rifle fire, and a bullet whooshed past my ear. I dropped to my stomach, then crawled backward into a bombed-out building and dropped down behind a portion of a standing wall.

"Don't move any part of your body, or the snipers will see you," Sultan shouted from where he and the other fighters were hiding.

The fighters took my security seriously, and over the last couple of days I had come to know some of them well. They didn't talk much about independence, but rather about driving the Russians out of Chechnya or avenging family members who had been tortured or killed. Like all the other fighters, they were volunteers. One young fighter told me how Russian soldiers tortured him when they came to his house to check his documents; they beat him until he was half dead and threw him into the Sunzha River.

If Sultan and the other fighters were frightened at being surrounded by Russian snipers, they never showed it. They didn't dig themselves foxholes because that was considered cowardly. They would liberate Grozny or die in the effort. And it wasn't only the young men who took up arms to liberate Grozny. At one point during the fighting, I saw an old man of about seventy-five with a white beard and mustache, dressed in a long tunic nipped at the waist. On his head he wore a *papakha*. He didn't carry a gun but wore a large curved dagger in his belt. Behind him marched some twenty young fighters with machine guns and hand grenades.

In the days before we set out, Sultan and the others had described to me how the Chechens surrounded each of the Russian military checkpoints. All villages had sent volunteers, they said. This wasn't a hit-and-run guerrilla operation but a carefully coordinated move, which had been months in the planning by Colonel Aslan Maskhadov and his staff. Everyone had been talking about it, but few believed it was for real.

"The Russians couldn't imagine that a few thousand Chechen fighters with hand grenades, launchers, and rifles could drive the Russian army out of Grozny," Sultan said, "but they always underestimated us." Later, Russian generals themselves praised Operation Jihad as an example of a remarkable attack.

While trapped in the ruins for those twelve hours on August 12, I kept thinking about Razyat and Malika. Life without them was unimaginable. Being so much older than I was, they were like second mothers. Sultan called to me to stay awake. "If you drop off, you could move an arm or a leg, and that would let the snipers know where you are."

My legs were falling asleep, and I massaged them, taking care not to cause any obvious movement. All around me lay dead bodies. Of course, I had seen plenty of death, but I had never watched a body change over a relatively short period. The victims had fallen in grotesque poses, and as the hours passed, the angle of their limbs shifted as rigor mortis set in. The nearest corpse to me was that of a Chechen fighter. Under the hot sun, dark blotches appeared on his face. As the hours went by, his body started to bloat, the smell of flesh became stronger, and I felt sick.

Each of those bodies rotting in the sun would bring such sorrow to families, even to later generations, just as the Deportation had done. I had lost so many friends. And now Razyat and Malika's fate was unclear. I refused to believe I wouldn't see them again. Of course, I wanted Chechnya's independence, but all this killing nauseated me. I had seen the suffering war inflicts on civilians who want nothing more than to be left in peace; innocent victims sacrificed on the altar of power-hungry leaders on both sides of the conflict. Ordinary people, including women, children, and the elderly, took the bullets and the shrapnel—not the generals or the politicians.

Taking in the scene before my eyes, I imagined Nana's sobs if something had happened to Razyat or Malika. Dada wouldn't show any emotions, but his heart would break. I imagined him saying, "So you went off to have fun and left your sisters to be killed in all that mess?"

Finally, after dark fell, the fighters said it was time to get out. We couldn't move forward any more. "There is no way we could cross the square without being killed," Sultan said. "We will return."

AROUND AUGUST 15, there was a lull in the fighting in our part of the city, which I saw as an opportunity to go back to Alkhan Kala to tell my parents I hadn't managed to find Razyat or Malika. This meant I had to cross the river again. An old women told me the only way to do that without being detected by snipers was to creep along the rusty, natural gas pipe suspended under the bridge by stanchions every ten feet or so. I managed to reach the bridge, which was guarded by Russian soldiers at each end. Wriggling on my belly, I reached the pipe and grabbed it. The rust scraped my hands as I swung myself around each of the stanchions, trying not to look down into the water. If I lost my balance and fell, I would be impaled on the sharp branches, bits of metal, and other flotsom that were piled up under the bridge. A shard of metal from the corroded pipe creased my right hand, and I clamped my eyes shut against the pain; I tightened my fists around the pipe. In all, it took me forty minutes to get from one bank to the other without being spotted.

On the other side, I crossed the railroad tracks, then dodged in and out of bombed-out buildings until I arrived at the Lokomotif Sports Stadium, now a pile of rubble. I could hear artillery fire on the other side of the city and the sound of firing guns. For several minutes I stood before the heaps of bricks and twisted girders, staring at what remained of the stadium where I had trained so often and won my first athletic competition. In those years, the future was mine. Excited faces cheered me from the stands. Now, I turned away to watch the column of refugees fleeing the city, exhaustion and fear on their faces, their few possessions strapped to them; old people being pushed in carts, children clinging to their mothers. It was so like the Soviet wartime films I had seen in my childhood of fleeing refugees in 1942 and 1943.

As I passed the central bus station, I joined the column of refugees heading in the direction of Chernorechye, a settlement south of Grozny. At the side of the road, I saw a Chechen man digging a big makeshift grave. It was a very hot day, the ground was hard, and rivulets of sweat ran down his face. Lying in the grass beside him were the badly decomposing corpses of a dozen Russian soldiers. The smell was horrific, and I looked on in amazement as he tried to clean up the area by covering them with earth.

"Their mothers would want their remains returned to the earth," he muttered. "Why shouldn't we bury them?"

Farther on, a woman, dressed only in a light blue nightdress, walked barefoot along the road. She was about thirty-five and surrounded by three boys, between the ages of around five and ten, whom I took to be her sons. In her arms she held an infant girl. I assumed she had fled from the nearby Railroad Workers' Hospital. The image of this woman stuck in my mind, symbolizing the tragedy of my country. Farther along, a young man was bending over his father lying on a homemade stretcher. The old man was apparently dead, and the son, holding a small book of verses, was reciting the *Ya Sin*, the Koranic prayer for the dead. Beside the young man were his brother, sister, and mother. He spoke softly, shedding tears as he read the prayer, which echoes through the towns and villages in Chechnya even today: *"Say: He will give life to them Who brought them into existence at first, and He is Cognizant of all creation. . . . Glory be to Him in Whose hand is the kingdom of all things and to Him you shall be returned."*

When he finished, the young man closed the book, placed it in the breast pocket of his jacket, and covered his father's face with a white cloth. Then the two brothers picked up the stretcher and pushed on in search of a proper burial place.

Farther down the road, I saw a man holding a handkerchief to his face; I could see blood pouring from his nose. Two small boys clung to his trouser leg, while he held a young girl to his chest. I walked over to examine him.

He had already lost a lot of blood. I asked him to give me a piece of cloth. He placed the little girl on the ground, reached into a sack that one of the boys carried, and tore off a strip from some clothing. I dipped the cloth into the cold water of a nearby spring and pressed a compress over his nose and forehead. I covered a small twig with another piece of damp cloth and pushed it into his nostril. "Hold it there," I told him. He lay down in the grass while I sat beside him for about ten minutes until the bleeding stopped. Then we got up and moved on.

When we finally reached Chernorechye, I decided to sit down on a nearby bench before taking the service road through the woods toward Alkhan Kala. I pulled from my pocket a folded piece of paper on which my father had written the prayer *Lak'ad Djaakum*. When I was a child, he had written the verses in Arabic with a transliteration in the Russian alphabet and made me recite them until I pronounced all the words correctly. As I said the prayer under my breath, I pictured my father sitting at the kitchen table and heard his voice.

Now hath come unto you a Mes-
senger from amongst yourselves: it
grieves him that ye should perish:
ardently anxious is he over you:
to the Believers is he most kind
merciful.

    But if they turn away, say,
"Allah sufficeth me: there is no
god but He: on Him is my
trust—He the Lord of the
Throne (of Glory) Supreme!"

Lak'ad djaakum rasulum min
anfusikum 'azeezun 'alayhi
ma'anittun hareesun 'alaykum
bilmu'miniyna raufur raheem.
Faintawallouw fak'ul hasbiyya
Allahu lailaha illa huva, 'alayhi
tawakkaltu wa huva rabbul 'arshil
'aziym.

I repeated the prayer three times, stuffed the paper back in my pocket, and rose to my feet to join the procession of refugees entering the woods. The road was a rutted one-lane path used by service vehicles. Buses and cars, top-heavy with boxes, suitcases, and pieces of furniture, bucked and stalled while people shouted for them to move on. You could almost reach out and touch the underlying panic. Suddenly, I heard the sound of helicopters; I looked up to see gunships approaching from the west. People screamed, dropped their bundles, grabbed their children, and ran in all directions. The drivers in cars or trucks seemed to go crazy, desperately trying to drive their cars along the narrow road, bumping into each other, ending up totally blocked. One of the helicopters began firing; a rocket exploded near a stalled bus filled with women and children, setting it on fire. The women started desperately breaking the narrow windows and pushing the children out, some in burning clothes.

My chest tightened in panic. I didn't know where to turn, whom to help. I spotted two small boys, who had been thrown out of the burning bus, screaming in shock. I grabbed them, pressed them to my chest, and ran into the woods. Through the branches I saw a second gunship flying low; the downdraft from its rotors shaking the trees. Maybe the gunners couldn't see us through the leaves, but they knew we were there. I looked around and saw an old bomb crater from a previous attack and dove into it, covering the two kids with my body. Then—a thunderous explosion, trees falling, wood chips and dirt pelting me. I waited a few moments, then rolled onto my back and tried to comfort the boys, who were whimpering with fear.

A moment of calm descended on us. I picked up the children and ran back to the buses. Several civilians lay dead at the side of the road. I returned the boys to the women who had escaped the bus during the gunfire, and they set off on foot for Alkhan Yurt.

The refugee column pushed on down the road through the woods, children and women crying, the men whispering prayers, everyone hoping the helicopters wouldn't return. This time, two fighter planes streaked out of the sky, diving sharply, bombing and firing everywhere. Again, everyone ran for cover, stumbling and falling. Several elderly men and women didn't try to run. They dropped to the ground, calling on Allah to save them.

"Hit the ground!" I yelled. "Open your mouths and cover your ears to keep your eardrums from rupturing."

A nearby crater wasn't big enough for everyone, so I squatted down under a big tree, hid my head between my knees, closed my eyes, and prayed. I heard the stutter of an assault helicopter; its shadow flickered above like an evil bird, its downdraft rattling the branches. Suddenly, there was the terrifying sound of large-caliber machine-gun fire. The bullets cut a furrow through the ground—parallel to my left leg—sending a swirl of dirt, twigs, and leaves into the air.

The cries of the wounded began to replace the roar of the planes. Children screaming like wounded animals from burns, a woman with a torn leg, a man blinded by a shell. "Help me! Help me! Help me!" That's all I heard. I wanted to block my ears. I felt overwhelmed. I had no instruments, no equipment, nothing. Never in my life have I felt so helpless.

Stop the bleeding! That thought ran through my head again and again. All I could do was rip shirts into strips, tie them above the wound, insert sticks in the knotted ties for a makeshift tourniquet, then drag the injured person to the road. There I flagged any moving vehicle, begging for transport to the hospital at Urus-Martan. Many drivers refused to stop; their vehicles were already overflowing with people. It was everyone for himself.

"Where are the parents?" drivers asked, as if it mattered when the child in your arms was dying.

"I don't know where they are," I shouted back. "Maybe they have been killed. Just get the children to the hospital, and we'll find the parents later."

About 4 P.M., I finally emerged from the woods onto the Moscow-Baku highway. A crowd of people waited there for relatives fleeing Grozny or for news any survivor could supply. I stood dazed, amid a sea of discarded belongings, a child's jacket, a single sneaker, a stuffed animal, a family photograph, and bullet casings everywhere. I could no longer feel my body. I looked down and saw that my shoes were coming apart, my toes sticking out in front. My brown trousers were torn, stained green from the grass I had crawled through, and caked with mud. A terrible heaviness enveloped me. I could barely place one foot in front of the other. I have no idea how long I stood there; maybe an hour, maybe only five minutes. A neighbor from Alkhan Kala stopped his car beside me. "Get in. I'll take you home," he said.

I don't remember much about my arrival home other than all the neighbors rushing out to meet me, full of questions. Zara said that they had watched the helicopters and planes strafe the woods, not realizing that I was there. Nana and Dada asked about Razyat and Malika. "I don't know if they are dead or alive," I said. They were silent. They saw the state I was in and didn't press me. "They are alive, I'm sure," Nana said.

Everyone wanted to know if I had seen Ali. He had been missing for almost a month. His brother Adam, who was four years older, had gone to look for him. Adam said that he was trapped in a cellar in Grozny with some of the fighters and that he was all right. Later, I learned that Ali had seen me but didn't want me to see him. He knew how furious I would have been for the worry he had caused us.

The next day, I told Nana I wanted to return to Grozny. "I've got to find Malika and Razyat. And I'll see if I can find Ali." She put the teapot back down on the table with a thud. "If they are dead, they are dead; if they are alive, they are alive," she said. "Hundreds of people went to Grozny to hunt for relatives and were picked off by snipers. I beg you, don't go!"

To refuse my parents' wishes was hard, but the more I thought about it, the more I knew I had to go. I should have been killed long ago, but for some reason—only Allah knows why—I was still alive. When you live in constant danger, a kind of metamorphosis of the organism takes place. I recalled an evening many days earlier, when Operation Jihad had just begun. A group of friends and I sat down to eat at the apartment of Natasha, a Russian neighbor of Magomed's. Though she didn't speak Chechen, Natasha behaved like a Chechen, always wearing a scarf and observing our traditions of hospitality. Her family had lived in Grozny for generations, so she had no reason to leave; this was her home. She was probably about forty-five, blond with gray eyes, and clearly wanted to bring us a little relief. "Feeding you is the only thing I can do," she had said, placing the bowl of soup in front of us.

Suddenly, a feeling of fear struck me. I sensed something terrible was about to happen. I pushed my stool back. "Let's go down to the basement for a little bit and then come back and eat." I tried to speak in a calm voice. Nobody moved.

"But we've only just sat down," Magomed protested.

"Just go! Get going!" I started yelling. Everyone looked at me in surprise. "Hurry, hurry!"

I stood up and made for the door. We stumbled down five flights of stairs. As we reached the ground floor, there was a searing whistling and an artillery shell plowed straight through Natasha's apartment. Everyone looked at me: "How did you know?" Natasha flung her arms around me and kissed me. I couldn't explain it any more than I could explain why I wasn't frightened to return to Grozny for Malika and Razyat.

Three days after I returned home—it must have been August 18—

I rose at 5 A.M., dressed in my running clothes, prayed, and left without telling anyone. I was determined to return to the capital to find my sisters and help the wounded. As I set out, the sky lightened, dissipating the clouds of smoke over Grozny. I ran along the back roads and paths into the city to avoid Russian fire. It took me a bit over two hours, and the surprising thing was that I didn't even feel tired.

Once in Grozny, I looked everywhere for Razyat and Malika but without success. No one had seen them. When I finally returned home a few days later, I discovered that Malika and Razyat had got back after I set out for Grozny to find them. They had survived thanks to a heroic Chechen FSB colonel, who brought them food and protected them from Russian soldiers. For days they huddled in the cellar. The colonel, like other Chechens who worked for the security services in cities throughout Russia, had found himself in an impossible situation when the war broke out. Some had resigned their positions; others, like my sisters' protector, had gone to Chechnya with the idea of secretly helping Chechens. Eventually they were found out and punished. Several months later, Malika and Razyat were devastated to learn that the colonel had been killed in a mysterious automobile accident.

Part 3

A Fragile Peace

Chapter 12

Rebuilding

I THINK THAT the August events, when the Chechen fighters liberated Grozny, finally convinced Moscow that it was time to withdraw from Chechnya. Their departure was negotiated at the end of August by Colonel Aslan Maskhadov with General Aleksandr Lebed, the pugnacious Russian general who later ran unsuccessfully for president. In November, Russian premier Viktor Chernomyrdin signed the agreement, which was full of lofty ideals about preserving human rights, the rights of ethnic minorities, and the right of self-determination. The main provision was that Chechnya's final political status would be put off five years, to be settled by the year 2001. Not unexpectedly, some in the Russian military protested, as did members of the security services. The fight was always against terrorism and bandits, they said; a troop withdrawal meant soldiers had died in vain. I understood Russia's humiliation and how its top military brass wanted to finish the job.

Following the withdrawal of Russian troops, the population struggled to return to normal. With the Grozny hospitals in ruins, I began working in the hospital at Urus-Martan. Right then, no one in Chechnya wanted to think about war. Everyone rejoiced. No more bombs, no more shelling, no more damp cellars. No more killings—at least, that is what we thought. People believed it was safe to rebuild, which we had done so many times throughout our history. In the coming months, the Russian military checkpoints disappeared. Planes, trains, and buses resumed service. Theaters and art galleries reopened in Grozny. Peasants returned to the fields despite thousands of mines. The elders stood up in the mosques, on radio and TV, urging us to get on with life. Time to stop grieving, they said; time to rebuild houses and get the children back in school.

In Alkhan Kala, as in all the other towns and villages, people wanted to reconstruct the mosques. My childhood friend and neighbor Khamzat Magommadov, who had made money before the war, ordered white stone from neighboring Dagestan. Those who could spare something also contributed. Malika made a special trip to Krasnoyarsk and persuaded Hussein to let his ten-year-old daughter, Khava, come to us so she could learn Chechen and attend one of the reopened schools in Grozny. That made me happy because I was increasingly convinced that if children did not know the language, Chechen culture would shrivel. Without culture, Chechnya would die. I was also glad to see my parents' renewed interest in life. "Time to get rid of all that rubble," Nana announced one morning, looking at the broken bricks, split beams, and twisted gate. "A reminder of bad times." I started to collect materials to rebuild my house.

We were all so busy rebuilding our lives that we tended to ignore the warning signals: The kidnappings and other crimes had already started before the war ended, and now they increased. On December 16, 1996, the brutal murder of six sleeping Red Cross workers in Noviye Atagi shocked us all. The killing of these workers—who had set up a field hospital; brought in medical equipment; provided food, water, and medicines; and hired some 200 unemployed locals—filled me with shame, as it did most Chechens. I went to Atagi the day after it happened. Women wept openly. "They came to help us," they said. I even saw tears in the eyes of some elders. No one was ever arrested for the crime. Witnesses reported that the gunmen spoke Chechen, which leads me to believe they must have been in the pay of someone who wanted to disrupt our upcoming presidential elections—among the many candidates could have been Doku Zavgayev, Moscow's puppet leader who felt betrayed by the Russian peace deal, or Zelimkhan Yandarbiyev, the acting president who was anti-Western and argued for putting off the elections—but nothing has ever been established against them. This barbarous act resulted in international organizations withdrawing their workers from Chechnya.

January 27, 1997, was the date set for our first presidential elections after the war. The main contenders included: Colonel Aslan Maskhadov, the military chief of staff; Shamil Basayev, the famous field commander; Movladi Udugov, the chief Chechen propagandist; Akhmed Zakayev, the minister of culture; and Zelimkhan Yandarbiyev, the acting president. I favored Maskhadov because I thought he was the most moderate and experienced.

The voting created amazing enthusiasm. Chechens came from all over, from Russia, Europe, the Middle East, and even the United States. Extra planes and trains were put into service. In the election, Maskhadov defeated Basayev in the balloting, which was deemed free and fair by official international observers. Later in May 1997, President Maskhadov signed a formal peace agreement with Russian president Boris Yeltsin. "The 400-year-old conflict has been brought to an end," he declared on national television. Life was going to improve; we were sure of it. In Moscow, Yeltsin was criticized by some of the hardliners for his words of conciliation.

But we were wrong. A peace agreement had been signed, the bombing had stopped, but beneath the euphoria over the end of the war, there existed a terrible malaise, which I observed every day in my patients. For those people whose relatives lay in mass graves or beneath piles of rubble, peace didn't exist. Thousands had gone missing. When there was no body to bury, no grave to visit, sorrow consumed their souls. Illness was skyrocketing throughout the republic. It seemed that the physical and mental stamina of the population, which had held up so well during the fighting, collapsed once the fighting was over. That winter, diarrhea, dysentery, and parasites attacked the population, along with the virulent form of TB that doesn't respond to antibiotics. Heart attacks and strokes felled people by the dozens. In our town, the hearts of seventeen people gave out in a twenty-four-hour period. Thousands struggled to survive without arms and legs. At least 10,000 people, many of them children, needed artificial limbs. Infants died when stress caused their mother's milk to dry up.

I began to realize just how sick the nation was. Pediatricians around the republic reported that from 1995 to 1996 a quarter of newborns suffered birth defects like cleft palates, harelips, stunted limbs, extra limbs, and missing internal organs. They and the other children without arms and legs were a large part of our future. Their defects would visit us generation after generation, as happened at Hiroshima and Nagasaki. I guessed the Russians must have employed poisonous chemicals, judging from the shriveled foliage, the respiratory diseases, and the lesions on the faces of children. Specialists claimed the military used Chechnya as a place to test all sorts of new weapons, including forbidden ones.

One morning, a tractor driver came into my office; the flesh on his hands was black and in places eaten through to the bone. He said he had been digging near storage containers on the side of the road between Grozny and the military air base of Khankala and found an intriguing phosphorescent object, like a box. "People say the containers are leaking," he said. I immediately sent the man to Moscow for treatment. Whether he survived, I don't know. Later, scientists found that the site had been used by the Russian military to store radioactive waste.

As a plastic surgeon, I was able to repair many birth defects, but often the deformities were too serious and I was helpless.

"What do you advise, Doctor?" asked a mother as she unwrapped her newborn baby and placed him on my table. Her hands shook. My nurse turned away in horror. The baby had an enormous head, a double harelip, a cleft palate, and small shriveled limbs which jerked every two or three seconds. His eyes looked out from the side of his temples, and he had two pairs of ears, a smaller set in front of the normal ones. Instead of nostrils, he had one large opening as a nose. I tried not to show my shock. I had seen deformities, but nothing like this.

The father, an unshaven man dressed in a grubby satin running outfit, watched my face.

"When you feed him, the food just comes out of his nose," he said. Now the mother waited for me to say something. I didn't know what to tell the poor woman. She appeared embarrassed, as though the tragedy was her fault. I didn't know what the parents expected of me. Perhaps they thought I could reconstruct the baby's face so it could eat, or perhaps they wanted me to give the baby a shot to put it out of its misery. I am also against euthanasia. I was powerless.

"It is in Allah's hands," I said. "I can't do anything for you."

"Thank you, Doctor," she said, wrapping up the baby again.

A week later, I learned that the baby had died.

After the woman and her family left my office, I recalled a conversation I had had with one of the French physicians from Doctors Without Borders. "The Russians don't need to bomb you anymore. In the future your people will die off like flies from the ecological devastation caused by the war," she had said. At the time, I thought she was exaggerating.

Treating the ill was a Herculean task. The economy had collapsed; 90 percent of men were unemployed. Half the doctors and nurses had left the republic during the war to find work in Russia. Either their nerves had given out, or they couldn't support their families. Unfortunately, war has placed a terrible strain on our traditions, especially relations between men and women. Once the factories had closed, men lost their jobs, forcing many women to become the breadwinners by trading in the bazaar. I knew a number of educated women—doctors, teachers, and others—who abandoned their specialties and went into small-time business to support their families. For a Chechen male, there is no greater humiliation than not being able to support his family. I was fortunate. I still had some savings left, but I knew they wouldn't last forever.

Friends suggested that I would do better to go to Moscow and work there, but my father's voice always reminded me about duty and I knew I was meant to stay in Chechnya. It was my duty to support my relatives. Most of them had no jobs, and those who did work, like Malika and Razyat, received no salaries. In all, I was responsible for thirteen people, not counting all the others who asked for loans they never paid back. I knew I had to make some money not only to support my family but also to buy much needed medicines and equipment for the hospitals. My friend Abek Bisultanov, who had made money from a car sales business, which he started after retiring as an athlete, collected more than $12,000. During 1997, I made several trips to Moscow to purchase medical supplies with his donation.

I decided that I would solve my financial problem by taking private patients for cosmetic surgery after-hours at the hospital, as I had done before the war. With the war over, everyone wanted to forget the ugliness. Stress speeds up the aging process, and when women looked in the mirror, they didn't like what they saw. Some of them came to me in secret, ashamed to be worried about their looks when so many people were suffering from the trauma of war. They dug into savings or borrowed money for the operations. I was sympathetic with this postwar desire to look good. Never again would I have a six-day growth of stubble because there was no water to shave, or wear damp blood-stained trousers, the matted sheepskin coat, or the boots that leaked. Now I took pleasure in shaving each morning and wearing a clean shirt and a tie.

I kept my fees low, which meant I never lacked patients. My price for a nose job, removing crow's feet, or a face-lift were a tenth of what the doctors charged in Moscow at the Institute of Cosmetology. As long as I had strength, I was determined to work. When I returned home, I would find relatives of the injured waiting in the street for me even after midnight, begging for my help. I grew weary; I was one man with limited strength. Once in the house, Dada would tell me of his friends who needed a doctor, mostly people who had been exiled with him in Kazakhstan. I knew his friendships from those times were sacred.

I took no money from my regular patients. Most of them were penniless. To overcome their embarrassment, they felt compelled to tell me their stories. This one had lost two children; that one a wife. This one's brother had been tortured; that one's daughter had been raped. "Please don't tell me," I implored them. "We all lost friends and relatives." I tried to control my irritation, which seemed to be growing with every passing day despite everything I did to curb it.

In addition to caring for civilians, I was called upon occasionally to treat Salman Raduyev, the controversial field commander I had operated on in the mountain hideout. Several months after the original operation, I had removed the scar tissue from the facial reconstruction. Not only was he an exasperating patient, never following instructions, but the association put my life in danger. One time after treating him, I found a note slipped under my door: "If you continue to keep Raduyev alive, the next time you'll be killed."

After Raduyev took hostages in the Dagestani village of Kizlyar in January 1996, he had risen to the top of the Kremlin's most wanted list. Journalists wrote constantly about him, and he appeared to revel in his reputation. He loved making up tall tales, even boasting about terrorist acts he had never done. After I told him not to mention my name, he said German cosmetic surgeons had traveled to Chechnya to operate on him, the same doctors who had operated on Michael Jackson. After that, people in Chechnya nicknamed him "Jackson" after the American rock star. In Moscow, the media called him "Titanik" because of the titanium plates and wires holding his skull together. Returning from medical treatment in Istanbul, he even tried to impersonate the late President Dudayev. For a while Raduyev claimed he was the reincarnation of Dudayev, aping his gait and mannerisms, and using his figures of speech until the fantasy wore off.

I could never make up my mind why Raduyev behaved as he did. People who knew him before the war said he was a well-educated, quiet man. Was he really crazy, or did he just enjoy acting out? Was he a religious believer, or was he using Islam for his own purposes like other unscrupulous leaders? Once while I was changing his dressings, I suggested he curb his wild talk, but he just laughed. It seemed that

Standing next to field commander
Raduyev (right), after an operation.

the press had made such a celebrity out of him that he had to live up
to his popular image.

Raduyev was a loose cannon, and there were innumerable assassination attempts against him. With so many enemies, it was hard to
know who was behind the attempts on his life, the Russians or the
Chechens. Raduyev claimed that I was the only doctor he trusted in
Chechnya, which meant that his men banged on my door at any
time of the day or night, demanding that I go with them to treat the
latest attack against him. We never went to the same place because
Raduyev slept in a different bed each night and rotated his guards almost weekly.

In April 1997, after he had returned from Istanbul, where he had
gone to get an artificial eye, he summoned me to a large house
guarded by 100 men outside Gudermes, the second-largest town in
Chechnya, about an hour and a half's drive east of Grozny.

Raduyev rose to his feet when I entered the room, ordered his guards out, and gave me a bear hug. His beard had grown back, and he wore dark glasses. On the small table next to his cot lay a pile of press clippings. "All stories about me!" he said, grinning. As usual, he was full of bravado. "So how are things, Tiger? Any problems?"

"The only problem I have is with you," I said. "People keep coming to ask if I know where you are."

He laughed, then launched into an account of his treatment in Turkey in 1996 and how the doctors in Istanbul had praised the way I had put his face back together. He removed his glasses to display the glass eye in the left socket, then handed me a brown envelope containing his x-rays. Examining his face, I immediately saw that an abscess had formed along the lower ridge of the left eye socket. His body was rejecting the titanium brace, which the Turkish physicians had screwed down to hold his glass eye. The implant must be removed, I said. He said he didn't have time to do it right away but that he would be back in touch with me in a few days.

Months passed before his guards arrived for me again. By now, the fistula oozed a yellow pus. I was concerned he would develop osteomyelitis, an infection of the bone, along the lower orbital ridge.

"I need to operate immediately before the infection gets worse and eats into the bone," I said. "I will have to go in through the mouth and enter the sinus walls. We will need to do a full series of tests—blood, urine—before giving you a general anesthetic."

"I'm healthy," he snapped. "I don't need tests. I don't have time for them."

There was no arguing with him. Reluctantly, I agreed to do the operation at the Gudermes hospital later that day, after 10 P.M. when the presence of his guards wouldn't frighten the other patients. The operation didn't go smoothly. When I opened up the fistula, I found that the infection had progressed into the orbital ridge, which I had to scrape clean. Instead of one hour, we labored for three. Moreover, there was excessive bleeding because Raduyev's blood lacked sufficient plasma, which kept it from coagulating—a condition I would have discovered through preoperation tests. By the time I managed finally to stop the flow of blood, I had broken out in a sweat. If Raduyev died, I would be blamed.

After the operation, I instructed Raduyev's guards to take him to the Ninth City Hospital in Grozny every day, so I could inspect the wound and change the dressings. Then they drove me back to Alkhan Kala.

Each day before Raduyev arrived at the hospital, his heavily armed men arrived to sweep the grounds, look for explosives under cars, and clear the corridors. He never stayed in the hospital. His guards whisked him in and out as quickly as possible. On the seventh day, I removed the stitches, thankful Raduyev's treatment was over.

However, a few days later, Raduyev began hemorrhaging and was rushed to the Ninth City Hospital. It turned out that he had once again disobeyed my instructions. After the fistula operation, I had told him to take things easy. Instead, he had gone to Sheikh Mansur Square and harangued the crowd, opening up the wound and setting off the bleeding. By the time he arrived at the hospital, he had lost so much blood that we ordered the mullah to read him the prayer for the dying.

Raduyev looked frightened. He liked to tell his followers, "We must die for the Jihad!" He was always ready to encourage others to sacrifice themselves. But looking at him now, I knew he had no desire to leave this life.

After determining he had insufficient plasma, I informed Raduyev, "We need blood urgently."

"No problem!" Raduyev waved his arms in the air. "My people will donate. Take fifty of them, one hundred, as many as you need—two hundred, if necessary."

I purposely did not tell Raduyev that two or three donors would be enough. Ordering his men to donate was a great opportunity to replenish the hospital's blood supply. We scrambled around for any container in which to collect the blood. Meantime, we dripped plasma into Raduyev, and he recovered well over the next few days.

Soon after his recovery, I learned about the rumors circulating that I was an FSB agent who had injected him with a slow-acting poison. I was furious.

"I don't like it," I said to him the next time he came to the hospital for treatment, "and I don't want to hear it anymore. If you don't trust me, there is no point coming to me. You have a lot of enemies. People are always trying to blow you up. How do I know they won't try the same thing against me?"

He apologized. "I'll tell my men to counteract the rumors," he said.

Raduyev was back on my operating table a few months later. This time, someone had planted a bomb in his car. The explosion killed the driver and a bodyguard. Shrapnel grazed his ribs and hip, and his face was burned horribly. I dressed the burns with my concoction of egg yolk and sour cream to help ease the pain and removed the dead tissue. Raduyev was a cat with nine lives, and it seemed that I was called upon to preserve them—a role I didn't enjoy.

IN THE SUMMER of 1997, I decided to take Zara, Maryam, and Islam for a vacation on the Caspian Sea in neighboring Dagestan. I believed that a week lying on the beach, soaking up the sun, and listening to the waves would replenish my energy and exorcise some of the terrible images that remained with me from those final August days in Grozny. For some time after the end of the first war, I had managed to suppress those images, especially if I was preoccupied with patients, but with the fatigue came depression. The week by the sea certainly helped, but soon after we came home, the images returned. As long as I was treating patients, I was all right. Then at the end of the day, as the light faded, the troubles started—slowly at first, then increasing with every hour. I couldn't sit still. I broke into a sweat. Sleep became impossible.

"You shouldn't take everything to heart," Nana said, finding me in the kitchen in the middle of the night. "The war is over. We are the lucky ones; none of us was killed."

What she said was true, but I had no control over the depression. My relatives didn't understand. Friends talked of rebuilding their houses or buying a car, and all I saw were planes dive-bombing us in the woods; all I heard were screams of terror.

Nana, my sisters, and Zara became so worried they suggested I go to the old mullah who lived in Alkhan Yurt.

"He has helped hundreds of people," Nana said. "People sleep in the street for days in order to see him. Lecha can get you an appointment." Lecha, my sister Raya's husband, had worked as a baker in Alkhan Yurt before losing his job.

At first I refused. The problem embarrassed me. Others had suffered far worse. In the end, I only agreed to seek the help of the mullah to calm Nana.

"The mullah has cured lots of children," she reassured me.

Two days later, Lecha and I left for Alkhan Yurt. The ruts in the road were filled with water, and we drove slowly. When I got out of the car, some people in the crowd waiting for the mullah recognized me. "It's the doctor," a woman called out. "Let him through!"

The crowd opened up. The gate into the inner courtyard of the mullah's house swung open, and I heard someone say, "Follow me." A figure loomed out of the dark and led me into a central room lit by a kerosene lamp on a table in the corner. As I removed my shoes, I felt warmth hit my face from the brick stove in the middle of the room. Bookshelves lined two of the walls, containing ancient Korans, some with leather bindings, others with broken spines, all in Arabic. Yellowing photographs of famous sheikhs and historic figures in Chechen history hung from the other walls. Next to them were what looked liked family photographs, women in Chechen national costume, men in tight-fitting tunics and *papakhas*.

"Please enter," said an old, hunched-back man with a neatly trimmed white beard. He came forward to shake my hand. Behind him stood a middle-aged man whom he introduced as his son. The old man—I guessed he was about eighty—wore a white Muslim prayer cap. Over his trousers, he wore the loose tunic of the Chechen traditional dress, and on his feet boots of soft black leather. I looked at his eyes, which held such a benign expression. Hundreds of wrinkles lined his face. I instantly felt as though I had known him all my life. There was something in his smile that made me feel he could help me. He invited me to sit down and called for his wife to bring tea. We sat at a small table in the middle of the room. On the table stood a transparent glass jar of water. The mullah's son handed his father a pair of glasses, two leather-bound copies of the Koran, a sheet of paper, and a pen.

"What are you suffering from?" the old mullah asked, after his wife had placed a glass of tea in front of me along with a small crystal jar of homemade jam.

I started listing my symptoms, but the mullah interrupted. "Did you see all those people out there?" he said. "They all suffer—irritability, depression, no interest in life, fear, agitation . . ." All my symptoms.

The mullah reached for a copy of the Koran. He flipped the pages, and when he found the passage he was looking for, he began copying it on the sheet of paper. His hand trembled as he wrote. When he had finished, he folded the paper, dropped it in water, and waited for the paper to absorb the water. While we waited, I heard a child crying. The door opened, and a woman entered carrying a young child. The face of the baby was crimson, and it gulped air, unable to stop crying. The old mullah stepped forward, placed his hand on the child's head, and muttered a few words of Arabic prayer. To my amazement, the child stopped crying.

As I watched the writing blur and the ink dissolve in the jar of water, I felt I was being helped. I didn't understand the Arabic words on the paper, but I had faith in the old man and I believed what was written in the Koran. "Take the water home; let it stand for three days," the old man said. "On the third day, remove the paper, dry and burn it, then drink a soupspoon of the water in the morning and at night. Come back and see me."

I did as the old mullah had instructed, drinking the water. I wondered what my professors in Krasnoyarsk would think if they could see me now. I had heard that many of them, formerly confirmed atheists, were now attending church.

A few days later, I began to feel better. My mood improved for a while. I slept more soundly. I can't explain all this from a scientific point of view. Thinking about it, I attribute the improvement to faith: my faith in Allah; my faith in the mullah's knowledge of the Koran; my faith in the time-honored Arabic words.

Despite the mullah's insistence, however, I didn't return for the second visit. Once I was feeling better, I became too busy and preoccupied to go back.

Chapter 13

An Eclipse of the Soul

I N T H E S U M M E R of 1998 I went to Moscow again, planning to spend three or four months learning the latest skin-grafting techniques. The timing was good because Zara was expecting our third child in late November, and I had to be back for the birth. I also hoped that old friends like Abek Bisultanov and Musa Saponov would help lift my spirits. Driving into Moscow from Vnukovo airport was a shock. After living for so long in Chechnya, I was conditioned to grayness. Moscow's prosperity disoriented me: the billboards advertising Marlboro cigarettes, the inflated promises from banks and airlines; the scantily clad girls advertising products on television, and everywhere flashing lights. Looking out of the taxi, I couldn't believe my eyes; in the next lane, an attractive young woman behind the wheel of a car was talking on a cell phone. Volvos, Jeep Cherokees, Mercedes shot by. Everything was westernized as Russia embarked on capitalism.

I attempted to buy a shirt in GUM, the large department store across Red Square from the Kremlin. Now designer stores like Calvin Klein and Escada lined the galleries. "Do you have a credit card?" the cashier asked, when I wanted to pay for a shirt. Embarrassed, I shook my head. I had heard of credit cards, but I had no idea how they worked. In any case, I didn't have one.

Instead of cheering me up, Moscow had the opposite effect. All the modernization reminded me how Chechnya had fallen behind. How could we ever enter the modern world? We were in the Stone Age. We had driven the Russians out of Chechnya, but how could we say we had won the war, when people had no work, suffered terrible diseases, and lived in bombed-out buildings? Ordinary Russians didn't seem to be suffering because of a lost war, at least not on the surface. True, in the provinces misery existed as it always had, but in Moscow everything glittered.

Russian colleagues I had known in 1993 at the Institute of Cosmetology now treated me coolly. In the past, we had worked together, eaten together, trusted one another. They knew what I had been through, but showed no interest in how I was or the conditions in Chechnya. When I entered Professor Frishberg's office, he merely looked up briefly, exchanged a few pleasantries, then turned back to what he was doing. He clearly couldn't wait for me to leave.

An old Russian friend, a colonel and a doctor of the Medical Corps whom I had met during my specialization at the Institute of Cosmetology, asked me to look at the x-rays of a Russian soldier wounded in Chechnya since he knew that I had a lot of experience with gunshot wounds. In an earlier operation, the doctors had used a titanium plate to mend a break in his lower jaw, but the wound would not heal. I told him the plate needed to be removed and replaced with a bone graft from his hip.

"Would you do the operation?" my friend asked. It would take place at the main military hospital run by the Ministry of Defense, and he would assist. I agreed.

On the day of the operation, after I had washed up, donned my scrubs, and was about to enter the operating room, my friend pulled me aside. "It's best not to say you are a Chechen," he whispered. "There are a number of high military officers—generals—walking around the corridors."

I could hardly control my anger. "You know that I am a Chechen, so why did you invite me to do this operation? After all I have been through, after all my people have suffered, am I supposed to be ashamed of being Chechen?"

My friend became flustered and apologized. "The patient is already anesthetized," he said. He was frightened I would refuse.

I performed the surgery because none of this was the young soldier's fault. I removed a piece of bone from the soldier's hip, shaved it to the right proportions, and fixed it to the jaw in place of the titanium plate. I achieved a perfect fit and was delighted. The operation complete, I removed my gloves and mask and then turned to the surgical team. "When the patient comes to, tell him it was a Chechen who operated on him. Let the medical staff in the hospital know. For now, my thanks. It was a pleasure working with you." I turned and left.

Sometimes people come into your life just at a time when you most need them. We believe people are sent by Allah to help us. A friend introduced me to Natasha Petrovna, an English instructor at the University of Moscow and a very committed Anglophile. When she wasn't teaching at the university, she gave private lessons to children. Each summer she escorted a group of kids to England. Previously, she had gone to Chechnya as a translator with a group of foreign officials, so she was familiar with the conditions there. One day, Natasha asked me if I would like to visit some Chechen children in one of the Moscow hospitals. "These are very severe cases, amputees. Many are paralyzed. I take them toys and sweets," she said.

She handed me a brochure put out by the Kabzon Foundation, a charitable organization raising money for the young victims of the Chechen war and bringing them for treatment in Moscow. I immediately recognized four of the children in the photographs. They had been my patients at the Ninth City Hospital in Grozny. I was happy they were receiving treatment in Moscow.

That Sunday, Natasha and I took a taxi to the hospital. The familiar smell of antiseptic greeted me when I entered the children's section. Apples, bottles of kefir, pieces of bread, and saucepans of leftover soup covered the window ledges. Some of the children lay on their backs; others were propped up against pillows. As always, relatives supplied food and care. Several parents sat on the bed next to their children, spooning them food. Children without relatives relied on the kindness of friends—people like Natasha—who felt sorry for them.

I entered a small ward where two beds faced each other along the walls. A boy of about ten, called Ali, caught my attention. His father held a book in front of him while the boy read out the Arabic alphabet. The father, an unemployed policeman from Grozny, told me he believed in miracles. He refused to believe Ali's legs would be paralyzed for life. He thought that if he could get his son to Israel, doctors there would cure him. He knew of people who had gone there. I didn't say anything. Taking a child overseas for treatment costs thousands of dollars, and the results are always uncertain.

Over the next few weeks when I visited the hospital with Natasha, I watched Ali progress. Lying on his back, the boy could hold a pencil between his thumb and index finger despite his paralyzed fingers and managed to write on a tablet that his father fixed above his bed. I was amazed by Ali's ability to grasp and remember Arabic words. Soon he was reading whole sentences. It was unlikely that he would ever walk again, yet he threw himself into life with such enthusiasm. His spirit seemed miraculous to me.

Listening to Natasha's stories about England gave me the idea of learning English, and I asked her if she would give me lessons. I knew that English would help me as a doctor, that I would be able to read the latest medical literature from abroad, maybe have an internship at some hospital overseas. As a boy, I had a fantasy about learning the language. Later, when I traveled abroad for sports competitions, I heard it spoken often. Natasha didn't respond quickly to my request because she had a heavy teaching load, but a few days later she telephoned me and agreed. We met every day for the next three months.

Studying was therapeutic, taking my mind off things, although sometimes I had trouble remembering words. Since the concussion, my memory was not what it used to be. As a medical student, I had no problem learning Latin, but English stumped me. "Keep repeating the words," Natasha said.

She suggested that I go to London for three months to be in an

English environment. I hesitated at first because of my family, but things seemed to be quiet in Chechnya. My family had always been very supportive when I wanted to improve my skills. I could go and return before Zara's due date. In the meanwhile, Malika and Nana would give Zara all the help she needed with Maryam and Islam, one of the advantages of an extended family.

Natasha had contacts in the British medical community and arranged for me to stay three months with a couple who were both doctors. All I needed was a visa to England. I filled out all the application forms and solicited letters of recommendation from the Chechen Ministry of Health and a Chechen company that promised to pay my expenses. Finally, I received a call from the British embassy and went to its chancellery across the Moscow River in the shadow of the Kremlin early in the morning. I was taken to a special annex that was divided into numerous cubicles. A consular officer beckoned me into one of these interview rooms, where he began grilling me for hours. Why did I want to go to England? Why did I have to study English in England? How could England be sure I would not defect?

All my reassurances about having a wife and children in Chechnya, of being responsible for elderly parents, didn't seem to convince him. My letters of recommendation carried no weight. Clearly, Her Majesty's representative was afraid that either I was a terrorist or I would stay in Britain.

"England may be a very beautiful country, but believe me, I'm perfectly content in the ruins of my native Chechnya," I told him.

By 2 P.M., my patience had worn thin, and I tried to break off the interview. The officer told me to wait. After ten minutes, a higher-ranking officer appeared and informed me that permission was denied. He stated that I had not answered the questions convincingly. He stamped the refusal in my overseas passport. I had no way of knowing it then, but that British stamp would be a signal to other foreign officials, which would produce more difficulties for me in the months ahead.

I dropped the idea of further specialization in skin grafting because

I sensed the anti-Chechen feelings among my former colleagues. Despite the pleasant distraction of my English lessons, I began to feel alienated from society in Moscow, and I developed a fear of being alone. I chided myself for not going back to see the mullah a second time, but I decided against going home because I knew my family would be upset to see me in this depressed state. I found it too painful to continue my visits to the hospital to see the children. Sadness over the fate of my people suffocated me; all those broken lives. Sometimes when I was alone—and it is hard for me to admit this—I broke out crying.

Natasha tried to distract me by taking me to museums and plays, but they didn't help much. I thought about returning home to Chechnya.

"You can't go back to Chechnya," Natasha said one day when we were sitting in a café after a visit to the Pushkin Museum. "With your talent as a surgeon, you will die there. You should move your family to Moscow, get into research, and go abroad on exchange programs. You need to expand your abilities."

"My family and I belong in Chechnya," I replied. "The people there are sick and need a lot of help."

"Then you should get some medical treatment for yourself," she said. "You need to find a good psychiatrist."

"I don't need treatment," I said.

I was wrong. Things came to a head one night a month later, in September, while I was staying with my distant relative Muslim Zhabirov near the Medvedkovo metro station. Without warning, I began experiencing an overwhelming feeling of sadness. I awoke with a start at 2 A.M., as if an electric shock whipped through my head, searing my eyes like a camera flash. A second later, it disappeared, and I was plunged into darkness, even though I was fully conscious. My heart raced. Frightened, I leaped out of bed and turned on the light. I needed air. I had to walk. Throwing on a jacket, I started for the door, then stopped. No, I couldn't go out; my friends would hear me and ask questions. Besides, it was dangerous for a Chechen to be out on the street, especially at night. I could be arrested, held up for money, even beaten up. I went to the window and opened it.

The damp air hit my face. I leaned over the edge. The streetlights through the trees shone on the wet pavement. There was a steady drizzling. Dark clouds hung over the apartment building opposite. A car drove by, its lights picking out the puddles. It occurred to me it would be so easy to jump and end it all. My tortuous existence seemed so much worse than anything I had suffered during the war. Several people hurried past. After all the atrocities, all the corpses, all the wasted lives, wasn't it time to move on to the next life? Then I thought of Nana and Dada, Zara, Maryam, and Islam. It was my duty to protect them. I imagined my body lying on the street, people crowding around, the police cars with flashing lights. I pulled the window closed.

I lay down again, unable to find a comfortable position, twisting and turning. Every few minutes I shifted, throwing off the covers. I dozed but was awakened by another flash. I looked at the clock. It was now about 2:15 A.M. I was drenched in sweat. A terrible darkness enveloped me, as if all meaning had been drained from life. An eclipse of the soul. I jumped out of bed and returned to the window. Now I really wanted to jump. I opened the window and took a breath. Then something held me back. An inner voice said, "Don't do it! Don't!" Maryam, Islam, my unborn child—what would happen to them?

I closed the window and sat down. I picked up a newspaper and tried to read; the words blurred, and nothing made any sense. I grabbed a book, skimmed the pages but understood nothing. The minutes ticked by. It was 3 A.M., and I felt desperately alone.

I am deceiving myself, I thought. I've got to shrug off this world. Back I stumbled to the window, this time, determined. I opened it for the third time. Other thoughts began flooding my mind. The Koran says that to kill yourself is a great sin. Your soul will not be allowed into paradise. Killing myself would make terrible problems for my friends. The police would get involved; they would want to know why I did it. They would question my friends and relatives.

My death—my weakness, my unforgivable weakness—would cast suspicion on all our family.

I could not do that to my parents, to my wife and children. I closed the window. I knew I was in grave danger. I had seen suicidal patients. I had read about young Russian soldiers going mad or committing suicide when they returned home after the war with Chechnya. In the morning, I decided to call a Chechen friend who worked in the Russian Ministry of Health and ask for help.

"I must be hospitalized immediately, or I won't survive another day," I said.

My friend said he would arrange for me to have free treatment through the Moscow Health Department. Together we went to the hospital located in the south of Moscow. The chief doctor referred me to his deputy, a pleasant woman physician. She asked if I wanted a private room, but I told her I needed to be with other people. She placed me in a double room with Sergei, a young Russian who had suffered a nervous breakdown. Later, I learned from the nurses that he was a regular patient at the clinic. Apparently, he had suffered a brutal childhood with alcoholic parents. We didn't talk much. He spent most of his time reading books and magazines.

I did not inform my family about what had happened to me because I did not want them to worry. Furthermore, it was almost impossible to communicate with Chechnya. Finally, I got a message to them through an acquaintance from Alkhan Kala who worked as an attendant on the Moscow-Grozny train, a thirty-six-hour trip. I told them I would be in Moscow a couple more months, but that I was all right, and they should not worry.

I stayed in the clinic for forty-five days, beginning in the middle of September 1998, while they dosed me with tranquilizers and administered injections to thin the blood flow to the brain and improve the memory. Most of the time I slept. When I wasn't asleep, I attended sessions with the psychiatrist and the hypnotist. Neither helped. The psychiatrist told me I was suffering from post-traumatic stress disorder, the aftermath of war. The diagnosis wasn't exactly news to me. I could have told him that. Unlike the old mullah, the psychiatrist lacked the healing touch, and I had no faith in him. For healing to take place, a patient must have faith in his doctor. The only things that helped were the recorded sounds of trickling water or singing birds, which I sometimes listened to through earphones. Toward the end of my stay, I flushed the tranquilizers down the toilet and started going to the clinic's well-equipped gym. In the worst of times—even in the midst of shelling during the war—exercise was the only thing that really helped. When I put in several hours of lifting weights, my mood would gradually improve.

Being a patient at the hospital gave me no protection from harassment. Periodically, I went to a kiosk outside the gate to buy snacks and some tomato juice. Up would drive a police car. The scenario was invariably the same.

"You don't have a Moscow *propiska* [residence registration]," the policeman would say, examining the documents. "You live in Chechnya. You must have a registration to be in Moscow."

"I know, I know, but I'm being treated in the hospital. You see I am wearing hospital slippers and pajamas. If you don't believe me, check it out with the clinic."

"We'll check it out at the police station. We need to check your fingerprints to see if you're on the computer."

That was my cue; the lead-up to the bribe. One hundred rubles (about twenty dollars) was the going rate. I pulled the note from my pocket, scrunched it in my palm, and held out my hand to the policeman.

"All right, then. Go get your treatment!" the policeman said, shaking my hand and taking the money.

ANOTHER CHANCE ENCOUNTER changed my life. In the late afternoon, patients met their relatives in the hospital courtyard. Given good weather, it was a pleasant place to sit and talk. Benches edged the pathways, along with flowers and shrubs. One day, I found myself sitting next to an old Chechen man who was being treated in a different section of the hospital. We started talking. We talked about the war, the Russians, our health problems. I confided to him that I didn't think the treatment was doing me any good. He gave me a quizzical look.

"I know what can help," he began slowly.

"What?"

"Times are different now, and we are not tied down by the old Soviet restrictions. You could go abroad."

I thought at first he was going to suggest some foreign recreation, as others already had. But his advice went off in an entirely unexpected direction. He looked at me intensely. "The only thing that will help people like you," he said, "is the hajj. Mecca can help you . . . a pilgrimage to Mecca."

Chapter 14

Mecca

I WAS READY to try anything. Mecca changes people's lives, everyone said. In October, after forty-five days in the hospital, Musa Saponov drove me to the Saudi embassy to apply for the visa. As I had already discovered with the British, obtaining a visa was a bureaucratic obstacle course.

"Do you have an invitation?" A consular officer, dressed in a navy blue suit and tie looked at my passport.

I shook my head. It was hard to picture each of the millions of Muslims who went to Mecca needing an invitation and visa.

"We have to consult the chief consular officer," he said. "Come back in four days."

When I returned, a second consular officer asked why I wanted to go to Saudi Arabia.

"To go to Mecca, to undertake the hajj. It's on the application form."

"The foreign office in Riyadh makes these decisions; come back."

I came back. This time the consular officer frowned at me as if he had uncovered something unpleasant. "So why should we give you a visa if the British refused you one?" he asked.

My patience was running out.

"I want to go to Mecca. It's a holy spot, and every Muslim is obliged to go once in his lifetime on a pilgrimage. You don't have the right to deny me this opportunity. Are you not believers?"

That ended the impasse. On October 23, the embassy issued me a visa signed by the consul.

I wondered if the Saudis had given me a hard time because I was Chechen. Maybe they believed I had no right to make the pilgrimage to Mecca. There are Saudis who don't regard Chechens as true Muslims. Both Chechens and Saudis are Sunni Muslims, but the Saudi interpretation of Islam is fundamentalist and strict. Some of them say that people who don't practice their form of Islam are not real Muslims.

Normally, rituals are performed before a pilgrim leaves for Mecca. You must clear up debts, resolve quarrels, ask those you harmed for forgiveness. You must pay for all your expenses out of your own pocket or, at least, have a sponsor. In short, you must be absolutely pure before you depart so you can enter fully into the spiritual experience of Muhammad's birthplace. I didn't have time to return to Chechnya if I was to catch my flight and reach Mecca in time for the pilgrimage. Fortunately, I had no outstanding debts or quarrels.

A Chechen friend who lived in the United Arab Emirates put me in touch with a family in Saudi Arabia who had hosted many Chechen visitors to Mecca. They invited me to be their guest. As my departure date approached, I grew apprehensive, not knowing what awaited me. I recalled an unpleasant encounter I had with two Wahhabis—that is what we called the Muslims from Saudi Arabia and other Middle East countries who arrived in Chechnya to promote Islam after the war ended in 1996. One of them limped into my office at the hospital in Grozny with a festering leg wound. He was accompanied by a friend. Both wore beards, camouflage fatigues, and spoke Russian badly. After I had dressed the wound, one of them handed me several sheets of paper, printed in Russian, describing the requirement for women to be fully covered.

"We have different points of view," I said after reading the information. Their attitude irritated me. Each nation has its own customs and traditions. Our women like bright colors, and if you ordered them to wear veils and be covered from head to toe in black, they would revolt.

"But it's written in the Koran," he said in his heavy accent.

"If you want to tell me how to live, don't bother coming to my office again," I replied. "I don't need instructions on how to behave toward my parents and my sisters or how they should dress."

After the two left, I couldn't get them out of my mind. These so-called Wahhabis were beginning to cause problems in Chechnya. They claimed our Chechen traditions contradicted the Koran. We insist our children show respect to their elders by standing up when they enter the room and yielding their place. They asserted this respect was misplaced; only Allah deserved such reverence. We welcomed the humanitarian aid we received from Middle Eastern countries, but we did not like it when they told us our Islam was not the true Islam. For 400 years we have fought against people telling us what to do. The Communists told us God didn't exist, only the Communist Party. Of course, we didn't believe that either, and we worshiped in secret. People like Dada risked eight to ten years in prison for secretly instructing children in the Koranic texts.

I had been told that the Wahhabis offered young men what we considered large sums—from $100 to $200 a month—to join their movement, which distressed the elders, who ordered the Wahhabis out of the villages. Many young men joined solely to support their families.

As my departure loomed, I cast these concerns aside and focused on what lay ahead. For fourteen centuries, Muslims have journeyed to this desolate valley where the prophet Muhammad was born, hoping to renew their faith and find inspiration. I don't think people in the West realize how much Islam has in common with Christianity and Judaism. We believe in one God, acknowledge the Bible, adhere to Moses's Ten Commandments. We agree with the Jews that Jesus was an important prophet, although not the son of God. Islam's main difference is we believe that 500 years after the birth of Jesus our prophet, Muhammad, appeared with a new interpretation of how we should conduct our lives. Although I was familiar with the five pillars of Islam—belief, prayer, almsgiving, fasting, and pilgrimage—I was apprehensive about the pilgrimage because I didn't know Arabic. How foolish not to have taken advantage of Dada's knowledge! I always said I didn't have time.

On October 28, I boarded a flight to Amman, Jordan, where I would have a layover before flying on to Jedda, the Saudi city on the Red Sea nearest to Mecca. On the plane to Amman, I sat next to Rashid, a Tartar from Kazan, capital of Tatarstan on the Volga River. He was a good-natured fellow, wearing a crumpled suit and old Soviet-style shoes. He said he was married to a Russian woman and had two daughters who were married to Russians. His love of hard liquor became obvious shortly after the plane lifted off: He reeked of cognac. He offered me some, but I told him I didn't drink.

I asked Rashid if he was going to Jordan on business. "No, no," he said, to my surprise. "I'm on my way to Mecca, although my wife doesn't want me to go." As the flight progressed, we talked at length about the pilgrimage. At one point, he conceded he didn't know Arabic and never prayed. He shrugged and burst out laughing. "So what? Allah will accept me! Allah will see my desire and know that in my soul I am pure."

"If your wife realizes you are going to Mecca in a drunken state, she will disapprove even more," I said. "And another thing—if you continue to drink in any Arab country, you'll probably be arrested!"

He looked at me, uncorked the bottle, and said, "If that's the case, I better finish it all now." He upped the bottle and drained it. Both of us broke out laughing.

It was late in the afternoon when we stepped off the plane in Amman, and the heat took my breath away. Rashid and I decided to go into town and rest before catching the plane for Jedda early the next morning. Rashid didn't have money for a hotel, so I offered to pay for a room, but he refused. Then I offered to take a room for myself and share it with him, but again he refused. He said he would rest in the little park beside a hotel, a grassy area with flowers and several benches. Since Rashid was an older man, I felt it my responsibility to stay with him.

We sat down on a bench, talking and watching the people go by. I felt as though I had already entered another world, the world of Islam. Women in veils walked by, and then some without veils. Everywhere there were palm trees, but little grass, and much red dust. As a child, I had heard about Mecca, Muhammad's birthplace, and Medina, where the prophet was buried.

A slight breeze rustled the palms. Looking up at the sky and seeing the Big and Little Dippers reminded me I wasn't in another world. If my family in Chechnya looked up, they'd see the same stars. I marveled at the vastness. Already I felt better. I thought of Dada and of my grandfather. They had wanted to go to Mecca but never found the means to do so. Now I was about to fulfill their wish.

After sleeping for a few hours, Rashid and I went back to the airport very early the next morning and boarded the plane for Saudi Arabia. Our jetliner arrived in Jedda early in the morning. Even though it was only 5 A.M., local time, the heat was withering. Rashid wanted to stay with me, but I explained I was being met by family friends and could not invite him. We said our good-byes, and he wandered off by himself.

Getting ready for Mecca, with
Salakh Mutabbakani (right).

Salakh Mutabbakani, the son of my host family, met me outside the arrival hall. He was a tall, portly man dressed in white robes and Arabic headdress. He had learned Chechen from his mother as a child, so we could converse easily. His mother, Zakiya, was the grandaughter of an emigrant who had left Chechnya for Turkey and later settled in Jordan, where she was born. She was married to a prosperous Saudi who was a distant relative of the king. It was a relief to get into Salakh's air-conditioned car. As we drove toward his house, the sun rose over the white stone buildings of the city.

In the early morning light everything sparkled. Salakh's large white house was on a street lined with palm trees. Salakh showed me into a large reception room with gold molding on the ceiling. Zakiya welcomed me like a long-lost son, seating me on a low couch draped with oriental rugs. Sinking into the piles of cushions, I felt immediately at home. After light refreshments they showed me to their spacious guest quarters, outfitted with washbowl, bath and shower, and a huge closet full of clothes for pilgrims in all different sizes.

The following morning over breakfast, I talked with Zakiya, a successful watercolorist. She spoke a pure, prerevolutionary Chechen, uncorrupted by the Soviet words and expressions we so often use today. The Soviet ban on speaking our native language meant many of our people grew up speaking a fractured Chechen. "You live in Chechnya, and you don't even speak the language properly!" Zakiya joked. Later, I visited Zakiya's daughter Raghad and met her children, who also spoke pure Chechen, even though they had never been there. I was deeply impressed that the language was being passed down from generation to generation, and I promised I would stop using Russian words.

Zakiya told me how her grandparents had left Chechnya long before the Russian Revolution of 1917 under the "Mukhadjereen" policy of encouraging emigration to Turkey. Ironic. "Our family couldn't get into Turkey," Zakiya related, "but we managed to make our way to Jordan, where there was a Chechen community."

The day after I arrived in Saudi Arabia, Salakh took me to visit the

Me with Zakiya Mutabbakani, who put me up in Saudi Arabia.

local hospital, where I donned scrubs and watched doctors perform an appendectomy on a woman. The hospital was very well equipped and clean. There I was offered a job by a doctor, who had opened a hospital in the holy city of Mecca to treat the many people who suffer heatstroke, dehydration, or are crushed by the crowds. The doctor said he was very short on specialists and could use my expertise. The offer flattered me, but I wanted to return to Chechnya.

The next day, Salakh and I left for Mecca. He was well versed in the Koran and was my guide. "Don't worry," he reassured me, "many pilgrims can't read the Koran. You'll notice guides leading groups of pilgrims and reciting verses in Arabic. The most important thing is to have faith." He instructed me to wash thoroughly, take a shower, cut my toe- and fingernails. Then he gave me two white sheets to wrap around my body. Before setting off, we prayed.

We traveled the twenty-five-mile route from Jedda to Mecca by car, moving very slowly as the road was congested with buses, cars, trucks. People had traveled here from around the globe, many spending their life savings on the journey. Later, I learned that the pilgrimage to Mecca, called for by the Koran, had encouraged Muslims to become renowned traders and travelers in the Middle Ages. Dozens of guidebooks were written to assist pilgrims with the journey. In the fourteenth century, Ibn Batuta, sometimes called the Muslim Marco Polo, journeyed 75,000 miles after his pilgrimage, farther than anyone else in the world had traveled at that time. He then wrote an encyclopedia of Islamic practices around the world.

We left our car in the huge five-story parking garage outside the city and continued on foot, passing the white pillars that marked the sacred territory around the holy city, where the killing of animals, or even the crushing of a bee or an ant, is forbidden.

Salakh and I, along with thousands of pilgrims, made our way into the square in front of the Great Mosque with its seven towering minarets, an ocean of humanity from all over the world, united in one belief. Muscular black men carried legless invalids on their backs like babies. Other infirm people were transported on wooden chaises or advanced in wheelchairs along a specially designated path. We entered the Great Mosque through the Gate of Peace and proceeded to the huge inner courtyard. As I heard the Azan (call to prayer) by the muezzin fill the air, my spirits began to lift. In the center of this inner courtyard stood Islam's most sacred spot: the Kaaba, a massive cube about fifty feet on each side, almost entirely draped in black cloth. Near the top of the cloth were embroidered citations from the Koran in large gold letters. I was overcome with awe.

At the corner of one wall of the Kaaba, a black stone, about a foot and a half in diameter, rests within a silver cowling. This is the famous Stone of Paradise, which is believed to be the only surviving piece of Abraham's original shrine. The Kaaba is an object of special veneration to which Muslims turn in our daily prayers. Thousands of pilgrims all dressed in white began circling the Kaaba in a counterclockwise direction. People on the outside of the spiral moved slowly at first . . . once around, twice, three times. Each time Salakh and I edged a little closer to the Kaaba and the sacred stone. With each rotation, our chain of people moved faster and closer to the center. Four times around, then a fifth swing. Each time we passed closer to the stone, raising our hands, and chanting the Shahad in Arabic.

On the sixth revolution, the swirl of people became increasingly disorderly as pilgrims struggled to get close to the Kaaba. A policeman stood above the crowd on a large stone step near the corner of the building, trying to keep order as the pilgrims jostled to reach the Stone of Paradise. I braced myself, determined to reach the stone. The force of the pilgrims' bodies propelled me forward like a powerful tide. Friends had warned me you had to be in good physical shape to resist the crush, so before leaving the Moscow hospital, I spent time working out in its gymnasium and swimming pool. Would I be strong enough? No wonder a special hospital was needed here. I had heard that some Chechens had gone to Mecca only to die of a heart attack, or slip and be trampled underfoot.

I pushed forward, my heart pounding, now on the seventh and final swing. I braced my body against the revolving mass, elbowing my way forward. On the Kaaba a series of sturdy belts, placed about half a yard apart, were bolted to the wall to steady pilgrims on the final approach. I grabbed one, then another, as I edged to the corner of the building. Salakh was pushed aside, and I lost sight of him as he drifted into the crowd. But I kept moving in the right direction, convinced my sanity depended on kissing the sacred stone.

Grasping belt after belt, I slid along the rough stone blocks of the Kaaba wall as I guided myself toward the silver cowling. I thrust my head through the circular opening, managed a fleeting kiss, then touched the Stone of Paradise with my hand. It felt smooth as polished crystal and was slightly indented from the millions of hands that had rubbed over it before mine. I said a quick prayer before the crowd shot my body forward again.

I fell back in with the other pilgrims. I felt changed almost immediately. The blackness had lifted; my head emptied out, and I felt relaxed for the first time in many months. People who saw me afterward said my face had smoothed out; the stress lines dissipated, the underlying tension gone. I can't really explain it.

When we found each other again. Salakh looked at me. "You come for the first time, and you get all the way to the sacred stone! You've performed a miracle. You should be a happy man. The stone is from heaven."

He said he had been to the Great Mosque six times and had never got so near to the sacred stone. He said that didn't matter because the important thing was to do the hajj. Before leaving Mecca, I spent several hours in prayer, begging Allah for help for Chechnya, our people, my family.

Looking back, I realize that my pilgrimage to Mecca introduced me to more than just the holiest shrine in Islam; it introduced me to the history of my religion and the work of Arabic scholars. While growing up in the Soviet period, the only thing I knew about Islam was what Dada had passed on to me from the Koran. The Soviet regime was militantly atheistic, putting all religions under pressure to close down their churches and places of worship. But the Communists couldn't eradicate all religious believers, who often had to study and worship in underground settings. As a result of my hajj, I began asking people about the history of Islam, and later in the United States I found material on the Internet and saw videos on the development of Islam.

I hadn't realized that 100 years after Muhammad's death in 632, the Muslim Empire had expanded into Iran, Egypt, all of North Africa, Spain, and Portugal. The extent of this empire was even larger than that of the Roman. The Muslim expansion was finally stopped in France at the Battle of Tours in 732, but Islamic rule continued in the Iberian Peninsula, especially at Córdoba in Spain, for nine more centuries.

By the middle of the eighth century, when the Dark Ages began to engulf Europe, Baghdad was the intellectual capital of the world. At the famous House of Wisdom, scholars from around the globe—Jews, Christians, Muslims, Zoroastrians, and Buddhists—studied astronomy, medicine, engineering, architecture, and mathematics.

I hadn't known that the Muslim scholars had translated and preserved ancient Greek texts, which laid the foundation for the Renaissance. The Muslims brought paper back from China and used it to record their discoveries, and created libraries with hundreds of thousands of books, far more than the relatively small libraries in the monasteries of Europe. The widespread use of paper allowed the development of letters of credit—the world's first checks—which permitted merchants to buy and sell throughout the empire.

What really astounded me was the groundbreaking advances in medicine. For example, al-Zahrawi, a prominent surgeon of the tenth century, wrote a medical encyclopedia that was used in Europe until the seventeenth century. He described such procedures as ligature of arteries, cauterizing to control bleeding, tracheostomy, stripping of varicose veins, management of liver abscesses, removal of kidney stones, dental extractions, implantation of artificial teeth. He used gold threads to secure false teeth because other metals would tarnish and cause a reaction. Pioneering work in ophthalmology was done by Ali Ibn Isa, who wrote a classic book on diseases of the eye—trachoma, conjunctivitis, cataracts—and prescribed treatments. Ibn al-Haytham, considered the father of optics, described how human vision takes place. Al-Razi proposed that disease was spread by airborne organisms, and created isolation wards in his hospital in Baghdad.

With excitement, I read a translation of the medical code of ethics, written by al-Tabari in the tenth century, which I found on the Internet.

The physician ought to be modest, virtuous, merciful and unaddicted to liquor. He should wear clean clothes, be dignified, and have well groomed hair and beard. . . . He should not join the ungodly and scoffers, not sit at their table. He should select his company to be persons of good reputation. He should be careful what he says and should not hesitate to ask forgiveness if he has made an error. He should be forgiving and never seek revenge. He should be friendly and a peacemaker. He should not make jokes or laugh at the improper time or place.*

*Shahid Athar, M.D. *Islamic Medicine,* page 8 et. seq., http://islam-usa. com/im3.html.

What Al-Tabari said about the obligation to patients accorded with so much I had learned at the Medical Institute in Krasnoyarsk, and also from Dada. The Arabic scholars were familiar with the early Greek texts, so I imagine that al-Tabari had read what Hippocrates had to say on medical ethics. His formulation went like this:

[The physician] should avoid predicting whether a patient will live or die, only God knows. He ought not to lose his temper when the patient keeps asking questions, but should answer gently and compassionately. He should treat alike the rich and the poor, the master and the servant, the powerful and the powerless, the elite and the illiterate. God will reward him if he helps the needy. The physician should not be late for his rounds and his house calls. He should be punctual and reliable. He should not wrangle about his fees. If a patient is very ill or in an emergency, he should be thankful, no matter how he is paid. He should not give drugs to a pregnant woman for an abortion unless necessary for the mother's health. If the physician prescribes a drug orally, he should make sure that the patient understands the name correctly, in case he would ask for the wrong drug and get worse instead of better. He should be decent towards women and should not divulge the secrets of his patients.

Some people today argue that Islam is a force directed against science and technology, yet it was apparent to me from what I learned during and after my pilgrimage to Mecca that some of the greatest scientists of the past were Muslim. When I returned to Alkhan Kala, not only did I feel much better, but I had a renewed commitment to medicine and a determination to put tragedy behind me and move toward a better future.

Chapter 15

Rising Crime

SOON AFTER I returned to Moscow from Mecca, I flew home to be with Zara for the birth of our third child. My relatives were very excited to hear about Mecca, especially Dada, who had always dreamed of going there. I downplayed my hospitalization in Moscow, as I didn't want people to worry about me. After Mecca, I wanted to put that behind me. I felt myself to be cured. On November 25, 1998, Zara delivered a baby girl. We named her Markha. I was so relieved she was normal, as so many Chechen children were born with defects. Markha quickly became Dada's favorite. As soon as she could crawl, she pushed open the door to his room, then turned around so he could lift her on his knee and give her candy. The other happy event that year was Razyat's marriage to Alikhan, a Chechen businessman with a job in central Asia. Since so many people in Alkhan Kala were in mourning, the families did not hold the usual celebration and Razyat and Alikhan left almost immediately for Alma Ata, Kazakhstan. We were sad to see them leave, but there was very little work in Chechnya.

In March 1999, I decided to fly to Krasnoyarsk, hoping to persuade Hussein to return to Chechnya for good. I had bought a small house for him on our street. He was reluctant at first, but when he realized how much his continued presence in Krasnoyarsk bothered Dada and Nana, he finally agreed to move Rita and his son, Adam, to Alkhan Kala.

I had another reason for going to Krasnoyarsk. As a result of the shocks I had received to the head during the war, my memory had deteriorated, and I occasionally suffered terrible headaches. After doing a brain scan, the doctors said I was suffering from a narrowing of the blood vessels, resulting in an insufficient flow of blood to the brain. They said the disruption of blood circulation was affecting my memory, and they recommended a course of treatment to increase the flow of blood to the brain. I was seriously contemplating staying on in Krasnoyarsk for treatment when I received a panic call from Malika. "Did you ever submit your name for the title of Merited Doctor of Russia?" she asked.

"Yes," I said. In 1996, the government of Chechnya had submitted the names of five doctors, including mine, to the Russian Ministry of Health to be recognized as Merited Doctor of Russia, one of the high honors in the Russian medical field. I had filled out the forms and hand-carried them to Moscow myself.

"The government is bringing a criminal case against you for that. They say it is inappropriate for a Chechen to be honored by Russia because Russia is our enemy."

Needless to say, I was astounded.

"They want you at the prosecutor's office," Malika said. "They have appointed an investigator for special cases, Mokhdan Baskhanov, to handle the case."

At first, I thought there must have been a mistake. I could hardly believe this constituted a criminal matter. I had met Baskhanov, an educated man with a degree from the law school in Sverdlovsk. One of his grandfathers was from Makazhoi, as was mine. We belonged to the same clan, which meant we should treat each other like brothers. I forwent treatment and returned home in May.

The morning after returning, I went to the prosecutor's office in Grozny. During the war, bombs had destroyed the main building, and the office had moved into a former kindergarten, surrounded by burned-out residential apartments. I picked my way around the fallen bricks in the courtyard, skirted the swings and sandbox, and entered the first floor. The only furniture in Baskhanov's office was a simple table, a chair, and a six-foot-high brown, iron safe in one corner. He rose to his feet when I entered. A heavyset man of about forty, dressed in a dark suit and white shirt, he invited me to sit down. As is customary, we inquired after each other's families before getting down to business.

"The Maskhadov government has asked me to open a case against you because you want to receive an honor from our enemy," he said, putting a piece of paper into his typewriter.

"Since when have we doctors become politicians?" I replied. "We haven't killed anyone. We don't go around armed to the teeth, and we are not stealing oil." I tried to control my anger and keep my voice polite. "The government of Maskhadov should be proud of us. It's a big plus that Russia recognizes our doctoring and our work."

"The government thinks it is inappropriate, which is why we are bringing a criminal case against you."

I jumped to my feet and walked to the window overlooking the street. A few armed guards were passing. I felt deeply insulted. I had stayed in Chechnya throughout the war while Baskhanov had left for Russia. He had come back only after the cease-fire of 1996, and now *he* was accusing me of fraternizing with Russia!

I took a deep breath and returned to my seat. "I don't understand," I said. "Doesn't the Maskhadov government and your office have more important problems to solve? There are so many kidnappings and murders. People steal oil all the time. You should be solving those crimes, not concerning yourselves with harassing doctors."

Baskhanov returned to the typewriter and began tapping out something on the keys. "You can go now," he said, without looking up, "but I will be calling you back." I got up to leave. "We are going to clear up this case," he said in a condescending tone as we shook hands.

As I left, I wondered whether Baskhanov might have been seeking a bribe. Most likely, he wasn't receiving any salary. Few people were. Bringing false cases against innocent people was how people who worked for the prosecutor's office supported themselves. He knew I was a plastic surgeon, and assumed I was rich. I believe that he instigated the case behind the back of the chief prosecutor with the connivance of Vakha Aigumov, a field commander who had been rewarded with the position of deputy chief prosecutor despite having only a tenth-grade education.

During the first war, I had had a run-in with Aigumov which I could not forget. At a time when the Russians were shelling Alkhan Kala, Aigumov addressed a crowd of refugees from Alkhan Kala in neighboring Urus-Martan, pretending that his men had won a great victory in our beleaguered town. "We have killed three hundred Russians and destroyed one hundred tanks," he declared from atop a tank. I hated boasting about killing.

"Why are you telling people that?" I contradicted him. "I have just come from Alkhan Kala. No tanks have been destroyed, and Russian soldiers are looting everywhere." After that, I became his number one enemy. I had no doubt he wanted me behind bars when I discovered his involvement in Baskhanov's accusation. I felt disgusted by what I considered an appalling abuse of power at the prosecutor's office. If I had been Salman Raduyev, with a private army behind me, or a notorious criminal like Arbi Barayev, they wouldn't have dared touch me.

I resumed working at the Ninth City Hospital in Grozny, where I learned that the other four doctors who had been nominated for Merited Doctor of Russia were so intimidated that they denied filling out the forms. Over the last months, relations between Chechnya and Russia had become increasingly tense. Under mounting pressure, Dr. Salman Yandarov, the chief traumatologist of the republic who had observed my first big operation, even suffered a heart attack.

A few days after my meeting with Baskhanov, he sent for me, but I refused to go immediately. "I'll come later," I told his men. "Right now I have too many patients. They are lining up outside my office. The corridors are overflowing with sick children and old people who will die if I don't help them."

Around 3 P.M. that day, I did go to the prosecutor's office, but Baskhanov wasn't there. His assistant said he had taken his children to a martial arts tournament. I waited for a while, then left. I heard nothing for a few weeks; then a messenger from his office delivered another summons. I ignored it. Two weeks later, I bumped into Baskhanov at the inter-city telephone center. He and his three bodyguards waited for me to finish my telephone call, then accosted me when I came out.

"If you don't show up at the prosecutor's office at nine on Monday morning, I will send my men to arrest you." His tone was arrogant in front of his guards.

"You have no right to talk to me in that manner, and I don't intend to come again tomorrow to wait for you. I already came, and you were doing your private business. I have a lot of patients, and they are more important to me."

"If you don't show up on Monday, I'll send guards," Baskhanov repeated. "You'll come without your feet touching the ground."

"I'm not coming!" I said. "You've got no authority. Go catch Arbi Barayev; go catch Salman Raduyev! They are walking around town scot-free. You have no laws for them, but you have them for me."

I was too angry to worry about tact. He had attacked my honor and that of my family by inferring that I was fraternizing with the enemy. He was a bully who wanted a payoff, and I was not going to comply.

"Send your guards; we'll see who wins," I dared him.

Two days later, three guards from Baskhanov's office showed up at the hospital. They seemed embarrassed and said they wanted me to know they had no quarrel with me personally. But they warned me that if I refused to go with them, Baskhanov would send a posse for me the next day.

"Tell the investigator I'll be waiting for his men tomorrow," I replied.

That evening when I went home, I told Nana, Malika, and Zara about the ultimatum. I did not tell Dada because I knew it would upset him too much. Nana wanted me to go to Moscow and hide for a while, but I refused. If I hid, people would think I had done something wrong. This was a battle I was determined to win. Later that night, I visited my friend Suleiman. He headed the Presidential Guard, which had been formed to restore order by cracking down on kidnapping, narcotics, and money laundering. The guardsmen were former fighters, and I had treated many of them during the war. I told Suleiman what had happened. "Don't worry," he said, "we'll fix it."

The next morning, about 100 of Suleiman's fighters, armed with rifles and rocket-propelled grenade launchers, pulled up in jeeps outside the hospital. I went out to greet them. The size of the force took me aback.

"You don't need so many. We are not going to take the prosecutor's office," I said. "One jeep in the courtyard is enough; the rest of you stay outside."

I went inside and began working. As I was operating on a woman who had fractured her jaw in a traffic accident, I heard a commotion in the corridor. I could hear someone shouting "Can't you see he's operating?" Moments later, ten or fifteen of Baskhanov's armed guards burst into the operating room. "Weren't you warned I was operating?" I shouted at them. "Get out of here!"

A group of my Chechen fighters came in, and one of them said, "Let's go outside. We can settle things there between ourselves. Don't bother Khassan. He's busy operating." After they and Baskhanov's men left the operating room, I finished setting the woman's jaw; then I went over to the window and looked out over the courtyard. Four military jeeps were parked in the lot on the far side of the hospital grounds. The investigator's men stood in a clump in the middle of the open area, while Suleiman's brigade encircled them. The voices drifted upward. I leaned forward to hear better.

"If you so much as touch a single hair on his head, we'll level your office with our rockets!" one of the fighters shouted. Then a chorus of voices:

"He's gone through the war!"

"He came to Bamut to treat us!"

"So we are all ready to die for him!"

Outnumbered, Baskhanov's men withdrew.

By now my case had become a cause célèbre. Everyone discussed it.

People in the prosecutor's office took sides. Baskhanov must have realized that things were getting out of hand. He had already appealed to the Ministry of Health, then to the chief doctor at the hospital, asking them to fire me, but they refused.

Three days later, two young men in dark suits, white shirts, and ties waited for me outside the entrance of the hospital. They explained that my presence was required at the prosecutor's office. There wouldn't be any problem, they said. I told them I was busy with patients for the next three days, but that I would be there on Wednesday.

Before going, I took the precaution of seeing a lawyer and drawing up an affidavit requesting that my case be assigned to another investigator.

When I arrived, there were several people gathered in the corridor outside Baskhanov's office, presumably waiting for the confrontation. After greeting Baskhanov politely, I sat down. "Listen, you have lost the case," I said. "Drop it. Otherwise you will be humiliated. Already people are joking about it."

Baskhanov jumped up from the desk, pulled a gun from his holster, and waved it in the air. Then he moved over to me and pressed the barrel of the pistol to my forehead. "If the Russians want to honor you," he shouted, "it means you're working for them. You're a traitor! You are guilty of insubordination and disrespect for the prosecutor's office."

I controlled my anger. "Shoot me if you want. I've been through everything. I've already been beaten and shot at."

Baskhanov lowered the gun and slammed his fist on the desk. He ordered the guards to remove me from his office. For several hours I stood in the corridor. Friends passed and asked what I was doing there. "Just standing," I said.

By now, I sensed that Baskhanov wanted to save face. He knew that journalists would get hold of the story and accuse him of abuse of power. He also knew I had operated on Raduyev, and feared I might call on him for help. Suleiman's brigade had frightened the leadership of the prosecutor's office.

After standing in the corridor for several hours, I was summoned to the office of the chief prosecutor, an experienced man, with a good reputation, for whom I had respect. He invited me to sit down. "Do you realize what kind of situation you have placed the prosecutor's office in?" he said.

"No, I don't know."

"I have only one request to you," he said. "Apologize to the investigator; then we will release you."

"No," I said, stubbornly, "I am not going to apologize to anyone. No one has the power to order my arrest without demonstrating that I have committed a crime, that I killed someone, kidnapped someone, or siphoned off oil."

He tried to persuade me by telling me that his deputy, Vakha Aigumov, was now supporting my release.

"Tell Vakha that I don't need his help either," I shouted. "You have arrested me. Now put me in prison."

The chief prosecutor said that he would take the matter to a higher level and that, meanwhile, I was free to go.

The criminal case against me finally was put aside. President Maskhadov declined to sign off on the proposal that we five doctors be recognized as Merited Doctors of Russia. Still, it always seemed to me ironic that the Russian government, in this case, treated me with greater respect than my own Chechen leaders.

IN JUNE OF 1999 my old friend Ruslan, who had been instrumental in negotiating with the Russians to save Alkhan Kala, was murdered. At the end of the first war, he had given up his post as chairman of the local council, saying he could carry on no longer because of lawlessness. He and his wife, Malizha, were driving out of town. A vehicle containing masked men had overtaken their car, swerved in front, forcing Ruslan to brake sharply. Then they forced him from his car and drove off with him, leaving Malizha unharmed. She sounded the alarm immediately.

The whole republic began looking for him. He was a well-known and respected figure. His picture appeared on television; friends begged for his release. People collected money for the ransom, but no one came forward to claim it.

Three weeks after Ruslan disappeared, I arrived home after a long day at the hospital in Grozny to be met by my brother Hussein. He was distraught as he recounted how he had found Ruslan's corpse while driving home that day with a carpenter, who was rehanging a door in my apartment in Grozny. "I glanced in the side-view mirror and spotted these two legs poking out from behind an oil drum on the shoulder of the road," Hussein said. "The body lay facedown in high grass. His wrists were pulled behind the back, lashed with wire."

Hussein and the carpenter eased the body over. "It was unrecognizable. The face was crawling with maggots," Hussein said, "the skin was all black, smelling so bad I wanted to throw up."

Hussein and the carpenter lifted the body into the back of the truck and transported it to the mosque. They laid out the remains on a carpet under a sheet in the courtyard outside the entrance.

"The body must have been buried, then dug up again, and dumped beside the road," Hussein continued. "There was earth in the hair and pockets."

Hussein said someone had sent for Ruslan's wife, Malizha. A crowd had gathered in front of the mosque to watch the tall woman with the long, blond braid down her back enter the courtyard flanked by several women. She approached slowly, as though frightened to lift the sheet covering the body.

A few feet from the corpse, she stopped, then let out a shriek. "The socks!" She focused on the feet. "Those are the socks he was wearing." She lifted a corner of the sheet. "Those are the trousers!" The two women on either side of her tightened their grip on her arm and led her away weeping.

Ruslan's male relatives removed the body to his house for the ritual washing before burial by a volunteer familiar with the Koran. This is a difficult job, especially if the body is in a state of putrefaction. The corpse is washed twice, as specified in the Koran—unless the person died in battle. In that case, the person is considered a martyr whose body may be immediately consigned to earth. After the ablutions, the body is wrapped in a white shroud for burial. Chechen families keep a bolt of linen cloth in their houses, knowing that the Koran warns that death is inescapable and you should always be prepared for it. The shroud is wound several times around the body, leaving the face open for viewing, but Ruslan's face was so disfigured it was kept covered.

I rushed to Ruslan's house. I couldn't bear to think that the bloated remains wrapped in linen were those of my friend. Ruslan had been my close friend and steadfast source of help and advice. And now he was gone, leaving Malizha and four children. Recently, Ruslan had seemed demoralized, saying that he was waiting for better times. We avoided talking politics. That's all people ever talked about: armed gangs, shootings, kidnappings, and the latest lies from Moscow. I couldn't stand it after a hard day's work. So we reminisced about old times, how we pulled tricks on Adlan, how in Krasnoyarsk, when Musa wanted to entertain a girl, he stole the champagne and chocolates that I kept as gifts in a suitcase on top of my wardrobe.

Ruslan and I agreed we would probably have to wait a long time before things returned to normal. President Maskhadov was a decent enough man, but he seemed powerless against the criminal gangs or the field commanders with their private armies. He failed to take draconian measures, such as arresting and trying the criminals, apparently fearing civil war. I came to regret that my old classmate Shamil Basayev hadn't become president. He was clearheaded, honest, and possessed the toughness required to impose order. We needed a strong hand.

As one of the most respected men in the region, Ruslan was mourned for two weeks, starting with the funeral the day after his body was found. People came from all over Chechnya. Cars blocked the road for half a mile. In the end people got out and walked. The body was conveyed by open truck, first to the mosque for the prayer for the dead, then to the cemetery. A rug was wrapped around the body. A black bourka, or shepherd's cloak of boiled wool, lay over the rug to ward off evil spirits. The family elders stood in the back of the open truck around the body.

A second truck, filled with religious singers, followed. They chanted the Declaration of Faith: *"La ilaha illallah Muhammadan Rasulullah"* (There is no God but Allah; Muhammad is his prophet). A long procession of cars followed the chanters. A funeral is a community affair with us. All are welcome to attend even if they didn't know the deceased.

At the cemetery, Ruslan's two brothers undid the white ties that kept the rolled rug around the body, pulled the rug gently away, and slid the body into the grave. In the grave, two elders eased the body into a niche, carved lengthwise into the earthen wall, placing the head to the north, and feet pointing south toward the Kaaba in Mecca. They worked under the bourka that was spread over the grave opening.

Finally, one elder emerged from under the bourka, while the other placed the white ties alongside the corpse and closed up the niche with wood planking before climbing out. The mullah said a brief prayer. Ruslan's father, followed by his brothers, shoveled dirt into the grave, then handed the shovel to the other mourners to take their turn.

There followed a three-day period—the Tezyat—during which people offered condolences to the relatives. Naturally, I went to visit the family. So many people were waiting that I stood in the street for a good while. The male relatives and town elders gathered under the awning of the outdoor summer kitchen, while the women remained inside the house. When it was my turn, I made my way with four or five other people toward Ruslan's father and brothers, who stood receiving the guests.

"May Allah bless him, make him glorious in the next life, and forgive him all his sins," I said in Chechen, following the tradition.

Afterward, the guests asked Ruslan's female relatives to make an appearance. As men are not allowed to be in a room with weeping women, Ruslan's mother and wife came into the yard with several other female relatives. Sadness flooded over me as I saw Malizha's tears.

On the fourth day—the day after the Tezyat—came the communal feast, which we call the Sagh'a in Chechen. People threw open their houses. Over this mourning period, the men had slaughtered two sheep and a cow, boiled the meat in large cauldrons in the open air, and distributed it to the mourners. The unconsumed portion—amounting to the greatest part—was later distributed, along with packets of sugar and sweets, among village orphans and the poor. Such benevolence, we believed, would be noted by Allah and would ease the passage of Ruslan's soul into paradise.

In the afternoon, a delegation of Muslim students, or *mutalibs*, came from the mosque and said a prayer in the courtyard. Then their leader, the *tourk*, chanted, "*La ilaha illallah, La ilaha illallah . . .*" The men began to form a circle, walking slowly at first, then picking up speed as the chanting of the *tourk* swelled, louder and louder. Faster and faster the men swirled to the mesmerizing rhythm of the *zikr* dance, transporting them into a state of spiritual ecstasy.

As I watched the *zikr*, memories flowed through my mind. I remembered how Ruslan and I had negotiated with the Russians. I remembered those times I had visited Ruslan on the way back from work: Malizha rushing to the kitchen, putting on the kettle for tea, mixing the batter for *lochmash* (fried pastry puffs), which we ate with dollops of sour cream. Out of the corner of my eye, I saw Ruslan's cousin slip away from the crowd, hide his face against a wall, and sob, his shoulders shaking.

Days later, when I visited Malizha to see if I could help her, she told me more about the abduction.

"I had warned him about a strange car that kept driving past our house," she said as she poured tea. "Sometimes the car just sat there watching the house. Once I got a look at the man driving and the other in the front seat. They weren't from Alkhan Kala. I had never seen them before. I warned Ruslan." Her eyes filled with tears, and she turned away.

I waited for her to continue. She described how they had taken the back road out of town, where there wasn't much traffic, when the car with the masked men stopped them.

"I began to scream, and the men pointed a gun at me. They said they would kill me. Ruslan said, 'Don't scream. I'll go with them.' He was frightened they would kill me, so he went. He never had time to pull out the pistol he carried." He didn't resist.

WE NEVER FOUND out who had murdered Ruslan, though most people guessed it was Arbi Barayev, on whom I had operated during the war in 1995. Barayev was a born killer, and his men were desperados with blood vendettas proclaimed against them for murder. They joined Barayev for protection against the avengers in an endless cycle of violence.

Looking at Barayev, you would find it hard to believe he was responsible for so many kidnappings and murders, including the four foreign telephone engineers whose severed heads were found at the side of the road in late 1998. He was a handsome man in his midtwenties, with refined features, always well dressed in clean fatigues. He owned a stable of expensive foreign cars, had several wives, and moved around with an escort of twenty to thirty guards. Everyone assumed that he was in the pay of Russian intelligence. "I work for whoever pays," he was reported to have said.

Barayev claimed to be religious, and during the war he grew a beard. However, nothing would convince me that a killer like him, who had caused so much suffering, was a true Muslim. I viewed him and his followers as opportunistic thugs who exploited Islam for their own purpose, and that purpose was power and wealth. He was an insult to our faith.

Barayev was popular with his men, but I think the war had conditioned him to kill. Then drunk on money and power, he couldn't stop.

The elders failed to curb his behavior. They begged him to leave town; his presence incited reprisals from the Russians. His relatives denounced him, which usually happens when someone refuses to obey the elders. The family announced in the courtyard of the mosque that if anyone killed him, they would relinquish all claims. There would be no blood revenge.

For a relative to go bad brings terrible shame to a family. I will never forget how one man confessed to me why he had killed his own son. This patient was fifty years old but looked like an old man with gray, lined skin, as if the lifeblood had drained out. He had been hit by shrapnel, and while I dressed his wounds, he told me the story. His son had become a heroin addict. The boy preyed on the villagers. I recalled that once he knocked on our door and, lying, told Nana that I had sent him to collect 500 rubles (about 150 dollars). She handed over the money, and he was gone.

"The elders ordered me to control him. They announced it at the mosque," my patient said. "I tried everything. I tied him to the bed and kept him in his room." The man's voice cracked as he spoke. "The villagers were demanding that I remove him, but where could I take him? What could I do? I had no way out. I shot him. It was the most difficult thing I have ever done."

This happened at a time when there was no rule of law in our society, and the central government was impotent, weak. If prisons, psychiatric hospitals, or treatment centers had existed, maybe the son could have been saved. But everything had been destroyed. No one in the village condemned the father. When the family elders sanctioned the killing, they did it to protect the community. There was already too much chaos.

"Allah will forgive you," I said to my patient.

Hearing my patient's story, I thought a lot about what makes some people go bad. War does terrible things to people not only physically but mentally, too. It also reveals each person's true character. I believe cruelty and compassion exist to varying degrees in every human being.

But in extreme circumstances, some people display incredible compassion and heroism, others cruelty and cowardice. Some Chechens, like Barayev, were born bad; others were pressured by the Russians and had no way out—*collaborate with us, or we'll put you in a filtration camp or kill your family.* I cannot even blame Chechens who collaborated with the Russians, though it makes me ashamed and sad when I think about it.

Part 4

The Second War

Chapter 16

War Again

B Y T H E M I D D L E of the summer of 1999, it was becoming clear that peace was wishful thinking and that sooner or later Russia would attack again. The signs were there: Russian troops were gathering along the Chechen borders, and Russian planes dropped bombs on what the Russian military spokesmen called "bandit-formation camps" around the republic. President Maskhadov seemed incapable of reining in the radical commanders or arresting gangsters like Arbi Barayev, or persuading Khattab, the radical field commander from Saudi Arabia, to leave Chechnya.

Adding to the unrest, the local police in the neighboring province of Dagestan were launching a campaign against Islamic extremists, forcing them into Chechnya, where anti-Maskhadov groups and criminal gangs welcomed them. The Islamic authorities in Dagestan, threatened by radical Islamists themselves, supported the crackdown. Earlier, many Wahhabi radicals, along with Dagestani opposition groups, had fled into Chechnya and set up operations in the town of Urus-Martan, their idea being eventually to overthrow the pro-Russian government of Dagestan and create an Islamic confederation in the North Caucasus.

Once more, fear gripped the republic. People began hoarding food. Many fled and sent children to relatives. I began dropping by the wholesale food market and picking up 100-pound bags of flour, sugar, and large boxes of macaroni. At the same time, I built up my stocks of basic medical supplies like lidocaine, surgical thread, and Polyglukin. I couldn't find a surgical saw and drill, so I would have to perform amputations and trepanations (holes bored into the skull to relieve pressure from swelling) with ordinary carpenter's tools, which were hard to keep clean and sterile.

Not knowing when Russians would attack put everyone on edge. Dada stayed glued to his radio. The only thing that appeared to distract him was little Markha, who toddled through to his room each morning, asking to be lifted on his knee. Nana, Zara, and my sisters became nervous, especially Malika, who lapsed into depression every time she saw the ruins of her beloved Grozny. The bombing panicked Hussein and Rita, who were not used to it. The slightest sound made them whisk Khava and Adam off into the cellar. It would take a while for them to tell where an attack plane was headed by the speed and sound of its engines.

Malika wanted us to go to the neighboring republic of Cherkessiya, buy a house there, and wait out the war. "They don't treat Chechens badly," she said of the Cherkess. We thought about leaving, but it wasn't practical. Nana said she couldn't leave the animals. And I knew many people would be depending on me for medical care when the war started. We decided to stick it out.

BY NOW, KIDNAPPING had reached epidemic proportions. Gangsters like Barayev, in partnership with Russian security services, made millions from ransoms and selling the corpses of the people they had murdered back to their relatives. When the *kontraktniki* signed up to fight in Chechnya, the Russian military promised bonuses. But the army was broke. By all accounts, military commanders gave the mercenaries freedom to loot and kidnap. The outside world heard about the kidnapping of journalists like Andrei Babitsky, a Radio Free Europe correspondent, or a Russian MVD officer like General Gennadi Shpigun, but never about the Chechens who were victimized 80 percent of the time. Back in June, the Chechen public had demanded that Maskhadov name the kidnappers and declare a war against them. He did nothing. The elders were beside themselves, addressing crowds out-side the mosque after Friday prayers and going on radio and television, urging people to stop the kidnapping.

Family and friends warned me, "If a guy wears a tie, builds a large house, and is a plastic surgeon, everyone assumes he is rolling in money. How can you drive around by yourself at night? You should carry a gun. You should have bodyguards. You should leave Chech-nya!" Early on, I had decided that I couldn't live my life worrying about being shot or kidnapped. I refused to walk around with body-guards or carry a gun. At the hospital we had only one gun, which we borrowed from the local police. The longer I had avoided death, the more fatalistic I became. As with most things, Allah decides.

Once I thought I had been kidnapped: At 2 A.M., someone ham-mered on the outside gate. When I opened it, I did not recognize the bearded man dressed in fatigues. A full moon illuminated everything, and on the other side of the street I could see a military jeep with three men inside. "We have a wounded comrade at the Ninth City Hospital," one of them said. "We were told you were a specialist. We need your help."

I told them to wait while I dressed and collected my things. By this time, Nana was up. "Are you sure it is safe to go? You don't know who they are," she said as I went out the door. I shouted not to worry.

The three fighters in the jeep didn't get out to greet me or introduce themselves when I crossed the street. Odd behavior for Chechens, I thought. They usually say hello. The bearded fighter pointed to a front seat. I got in, and he sat in the driver's seat, gunned the engine, and the jeep shot forward, tires screeching. The men in the backseat didn't address me but spoke together in low voices. The needle of the speedometer hovered around sixty miles an hour, with the driver swerving and braking to avoid the potholes in the road. I held on tight and braced myself against being thrown into the windshield. At the ap-proach of the military checkpoint at the edge of Alkhan Kala, the dri-ver accelerated. He's running the checkpoint, I thought. This is it. I'm being kidnapped.

The needle of the speedometer shot up to seventy-two miles an hour. A guard at the post stepped into the road, then jumped back, never raising his gun. The kidnappers often worked hand in glove with the Russian military. My first thought now was how to behave. Don't let them see any fear, I told myself. Don't anger them. Keep calm. My heart pounded against my ribs, and I took a deep breath.

The words of my judo coach before a match raced through my mind. "Center yourself." Without closing my eyes, I prayed. "Please, Allah, don't let this be a kidnapping."

The idea of another detention scared me. Memories of the pit haunted me. Images flashed before my eyes: my picture on television with the other abducted victims; relatives and friends begging for my release on the air; my patients collecting ransom money. Then I thought of my patients: the old man with the massive gash on his hip, from which I drained gobs of yellowish, foul-smelling pus everyday. And what about the three old men with urinary blockages who needed their catheters changed? Or the twelve-year-old boy with the wound on the side of his head from an antipersonnel mine? I needed to check for purply red blotches, indicating the onset of infection. If sepsis set in, he could be dead in five days. I was so busy making a mental inventory of my patients that I didn't see the jeep had turned onto the street toward the Ninth City Hospital. This was not a kidnapping after all. I sank back in the seat and let the tension drain from my muscles.

At the hospital, I reassembled the wounded fighter's shattered jaw while his comrades smoked outside the operating room. Later, driving me home, they broke their silence, telling me how amazed they were that I had agreed to get into the jeep with them. I didn't tell them how terrified I had been.

I BECAME CONVINCED of Moscow's role in the kidnapping business when Barayev's thugs tried to arrange an abduction of Dima Belovetsky, a Russian journalist friend of mine. Dima worked for the Russian monthly magazine *Ogyonok* and often came to Chechnya. My friend and neighbor Musa Muradov, the editor of an independent Chechen newspaper, *Groznenskii Rabochii*, had introduced us. Dima had been a judo fighter before becoming a journalist. It turned out we had fought in the same competitions, though I didn't remember that until I saw his picture in my photo album. He had a distinctive stance, crouching forward like a lion ready to pounce. Since retiring from athletics, he had put on weight, which is why I didn't recognize him at first in my living room over tea. He pressed me about my operation on Raduyev. I didn't want to tell him, but in Chechnya when a friend makes a request, it is difficult to refuse. I even showed him x-rays and persuaded Raduyev to give him an interview. To my distress, he published a huge article about the operation, which certainly didn't endear me to the Russian authorities. In the summer of 1998, he arrived in Chechnya, seeking an interview with Shamil Basayev and Khattab. As always, he dropped by my house. Zara prepared dinner, and we sat around talking all evening. We were about to go to bed when we heard banging on the gate.

When I opened the door, I found six men outside. I immediately recognized them as members of Barayev's gang I had seen driving around the village in their latest-model foreign jeeps.

"You've got a guest here?" one of the men said out of Dima's earshot. "How would you like to earn some money? Hand him over. We'll give you five thousand dollars." In my opinion, Barayev's men were carrying out a Russian assignment to put a chill on journalists reporting independently from Chechnya.

My anger rose. "How could you come to my house and ask such a thing? He's my guest."

"There could be more money later."

"Over my dead body, and my clan will retaliate if you touch my guest! Come back here, and I will shoot you all!" I shouted back.

"We were just jesting," they said when they saw how angry I became. But I knew they weren't joking. Underneath they were deadly serious.

"Tell Arbi not to send such envoys to me anymore. Now get out!"

I didn't want to alarm Dima because he was my guest, so I told him that some guys had just dropped around with a medical question. The whole incident made me ashamed. It seemed that whenever a foreigner or Russian journalist came to Chechnya, someone tipped off the kidnappers. This information could only have been obtained from the security services. How better to prevent humanitarian workers or journalists coming to our country than to kidnap a few? Kill a few? Little by little we were being isolated from the international community, which until now had been more or less sympathetic to our bid for independence.

ON AUGUST 2, 1999, legendary Chechen commander Shamil Basayev made what most people, including myself, considered a fatal mistake. With a force of about 2,000 men, he attacked Dagestan, which was teetering on the edge of chaos as major ethnic groups, religious extremists, and criminal gangs struggled for power. Since Dagestan received some 80 percent of its budget from Moscow, it did Russia's bidding, launching a vicious counterattack against the Islamic extremists. I was surprised that Basayev, who wasn't an Islamic extremist, would have made such a miscalculation. Five percent of Basayev's force were Chechens; the rest were the Dagestanis who had fled their province during the crackdown and now hoped to return with his help. Basayev had been led to believe that antigovernment factions in Dagestan would support him. However, he and his men ended up retreating to Chechnya on September 15.

Everyone criticized Basayev. Later, when the leader of the Dagestan opposition group ended up in Moscow, we all concluded that he had been paid off by Moscow to deceive Basayev, thus giving the Russians an excuse to move their troops into Chechnya. Once again the Kremlin had played its "divide and rule" card, pitting one faction against another, thus preventing a united front.

After Shamil Basayev's assault on Dagestan, any hope of avoiding war dissipated. By now I think most people didn't even care about independence anymore. All we wanted was to get on with our lives, but war became inevitable after the bomb explosions in Moscow and other cities. The first car bomb went off in Manezh Square at the end of August, killing one person and wounding several others. This was followed by the explosion at a Russian military barracks in Buinakask, killing sixty-two Russsians, including women and children. Chechen terrorists were blamed for both.

The next two bombings were horrendous, blowing up two large apartment buildings in Moscow, killing some 300 people in all. I had just finished operating when one of the doctors came to the door with the news.

"Something terrible has happened." His face was pale. "It's on television." I washed up, then hurried down the corridor to the men's ward. People pressed into the small room, standing on chairs, perching on beds to see the small television mounted on the wall. It was like a scene from hell: ambulances racing through the streets, policemen, firemen, and rescue workers stumbling through the rubble with little hope of finding the bodies, weeping civilians in their nightclothes.

I closed my eyes, feeling nauseous. There was no doubt Chechens would be blamed, and I feared for friends and relatives in Moscow. At that time some 200,000 Chechens lived in Russia, 100,000 in the Moscow metropolitan area. I decided to try to call Abek Bisultanov. In the street people hurried toward the telephone station. I grabbed my car and drove to an inter-city telephone center outside Grozny, hoping for a shorter wait.

"Baiev!" The telephone operator announced after I had stood in line for two hours. "Booth number four."

I entered the booth and picked up the phone. The operator connected me to Abek's number in Moscow. When he answered, I could hardly hear for the hysterical shouting from the adjacent booths. The woman's voice rose to a frenzied pitch in the adjoining booth: "What do you mean he has disappeared? When did they take him?"

I clamped my fist over my ear to cut out the noise.

"This place is teeming with uniforms!" Abek was saying, at least that's what I think I heard. The line was full of static. "Nineteen policemen for every Chechen," he shouted. "It's a pogrom! They are rounding us up. Police are blocking railroad stations, airports, and roads in and out of Moscow. Chechen businesses are being dissolved and . . ." The telephone went dead.

As I drove home that evening, Dada's words echoed in my head: "They want to get rid of us." I learned later that in one day the Moscow militia checked 26,561 apartments, 7,908 storage areas such as basements and semibasements, 180 hotels, 415 hostels, 548 places of entertainment. Taking part were 14,500 employees of the GRU, the military intelligence service, and 9,500 members of the Russian Interior Ministry's armed forces. They worked twelve hours a day with no days off. For almost six months, Abek didn't leave his apartment, relying on a few kindly Russian neighbors to bring him food. His money ran out because he could no longer travel to Poland to buy cars. Moscow's crackdown on Chechens was good business for the local police, inflating the average bribes from $50 to $100. Chechen males sewed up their pockets to prevent the police from planting narcotics on them.

Friends described the scene on the streets of Moscow when the police spotted a Chechen. "On the ground, legs apart!" Then the arresting officer summoned a passerby. "Citizen, we need you to witness what we have found on this criminal" would be the next request. Then, like a conjurer pulling a rabbit out of a hat, the officer would withdraw a packet of marijuana, heroin, or explosives from under the suspect's waistband. Some 3,000 Chechens were arrested in Moscow alone, including doctors, professors, and teachers. Clearly, it was now out of the question for me to travel to Moscow to buy much-needed medical supplies. I would have to make do.

For Chechens to have committed these horrendous crimes didn't make sense to anyone, at least in Chechnya. Why commit crimes or terrorism at a time when the international community was beginning to show sympathy for our cause? Several Russian journalists asked the same question. An article in *Moskovskíí Komsomolets* two days after the bombings hinted that the Russian security police had actually planted the bombs. The article noted that the explosions looked as if they had been cribbed from a Soviet secret police manual and planted by someone trained in their methods.

I remain convinced that the Russian security services blew up those apartment buildings to prepare the Russian people for war, to influence public opinion, and to lay the groundwork for the national election of March 26, 2000, which resulted in Vladimir Putin becoming president. Of course, I can't prove anything. It seems unfathomable to kill innocent civilians for political ends, though a reading of history would tell you that it has happened often enough in Russia.

BY SEPTEMBER 1999, the Russians began bombing Grozny again. Every day it increased, far heavier than anything we had seen during the first war. Finally, by the middle of the month, our minister of health ordered us to close the Ninth City Hospital and return to our villages to set up medical centers there. I packed up my operating table and some supplies and drove to Alkhan Kala. Several doctors and nurses said they would join me there.

On Friday after prayers, I mounted a platform in the courtyard of our mosque and appealed once again to the people for help. "We'll restore the old bombed-out hospital building, but I can't do this without your help," I told them. "We need volunteers to mend the roof, reconstruct and paint walls, rebuild the toilets. We need everything: beds, bedding, cheesecloth, bandage material, any medical supplies."

When I descended from the platform, a tall middle-aged man with graying hair was waiting for me. Nuradi Isayev was a revered figure in town, a man with a knowledge of all the religious rites associated with the dying; in short, the equivalent of an undertaker. No one paid him for his services. Preparing people for the next world was his private mission.

He had been employed for years at the DOK wood-processing plant, before it was forced to close down. Now he said to me, "Let me organize security for the hospital. I'll find reliable people. We'll guard the hospital and make sure that everyone obeys the rules for keeping the place clean."

He was married with two sons: Akhmed, the older one, had a job as a security guard for a factory in Grozny; Zelim, the younger one, was ten years old. During the first war, a bomb blast threw Zelim off the roof of their house. He broke both his arms, which were never properly set. As a result, they were abnormally short when the bones mended. I always swore that as soon as the fighting stopped I would find treatment for the boy.

Once again the townspeople rallied. They delivered sheets, blankets, pillows, items saved over a lifetime for their children's marriages. There were more volunteers than I could use. The most important piece of equipment at the hospital was the generator. Zaurbek Aslanbekov, our volunteer electrician, had acquired an old military generator from a neighbor who had bought it from a Russian officer when he left Chechnya in 1996. It was far larger than we needed, and guzzled fuel. If ever there was a temperamental piece of equipment, it was this generator. Zaurbek kept a collection of broken-down generators in his little workshop, which he cannibalized for spare parts. I never asked him where he found the fuel, but we always seemed to have enough.

Our volunteer cooks were two sisters, Roza and Zarema Asayeva. "The only thing I can do is sew and cook," Roza told me. The two women traveled several miles every day to work, often through gunfire. Zarema had worked at the Fourth City Hospital in Grozny.

Several people offered to be my driver. "Here's my car; I'll help you any way I can," said Avalu Isayev, one of Nuradi's nephews who owned a late-model Zhiguli. I didn't like putting his life in danger, so most of the time I drove myself. Alavdi, one of the security guards, hauled water from the spring. Nuradi placed guards next to the water troughs at the entrance of the hospital to see that people washed their shoes before entering.

All the refugee women from Grozny and surrounding villages flooding into Alkhan Kala meant there were more women having babies, so I decided to section off a small space in the hospital as a maternity ward to give them privacy, under the care of Zina Aduyeva, our volunteer gynecologist. Whenever a baby was born, we all rejoiced to know that amid all the destruction, new life was coming forth.

Cleanliness became my obsession at the newly renovated hospital. The nurses joked that the place was cleaner during the war than before. I insisted we start the day in clean scrubs with the floors of the hospital mopped. Each night, the nurses took my scrubs and several pairs of sheets home, boiled them over their wood stove, hung them up to dry, and ironed them with a nineteenth-century iron filled with hot coals. Grozny no longer produced electricity. Only a few people with small generators at home had power.

I brought to the hospital two pieces of sheet metal from home, and a metal worker fashioned them into a primitive stove. This stove was essentially a large metal box on four legs, with a small door in front, and an exhaust pipe leading out a window from the back. It didn't hold heat for very long after the embers died down but was quick to warm up. My volunteers, who risked being blown up by the mines, gathered wood every day for fuel. We stacked these green pieces under and around the stove to dry out.

Of course, controlling the dirt was a huge challenge. At the end of the day, blood soaked my undershirt, and the floors sloshed in it. Still, I was convinced that neatly ironed hospital dress reassured the patients and their relatives. Certainly, I felt better wearing clean scrubs. So did the nurses. Outside, mud, slush, and rubble reigned. Despite all the boiling, the odor of putrid flesh lingered. I could never determine if the stench actually permeated my scrubs or only existed in my head. I dreamed of hot showers and steam baths.

BY THE END of September 1999, I knew I had to get my family out of Alkhan Kala. Yeltsin's newly appointed prime minister, Vladimir Putin, vowed: "We will pursue the terrorists everywhere. If, pardon the expression, we find them in the toilet, we'll drown them there!" Longing for law and order, ordinary Russians loved his tough talk. Contrary

to the atmosphere during the first war, Russian public opinion supported tough action against Chechnya. It was only a matter of time before Alkhan Kala would come under heavy attack again. Russian tanks,
artillery, and forces had taken up positions along the ridge and had begun lobbing shells into the town. I believed that the second war would
be more brutal than the first. Russian public opinion had turned against
us, and we had lost all hope that the United States or Europe would put
pressure on Russia to halt the fighting.

People were pouring out of the town. In the end, Nana agreed to
leave our animals and accompany me if I would also seek refuge in the
neighboring province of Ingushetia. Lyuba, an Ingush doctor who had
worked in Grozny with me at the hospital, said she would try to find
some kind of accommodations for us. I removed the rear seat of my
Niva and packed Zara, our children and Hussein's, and Nana in the
back. I said I would return for Malika and Dada after I had found a
place to stay. We left early in the morning to avoid traffic during the
two-hour drive. Even so, the Moscow-Baku highway was backed up,
and the Russians fired random shots at the refugees' columns. At the
Chechen-Ingush border, buses and private cars waited for days, in lines
three abreast that extended for miles. Their roofs were loaded with
mattresses, bedding, cardboard boxes, trunks, and pieces of furniture. I
decided to risk cutting across an open pasture despite warnings from
other drivers that the field was full of ruts. Fortunately, the Niva is a
high-slung vehicle, and I managed to get through the shortcut and
over the border into the Ingush capital of Nazran without mishap.
Russian military tents dotted the field adjacent to the border post.

One look at the streets of Nazran, and we knew we would never
find a room there. Refugees slept in makeshift tents, in cardboard
shelters, or under plastic sheeting. Others took shelter in their cars or
trucks. The roads were awash with mud. Lyuba suggested we try the
village of Troitskoye, located ten miles outside Nazran. The first room
we inspected had no water or electricity. Moisture from the newly plas-
tered walls oozed down their surface. We all spent that first night with
Lyuba's mother, who told us about two rooms for rent in the village.

The next day, I drove back to Chechnya for a gas ring, mattresses, blankets, a few pots and pans, and a large aluminum basin for washing. On the return trip to Ingushetia, Dada and Malika followed me in his old Zaporozhets car. At the border, we could not take the shortcut because his car was too low and not powerful enough. We waited in line, hour after hour, the idling engines filling the air with exhaust. Dada's car overheated several times, and we had to beg for water to refill the radiator. I passed the time walking along the lines of cars to the border post, which was manned by Russian troops and Ingush police. I watched with disgust as the Russian soldiers turned back the refugees unless they produced a bribe. Most of the drivers paid up without protest.

An exhausted-looking man, unshaven with greasy hands, was arguing with one of the Russian border guards at the crossing. I glanced at his truck. It was packed with clothes spilling out of broken cardboard boxes, a mattress, a plastic chair, and a crate of chickens. By the time they got to Ingushetia, the chickens would probably be dead, I thought. An elderly man and woman—apparently the man's parents—slumped semiconscious in the cab.

"They need to go to a hospital! Can't you see they are ill!" the man's voice cracked in desperation. "I don't have any money. Can't you see? No money! No money! I have no money!"

"Everyone pays to go through." The young border guard, who couldn't have been more than twenty, stood his ground.

As the argument progressed, the line of cars stopped moving altogether. Soon the drivers began leaning on their horns, the noise deafening. The border guard finally looked up, concluded the situation was hopeless, and reluctantly waved the truck through. As I observed the scenes of human misery, I recalled Mecca and tried to rekindle that sense of calm and hope I had felt after the pilgrimage, but the fate of my people filled me with sadness.

When I got back to Dada's car, I saw his face was flushed and beads of sweat dotted his forehead. He needed to urinate frequently because of an enlarged prostate, though he always held back, refusing to go by the side of the road. I took him to a quiet spot in the field by my car.

After seven hours, we finally made it across the border. Nana and Zara had taken the two rooms that Lyuba had found, and we were lucky to have a roof over our heads. Later, I visited one of the refugee camps that the Russians and Western humanitarian organizations had set up near the border. Refugees slept in large tents with three-tiered bunks, warmed by potbellied woodstoves. Many had brought their animals, which were penned up in enclosures near the border. Mud was everywhere. There was no way to keep clean, no privacy, no way to escape from the smell of human excrement. Dysentery and tuberculosis were in the air.

I made a quick visit to the medical tent, where some of my old colleagues worked with the Red Cross and Doctors Without Borders. A long line of people waited to see the doctors. An emaciated-looking woman holding a handkerchief to her mouth caught my eye. She uttered a hollow cough, which seemed to originate in the depth of her lungs. TB, I thought, as I looked at her dry skin and feverish eyes. At least 25 percent of the population had contracted tuberculosis.

Another medical tent housed shell-shocked children, about twenty of them sitting on planks laid across bricks. The woman doctor tried to engage them, but they stared with vacant eyes. "Most of them have lost their parents," the doctor said, pointing to a young boy, about five, and his sister. "Their parents were killed in front of them. Sometimes they play with the others; then suddenly they stop and burst into tears."

I stayed in Ingushetia only two days. I needed to get back to Alkhan Kala to oversee the renovations of the hospital. I knew if I told Nana I intended to return to Alkhan Kala, she would insist on coming with me, so I said that I was going back to pick up more supplies and would come back to Ingushetia. She didn't believe me. She knew me too well.

"If you go back there, I insist on coming with you," she said. "If I stay here, I will worry all the time. Someone has to look after you."

In the end, I relented, and she and I made our way back to Alkhan Kala.

I hated the idea of subjecting Nana to the misery of war, the bombing, the cold cellar. Nevertheless, she and I went back to living in my house in Alkhan Kala, where she would slip outside to her stove in the courtyard between raids to cook up soup.

Chapter 17

Reaching a Climax

A T THE BEGINNING of October 1999, the hospital was
ready. That first day, I invited the ten doctors and twenty
nurses who had accompanied me from Grozny into the lit-
tle area off the operating room, which I would use as an office. I wanted
them to understand what they were getting into. I had made my decision to stay, but that didn't mean that everyone else should. When it
comes to risking one's life, each person weighs things differently.

"In the first war," I said, "doctors and nurses were killed, and I can
assure you that the coming war is going to be much worse."

The room fell silent. Then one doctor asked why I assumed the
worst would happen to us.

"Did you go through the last war?" I asked.

He shook his head. Imagining war when you have never experienced it is impossible.

I took a moment to reflect, then continued: "I want you all to
know that if you decide at any point to leave, I will not hold it against
you. You are free to leave anytime. You don't even have to inform me.
Just go. I am not going to try to keep you here."

FOR ALMOST TWO weeks, a pleasant calm fell over the town of
Alkhan Kala. A sense of fellowship developed among all of us. Rather
than sitting at home waiting for the next round of shelling, we worked
together. We were doing something useful. Our spirits rose. At the hos-

pital we dealt with ordinary matters—stomach ailments, colds and coughs, dressings that needed to be changed—while the Russians looked at us through their binoculars from the ridge. Only the thud of artillery in the distance, broken by occasional sniper fire, reminded us of the approaching conflict.

The calm was too good to last. One afternoon, I sat with my nurse Rumani Idrisova and staff around the table drinking tea and eating soup. On the table was a box of chocolates Nuradi had brought for the nurses. A few days earlier, Rumani's husband had visited the hospital to try and persuade her to return with him to Ingushetia. They went off into an empty room and talked for nearly two hours. When she came out, she was smiling. "I'm staying," she said. "My place is here."

Several streets away, on Mira (Peace) Street, one of the main thoroughfares in the town, people gathered following the funeral of a young boy who had stepped on a mine while collecting wood. A crowd of people on the streets was always an invitation for Russian fire. The mourners should have known better, but the exchange of condolences after a death is one of our important traditions.

Suddenly, there was an enormous explosion. We rushed away from the windows and into the corridor, then squatted on the floor with our backs to the wall. We veterans of the first war were determined to stay calm, to finish our soup. Razyat Almatova, one of our local volunteer nurses, couldn't lift the spoon to her mouth because her hand shook so much. Fear was contagious, so I cracked a few jokes, which I don't think she appreciated.

Within five minutes the wounded began arriving, some in the arms of relatives, others in carts or on stretchers. There had been no warning—a mortar is silent until it explodes close to the ground, spraying shards everywhere, shredding human flesh. There were at least seventy casualties; some killed and some with limbs hanging off. Relatives elbowed their way into the passageway, stumbling over the bodies strewn every which way on the floor. I was confronted by endless wounded and didn't know where to begin; I felt disoriented; my head began pounding. The first thing to do, I told myself, was to identify the victims who had a chance of survival. Slowly, I pulled myself together.

"Move away; give the doctor room to work!" Nuradi shouted. He never lost his head. Some of the nurses panicked, running aimlessly in all directions, grabbing the stands with hanging drips.

"Forget the stands!" I shouted. "We don't need the drips yet. Grab the rubber tourniquets. Stop the bleeding! First of all, stop the bleeding!"

With Nuradi at my side, I operated along with the other nurses and doctors until 3 A.M. I was only too familiar with this ghastly work: stuffing gauze into wounds, clamping off major blood vessels, cauterizing smaller ones, peeling back skin, and sawing through bone. There was no time to swab the floor, which was slippery with blood. We wrapped up the severed limbs for the relatives.

THE MORNING FOLLOWING the attack on the mourners, I left on foot for the hospital after a few hours' sleep at home. The sky was blue except for the smoke billowing over Grozny. The silence was unnerving after the attack, as though something terrible was still about to happen. My throat felt raw, and my eyes burned from the smoke. We can expect lots of asthmatics and children with trouble breathing today, I thought. I found the hospital very quiet when I arrived. Raisa, our cleaning woman, had mopped the corridors, and all traces of yesterday's bloodbath were gone. I made my way to the office to confer with the staff. Every morning, we met for five to ten minutes to discuss the day's activities. Nuradi met me at the door, his face downcast.

"Everyone left in the night," he said. "All the doctors and almost all of the nurses are gone."

"After last night, I half expected it," I said. I made a quick calculation. Now I was the only doctor for the 100,000 people who lived in Alkhan Kala and the six surrounding villages. I had eight nurses, most of them local women. Losing the doctors and nurses upset me at first. However, I soon realized that I was better off with a small group of people I could depend on. If they hadn't lost their heads during the massacre yesterday, they could surely face anything.

Rumani was the only nurse with wartime experience. She had worked in the burn unit of the Fourth City Hospital in Grozny during the first war. Zara Akhigova, on the other hand, had taken only two nursing courses by August 1999 when the war resumed. The first time I asked her for surgical clippers to clean off bone shards, she passed me pliers for pulling teeth. She was horribly embarrassed.

The next day, I brought her a medical textbook from home. "Here, learn the names of all these instruments by tomorrow," I said. She was a quick learner and turned out to be one of my best nurses.

Another dedicated nurse was Maryam Utsieva, who lived near the hospital. Day or night—whenever the shelling started—she made her way there. Zarina Baligova was an unexpected surprise; she started working at the hospital when her brother was seriously wounded. After he was released, she volunteered to stay on to nurse the others. In addition to the nurses, my nephew Ali, who was halfway through his second year at medical school when Grozny was laid to ruins, offered to help.

One mainstay of my team was Said-Ali Aduyev, the brother of Zina, our volunteer gynecologist. Said-Ali was a village dentist who lived next

Operating under fire. Left to right: me, my nephew Ali, nurses Rumani Idrísova and Markha Chalaeva, and Said Ali, the dentist turned surgical assistant.

door to the hospital. He had stayed at home to look after the livestock when the rest of his family left for Karachayevo-Cherkessiya, a neighboring Caucasian republic. I never had to call on him; he always knew when I needed him.

The shelling of Alkhan Kala and the surrounding villages intensified with each passing day. When one evening the Russian news claimed that Chechen fighters were blowing up cisterns of ammonia in Grozny, I suspected this meant the Kremlin was preparing the Russian public for the use of poisonous weapons, for which the Chechens would be blamed. Soon we saw a huge ash-colored cloud over the capital. For days, it hung there. The smell of explosives filled the air, causing breathing difficulties, strange skin eruptions, and unexplained deaths. I had treated many patients with mysterious skin eruptions that I assumed were caused by the defoliants the Russians sprayed on the trees. I never treated anyone injured by one of the terrible vacuum bombs they had started to use. The shock wave from the explosion was so powerful it collapsed buildings and sucked bodies out, smashing them against stationary objects. Colleagues told me how you would find people dead in a cellar with no evident markings on them, though their organs were atomized inside their bodies.

Apparently, we were bombarded because the Russians thought Alkhan Kala was a hotbed of fighters. Smoke billowed over the valley, and at night flames from the burning houses lit the sky. People spent days and nights huddled in cellars, where the atmosphere was so close it caused the skin to turn a dull gray and the muscles to lose elasticity. It didn't matter how many layers of clothes you put on, you always felt cold. Nana insisted she was all right, but I could see by the color of her face that her heart was bothering her. For several years, she had suffered from high blood pressure. Lack of sleep distorted people's thinking, ruined their concentration, made them irritable and depressed. As soon as you fell asleep, the shelling began. Go to the latrine, and you could be shot. Half the time the wounded couldn't be moved to the cellars. Neighbors often crowded into our cellar. Everyone talked nervously to drown their fear. The repetitive conversations about the war grated on my nerves. The Russians this, Maskhadov that, Basayev, Putin, Clinton . . .

"Let's talk about something pleasant," I urged.

"What's pleasant?" one of my cellar comrades responded.

"Beautiful places?"

"What beautiful places? Everything is rubble."

"Beautiful women!" That at least got a laugh.

I had heard it all before: who's hurting, who's dead, who's wounded, whose house was destroyed. My nerves were raw. The moment the shelling stopped, I rushed to the hospital. Sometimes I lost patience with the nurses, screaming at them for no reason. I fought against these outbursts, knowing I had to find some other way to relieve tension. Doing push-ups between operations helped.

"You must listen to music with a strong rhythm," Dada had told me during the first war, "not all those slow songs you like."

I tried to follow his advice now. However, when I played the music on my small battery-run recorder during breaks between operations, Nuradi complained. "People will think we are having a good time and they are suffering so much," he said.

With each passing day, I became more exhausted. If I had two or three hours of sleep a night, I considered myself lucky. Often I was so tired that sleep was impossible even if there was quiet for a few hours. I worried about my waning ability to feel my patients' suffering, that compassion had been replaced with irritation. And as if the shelling were not enough, the civilians were also victims of looting, rape, and killing by the *kontraktniki*, in particular the infamous Shamanov Division camped on the heights not two miles from the town. Fifty percent of General Vladimir Shamanov's 5,000-strong division were regular soldiers; the others, convicts released from prison to fight in Chechnya. A patient told me she had overheard a regular officer try unsuccessfully to control the mercenaries during the siege of Alkhan Yurt when the mercenaries went on a rampage, killing scores of people.

"They are civilians; we are not supposed to harm them," the officer had said.

The mercenary chortled: "But this is war. We can do anything in war. Just try and stop us."

I will never forget the face of the woman who came to the hospital because of a leg wound. Her skin sagged; her nose and mouth drooped. Wisps of dirty gray hair straggled out from under her scarf.

"How long have you had the wound?' I motioned her to lie down on the examining table. She dragged her legs stiffly and raised herself onto the table. She didn't reply, just stared at the far wall. Her husband had told the nurse the wound had gone untreated because they couldn't leave the cellar for a month.

I lifted up her skirt to examine her leg, revealing dirty gray pantaloons with holes everywhere. I unwound the dirty rag covering the gash in her leg. Decomposition had set in, and the odor of dead tissue filled the room. I gave her a shot of local anesthetic and began to cut away the blackened flesh.

"Doctor, what are you doing to me?" Her head shot up. For a moment, her eyes focused on my face, then returned to the wall.

"I am cleaning your wound," I said, dropping a piece of dead flesh into the bowl Razyat held out. "We saw how they were shelling your village. It was hard to believe anyone survived."

Her head shot up again. For a minute, she said nothing; then she looked at me and said, "I don't know where my daughter is." Her voice was flat. "They were all drunk, four or five of them. My husband tried to protect her, but they beat him over the head with their rifle butts." She fell silent.

I finished cleaning the wound, doused it with a saline solution, and bandaged it. "We'll change the dressing tomorrow." I turned away, not wanting her to see the anger on my face. Razyat helped her from the table.

"They raped her in front of us," the woman said, walking to the door like a robot.

She didn't cry. She recounted the rape as though it had happened to someone else's daughter. She lay zombielike in the hospital for a month, never leaving her bed. Periodically, she burst out, "General Shamanov told his men, do what you like."

When the wound had healed enough for her to leave the hospital, her husband came to take her home. He looked about fifty, but he was probably a lot younger. I couldn't imagine what it must have cost a father to watch his daughter being raped and being helpless to stop it.

"Thank you, Doctor, for what you have done," he said. "My house is destroyed, and I have nothing to give you."

"I don't want money," I said. "Your wife is psychologically ill; she needs some medicine." He nodded. He said nothing about his daughter. I was reluctant to ask.

Thinking about this incident made my blood boil, and for weeks I couldn't get it out of my mind. Residual rage burned in me when a Russian *kontraktnik* was brought to the hospital. He had been extracting bribes and terrorizing civilians at a checkpoint. In retaliation, Chechen fighters had shot up the post. A bullet had passed under this *kontraktnik*'s armpit, avoiding his flak jacket, and piercing his lung.

"I don't want to be treated by bandits!" he screamed as Rumani gave him a shot to relieve the pain. "Son of a bitch! Bastard !" he shouted at me.

A Chechen fighter standing in the corridor shouted out to me, "Let him die!" For a moment, I was tempted. The world would be a better place without this monster. He wouldn't rape any more women or children. But then I remembered Krasnoyarsk and the words of the Hippocratic Oath engraved on the wall at the medical school. If I started deciding who would live and who would die, where would it end?

"I am a doctor," I replied. "It is my job to treat whoever needs help. Allah will punish him."

DURING THIS PERIOD of intensive bombing, I continued to do my medical rounds, sometimes on foot and sometimes by car. I had learned to read skin and tissue: to interpret discharge from an injury, to know that roughness and a lack of elasticity under my fingers as I probed a wound meant the flesh was damaged. The way a surgeon cuts into the tissue, being careful to save the blood vessels, determines how long the wound takes to mend. Sepsis can progress with lightning speed, so I visited patients like Sultan Ganayev daily to combat his infection. He had a large, open wound at the level of his right hip that had spread to his lower spine. I did battle with his dying flesh. The smell of pus and dead tissue was so strong, visitors gagged and left the room. The constant shelling had undermined Sultan's nervous system, and his body was struggling with the spreading infection.

"Leave me up here. I'm going to die anyway. You get down into the cellar." He would yell at his wife and grown children every time the shelling started. The eldest son never left him, not even through the worst shelling.

One day as I drained the pus into the bowl, Sultan turned to me and said, "Khassan, tell me the truth. Am I going to die?"

"Of course not," I said. "Your wound is getting better."

He grinned. "As soon as I am well, I will take you to my vineyard; then you will have as many grapes as you can use," he said.

"I look forward to it," I replied.

I never told my patients they were dying because I felt that it destroyed all hope, and healing needs hope. I believe that telling the truth often encourages death. Especially the onset of cancer. There is no word for cancer in the Chechen language. The Russians call cancer *rak*, the same word as crab. In Chechen we call cancer "the unmentionable" and hide it from the patient.

I never gave up on Sultan, though I didn't hold out much hope for those grapes. I continued to struggle for his life, believing in miracles. Under different conditions I might have saved him, though he would have spent the rest of his life in a wheelchair.

As the weeks passed and the casualties streamed in, our medical supplies started to dwindle. I turned to Dada's age-old remedies. I cleaned wounds with sour milk and applied honey to help close them. On burns I used egg yolk and sour cream. I advised people to urinate in a container, let the urine stand for a week, and apply the sediment, which settled at the bottom, to their wounds. I also used herbal solutions made with oak bark, coltsfoot, or sage as dressings. When our surgical thread was gone, I appealed to the townspeople for ordinary thread, which we disinfected by boiling. When the disinfectants gave out, we mixed weak, medium, and strong salt solutions. To dress wounds, I used ordinary household supplies.

During this period, our team experienced tragedies of its own. One night when Nuradi walked me home, he told me that he hadn't heard from his older son, Akhmed, in weeks. Nuradi always insisted on accompanying me, even though I would tell him it wasn't necessary.

"I tried to get messages to him," he said. "I want to go to Grozny and look for him."

"It's too dangerous," I said. "Too many Chechens have been shot going to Grozny to look for their relatives."

In the end, Nuradi agreed not to go. Then one day he asked me to go home with him. When he stopped in front of his house, eyes downcast, I guessed what was coming.

"Some local fighters came from Grozny," he said. "They reported that several young men from Alkhan Kala were buried in the central stadium." The Dinamo Stadium in Grozny had become a temporary burial ground for Chechens until it was safe enough for the relatives to remove the bodies for a proper burial. The news of Akhmed's death was closely held. Nuradi's elderly mother was not informed for fear it would give her a heart attack. One day when she sat outside in the street, friends approached with condolences. She died a month later from the shock.

Alavdi's eighteen-year-old sister died when a shell hit their courtyard. She was sweeping the yard, and he was inside the house. The shock wave knocked over the young woman, shredding her body before his eyes. He rushed to the hospital with her mutilated corpse, in a state of shock, thinking I could help, but it was far too late. Nuradi tried to calm him down. Alavdi didn't know how he was going to inform his parents, who lived in another town.

Sometimes I felt that the whole population was verging on nervous collapse. Children walked around in shock, either retreating into silence or crying nonstop. The milk of nursing mothers dried up. One day, I saw a nine-year-old boy with half a head of white hair. His mother said it had happened overnight. Another, a seven-year-old boy, had been so frightened by bombardment that the left side of his face twisted over to the right, leaving him with a disfigured, wry mouth. I had no tranquilizers or medication to calm people down, nothing to curb the outbreaks of violence brought on by stress, as in the case of Salavdi Kadirov, a weight lifter, whose brothers asked me for help. My only advice was to tie him to his bed, which, with such a bull of a man, required the help of several men. On the street, the first Russian sniper would have picked him off. Some people treated their nerves with alcohol, for which I couldn't blame them.

NOVEMBER 25, 1999, brought a harrowing bombardment. I thanked God that most of my family was safe in Ingushetia. "From the sound of the explosions, the shelling is following a full-coverage pattern," I told Nuradi. "The Russians have mapped the town into squares and are systematically directing their barrage from quadrant to quadrant. They'll probably hit the hospital, and in another few minutes my house will fall in the target square."

"I'll hold the fort here," Rumani volunteered. "Go home quick and warn anyone who is there."

I ran home as fast as I could. There I found Nana, friends, and neighbors gathered around my television, which I had managed to hook up to an old Japanese generator. The electricity had been out for months. My friends were waiting for the 9 P.M. Moscow news, anxious to learn how the Russians were reporting the war.

"Get into the basement," I yelled. "The shelling is moving this way."

"Can't it wait until after the news?" one of my neighbors asked.

"No!" I ripped the plug from the generator. "Get down there immediately!"

About 9:50 P.M., a missile smashed into the house with a deafening explosion. Two minutes later, a second rocket hit, smashing through the top of the basement. A blinding flame flashed through the cellar as the rocket rammed through the ceiling. That was followed by an explosion that tore off the corner of my house, causing the basement ceiling to crack. The women screamed; we all crowded into the far corner, praying out loud.

A third hit, and it would be over. People clung to one another in silence, eyes closed, waiting for the end. But we were lucky. Allah heard our prayers. There was no third missile. I struggled to push open the steel door, which had crashed shut, but it was blocked by rubble that had fallen on it. Above, I could hear voices, and when our neighbors finally freed us, I stumbled out, tripping over fallen bricks and what used to be the table of the summer kitchen, choking on the dust and acrid smoke. What greeted me was a terrible sight: My house was partially destroyed; the upper floors and roof were gone, and only the ground floor, constructed of reinforced concrete, was left standing. My parents' house was leveled. So much time and energy rebuilding the house! One minute, and it was rubble. Nana had taken such pride in the wooden roof I had built out over the courtyard at the back of the house.

Where do we live now? I thought as I looked at a broken dinner plate lying under a fallen roof beam. We build; the Russians destroy. Then we build again; the Russians destroy again. Some people can't take it; they have heart attacks and die. Others are defiant. "We will rebuild our house, and this time it will be an even better house than the one the Russians destroyed," they say. The process becomes a way of life. We have been doing it for centuries. But right now, rebuilding wasn't on my mind. The wounded would be pouring in.

Fallen bricks, plaster, and collapsed beams blocked the front of the house. I scrambled over the mess into the back and climbed over the fence. The road and path behind the house had disappeared under fallen debris. Houses burned on either side of me as I ran. Men with buckets of water were trying to extinguish the fire at Hussein's house. At the time Hussein and Rita were in Ingushetia, along with their children. He and Malika returned to Alkhan Kala a little later.

Consulting Chechen fighters after an amputation during the second war.

In those awful days, we all expected tragedy, even death. When death arrived, it wasn't the kind of shock someone experiences with a plane or car crash. For people surrounded by tragedy, death is a natural event, something happening to everyone. You are not alone. In the house across the street, someone was killed yesterday. In the house next door, three people last week, and in one house, a whole family. Every Chechen family had its deaths. In these extreme circumstances, you realize the fragility of life. You recognize what is important, what is superficial. What is true, and what are lies.

I eventually managed to make my way through the debris and arrived at the hospital, which was only partly damaged. It was now past 10 P.M., and I went back immediately to the operating table. I worked throughout the night and into the next morning. As the wounded were brought in I noticed a woman in a beige overcoat and floral head scarf. She stood against the wall, her eyes cast down; she didn't seem to be with anyone.

Fourteen hours later, I left the operating room, exhausted. My last operation before taking a break was to extract pieces of shrapnel from a young boy's back, a tricky job since four of the shards were close to the spinal column. I didn't want to risk paralysis so I decided to leave them in. As I walked down the corridor, the woman in the head scarf looked up. "Doctor," she said, "when you get a free minute, I need to talk to you."

"Later," I said.

"Please, Doctor, I need to talk to you in private." She blocked my path. "I can see how busy you are with all the wounded. I am so embarrassed."

She must have been wounded in her private parts and didn't know how to tell me, I thought. In our country, women don't discuss female problems with a male doctor. Nor do men and women talk with each other about such things as childbirth and sex. I assumed the women talk about such matters among themselves. They have close friendships.

Now I looked more closely at the woman. "Umazhova?" I asked. I realized that I had seen her often around town. She had quite a reputation for organizing protests and for talking back to the Russians, accusing them of breaking their promises. Her first name was Malika, but everyone called her by her family name, Umazhova. She nodded.

"Come on, I'm a doctor," I said. "Everybody here is having a terrible time. You can tell me your problem." A Russian bombardment was not the time for female modesty, I thought. I took her elbow and

led her into the room that served as my office. She sat on the edge of
the chair, her hands fidgeting in her lap.

"There's a member of our family who has been wounded,"
Umazhova said. "She's like a daughter to me. She is our breadwin-
ner." She paused. "I am embarrassed to tell you."

"Bring her in," I said, rising to my feet. "We'll treat her; no
problem."

"I don't think you understand, Doctor," Umazhova went on. "It's
Zoyka."

"Zoyka? Bring her in . . ." My patience was running out.

"I can't," she said. "You see, Zoyka is a cow. She's really a member
of the family. A piece of shrapnel has lodged in her neck, where it
meets the shoulder."

So that was it. A cow! "I don't operate on animals," I said. "I simply
don't have time."

Her eyes filled with tears. "It's really awkward for me to come here
and burden you with our problems, particularly since there are so
many here on the edge of life and death. But please understand,
Doctor, Zoyka is our life too. Without her, my five children will go
hungry."

"I can't leave the hospital; more wounded will be coming in," I
protested. I felt myself weakening. I knew very well the importance
of a cow in a Chechen family. I was always lecturing the townspeople
about keeping their animals indoors during a bombardment. I think
it was the mention of her children that broke me down.

"All right, all right. But I've really got to make it as quick as possible."

A friend of Umazhova's drove me to her house on the outskirts of
town. Nearly all the houses along the way were either damaged or in
ruins. Shrapnel scars scored the walls of Umazhova's house; windows
were shattered. We entered the courtyard through a pitted iron gate.
I looked around. No sign of a male presence. If Umazhova had a husband, either he was off fighting, or he had been killed. She told me
she had a bedridden mother.

Zoyka lay on her side in a makeshift barn on the far side of the courtyard, where she had fallen when she was hit. She was a ginger animal with a splash of white down her forehead. Her coat was groomed to a silky softness; not a splatter of cow dung or mud on her. Two braids intertwined with red ribbons hung over her forehead, as though she awaited a prospective suitor. I wondered if she was decked out especially for me, or if the ribbons were meant to ward off "the Evil Eye." A copper bell hung from her neck. Just below the leather strap holding the bell I saw the wound. It was deep, penetrating almost to her spine.

Umazhova squatted on her heels in the mud and began stroking the cow's head. "There, there," she crooned. "Doctor has come to help you. Soon you'll be better."

"We'll have to tie her feet so she won't thrash around." I knelt down, opened my bag, and began selecting the instruments.

Umazhova patted Zoyka. "That's not necessary. Better that I stroke her and talk to her. She understands everything." She put her face close to the cow and rubbed her neck. "You understand, Doctor is here to make you better. You be a good girl."

The cow's large brown eyes stared up at me, imploring, full of trust. My heart went out to the cow. I had seen that look before in the eyes of childhood friends who ended up on my operating table, so shattered I couldn't do anything to save them.

Right now, I was not taking any chances on Zoyka being a good girl, so I anesthetized the area of her wound. Usually, I hunt for shrapnel before anesthetizing. That way, you can tell by the reactions of the patients when you are getting near. I widened the wound, which was about two inches by two inches, to make it easier to remove the shrapnel. Then I inserted my forceps in the opening, where I found a large piece of metal, its edges sharp as a razor. I worked slowly. A cow's neck was unfamiliar territory. I didn't want to cut into any veins or arteries. While I worked, Umazhova's children watched from under one of the trees. Once I had removed the shrapnel, I probed the hole with my index finger to see if I had missed any pieces of metal; then I cut away the dead tissue and doused the wound with a saline solution. Throughout the hour-and-a-half procedure, Zoyka remained calm. I was amazed. Afterward I explained to Umazhova what to do in the days ahead and how important it was to change the dressing daily.

As Umazhova's friend drove me back to the hospital, I saw the five children standing in the street near the gate. The oldest boy must have been about fourteen. They watched in silence as the car drove away. For a moment, my fatigue lifted. I felt at peace after treating Zoyka; Umazhova's children would be able to get their milk.

As we drove back to the hospital, I turned my head toward the mountains. They always had a calming effect on me, letting me reflect and collect myself. Usually, you could see their snowcapped peaks, but today they were hidden by a layer of haze. Would those mountains continue to protect us, as they had throughout our history? Or would that mighty Caucasian range be defeated by bombs and rockets and the fumes from burning oil refineries?

After operating on Zoyka , I worried people would learn that I was treating animals. Cows, sheep, dogs, cats, geese; they were also victims of war. If I wasn't careful, I would end up running a veterinary clinic. Inevitably, news of Zoyka's operation spread around town. Three days later, Abubakar came to me about his horse. Abubakar was the owner of a fancy racehorse, which he boasted took first place in important races in Dagestan, Ingushetia, and Ossetia and was worth $3,000. The horse had received two wounds in the shoulder; the more serious was four inches deep, right down into the muscle. I was reluctant to treat the horse, but I didn't know how to refuse because Abubakar was a volunteer worker at the hospital.

"Get the horse ready, tie it up, so it doesn't struggle and I can work quickly," I told Abubakar when I reluctantly agreed to his request. "Its legs are so slender they'll break easily."

Abubakar's horse was no Zoyka. It took ten men to hold it down. I fished into the wound and removed the shrapnel, and doused it out with a saline solution. After that, the horse stood up.

A few weeks later, there was Umazhova outside my operating room again. "Zoyka wants to thank you," she said, smiling. She handed me a big aluminum can of milk, a crock of sour cream, and a packet of cottage cheese.

"I am glad she is recovering," I said.

Umazhova beamed. "Zoyka understands everything," she said. I almost believed her.

But after treating Zoyka and Abubakar's $3,000 racehorse, I told Rumani to spread the word: Doctor will do no more operations on animals! "You've got to protect me," I implored her.

I WAS BECOMING increasingly pessimistic about peace in Chechnya. The United States and Russia were busy worrying about the reduction of nuclear warheads, terrorism, and other issues around the world. Human rights abuses in Chechnya were pushed out of mind. According to Russian officials, their forces were merely engaged in pinpoint bombing of rebel camps in Chechnya. But every day, I treated civilians who had been maimed. Every day, I heard another story about a rape, a family executed for a shortwave radio, a young man thrown into a filtration camp.

Russian propaganda grated on my nerves. I wanted to do something to counteract the lies, so I started videotaping with the help of my nephew Adam, the third of Raya's four sons. Adam was a brilliant athlete, winning the All-Russia Tae Kwon Do Championship four times. Everyone loved him, especially the kids in the town, to whom he gave free tae kwon do lessons. "We must get them off the street and give them some goals in life," he said. Adam's younger brother Ali worshiped him. Adam dreamed of being a journalist, and he had developed a relationship with the British news agency Reuters, to which he supplied exclusive footage. By the end of 1999, the Russians banned westerners from entering Chechnya, so Western news organizations had to rely heavily on locals to fill the gap. That was a great opportunity for Adam, who proved fearless, but it was dangerous work.

I worried about Adam all the time. "You are taking too many risks. You must stop. We'll get the film out later," I said.

Whenever we had one of those conversation, he would look at me with his charming smile and make promises he didn't keep. One day, we sat together in my office drinking tea. He had just returned from taking film to Ingushetia and regaled me with the trouble he had encountered at one of the checkpoints. He took a long sip of tea, then turned to me. "You like your job, don't you, Uncle?" he said.

I nodded.

"And you take risks for it, don't you?"

"You know I do. I can't avoid it."

"I promise I will be careful," he said, "but it's important the world knows what is going on here."

He was like me. Stubborn. I knew he wasn't going to stop. You tell people what they want to hear, then go on doing what you believe is right. After that conversation, I avoided the subject.

In addition to making the videos, which I hid in the basement in boxes of broken crockery, I started writing a journal. The thought of all the civilian suffering going undocumented ate at me. Knowing I could die at any moment, I wanted someone to know what we had been through. Eventually, Western human rights organizations would ask questions, and I wanted some documentation. I would write a few lines at night after work, or by candlelight when I was in the cellar, some of them in a private code in case the journal fell into the hands of the Russians. I recently decoded the entries that give some sense of what our daily life was like.

November 30, 7:00—Once again intensive bombardment of Alkhan Kala; we did not sleep all night: we could hear shells exploding nearby. We sat in the cellar, five of us in all, including three of our neighbors.

9:00—Went to hospital; six new wounded patients arrived; I operated on them. Throughout whole day, the Russians conducted intensive bombardment of Alkhan Kala and Alkhan Yurt. Later, military helicopters carried out powerful rocket strikes against Alkhan Yurt; on same day, Chechen fighters destroyed a Russian helicopter, tanks, and armored personnel carrier.

17:00—Yusha (our elder) came back from Mozdok after meeting with General Shamanov, who promised the bombardment of Alkhan Kala would stop in three days.

20:25—I came home and sat in the cellar with Nana, Alavdi, Kuchal, and Sanet. The night sky was lit up by illumination flares shot up by the Federals. All around quiet.

Days later:

December 11, Alkhan Kala, 10:00—I spent the night at the hospital after operating on wounded most of the night.

11:00—I went to a meeting with the Federals; after that, I drove to the hospital at Zakan Yurt with a lieutenant colonel, Igor, for medicines. The director of the hospital, a Russian colonel Alexei Alexeyevich, was completely drunk; it was impossible to agree with him on anything; shortly thereafter, the nursing staff connected him to a drip to lessen the intoxication. We had to come home with nothing.

12:00—Returned to the hospital and changed bandages.

15:00—A delegation of Russian military, headed by General Gennadi Troshev, the deputy commander of Russian troops, addresssed a town meeting and announced that shortly gas and electricity would be restored to Alkhan Kala, children would be able to go to school, and people would get medical treatment.

In answer to this, Malika Umazhova told the general to his face that all these words and promises were absolute lies. She expressed the general opinion that the military everywhere offer idle promises about ending the shelling and then violate these promises.

23:00—Got home very tired. Outside, the night is starry, cold. On the outskirts of town, the Federals launch illumination flares into the sky. From time to time, machine-gun fire.

And toward the end of the month:

December 24, Alkhan Kala, 8:00—Went to work; rebandaged the patients and operated on the wounded from Alkhan Yurt. Yes-

terday driving by Alkhan Yurt, I was devastated by a terrible sight—
many houses were rubbed off the face of the Earth. Whole streets
of burned-out houses. Dead cows were lying along the road. As a
result of the shelling, graves and headstones were destroyed. Alkhan
Yurt made me think this was a second Samashki.

18:00—The Federals (in this case a Muslim from Bashkiriya)
brought a young man from the village of Kirovo on an armored
personnel carrier. He had a penetrating wound in the buttock
with damage to the urinary bladder. The wounded man needed to
be operated on immediately, but our conditions would not allow
it. We got the commander of the personnel carrier to take the
wounded man to the hospital in Zakan Yurt. I had to go along as
a guide.

20:30—I got home.

23:40—Occasionally you can hear gunfire. On the outskirts of
town, the Russians are firing illumination flares. Today is the 15th
day of Ramadan and the second day since natural gas has been restored. That's a great joy during this difficult time.

Conditions worsened steadily. I had the feeling that we were reaching a climax, though what it would be I couldn't foretell. How could
Chechnya, a country of less than 1 million people, hold out against
Russia? Also, I had begun picking up rumors that extremists like Arbi
Barayev were criticizing me personally for treating Russians. Most
people, including our field commanders, understood my duty was to
treat the wounded—friend or foe. How long that understanding could
last, I didn't know.

Chapter 18

Double Jeopardy

O N THE EVENING of December 31, 1999, I left the hospital around 11 P.M. Rumors had it that the Federals would stage an all-out assault on New Year's Eve to honor the Russian soldiers who had died in the storming of Grozny five years before. With everyone in their cellars, an eeriness permeated the streets. I had hoped the snowfall earlier that day would camouflage the grayness and lift our spirits, but the flakes turned to slush on the ground. Over the previous week a stream of wounded had poured into Alkhan Kala and surrounding villages. Under cover of darkness, relatives transported the injured on foot through the frozen swamps along the river to avoid the military checkpoints and the snipers, who treated any moving object as game.

At the stroke of midnight, flares rose all over Chechnya like fireworks, followed quickly by bombardment. At 2 A.M., Nuradi found me at home and announced an influx of wounded. We hurried to the hospital, darting from building to building to evade the exploding shells. I was able to treat all the injured in an hour, then return home. Later in the day there were more casualties, so I was at the hospital from early evening until 11 P.M.

These days, we all slept in the cellar. That afternoon, Nana had ventured out and had prepared some soup on the stove outside in the courtyard. After eating, Hussein, Malika, Nana, and I curled up on the sheepskins to catch some sleep. At 6 A.M. on January 2 we were awakened by Nuradi banging on the cellar door.

"Barayev entered the village with all his men, about three hundred of them," Nuradi said after I opened the door to let him in. "He claims that Operation Jihad has started again and that towns all over Chechnya are falling."

"Do you believe that?" I asked. Nuradi laughed bitterly and shook his head.

Barayev was nothing but trouble. We all wished the Russians would eliminate him, but he always seemed to escape their net. Most of us suspected he worked for the Russian secret police. Moscow claimed it wanted him dead, but every time the Russians launched a *zachistka* or clean-up operation in Alkhan Kala, Barayev knew about it ahead of time.

"The Federals will use his presence here as an excuse to attack," I said.

"They have already set up a cordon around town," Nuradi continued. "The Russian troops are deployed along the Sunzha and on the heights overlooking the town. It's a pincer movement," he said. "And people are beginning to panic. They don't know where to go, how to escape."

"We have to move the patients," I said. "About half are fighters, the rest women and children. The fighters will be massacred by the Federals, and any young men will be sent to the filtration camps. Go to the hospital and prepare them. We'll need transport."

Immediately, I sent a messenger to neighboring Kulari, about twenty minutes away on foot, to summon help in getting the wounded over the suspension bridge. I told Nana, Malika, and Hussein to wait. I would return for them as soon as I had finished transporting the patients. I removed my Niva from what was left of the garage, took out the seats, placed a mattress on the floor, and left for the hospital. If the patients were ambulatory, I could fit five or six in the car; if not, only three or four.

The Russians had closed the roads out of town, leaving the rickety footbridge over the Sunzha as the only means of escape. It was still dark when we loaded the first three patients and drove to the river to meet young volunteers from Kulari who would help them across. A few yards downstream from the bridge, a tractor and a large truck were stuck in the middle of the river where they had tried to cross. We slipped the three men off the mattresses onto blankets, then tied a large knot at each end as a hand grip. At that time in the early morning, the bridge was clear. After receiving a go-ahead from someone on the opposite bank, the volunteers picked up the wounded. Then, single file, they advanced step by step across the suspension bridge, a precarious operation. The slightest wind swayed the bridge. In the past, fleeing refugees had lost their balance and fallen into the icy water below.

We completed about fifteen such runs before lunchtime, transporting all seventy patients across the river. Word of Barayev's arrival had created panic in Alkhan Kala, and many people rushed to the bridge to flee. At about 1 P.M. I started home to give the car to Hussein so he could get the rest of the family out of town. As I drove past the abandoned wood-processing plant, an old woman flagged me down. I ground to a stop.

"Barayev is looking for you," she said, wringing her hands. "Don't go to the hospital. You have to escape."

"I can't do that. There are too many wounded left in the houses."

"You'll be killed. No one will criticize you if you leave. The people will understand." The old woman started to cry.

"I can't," I repeated. "Don't worry."

I was always touched by how protective the townspeople were. People like this old woman made me more determined than ever to stay. I put the car back into gear and drove toward home.

As soon as Hussein had driven off with Nana and Malika, to the footbridge that would take them to Kulari, I left for the hospital on foot. At the entrance I saw crowds of bearded fighters, Barayev's men. In the far corner of the building, Zaurbek Aslanbekov was removing the generator from his little workshop and loading it into his car. Bless him, I thought. He guards that generator better than his family; he won't allow it to fall into Russian hands.

"Stop. Leave that!" Five fighters bounded forward. "We'll need it."

Zaurbek tried to protest but finally turned and carted the machine back into his workshop.

"Look, there's that *kozyol* [goat]," a voice called out. Arbi Barayev, who stood in a group of ten fighters, had spotted me. He had grown a beard since I last saw him driving around town in a foreign jeep, but I recognized him from his height and clean fatigues. He pointedly refused to greet me.

"Turn him around and tie him up." He waved his Kalashnikov rifle in the direction of the hospital entrance. Barayev's men moved toward me. Two of them grabbed my arms. Three more propelled me forward by pushing their rifle barrels against the small of my back. Once we were inside the building, Barayev stepped forward, pointed his rifle at my feet, and fired a round of bullets into the wooden floor.

"He deserves to die," he said to his men, who crowded into the narrow corridor to watch. Now he pointed his rifle above my head. "He has opened a hospital for Russians soldiers." A round of bullets tore through the ceiling. "He is treating our enemies." Another burst to the ceiling. I felt the bullet wheeze over my head, then the spent casing hit the floor. "Assemble the emirs."

My heart pounded, and I felt a tightening in my chest. I knew I was about to die. To die at the hands of the Russians in the name of independence was one thing; to be mowed down by Barayev would be a useless end. Life meant nothing to Barayev. He had once gunned down someone blocking his car in traffic.

Barayev's men marched me into my office and pushed me into the far right-hand corner of the room. I stood in the corner with my back to the wall, flanked by two guards cradling rifles. I couldn't see Arbi Barayev's face; he sat with his back to me. He had commandeered my chair at the head of the table, the place where I addressed the staff each morning. The room felt glacial, the kind of cold that penetrates your bones. Under my bloodstained scrubs, I wore several sweaters. My feet felt numb, and I tensed my muscles to stop my limbs from shaking. The last thing I wanted was for Barayev and his henchmen to think I was frightened.

Barayev placed his six senior lieutenants on either side of the table, rifles propped against the chairs. He had selected these bearded men in black woolen ski caps from his private army to make up a shariat court. He called his men emirs. *Emir* is not a Chechen word; in Arabic it means "commander." Barayev referred to himself as chief emir. Frankly, I doubted that Barayev would recognize a shariat court if he saw one. The judges of a shariat court must know Arabic and be able to read the Koran in the original. There was no Koran in evidence, and the proceedings were a charade meant to appease the people of Alkhan Kala, who would protest Barayev having executed their only doctor. He could declare: "The shariat court found him guilty. It was the court's decision. Allah's will."

Barayev sat addressing his men. "We are here to judge this man. He is a good surgeon, but he is running a hospital for the enemy." He turned to the man on his right. "I am asking you all to voice your opinions."

The first man stood up. "The Russians drive up to his house in a personnel carrier. He jumps on board, and they drive off together," he said. "It's clear to everyone he is working for them."

"During an Operation Jihad we have the right to put traitors to death," said another.

"We are at war, and according to any military tribunal, he would be condemned to the firing squad for saving the lives of our enemies," blurted out a third.

"He is treating Russian pigs. Execute him," declared a fourth.

The list of my sins was punctuated by rounds of mortar fire outside. The Russian attack against the Barayev contingent had begun at the edge of town near the grain elevator. I heard an explosion, which turned out to be the blowing up of an armored personnel carrier.

Shortly, more wounded were brought into the hospital, and I could hear yelling in the corridors.

My so-called judges weren't natives of Alkhan Kala and had no idea what I had really been doing. They were intimidated by Barayev and mouthed his opinions: "Traitor. Works for our enemy. Deserves to die."

But Barayev and his family were from Alkhan Kala, and he knew full well whom I treated. He knew that if I mounted a Russian personnel carrier, I was conveying wounded to the hospital and not committing treason. He knew I treated Chechen fighters, women, and children. He was not stupid. Just flexing his power and love of blood.

"So we are all in agreement that you should be executed," Barayev announced when his emirs had their say. "The shariat court now gives you the right to have the last word," he added. "What do you say?"

I think he expected me to beg for mercy. But I was determined to say what I thought of him and his "court." I had nothing to lose. Whatever I said or did wouldn't make any difference. The decision had already been made. What did surprise me, though, was that Barayev was more concerned with his "shariat court" than with the fighting between the Russians and his men, which was clearly intensifying.

"I opened a hospital for my fellow townspeople and refugees and people who needed my help," I said above the gunfire. "Today I evacuated seventy patients to save them from the Russians. Half of them were Chechen fighters. The townspeople know very well I am not a traitor. They know I operate on them. So for you to say that I am a traitor is nonsense.

"I live by the Koran. It's true I am not a scholar and I have not read the Koran completely, but I do know that it says to do good to others. The Koran says to help the needy. You don't have any idea what's written in the Koran. Your law is the law of the Kalashnikov. You came here to execute me. Your presence will bring casualties to the people of Alkhan Kala, and you are going to kill me so I couldn't help them."

The emirs fidgeted and stroked their beards.

"And one more thing," I added, speaking directly to Barayev. "Have you forgotten that in 1995 when you asked for help, I operated on you; how I removed a rifle bullet from your neck? Saved your life? You order me to be put to death—strange way to express your gratitude! Have you forgotten that people suffer the same as you and ask my help?"

At that moment there was another explosion, this time nearer to the hospital. The window frames rattled. The emirs looked at each other in surprise but kept silent. They may not have known about my help to Barayev. As I stood in the corner wondering what Barayev would do next, panicked voices filled the corridor. "Where's the doctor? We need a doctor!"

A door slammed, and I heard the sound of someone running down the corridor. Barayev jumped to his feet, strode to the door, and flung it open. A Barayev guard shouted, "Wounded fighters! Four fighters and two Russians."

Barayev turned to his emirs. "Guard him," he said. "He can treat our people first; then before leaving, we'll execute him."

I hurried to the operating room and began working. An hour later, Rumani appeared unexpectedly. "They told me in Kulari that you were still here, so I came back," she said. "I knew you would need help." I was glad of Rumani's help but worried about putting her life in danger.

When I saw that Barayev's guards had put one of his men on a mattress next to the Russian soldiers, I braced myself for trouble. "What are you going to do with him?" one guard asked, nodding toward the young Russian soldier with shrapnel in his back and legs.

"I am going to operate on him," I said.

"Don't touch those pigs!" he shouted.

"They are injured. It's no difference to me who they are."

"What do you mean? Are you telling me I'm a pig too?"

He grabbed his rifle and waved it in my direction, discharging one round into the ceiling. "I'll shoot you!" he screamed.

I rushed over and grabbed hold of his rifle. As we struggled, some of my volunteers came running. "Leave the doctor alone!"

Barayev's man was weak, and I managed to wrestle the gun from him. "In this hospital I give the orders!" I yelled. "Whether you like it or not, you will obey my orders!"

One of the young Russian soldiers who had watched my confrontation with Barayev's men called out in my direction, "Doctor, leave us be. Don't create problems for yourself."

"There are no problems," I said. "And I am going to fix you up next."

For the next thirty-six hours, Rumani and I worked around the clock in the operating room, taking only an occasional catnap when our concentration gave out. While we operated, Russian artillery pounded the town and Barayev's men fought gun battles with the Federals. The window and door frame of the hospital blew in; then the sandbags we had piled against the outside walls of the operating room fell down; then the roof took a direct hit. The houses surrounding the hospital, which gave us some protection, took numerous hits and finally burst into flames. In this commotion, Barayev disappeared. Even his own men could not find him.

Around 2 A.M. on January 4 Barayev's men picked up their wounded and left, abandoning twelve of their dead in the corridor. Undoubtedly, they would have shot the two Russian soldiers if I hadn't been there. Later, some villagers told me how they had watched Barayev and a wife being carried across the Sunzha on a military stretcher—like royalty, they said with disgust. His fighters and the wounded waded across the river, icy water up to their chests. Although it was 2 A.M., it was as light as day because of the Russian illumination flares. Some locals went up to the Federals, told them Barayev was leaving, and asked why they didn't kill him. "We don't have orders," came the answer. But it was all right to fire on peaceful civilians. I heard that when Barayev and his men reached Kulari, the elders refused to let them enter the village. "What you did in Alkhan Kala was enough," they said.

"In that case, get us cars and drive us to the next village," Barayev replied. The others agreed, and soon afterward, Barayev and his men disappeared.

I left the hospital for the first time in two days later that morning. It was 9 A.M., yet I could hardly see for the clouds of smoke from burn-ing buildings as I walked around surveying the damage. Ash covered everything. The sound of people crying and dogs barking filled the air, and in the distance I heard the rumble of gunfire. The fumes burned my throat. The place was unrecognizable. Wires, broken walls, tree branches, and burning wood blocked the way. Everywhere houses were on fire, fences were down, and people's belongings littered the courtyards along with dead animals. A blood-soaked cow with a bloated stomach lay in our neighbors' backyard. People hurried past me in a panic, anxious to find shelter for the injured, before the next *zachistka*, the mopping-up operation following the destruction of the village. I started home about noon. Nearing my house, I saw a column of military vehicles moving along the highway toward town.

Suddenly, I heard shouts and saw several hundred soldiers spread out around the block. Five of them broke out of line and advanced toward me, brandishing their weapons. Three wore black woolen masks, and two had black greasepaint on their faces.

"Freeze! Don't move!" barked one of the masked men, jabbing his rifle in my chest. "Your documents! Hand them over! *Bystro* [Quick]!"

"I don't have them. They burned up in my hospital."

"Who are you? A doctor?" a heavily built trooper asked.

"I am a surgeon. I live in Alkhan Kala."

The two men with uncovered faces had red blotches on their cheeks and bloodshot eyes. They were drunk, and I knew I was in for trouble.

Their eyes dropped to my blood-soaked scrubs. "So you've been operating on Wahhabis?" one of them said. "Well, Doctor, you've come to the end of the line. Now you'll be operating on bandits in paradise."

"I operate on all who need help. I've operated on your soldiers, and civilians, and Barayev's men too." I was so tired I hardly thought about what I was saying.

"So you operated on Barayev's men?"

I nodded. At this, the stocky *kontraktnik* in the mask struck me so hard against the chest with his rifle butt that I was thrown backward into the slush. All five soldiers immediately gathered around, kicking and punching me. Protect your head, I told myself. They probably did not beat me for more than five minutes, but it seemed like hours.

"Get up!" a greasepainted soldier shouted. "*Bystro!*"

With difficulty, I struggled to my feet, all covered in mud. The pain was so excruciating I thought they had broken my ribs.

Then the soldiers started arguing. "Shoot him!" one of them yelled.

"No, don't shoot him!" another said. "Let's take him with us. They won't fire if they see we have their doctor with us."

One masked *kontraktnik* grunted, "Let's go."

They grabbed my arms and pushed me in front of them. We marched slowly down Ulitsa Lenina (Lenin Street). Along the way, the mercenaries kicked in gates and searched the houses for fighters, yelling obscenities at the inhabitants. They were jumpy, making sure I was visible, on the radio all the time to their command post. We followed Lenin Street for half a mile, past the mosque, then right and down Nuradilova Street. I pointed out the hospital, which they insisted on entering and searching. "Twelve Barayev men dead," the masked leader radioed to his command post.

"Collect them, and we can trade them for Russian soldiers," came the reply.

When one of the masked *kontraktniki* saw the two wounded soldiers I had treated lying in the corridor, he yelled, "What are you guys doing here?"

"Don't shoot," they cried. "We are Russian soldiers."

I interjected. "They are wounded and have undergone very serious operations."

The *kontraktniki* laughed at me and radioed for transportation. When the armored personnel carrier arrived, they dragged the soldiers from their mattresses and manhandled them into the vehicle, the soldiers screaming in pain.

"Don't throw them around like that," I said. "They have been seriously wounded."

"While we fought, you've been shirking here, you fucking traitors!" The mercenaries yelled at the soldiers.

After the hospital, we continued down the street. An elderly woman emerged from one of the houses and called out to me in Chechen, "What are they doing to you?"

"I am a human shield," I said.

The old woman let the *kontraktniki* have an earful in broken Russian. "He's our doctor; leave him alone. He's treated your people too." She started down the street shouting in Chechen to anyone who would listen. "They are holding our doctor. Doctor is a prisoner!" Soon more women, followed by a few elderly men and several children, gathered.

"Move back, or we'll shoot," a masked mercenary commanded. "Go back to your houses."

But the women were insistent and angry; their comments came thick and fast:

"He's treated your injured!" screamed a woman holding two small children by the hand. "You have no right to touch the doctor!"

"He treats women and children."

"Shoot our doctor, and you'll have to shoot us all!"

The women's cries began to rattle the *kontraktniki*. By now, some thirty women, along with their children, surrounded the Russians. The village elders couldn't get a word in edgeways. Everyone shouted at once. Several children, terrified at the sight of masked soldiers, began crying. The soldiers waved their rifles wildly and shot into the air. I prayed that the instinctual reluctance to shoot women and children would force them to hold their fire. But I knew the mercenaries were not normal people, especially when full of liquor. They could do anything.

"Stand back!" a masked soldier yelled.

"Let him go!" countered the women. "Release him!"

It was 3 P.M. By now, the soldiers had had enough. They conferred hurriedly with one another; then the leader turned to me and said, "*Nu ladno, idi* [Okay, get going]!" The women had saved my life. During the *zachistkas*, the women were always ready to mount a protest in an attempt to stop the Russians from arresting or killing a man. Many of us owed our lives to them.

My confrontation with Barayev and the mercenaries had so exhausted me that I staggered home and stumbled into the cellar hoping to lie down and sleep. Everything in the cellar—my clothes, the mattress, the sheepskin—was damp and cold. I tossed and turned most of that day, never finding a comfortable position. When night came, dreams of blood, cries, explosions plagued me, and I kept waking up. Finally, I rose and went outside; my watch showed 3 A.M. Deadly quiet hung over the town. Twice in two days I had escaped death, and I said a prayer of thanks to Allah, but I knew that Barayev wouldn't forget. He had sworn to kill me. Sooner or later he would do it. I had to start making plans to leave.

Chapter 19

Descent into Hell

VERY TIME I had thoughts of leaving Chechnya, something intervened, or maybe I was just incapable of making
that decision. This time, it was the stream of townspeople
who arrived at my house to find out how I was the morning after my
run-in with Barayev and the mercenaries Several women started crying, thanking Allah I had escaped death. Their concern made me realize that I could not abandon them. To leave would be to betray them.

I went from house to house the next week, treating the wounded.
The hospital was not yet repaired from the rocket attack of November
25. Seven houses on our street had taken direct hits. Grief engulfed the
town; combined with the muddy streets and smoke in the air, there
seemed not even enough oxygen to breathe. Funerals took place on
every street. Many of the deaths were from heavy weapons directed at
the village for no obvious purpose. On January 9, a Russian personnel
carrier rolled up to the damaged hospital with an old Russian woman
and dumped her, stark naked under a blanket, in front of the door. The
soldiers said she was from the Kirova settlement and had lain in rubble
for four days after being hit by a sniper. I told them my hospital was
out of commission and pleaded for them to take her to a Russian hospital. They ignored my protests and drove off.

Nuradi made a corner for the old woman in the hospital with plastic sheeting and sandbags. The nurses found warm clothes for her, and
I managed to extract the shrapnel from her shoulder and clean up the

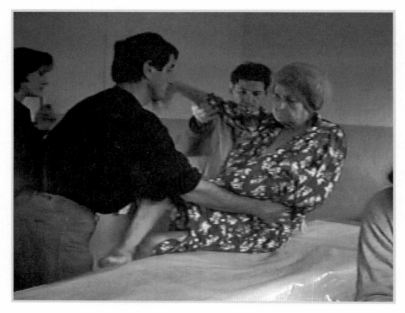

Most of my patients were peaceful civilians. Here we prepare an elderly
Russian woman for surgery.

wound. She said she would see to it that I was written about in the
newspapers and that people knew the truth about Chechnya. I
thanked her, thinking that no one could possibly know the truth about
Chechnya.

While the townspeople struggled to clear up the debris, bury the
dead, and care for the wounded, the *kontraktniki* marauded under
cover of the *zachistka*. They stripped the houses, loading all movable
possessions into their military trucks. I was walking home from the
hospital one day when an old woman rushed up to me and said, "A
Russian troop carrier is parked in the courtyard of your house. The
soldiers are taking everything out. We tried to stop them, but they
threatened to shoot us."

When I arrived, a crowd of women and elders were shouting at the
soldiers. The soldiers ignored them. Out went our china, clothes, tele-

vision, VCR, even my sports trophies and medals. I watched helplessly as the soldiers drove off.

The next day, some fifty Russian soldiers commandeered what was left of my house and turned it into a bunker to protect them while carrying out the *zachistka*. The walls of the ground floor, which I had originally built with reinforced concrete, were still standing. To protect against stray bullets and shrapnel, they blocked the windows with sandbags made with flour sacks, which they had taken from our store-room, dumping the precious ingredients on the floor.

Several days later, the Federals withdrew after completing their mopping-up operation. Nana returned from Kulari with Malika and Hussein to inspect the damage. The place looked as though a tank brigade had swept through it. Flour all over the floor; macaroni on the sofa; jars of fruits and vegetables Nana put up for the winter splattered everywhere; dishes smashed; family photographs strewn all over the courtyard and trampled by muddy boots; feathers everywhere from the chickens that the soldiers had killed and eaten. They had even pried up the parquet flooring for firewood. Moreover, they hadn't bothered to use the toilet but had relieved themselves anywhere, including in some of the fancy crockery Nana kept for guests. It was an abomination, but one familiar to every town and village in Chechnya.

With the help of friends, I rehung the iron gates, which had been knocked off their hinges. Our family started cleaning up as well as we could. Then Nana and I went inside the house. It was dark, so we lit a kerosene lamp and sat down on a pile of rubble, both of us lost in thought, too exhausted to talk. I was worried about her, about everything she had been through. Again, the thought of leaving Chechnya entered my mind. How much more could I take? A loud noise interrupted my thoughts. I rushed outside to find that an army personnel carrier had just plowed through the gates again.

"Stay put! Don't come out, or we'll shoot you like rabid dogs." Three *kontraktniki* jumped out of the vehicle, guns at the ready. "Up against the wall!"

Let them take what they want, just so long as they don't execute us,

I thought. It turned out that the *kontraktniki* had returned for some hardwood flooring they had piled up in the garage, probably for use as fuel or to sell for vodka.

OVER THE NEXT weeks, things were more or less calm—that is, as calm as things can be during war time. The elders kept lists of those who were wounded or who had died, informing the relatives if possible. People searched for their lost loved ones in the makeshift morgues, desperately collecting money to pay for the return of the bodies for burial. They paid a fee just to enter the building where the bodies were lying. Prices to buy back the bodies depended on the importance of the individual. A dead field commander fetched the highest prices, then a fighter, followed by ordinary civilians. It was an unconscionable trade. I heard of many cases in which the body had organs missing.

While relatives searched for their dead, I continued my struggle to treat the living, including the old Russian woman whose shoulder was in such bad shape it needed several skin grafts. Then at 6 A.M. on January 31, 2000, Nuradi summoned me urgently to the hospital. "Come quickly! The wounded are pouring in!" he said.

When I arrived at the hospital, I saw dozens of wounded lying like displaced cordwood, some on top of others, along the corridors of the ground and second floors The hospital didn't have room for all the wounded in the corridors, so many lay on mattresses outside, their blood forming crystals of red ice on the snow. They had come on sleds, on the backs of comrades, on stretchers devised from jackets and poles. The shock of this scene disoriented me. Whom to treat first? How could we possibly alleviate pain now that our anesthetics were all but gone? For a few moments, I was paralyzed.

"There are about two hundred here already," Nuradi informed me, "fighters and refugees from Grozny. And a few wounded Russian soldiers, too, which our guys dragged with them. More are arriving."

I had walked into my recurring nightmare. I looked down, expecting to see the snakes. I will wake up, I thought, fighting the panic. I took a deep breath. All I could do was work as long as Allah gave me strength.

Even in war life goes on: Grozny after the bombardment. (Laurent Van Der Stockt/Gamma Presse Images)

What I learned in the next hours was that some 4,000 people had escaped from Grozny during the night. This group included 2,000 fighters, under the command of the major Chechen field commanders, including Shamil Basayev; countless refugees; some 50 Russian soldiers, some 20 of them wounded; and several foreign journalists. Since the start of the second war, round-the-clock shelling had pulverized the city in an attempt to drive out the fighters. Hardly a building remained, only truncated walls, gaping windows, and smoldering rubble. The once-thriving capital had been reduced to a wasteland. No food, no electricity, no water. Thousands were trapped in cellars along with the rats. In the last weeks, deep-penetration missiles and vacuum bombs killed thousands, and Shamil Basayev finally gave the order to evacuate. The plan was for the Chechen fighters to retreat to the mountains and launch guerrilla attacks from there.

It was snowing hard when the evacuation began. Shamil Basayev and several other field commanders, including Lecha Dudayev, the nephew of Chechnya's late president, led the way. The fighters edged along a narrow path leading south from the city, following the Sunzha River past the settlement of Kirova. The going was difficult because for three days it had been snowing, and in places they plunged up to their knees. The Russians had mined an open field near the river, about three miles short of Alkhan Kala. Later, a Russian general would tell the press that they had "tricked" Basayev into crossing the minefield. That wasn't true.

Basayev and his men knew about the mines, but the snow had been disorienting and they lost the trail. The field commanders convened to discuss the best way to continue. Someone suggested sending the Russian prisoners ahead to trigger the mines and forge the path for the others. Lecha Dudayev and several other field commanders disagreed. They contended that intentional killing of weaponless Russian soldiers contradicted the spirit of Chechnya's struggle for independence and the Muslim faith. Shamil Basayev agreed, saying that as a senior commander, he should be the one to lead the procession across the minefield. So they pushed on. To protect the life of their leader, two of his bodyguards rushed forward, sacrificing themselves on the mines but opening up a safe path. A few yards away, another mine detonated, shattering Basayev's right foot and ankle. In the ensuing panic, people started running in different directions, setting off still more mines. Lying in the snow, Basayev called for calm. "Stop running!" he shouted. Volunteers pushed through the snow, forging a safe path; many died when they trampled on invisible, live mines.

Meanwhile, Russian snipers and tanks on the ridge to the east fired at the fleeing people. When it was over, some 170 lay dead on the field. The mines made it impossible for relatives to collect the corpses. Bodies were not retrieved until many months later.

Ultimately, some 300 severely wounded reached my hospital. I edged my way down the corridor to assess the damage. Blood splattered my trousers and oozed into my shoes. Looking over the wounded, I was struck by their stoic reactions. Few struggled or yelled for painkillers. Some read from the Koran, while others comforted their comrades. The fighters were mostly young boys from villages throughout Chechnya.

The whole scene sickened me. The war was claiming Chechnya's best. These were youths, not more than eighteen or nineteen years old, just out of school. My eyes fell on a young fighter drifting in and

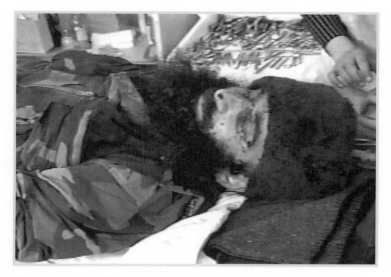

Field commander Shamil Basayev, near death, awaits amputation of his right foot.

out of consciousness near the door. Next to him lay a young woman with a shattered foot. His face was pale from loss of blood, and his eyes held that wide-open look heralding death. I called to Nuradi to get him onto the operating table.

"No. No," the young man murmured. His voice was faint, and I leaned close to hear him better. "Take her," he said, indicating the young woman.

"Your situation is more serious than hers."

"Take her first," he insisted, as his eyelids slowly closed. This boy's nobility in ceding his place filled me with pride but also with anger and a terrible sadness.

"Make a list of the worst off!" I called to the nurses. "Get everyone's name. Whoever has lost the most blood, bring to me first. Hurry! Check everyone! Check the pulses."

As I worked, townspeople arrived to give blood. The first person I operated on was a fighter whose legs were shattered at the knee joint. There was no way to salvage his legs.

The second patient on my operating table was Basayev, whom the Russians were so eager to kill they had announced a $1-million reward for his capture. Life takes strange turns. When I knew him as a schoolboy, he was so quiet and was consumed by soccer. On this day, I barely recognized him lying in the corridor. His face underneath the matted beard was caked with blood, dirt, and gunpowder. His hands, frostbitten, were wrapped in rags.

"Is that you, Khassan?" he asked as I bent over. The explosion had blinded him. "Don't operate on me first. Deal with the young guys before me."

"You've lost too much blood," I replied. I slipped on the blood pressure cuff: 60 systolic over 40 diastolic, a near-death reading. He had probably lost 50 percent of his blood; another half hour, and he'd be dead. I had to work fast. He was suffering oxygen starvation as a result of failing circulation.

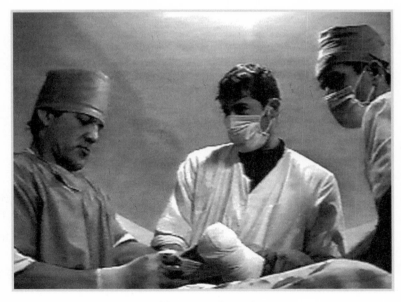

Bandaging an amputee assisted by my nephew Ali.

Under the dirt and gunpowder, his skin was paper white, contrasting with his full black beard. I removed what remained of his combat boots. The sole of his right foot was shredded, hanging by tendons and soft muscle tissue, exposing shattered fragments of the tibia and fibula.

"In pain?" I asked. "You are so quiet."

He shook his head. "I don't want to interfere with your work," he whispered.

"I'm going to have to amputate your leg above the ankle," I said.

"Do your work," he said, "but if there are others worse off, take them first."

We hooked up two IV lines of glucose and Polyglukin to his arms; then I ordered my nurse to check his blood pressure every three minutes and shout out the readings. We managed to get it up to 80/60.

By this time, word had leaked out that Shamil Basayev was among the wounded. Several Western journalists stormed into the operating room, madly clicking their cameras in an effort to capture the picture of Russia's nemesis. I ordered them to leave. The only person who recorded the entire operation with a video camera was my nephew Adam; Reuters later distributed his footage around the world.

Rumani split Basayev's right trouser leg, heavy with blood and snow, from the ankle to the knee and rubbed iodine over the operative field directly above the right ankle joint. Then I injected the area with lidocaine and made a vertical incision with a scalpel along the tibia bone. Next I started to cut, layer by layer, through the muscles, the fascia connecting tissues, clamping them, and step by step, sewing up the loose fragments of the cut muscles simultaneously with the blood vessels and arteries in the amputation area.

I was assisted by my nephew Ali, who immobilized Basayev's leg while I scrupulously scraped the flesh and muscle away from the bones along the line of amputation some seven inches above the ankle. Next I took my carpenter's hacksaw and sawed through the two leg bones. Finally, I sewed a flap of skin with surgical stitches to the healthy tissue around the stump and inserted drainage tubes fashioned from fingers of a pair of surgical gloves. As soon as I had finished, Basayev's guards rushed him from the building, knowing the Russians would be hunting for him everywhere. As they left, Rumani quickly wrapped the severed foot in plastic and handed it to Basayev's relatives for burial.

It turned out that Vakha Aigumov, my old enemy from the prosecutor's office, was third on the operating table. He had left his prosecutorial job to command 100 fighters in Grozny and fled the capital in the general retreat.

"Do what you must," Aigumov said when I told him I would have to amputate his leg. Still, I didn't want him or his relatives to think I was taking revenge, so I called in his brother to look at the leg. He agreed that the amputation was necessary.

I worked all that day, and throughout that night, to the groans of the wounded and the dying as the mullah and the elders intoned the words of the Koran. During those hateful hours, many of the famous field commanders passed through my hospital. Abdul Malik was brought in wounded; others like Hunkar-Pasha Isparilov and Lecha Dudayev were brought in dead; Ruslan Gelayev survived and hung around the corridors. Ali, Razyat, and my other volunteers moved among the living, adjusting the tourniquets and cleaning wounds.

I received word that several nurses and doctors, including Oumar Khanbiev, the Chechen minister of health, were on their way from Grozny to help. That was cheering news, because my strength was fading, and my arms ached from sawing. In addition to the amputations, I performed brain surgeries using a carpenter's hand drill.

Before long, I had cut through so much bone that the teeth at the center of the hacksaw blade became dull. I didn't have a second blade, so I started bearing down hard on both ends of the saw, easing up on the middle. I got so used to this three-part stroke that the sawing motion became automatic. For twenty-four hours, I didn't leave my operating room; nor did I drink or eat. I couldn't face the scene in the corridor. Finally, someone placed a cup of strong tea laced with sugar in my hand, and I squatted in the corner for a few minutes. Every second, every minute was a man's life. I lost all sense of time. My hands felt increasingly heavy, dead weights, reluctant to obey. My fingers fumbled

Still in bloody gloves, I take a break during the marathon operating session.

with the thread. I prayed that I wouldn't pass out in the middle of an operation. human

About twenty-seven hours after the crisis hit, I heard a roar overhead. "Please, Allah, let me finish this patient," I said under my breath. I felt dizzy. I quickly stitched the flesh together and tied off the thread. Then I sensed myself falling. The next thing I knew, I was outside and Rumani and Razyat were rubbing my face with snow. The cold revived me, and I stumbled back to the operating room.

We had run out of surgical thread, and I was now using ordinary thread soaked in alcohol. Working with the wet thread proved difficult and annoying. By this time, I had sewed so many wounds without gloves that cuts developed between my fingers. The blisters on my hands were bursting and turning into small wounds. And still no sign of the doctors and nurses from Grozny. I feared they had been unable to reach Alkhan Kala.

On the second day, February 1, I operated without a break until about midnight, when I fainted a second time. Again, the nurses rubbed my face with snow, and I went back to work. By the third day, I had performed sixty-seven amputations and seven brain surgeries. The severed limbs piled up for Nuradi to bury in the corner of the hospital grounds with a quick prayer near the fence.

After two days with hardly a break, my strength gave out. I could no longer control my hands, and my arms developed spasms. There was still no sign of the doctors and nurses from Grozny, and Rumani insisted I get some sleep. She said I was of no use in my current state. Stumbling home at 4 A.M. February 2, I breathed in cold air and ash. A fresh snow had fallen, and the sky was clear. Flames and rebounding flashes of artillery fire mingled with the stars. I was indifferent to the gunfire and explosions around me. All I could think about were the dead and the mangled in the corridor with their dangling extremities.

AFTER I ARRIVED home, I tried to wash my hands. The pain was excruciating. Malika took my bloodstained clothes to wash. "Don't touch them," I said. "Keep them as souvenirs of what we have been through." I fell into bed, so exhausted I couldn't sleep. I was used up. It was so dark I hadn't noticed the blood on my undershirt. When I woke up, a few hours later, I found that my chest was covered in dried blood; under my nails and between my fingers—more blood.

After a quick breakfast of tea, cheese, and bread, forced on me by Nana and Malika, I trudged back to the hospital at 9 A.M. February 2.

I knew that we had to get the wounded out of the hospital; otherwise they would be killed when the Russians moved in for the zachistka. Some forty men hid in the storage area under the vegetable depot. Relatives and volunteers around the village hid others under the floorboards, hoping they wouldn't suffocate once the boards were nailed down again. Any male between the ages of ten and sixty risked being detained, executed, or ransomed off.

We loaded three buses with wounded fighters and several women and children, hoping to transport them to the hospital in Urus-Martan. By this time, the doctors and nurses from Grozny had appeared. They had arrived earlier but were hiding out in the town until now. They were ready to accompany the patients. Although many civilians were wounded, we gave priority to the fighters because we knew what would happen to them if they fell into the hands of the Russians. Those fighters who wouldn't fit in the buses hid in the village. We had been told that Bislan Gantimirov, an ethnic Chechen who had been appointed the Russian government's representative in Chechnya, would give us free passage to transport the wounded to the hospital. Gantimirov, a former mayor of Grozny, was an unpopular figure in Chechnya. We were informed that the Russians would begin a *zachistka* at 3 P.M. I wore my hospital uniform and took a seat in the first bus. A military jeep containing two of Gantimirov's men led the way. The convoy descended the hill leading to the bridge over the river a mile down the road to Urus-Martan. At the bridge, two more of Gantimirov's representatives flagged us down.

"Three buses are here with the wounded fighters," one of them shouted into his radio after we stopped.

"Have they got the guns?" Gantimirov's voice came back over the airwaves. "They must surrender one weapon for each passenger on the bus."

"We have no weapons," I said. This was the first I had heard about weapons.

"No weapons," Gantimirov's aide reported.

"Then turn the buses around and have them return with the guns," Gantimirov ordered.

"Let the buses stay here, and we will go back for the weapons," I said to Gantimirov's aide. "The patients are suffering. We have no painkillers, and the road is very rough."

"Orders are that you return to Alkhan Kala," he said.

I looked at my watch; it was already noon. I didn't understand why Gantimirov was insisting we return to Alkhan Kala. I didn't trust him. But at that moment we had no options. After agreeing to have the buses back at the bridge by 2 P.M., we turned around, drove back to Alkhan Kala, along with the jeep carrying two of Gantimirov's men. We parked in front of the hospital, where hundreds of people had gathered.

"We have to gather up the weapons immediately," I said after descending from the bus. The crowd as well as the passengers inside the bus were silent. It would take a lot of persuasion to make them hand over their weapons, probably hidden with friends in the village.

"Where are the guns?" I asked. Still no one replied. "Hand them over, or we'll not be allowed to pass."

"We won't give up our weapons," one of the passengers said. Others echoed agreement.

"For the sake of Allah, if you don't, a lot of you will die. A life is more important than a weapon."

After some argument, the fighters reluctantly agreed, and volunteers fanned out around town to collect the weapons. Within half an hour the vehicle was full of guns. Just as we were about to depart, a woman ran up to us to say that the *zachistka* had already started, that people were being beaten and taken away.

"Get Gantimirov on the radio," I yelled to his representative.

He tried to reach him, but there was no answer. "We have to find him," he said. "I'll go with you."

"I don't want you going alone; I'll go with you," said Hasilbek, my father's old friend. I was grateful for his company. Gantimirov didn't know me, but Hasilbek would command respect. In his gray sheepskin *papakha*, the village elder cut a distinguished figure. We climbed into the jeep, headed for the bridge and over the river to the settlement of Partizanskaya, where Gantimirov was supposed to be. Time was running out.

Since our earlier trip to the bridge, the Russians had dug in, with tanks lined up along the river, their gun barrels pointed toward Alkhan Kala. We flashed the lights of our car, praying they wouldn't fire on us.

We found Gantimirov behind a service station where the Russians had established temporary headquarters, conversing with a group of high-ranking military officers. In the nearby field, drivers sat in their tanks, awaiting orders to advance. Across the road, some fifteen or twenty Chechen women who had been detained on their way back from Ingushetia stood in a group with their sacks and boxes at their feet. A sense of anticipation filled the air. No one was smoking; no one was talking. Gantimirov and the Russian officers turned to look at me.

"We thought we had an agreement with you that we could take the wounded to the hospital in Urus-Martan before two oclock." I addressed Gantimirov in Chechen. "You know that if they are still there when the Russians arrive, they will be slaughtered."

"The operation has begun," Gantimirov snapped. "I can't help you. You should have collected the weapons when you were told."

"We came here for your help. If you don't help these men, they'll be sent to a filtration camp and tortured to death." Anger rose in my stomach. We were being double-crossed. Thinking I was about to hit Gantimirov, Hasilbek jumped between us. Gantimirov scowled, walked back to a jeep, and got in.

"You are to blame! It's all your fault!" he shouted, rolling down the window and sticking his head out. "Blame yourself, doctor!"

We had to get back and tell everyone what had happened and get the buses removed.

I turned to a Russian colonel and said, "At least let us get the women and children out of Alkhan Kala and to a hospital."

He clicked on his radio to ask permission. "No one is to leave until after the cleanup," came the reply.

I looked around and saw the group of women a few hundred yards away. I called to them in Chechen: "Try and get back to the village and tell the people in the buses what's happened! There are still wounded at the hospital. Get them hidden! You'll have to go to Kulari and wade across the river. The Russians have blown up the suspension bridge."

One young woman managed to slip away while Hasilbek and I went from one officer to another, hoping to get permission to return to Alkhan Kala. No one wanted to talk to us. On high alert, they communicated back and forth on their radios, monitoring the operation. If we listened carefully, we could follow some of it: a skirmish here, an arrest there, intermittent gunfire. Suddenly, we heard a major, standing not far from us, bark into his radio, "Have you found that fucking bandit doctor yet?"

Hasilbek looked at me.

I grabbed the zipper on my jacket and pulled it all the way up. I didn't want the top of my scrubs to show. It was so cold that day I had put on wool pants over my scrubs. We could hear the reply come over the major's radio: "We are here outside his house. His mother says she hasn't seen him for two days."

"Go house to house. Find him!" the major said. "He is operating on bandits."

It was amazing. They were so busy organizing the assault on the town that they hadn't even asked to see our documents.

"Let our doctor go!" A voice called out from the group of women on the other side of the road. Her words floated off into thin air. My heart jumped, but the major paid no attention. Hasilbek rushed over to alert the women of the situation. Now they yelled, "Let our neighbor go! He isn't a fighter. He has a family."

All our efforts to return to the village failed, and I prayed that the young woman had made it across the river to warn Alkhan Kala. Around 6 P.M., the three buses arrived, followed by ten closed military trucks. I was sure they contained prisoners from Alkhan Kala.

"Where are you taking the buses?" I asked a general standing nearby, an ominous feeling sweeping over me.

"To Tolstoi-Yurt," he replied.

"But there are seriously wounded people in the buses; they need to go to the hospital in Urus-Martan."

The general shrugged his shoulders and walked away.

Tolstoi-Yurt was where the Chernokozovo filtration camp was located. The Russians had created no fewer than twenty-two such camps in Chechnya, some located on the grounds of Muslim schools, others in the basements of large stores. The most infamous camp was Chernokozovo. Theoretically, the purpose of such camps was to weed out the fighters from peaceful civilians. But in practice, anyone taken to a filtration camp was presumed guilty and was beaten and tortured. I knew only too well what awaited the wounded in the buses.

Gantimirov had handed the fighters over to the Russians. They never would have relinquished their weapons if they thought they were going to Chernokozovo. I walked over to the buses to break this bad news. I said that it was out of my hands, that I was helpless. Later, one of the doctors accused me of helping send them to the filtration camp, an accusation that devastated me.

After the buses departed, the Russians allowed Hasilbek to leave. A column of soldiers marched me across the road to an abandoned farm surrounded by a high brick wall. As we walked, they cursed me.

We walked through a gate and into the enclosed area, where a battered steel shipping container was standing. They pushed me inside the container, which they had fashioned into a lockup with a single window covered with bars. Outside, an icy wind was blowing. I crouched in the far corner and pulled my knees to my chest, trying to keep warm. My limbs soon became numb, and I rubbed them to bring the circulation back, but it didn't help much. Periodically, light from a flare shone through the bars, casting strange patterns on the walls, and in the distance I heard the thud of gunfire. Sleep was impossible. Maybe tomorrow I would find myself in a filtration camp along with my patients, I thought. Gantimirov's words circled through my brain: "You are to blame! It's all your fault!"

Around 9 A.M. the next day, February 3, I heard the voices of women outside, mixed with male protests. I couldn't hear exactly what was being said, but I guessed the women were demanding my release. Half an hour later, the end door of the container swung open.

"Out!" a Russian soldier commanded.

I tried to stand up but fell over on my side. I was so cold. "Give me a little time to get the blood flowing," I said, rubbing my legs.

"Get up before we beat the shit out of you!" the soldier yelled.

I staggered from the container. "You bandit, we should shoot you!" the Russian soldier shouted. Not a word about why I was being released. The women rushed to surround me. "You as well!" the soldier waved his Kalashnikov in the direction of the women.

The women and I returned to Alkhan Kala on foot. Approaching the hospital, I saw a splash of color—a line of men's trousers, jackets, T-shirts, and boots—draped over the fence surrounding what was left of the hospital. A woman said the Russians had stripped the wounded, beaten them, thrown them half-naked into trucks, and driven off. "When people came looking for their relatives, they could tell by the clothes that they had been there," she said. Somewhere the Russians had heard that Wahhabis, for religious reasons, didn't wear underwear, which is why they insisted on stripping the prisoners.

The young woman who had volunteered to warn the people in the buses had made it back to Alkhan Kala, but not in time to save all the wounded. Only a few had managed to slip through and hide in the village before the *zachistka* started.

The first thing I did was to rescue my instruments from the hospital. Some young boys surveying the ruins warned that the Russians had mined the building and booby-trapped the corpses. Move them, and they would explode, they said. Hasilbek and some of the other elders tried to prevent me from entering. But I had no choice; I had to get my instruments. I climbed through a window. Seven corpses lay on the floor in the passageway. Stepping around the trip wires, I edged toward the operating room, which was in shambles. Blood was splattered on the walls. Piles of soiled clothes lay on the floor, along with fallen plaster, passports of the men I had operated on, and dozens of unexploded grenades which could go off at any moment. I threw the passports into a cardboard box, along with ten surgical clamps, bandages, tourniquets, a scalpel, and a few other instruments, and tiptoed out.

Once I was outside, a nurse called out, "Come and see what they have done!"

I followed her down the steps of a makeshift dugout in the hospital grounds. There I found seven of my patients, lying dead, executed at point-blank range, among them the old Russian woman. The sight of her lying there in her blood-soaked robe was a terrible blow. I had fought for weeks to save her life, and in one second it was wiped out.

THE NEXT MORNING, a group of people assembled outside my house, seeking help. My limbs felt weak, my hands swollen, my shoulders and back ached. I went out to speak to them. "I can't do this any longer. I don't have the strength in my hands," I said, holding them up to show the relatives of a young boy whose lower leg had been blown off by a mine.

"Khassan, we don't believe that," the boy's brother said. "Won't you just come and see him?" Their insistence irritated me. They demanded things I could not do. I always tried to make myself appear strong for their sake, but underneath I was as weak as they.

"Just take a look at him," they begged. Reluctantly, I agreed.

They drove me to their house, along with my nurses Rumani and Markha. The young man lay on the kitchen table. They had hooked up a car battery to provide light. His brother said he was nineteen years old. He was a tall, good-looking boy. The smell of gangrene filled the room. His blood pressure was dropping; his pulse almost impossible to find.

"His leg needs to be amputated at the thigh. He has lost so much blood already, he may not survive."

"If he dies, that's Allah's will, but there could be a chance if you operate," his brother pleaded.

What could I do? I doubted the boy would survive, but the relatives believed in miracles. They would be disillusioned if I didn't try.

"We're out of painkillers. Someone go out on the street and see if anyone has any lidocaine, novocaine, anything," I said. I ordered Rumani and Markha to prepare the patient for amputation.

As I worked, his blood pressure fell to 60 over 40, and his eyes rolled to the back of his head. "We're losing him!" I yelled. Every time his blood pressure dipped, we stopped the operation and tried to raise it with Polyglukin. Markha's blood was compatible with the boy's, so she gave him 400 cubic centimeters.

While fighting to save the boy's life, I felt a surge of adrenaline. The pain in my hands disappeared. The operation was difficult. At the trickiest moment, when I was about to tie off the femoral artery in the leg, the light from the car battery gave out. A neighbor lent us a flashlight, but it was weak; I had to bring it right up to the wound to do my work. When the operation was finished, I was bathed in sweat and couldn't straighten my back. But the relatives were appeased and tried to express their thanks by forcing the keys to their new sports car on me. I refused, saying, "What I did is for Allah. Thank him."

Over the next days, I treated patients in their homes, aware that the Russians were looking for me. One of the people I visited was Vakha Aigumov. He looked shamefaced when I examined him on a cot in the cellar of his house. As I unwound the bandages on his stump, I sensed he wanted to tell me something but found it hard to express himself.

"I am ashamed of how we acted with you," he blurted out.

I was glad Vakha recognized that mistake. Dada never tired of telling me, "Khassan, you see, good always triumphs in the end." A reassuring thought when all around me I saw nothing but suffering and brutality.

By the time I had dealt with the urgent cases, my back was in agony again. My nurses now pressed me to leave Chechnya. "You have treated all the serious cases. We'll look after the dressings," Rumani said. "It's dangerous for you here." But I couldn't escape because the town was surrounded by Russian troops.

On the morning of February 8, Hasilbek's son, Isa, drove Rumani and me back to my house after an amputation. The snow had melted, and water filled the potholes and craters. I saw a strange car parked outside our house, a red Zhiguli. I told Isa to slow down. You could never be too careful. Malika stood at the gate, and next to her was a clean-shaven stranger dressed in well-pressed khakis. From his dark hair, pale skin, and prominent nose, I recognized him as Chechen. Isa stopped the car, and I got out.

"There he is." Malika was pointing at me. I greeted the man in Chechen.

"I have come from Nazran," he said, shaking my hand, "to help you get out of Chechnya."

"What is this all about?" I asked.

"I am a colonel in the FSB. My name is Ruslan." He explained that he had been born in Alkhan Kala but had spent much of his career working in Moscow. His superiors had ordered him to Ingushetia to attend a special meeting with the military authorities in charge of the North Caucasian Military District.

"They want your arrest," he said. "I told them that you were a doctor, that you upheld the doctor's oath and were obliged to treat everyone. They said they didn't give a damn about any medical oath or any international convention; that you were saving fighters and had to be stopped."

Although Ruslan Temirkhanov was an employee of the Russian security services, I felt I could trust him. I sensed he was like the Chechen security colonel who had helped Malika and Razyat when they were trapped in Grozny in August 1996. I invited him into the house, but he shook his head.

"We have to leave for Ingushetia right away," he said. "We don't have time; the borders are being sealed. Once it gets dark, it will be difficult to get out. I'll stay out here and have a cigarette while you get ready."

I told Malika to find Adam, who needed to send some videotapes of the operation on Basayev to Reuters from Ingushetia. If possible, I wanted to persuade Adam and Ali to leave Chechnya. Ali was putting himself at risk not only by helping me in the hospital but also by helping Adam to transport film to Ingushetia. I rushed inside, changed my clothes, and grabbed my passport. I hated to leave my medical bag but to carry it would give me away immediately. Nana and Malika were relieved that I was leaving for a safe place to join Zara, Dada, and the children.

When Adam showed up, I explained to Ruslan that I needed to take him with us. Ruslan was unenthusiastic. "There won't be room for him. I've got to pick up three wounded men and get them across the border, too," he said.

"We'll manage," I replied. "Adam can sit on my lap."

We got into the car and drove off in search of the wounded fighters. We picked them up one by one at different houses and squeezed them into the backseat. They were all clean-shaven and dressed in ordinary clothes.

"You're taking an incredible risk," I said to Ruslan, once we were on our way.

He shrugged. "I have worked for the FSB for many years. During the first war, they wanted to send me to Chechnya, but I refused. Then when this second war broke out, I decided I would use my position to help a few individuals."

I fell silent and gazed out the car window. What was there to say? It seemed that Allah had sent another person to save me.

Part 5

Refuge in America

Chapter 20

My Escape

A S WE DROVE down the hill with the three wounded men toward the bridge, an empty bus approached us. The driver flashed his lights and flagged us down. In the mirror we saw the bus stop, so we braked and backed up. The driver turned out to be one of my old schoolmates, Khamzat Lasanov. He said he had just come through a checkpoint at Kulari and had heard the guards talking about me over their radios.

"They claim you are sneaking wounded fighters out of Chechnya and must be arrested," he said. "They have circulated a description of your car, the license number, to all the checkpoints. Be careful! They're after you!"

Ruslan turned to me. "We better go back and return the men," he said. We hated to do this, but there was no alternative. The wounded men understood. Ruslan turned the car around and sped back to Alkhan Kala, leaving the men at the houses where we had picked them up only minutes before. I now started worrying about Adam's videotapes, which were the size of tape recorder microcassettes.

"Let me have those tapes," Ruslan commanded. "You'll be checked. I won't be. If the guards find them on you, you'll be executed on the spot." He took a packet of Marlboros out of his left breast pocket and emptied the cigarettes into the glove compartment. Then he put the two tapes in the packet and stuffed it back into his pocket. "Ready?" he asked.

It was a little after 3 P.M. and was beginning to get dark. I thought for a moment. "Whatever will be, will be," I replied. "Let's go."

A MILE FARTHER down the road, at the military checkpoint, soldiers flagged us down. "Get out, one by one. Hands up! Flat on the ground!" they shouted after we stopped the car.

"Open the hood and the baggage compartment immediately!" one of the soldiers yelled. After searching the car, they demanded our documents. While the soldiers were scrutinizing them, I looked around and saw an empty house nearby with rifle barrels pointed out the windows. On the roof, soldiers had taken up their positions. They had assumed we were carrying fighters and were ready for us.

One of the soldiers withdrew a few yards and clicked on his radio. "We have here an FSB colonel and two civilians, not fighters," he said.

He returned, handed back our documents, and waved us on. Apparently, these soldiers had not yet been informed that the name of the "bandit doctor" they were looking for was Baiev. Thank goodness I had abandoned my medical bag at home!

At the next post, the soldiers took one look at Ruslan and didn't bother to check us. At the third post, they signaled us to stop the car. Ruslan braked, then opened his window. "There is intensive shelling down the road at Shaami-Yurt," the guard told him. "You can't go on. It's too dangerous."

"We'll risk it," Ruslan replied.

"Don't say we didn't warn you."

We drove at breakneck speed. Over the roar of the engine we could feel the repercussions of artillery. Tracer flares lit up the sky. We passed another six checkpoints before crossing the border into Ingushetia. I gave Ruslan the address where my family was staying in the village of Troitskoye outside the capital of Nazran. When we arrived at the house, I invited him in, but he said he had a meeting. Then he looked up and repeated the address to commit it to memory. "I promise I will return," he said. "Then we can sit down and get to know one another better." As I watched him drive away, I doubted we would ever see each other again. Adam left immediately to hand his tapes over to a Reuters representative.

When I entered the house, Zara, Maryam, Islam, and Hussein's two children, Khava and Adam, were lying on the floor watching television. They all jumped up to greet me. Markha was lying asleep on a rolled-up mattress. I told Zara briefly how I had escaped, then went into the next room to greet Dada, who lay on a cot, crutches propped next to him. I flopped down on the mattress.

I assured him that Nana, Hussein, and my sisters were all right. Then I told him what had happened. Dada looked puzzled when I told him about the order for my arrest. "But you're a doctor. You operated on Russians. Maybe they don't know that," he said.

"They don't care who I operated on," I said, "Russians, the Russian-speaking population, Chechens—they don't care. For them it's war, and where there is war, there is lawlessness, hatred, and evil."

Dada shook his head. He reached for his crutches and swung his legs off the bed.

"I'll go to Mozdok," he said, referring to the town in the neighboring republic of North Ossetia. "I am an invalid of the Great Patriotic War. I'll talk to General Shamanov; he will listen to me. I'll go to the top commander and tell them not to hunt you down. I'll get a piece of paper from them saying you are not to be pursued."

Poor Dada, he didn't understand what kind of world the war had now created. He was still living in the Soviet Union. In that bygone era, with a semblance of order, a complaint to the Communist Party might bring results.

"It's unrealistic," I said. "To get to Mozdok is impossible. If you can't even go to the bathroom alone, how can you go to Mozdok? All the roads are closed. The borders are patrolled, and the guards are not letting any Chechens through. You're going to say, 'Please, my son shouldn't be pursued'? Everyone in Chechnya is being tracked down; nobody is safe."

Dada fell silent. "It can't be," he said when he finally spoke. "There are generals there; the Russians are intelligent people. Talk to them."

"Dada, people are lining up for days, for weeks, trying to get news of their sons who disappeared on the battlefield or who are rotting in filtration camps. At least I'm not in a camp."

Dada dropped his head in his hands.

"It's a different world now, Dada," I said.

His shoulders slumped. He replaced his crutches against the wall and got back on the cot. After that, he didn't talk for a long time; then he asked me to tell him everything that had happened in Alkhan Kala: who had been killed, who wounded, who had been made an invalid. He shook his head in disbelief as I described the devastation.

"This war won't end soon," he said.

That evening, Zara told me how she and Khava had trudged through the mud for half a mile to haul water from the river for washing clothes. With five children, one of them an infant, laundry was a full-time job: heat the water, scrub everything by hand, and hang it around the single gas ring to dry. For drinking water, they went even farther, to a spring a mile away. Electricity was spasmodic, but thank God for gas so Zara could prepare food. I could see that she was exhausted, but she didn't say anything. She knew how lucky we were compared to so many others.

That night, I slept badly. Outside, a thick fog pressed against the windows of the house. The planes taking off and landing at the nearby airport woke me intermittently, my heart pounding. Lying there, I thought about Ruslan and the risks he had taken to help me, and I wasn't the only person he had helped. He brushed off my thanks, insisting that what he had done was nothing.

Each morning, I awoke more exhausted than when I lay down. The news out of Chechnya was depressing, especially concerning the massacre at Saadi-Qotar, also known by its Russian name of Komsomol'skoye. Before leaving Chechnya, we had all seen the smoke and flames rising from the burning houses but didn't know exactly what had taken place. It turned out that the Russians received a tip that some 1,500 fighters intended to enter the village to get food on their retreat to the mountains. I heard that field commander Gelayev, who had passed through my hospital on January 31, was among them. Once the fighters arrived, the Federals sealed off the town in the dead of night and permitted no one to leave.

As the Russians began shelling, a crowd of women and children approached the troops, pleading for safe passage out of the town. They were refused. The Federals also prohibited any of the villagers from neighboring towns to bring in relief supplies. For a week, the Russians made the residents live under open skies alongside the Federal lines, in effect turning them into human shields. By the time the bombardment ended, not a house remained standing. About 800 fighters escaped, but 700, along with hundreds of civilians, were killed.

I didn't know which was worse: being in Chechnya under the shelling or in Ingushetia unable to help the wounded there. Despair started to envelop me. Whatever happened, I feared my mental state would become worse, and I would end up incapacitated, as I had been in Moscow after the first war. Work had been my salvation—I needed patients as much as they needed me. Treating them kept my depression at bay; if I stopped, the demons would return.

I borrowed instruments from a local hospital and started treating the wounded Chechens who were housed in villages around Ingushetia. Although the official crossings were closed, relatives managed to sneak them in over secret paths. Traveling from village to village, sleeping in different places every night, was also a good way of keeping the FSB from finding me.

I also performed some operations in the hospital during my stay in Ingushetia. "Is that Khassan?" someone called out from a stretcher being carried into the hospital. "We've never really met, but I'd recognize your voice anywhere," he said. It was the young man whose leg I had amputated—my last operation in Chechnya; the one I didn't want to do. The young man was alive and well.

THE DAY AFTER I arrived in Ingushetia, Adam introduced me to a journalist he knew, Karina Melikyan. Her father had been a TASS bureau chief in Washington, D.C., in the 1960s, and she had learned

English as a child. Now she worked for Reuters and wanted to interview me. Though talking to the press was risky, I agreed. I wanted people to know the truth about Chechnya, and I wanted to draw attention to the fate of the doctors and fighters who had been corralled into the filtration camp at Chernokozovo. Our first meeting took place outside the entrance of the Ingush Republican Hospital in Nazran, where Karina and Adam photographed me in my scrubs. They suggested I also have a meeting with the representatives of Physicians for Human Rights, Human Rights Watch, and Amnesty International. I agreed to do that too.

The morning of the meeting, I dressed with care in a dark suit, white shirt, and tie. Fortunately, I had sent some of my clothes with Zara and the rest of the family when they left. I assumed that all Americans living in a wealthy country would be well dressed, especially for an official meeting. I was surprised when I walked into the hotel lobby and saw the human rights people standing there unshaved and sloppily dressed. Still, they smiled and made me feel welcome. I suggested we meet in a café rather than in the hotel, which I was sure was bugged. Sipping tea in the café, I described my hospital, the abuse of civilians, and the doctors taken to the filtration camp.

We decided to give a full-blown press conference and invite Western and Russian journalists who were in Nazran waiting to cross the border into Chechnya, something barred by the Russian authorities. We hoped that publicity would shame the Russians into releasing the doctors and patients who had been transported to the Chernokozovo filtration camp before I fled. Many journalists attended the press conference. I learned later that the Russians released the doctors after holding them for a week, and the patients a week after that. A little free flow of information goes a long way.

OLD FRIENDS IN Ingushetia kept telling me that I had aged during the war. Looking in the mirror, I saw my face had shrunk and a network of wrinkles covered my cheeks. Peter Bouckaert of Human Rights Watch was even more emphatic. "You're ill!" he declared.

I laughed. "What do you expect? I've been under fire for a half year. Take a look at my hands," I said, showing him the blisters on my palms and the cuts between my fingers.

"How can we help you?" asked Doug Ford, the leader of the Physicians for Human Rights team. An energetic lawyer, he was taking depositions from Chechens about conditions and abuses. He was always ready to help.

"I need rehabilitation," I said, "but it's impossible to get it here. I dream of a quiet place where I can get some treatment."

"How about the United States, if we can arrange it?" he said. "There you could get some rehabilitation, observe some of the facilities there. Maybe even tell people about what's going on in Chechnya."

A doctor on Doug's team pulled me aside. He told me that he had escaped from Iran and gone to the United States. "If you get to the U.S., stay there," he advised. "American doctors earn a lot of money— between $150,000 and $200,000 per year." An unheard-of amount of money, I thought, but ending up in America was far from my mind. All I wanted was to rest and to return to Chechnya.

Soon word came from Washington that I was welcome there whenever I could make the trip. I told Doug and Peter I had a few patients to attend to, but that I would be free at the start of April. I hated to leave the family again, but they saw my exhaustion and realized that I had to recover my strength. In mid-March I flew quietly to Moscow. There was some risk in going there, but I was counting on the protection of the human rights organizations and the fact that in Russia, the left hand often doesn't know what the right is doing. Someone— probably Karina—must have informed the press that I was arriving, and I was met by three reporters from the NTV independent television channel. I spoke to them reluctantly, knowing that if I talked too frankly, it would alert the Russian authorities. That night, NTV announced, "Today a famous doctor from Chechnya who has a great reputation with the Chechen field commanders arrived in Moscow." The news item stressed the words *Chechen field commanders.* That was not good news.

Shortly, another news item caused problems for me. This one announced the arrest of Salman Raduyev as he was trying to leave Chechnya for Azerbaijan. This news, plus the report linking me to Chechen field commanders, drove me immediately underground. It seemed that I could never escape problems with Raduyev. His death had been announced so many times, only to be followed by his resurrection, that no one wanted to believe he had really been caught. Journalists tried to contact me, knowing I had worked on his face and would recognize him. But I agreed to talk only to my friends Musa Muradov and Dima Belovetsky. One look at his face on the television screen, and I knew it was definitely Raduyev.

From that day on, I never spent more than one night in any one spot while in Moscow. Friends screened all my phone calls and never allowed me to go out alone.

Human Rights Watch organized a secret visit for me to the U.S. embassy. I was hustled through a side door, away from the line for visas outside the embassy, which was as long as the crowds at the Lenin Mausoleum. A U.S. marine escorted me to a friendly woman consular officer, who indicated I might be granted a visa very soon. Three days later, Karina called, and we went back to the embassy. When I emerged again through the side door on Devyatinskii Lane, I had an American entry visa in my Russian passport.

A week after I arrived in Moscow, I received a call from Zara, telling me that Nana had fallen ill. Malika and Hussein had driven Nana from Chechnya to Troitskoye, in Ingushetia, stopping several times along the way to revive her. Her blood pressure was elevated—about 220 systolic—and she was suffering chest pains. "She says she is going to die and wants you near," Malika reported. This was the first time Nana had ever summoned me, so I knew it must be serious. I told deputy chief Sasha Petrov of the Human Rights Watch office in Moscow that I would have to either postpone the trip or cancel it altogether. Postponing was no problem, he said. I flew back to Ingushetia.

Malika and Hussein had tried to take Nana to several hospitals, but all were full. When I finally arrived and saw her lying on a mattress on

With Dada and Nana in happier days.

the floor, I could hardly control my tears. She needed intensive care. She had insisted on staying on with me throughout the war, preparing meals, sharing the damp cellar, keeping me going. I was to blame for her state and decided to plead directly with the minister of health of Ingushetia.

When I visited the minister the next morning, I said, "Considering all the time I have spent working on patients in Ingushetia, I am disappointed that you can't find a place for my mother." He appeared embarrassed and said he would give orders for her to be admitted immediately. For a week, I remained with her in the intensive care unit. After a few days, her pressure began to drop, and she showed signs of recovery. One day we went outside into the hospital yard. It was a beautiful day with the sun shining, the smell of spring in the air. Patients and their relatives sat outside on benches in the hospital yard. We managed to find a bench near the corner of the building. Nana insisted she was much better and urged me to leave for America. I was reluctant, still worrying about her health. I was also apprehensive about leaving Zara and the children for a few weeks. They accepted my decision stoically; for so much of the war we had been apart.

On April 8, 2000, however, I returned to Moscow to complete preparations for what I thought would be a monthlong U.S. visit. Nine days later, friends drove me to Sheremetyevo international airport. The day was bright, and the old women were out with their twig brooms sweeping up the refuse that surfaces once the snow melts. Although my papers were in order, I had a deep foreboding. Compared to Grozny airport, Sheremetyevo was enormous, and I felt disoriented among the travelers in line with their baggage. Announcements boomed over the loudspeaker in different languages. What am I doing here? I wondered. The Aeroflot jetliner was scheduled to leave for Washington in about two hours, at 4 P.M. My friends promised to wait in the departure hall until they saw me pass through customs.

My two suitcases went through the x-ray machines without a hitch. One hurdle passed, I thought; no police provocateur has stuffed narcotics in my bag. I waved to my friends to leave, forgetting that I still had to go through Passport Control. The lines moved slowly, broken only by the rhythmical click-clack of the uniformed guards as they stamped the passports. Finally, my turn. The woman FSB border guard had a pleasant face. Perhaps it would be all right, after all.

She reached for my passport, flipped the pages, then stopped and looked at me . . . then back to the picture, then back to me. My temples tightened. I scanned the lines at the other booths. They moved slowly, but they moved. My line had stopped altogether, and several people behind me switched to other lines. Holding the passport in her hand, she reached for the telephone. I couldn't hear what she was saying behind the glass, but the old fears returned. A few minutes later, a uniformed woman, whom I judged to be in her fifties, entered the booth and took my passport.

"Young man, follow me!" she barked. The idea of going to the United States is going to end badly, I thought, as I followed her to the end of the hall. She opened a door and ordered me in.

"Stay here," she said, leaving the room and closing the door behind her. The room was empty except for a sofa. I sat down. I guessed a hidden camera was monitoring me to see if I acted nervously. Half an hour later, she returned, accompanied by a pleasant-looking, middle-aged man in plain clothes who introduced himself as a colonel in the internal security service. He held my passport in his hand.

"Are you Baiev, Khassan?" he began.

"Yes."

"Where are you flying to?"

"To America."

"For business, or did someone invite you?"

"I'm on vacation. I'm going to America for recreation." I glanced at my watch. It was 3:15 P.M.—boarding should now be under way. I guessed the idea of a Chechen having the money to travel when ordinary Russians did not must have grated on the colonel.

"Where do you live at the moment?" he continued.

I tried to mislead him. "In Vladikavkaz, North Ossetia." I spoke calmly, but underneath I was nervous, knowing that the Russian authorities were after me. I decided to counterattack. "You know there is one thing I don't understand," I went on. "Why are you holding me here? Is it because I am from the Caucasus? My things have been checked, and I have nothing suspicious on me. If my plane leaves without me, I'm going to complain to the prosecutor's office."

He brushed aside my remarks. I didn't have the impression that he was angling for a bribe. But I knew Moscow had an unofficial ruling against allowing Chechens to travel abroad because of the war. He stared at me, then popped the most dangerous question of all: "When did you leave Chechnya?"

"In 1996," I lied. My international passport, valid until September 2001, had been issued by the Russian authorities in Grozny in 1996. "I left in 1996 to take a job as a dentist in North Ossetia." Another lie, but a plausible one.

It was now 3:25 P.M.; boarding must be coming to an end. The colonel left the room for a few minutes. I figured he was checking to see if my replies tallied with the information in his computer. Would he find an order to arrest "the bandit doctor"? The minutes dragged by like hours. I was so afraid the airport computer would betray me; that I would be arrested on the spot and thrown into prison. Then suddenly the door opened again, and the colonel reappeared. He was expressionless. He handed me my passport and announced I was free to go. Apparently, the arrest order still hadn't caught up with me.

Worried that I wouldn't find the right gate, I asked him to escort me to the plane. When we arrived, the door was closing. I was the last passenger to board and took a seat in the rear. I sat there tense, desperately trying to control myself until the plane finally roared down the runway. I have managed to crawl out of hell, I thought, as I watched the silver birches disappear beneath the wing of the plane.

For the next nine hours, I spoke to no one. A girl across the aisle tried to strike up a conversation, but I ignored her. In the seat in front, some Russian professors and academics ordered drink after drink, becoming so loud that a group of American tourists complained to the flight attendant and went to sit somewhere else. I couldn't sleep. I found it hard to believe that I was actually going to the United States.

AN HOUR BEFORE landing, I looked out the window and saw the ocean. I had seen the skyscrapers and huge buildings on television, and I had met a number of aid workers. Everyone said Americans were open and friendly, but I didn't really know what to expect. Human Rights Watch had made plans for Misha, a Ukrainian doctor living in the United States, to meet me at the airport.

Crowds of people, all different colors and nationalities, milled around the arrival hall at Washington's Dulles airport. I approached a group of Russians from my flight, hoping for help when I came to the customs officer. At the immigration booth, the officer took my passport, glanced at it, then ordered me to follow him into a large hall. "Wait there," he said, pointing to a bench. I sat on the bench for about four hours, watching the customs officers spread people's belongings on the tables and examine them. I wondered what had happened to my luggage.

Sitting on the bench in the customs hall, I had my first impression of America. The first thing that struck me was the amount of light everywhere, whereas in Russia the public buildings were dark and somber. All around me were people from different countries, speaking different languages, some dressed in their national costumes. Everyone looked so well fed, overweight by Chechen standards. Finally, an officer appeared with my baggage, dumped it on the table, and gestured for me to open it. He pulled everything out, cuffs, collars, belts, the soles of shoes—everything was scrutinized.

Because I'm Chechen. That crazy thought entered my head. I had escaped the Russians only to fall into the clutches of the Americans.

Five hours after disembarking, I emerged into the airport lobby, supposedly a free man. I looked around for someone to greet me. No one. Misha was nowhere to be seen. I wondered why he hadn't checked with the Aeroflot representative. I vacillated between terror and humiliation.

"Help me," I blurted out to a police officer. "Russian." He led me to the Aeroflot agent, who was about to go home. I quickly explained my problem.

"Don't make a fuss," the agent advised. "They can send you back to Moscow on the next plane." And, no doubt, the FSB would be there to meet me.

It was 2 A.M. in Washington, 10 A.M. in Moscow. The Aeroflot agent allowed me one call. I telephoned Karina in Moscow. She called the Human Rights Watch representative in Ingushetia. He called Rachel Denber, the Human Rights representative in New York. Rachel, who speaks excellent Russian, persuaded the Aeroflot agent to take me to the nearby Marriott Hotel. I was exhausted, disoriented, and hungry.

The Marriott receptionist handed me a white card to open the door to my room. I had never seen this type of magnetic key before. I inserted the card into the slot, thinking the door would swing open. I must have stood in front of the door for ten minutes, not realizing that I was supposed to pull the card out quickly and turn the knob.

"Help! Problems!" I said to a woman passing by. She smiled and showed me how to open the door.

The room contained a TV in a cupboard and a large refrigerator with nothing in it. Fortunately, I had saved a few pieces of bread from the plane.

At 7 A.M., I received a call from Rachel, who told me that room service would bring me breakfast in my room and that Misha would call later on and take me to the Washington Hospital Center, where I was scheduled to stay and to observe operations under the auspices of the Washington office of Physicians for Human Rights.

When Misha arrived several hours later, he explained that he had waited for me at Dulles for an hour the night before but could find no sign of me, so he went home. On our way to the hospital, we drove through the center of Washington. This was the first time I had seen the White House and the Capitol close-up, and I marveled at the beauty of the city.

"You should be careful; this hospital isn't in a good neighborhood," Misha warned me.

I had to laugh. "America! Danger here too?"

Chapter 21

Hard Choices

T HE WASHINGTON HOSPITAL CENTER is a huge complex
stretching many blocks on the southeast section of the city.
Misha escorted me to the fourth floor of the living quarters,
where I would be staying. My room had three narrow beds and an old
television, and there was a bathroom down the hall. It reminded me of
a student dormitory in Russia. He left me to unpack and get settled.

Loneliness washed over me. Chechens are not used to living alone.
Americans, as I was to discover, have a great respect for privacy, but
all I wanted was human contact. I would have settled for strangers in
the two other beds—anything not to be by myself. I missed my family. I missed the wounded. I even missed the ruins.

Dr. James Cobey, my host, showed me around the hospital. I was
excited because I had heard so much about the advances in U.S. medicine. The moment I entered the main building, I felt exhilarated.
Breathing the smell of disinfectant temporarily stopped me from
thinking about Chechnya, and worrying about my extended family.
The smell at the Washington Hospital Center was different from that
at Russian hospitals—it wasn't as strong. Certainly, it was different
from the odor of dried blood at my hospital in Alkhan Kala, which,
despite all the scrubbing, would never go away. My host, an orthope-
dic surgeon, arranged for a Russian-speaking anesthesiologist, Sasha,
to be my translator.

The conditions under which surgeons work in the United States amazed me. Not that I think American surgeons are any more skilled than Russian or Chechen surgeons, but what conditions! What I could have done with such equipment! So many lives I could have saved. Dr. Cobey showed me some twenty operating rooms, each for a different specialty: one for cardiology, another for transplants, and so on. Every procedure had its specialist. Nurses had assistants and assistant-assistants. Surgeons would arrive, perform their operation, and leave. It was dizzying. No one yelled or shouted. Everyone knew what to do. And monitors were everywhere. An analysis at the touch of a button. In Chechnya, we waited days, sometimes weeks, for test results.

Observing the array of flickering and beeping monitors around the operating room, I wondered if the American doctors weren't allowing machines to think for them. Were they losing touch with patients and that intuitive sense that tells a doctor what's wrong and how to cure it?

Though being in a hospital atmosphere helped lift my spirits, certain things unsettled me. Seeing the orderlies toss into the trash half-used supplies—such as suture thread, operation masks, head caps, shoe coverings, or glasses—made me angry. Couldn't they have gathered up the unused supplies and sent them off to a needy part of the world? I could have used that discarded thread to sew up dozens of wounds. Observing the doctors and nurses prepare a patient for a medical procedure, such as a tracheotomy, made me tense because the preparation took hours. The doctor was so calm, as if he had all the time in the world, drying off the operative field and marking the skin with such deliberation. "Cut, for God's sake," I said to myself, my fingers itching to take the scalpel.

I had become so conditioned to the life-and-death situations of war, I wondered if I would ever readjust to normal hospital conditions. Before the war I was known for being even-tempered. Now I found myself overreacting to everything. The day a medical helicopter transported a road victim to the hospital, I could hardly control myself. The man's leg was broken, and he was bleeding profusely.

The emergency room doctors stopped the bleeding and bandaged him. Then they discharged him.

"But the man is in terrible pain," I whispered to my translator, Sasha. "Why aren't they putting a splint on that leg?"

Sasha shrugged and said. "Maybe they are taking him to another hospital."

"Let me put on a splint," I said. "Ask them if I can."

Sasha burst out laughing. "They won't let you anywhere near him because it would be breaking the rules. Without medical insurance, a patient gets second-class treatment; without a license, you are not even considered a doctor here."

"I've seen enough," I told Sasha. "I can't watch this; let's go." Sasha was right. In America, I can't touch a patient. Everyone here is terrified of lawsuits.

With every passing day, I felt myself becoming more nervous. At night when an emergency helicopter would land on the roof of the hospital complex with an accident victim, I would jump up in bed, my heart racing, fearing a bombing in the next few seconds. The walls would close in on me, and I could hardly breathe. When this happened, I headed downstairs and out into the street. Exercise was the only thing that helped.

The security guard at the desk downstairs would try to stop me from going out in the early morning hours. I could hardly understand a word of her English. I pointed to the door. I didn't care what time it was. I had to get outside. Once on the street, I jogged sometimes until the sun rose over the city.

One evening when I was out jogging around 10 p.m., I decided to depart from my usual tour around the hospital and continue along the road for some distance. I found myself in a street of row houses. Elderly people sat on the sidewalk outside, and kids played in the street. Suddenly, six black youths stepped into the road, blocking my path, gesticulating, and shouting words I didn't understand. They wore long baggy shorts, bright T-shirts, and their hair was in cornrows. But there were no rifles, no hand grenades. I wasn't frightened.

My lack of fear had nothing to do with being brave. It was as though the wars in Chechnya had inoculated me against physical fear, at least as far as my own safety was concerned. The largest youth stepped forward. The group refused to let me pass. Finally, I rolled up the right sleeve of my T-shirt and flexed my biceps, which had benefited from years of athletic training. Then, with all the force I could muster, I slammed my right fist into my left hand.

"Come on!" I shouted in Russian. "I'm going to get you!"

They looked taken aback and began talking to one another. Then they shouted something at me, turned, and walked away. I don't know whether it was my biceps or my Russian threats that stopped them. They probably thought any white man who jogged through their neighborhood at night was crazy, which is what my friends said when I told them what happened.

IN THOSE FIRST weeks in Washington, when I wasn't observing at the hospital, I had frequent talks with people about Chechnya. Amnesty International, Physicians for Human Rights, and Human Rights Watch arranged meetings for me, which included a trip to Boston in May. My speaking out was a way to promote their agenda, and I was anxious for influential Americans to know about the abuse of civilians in Chechnya. I had hoped that the United States, with its concern for human rights, would bring pressure to bear on Russia to stop killing civilians. The people I talked to included two senators, John McCain and the late Paul Wellstone. I also met Dr. Zbigniew Brzezinski, former national security adviser to President Jimmy Carter and a severe critic of Russia's human rights violations.

At my meetings on Capitol Hill, senators and representatives listened politely behind their large mahogany desks, nodding their heads in sympathy. I had the feeling they knew as well as anyone else what crimes were taking place in Chechnya, but chose to ignore them. Diplomatic relations between Russia and the United States were improving, and no one wanted to jeopardize them.

"You have to understand that Russia is a nuclear power. For many

I met the late senator Paul Wellstone (right) and Maureen Greenwood (left) on Capitol Hill in April 2000.

years their missiles have been targeted on us, and they could be retargeted again at any time," one senator told me. "Furthermore, a lot of people in Congress think Russia is fighting against Islamic extremists."

"Why are you so frightened of Russia?" I asked. "We Chechens don't have atomic bombs, planes, or tanks. We fight them with Kalashnikov rifles." The senator nodded and smiled.

"You're sending money to Russia, and that money goes to the war," I added. "The Russians say they need your aid for old-age pensioners, but that's not how they use it. They spend your money on the war. They sell their new arms to foreign countries and use their old weapons on Chechnya."

Several people suggested I should become Chechnya's representative in Washington, but that was the last thing I wanted to do. I was willing to speak out against the excesses, but I didn't want to become involved in political maneuvering. Furthermore, at that time I still planned to return to Chechnya. As a doctor, I was ill equipped to deal with the political infighting that appears to be inevitable among various groups, especially in a war-torn country like Chechnya where people support different factions and promote different solutions. All I knew for certain was that medical personnel in my country, and in many other areas around the world, were on the front lines. Warring sides targeted and killed them in direct violation of the 1948 Geneva conventions.

Before long, the meetings in Washington became exhausting. At night, I tossed and turned, the images of war rising before my eyes. Once, in a moment of weakness, I started out to buy a bottle of vodka. The night before, I had had an upsetting conversation about events in Chechnya. Drinking violated my religious convictions. I knew perfectly well that if I drank, I would feel much worse afterward, but for that moment I wanted to forget everything. Finally, after much debating with myself, I managed to suppress the desire.

I asked Doug Ford from Physicians for Human Rights to cancel all my appointments and find me a psychologist, someone who could help alleviate my despair. As soon as I walked into Dr. Judy Okawa's office, which was decorated with children's pictures, I believed she could help me. "Dr. Judy," as I called her, heads the Center for Multi-Cultural Human Services in Falls Church, Virginia, just outside Washington. The clinic specializes in treating people who have suffered torture or severe trauma. (According to the United Nations, torture is practiced in more than 100 countries around the world.) Dr. Judy had the same gift of healing and consoling as the mullah of Alkhan Yurt. With the help of a translator, I was able to express things I had never talked about before. Just talking about them helped.

She invited me into the room next to her office, which contained a closet full of plastic toys. "Choose some figures and place them in the sandbox," she said. I selected a two-story house, a child on a swing, a woman with a baby in her arms and inserted them into the sand. Then I placed a dove on the roof of the house. Arranging the figures in the sandbox filled me with sadness. Dr. Judy asked me why I had selected those particular items, and I told her that was how life was before the war. Then I picked a dolphin and a shark and placed them with the others.

"Why those?" she asked.

"The dolphin is a kindhearted creature that likes to approach human beings," I said. "The shark is bloodthirsty and reminds me of a military vehicle that kills people." I don't know what it was about this exercise, but my throat constricted. I felt the tears well up behind my lids, and I hid my head in my hands.

An American friend of mine expressed surprise that someone from Chechnya, where men are ashamed to display weakness, would consult a woman psychologist. For me, it was easier to reveal weakness to a woman than to a man. I even told Dr. Judy about the vodka. "No, no!" she scolded me. "Working out physically is the best medicine for stress. If you begin to feel like drinking, run around the block." Of course, she was right.

AFTER THREE WEEKS in a room at the Washington Hospital Center, I went to live with Larry Ellis and Chris Reichel, a couple from Silver Spring, Maryland, a suburb of Washington. For many Chechens passing through Washington, Larry and Chris provide a home away from home. Any Chechen can count on a bed or a meal at their house. Once I was living in their small basement apartment, I felt less tense. At the same time, I made contact with the one community of Chechens living in New Jersey.

"Allah saved you so you could come to America," Hamid Ozbek-Umarov said, rising from the couch in his living room to greet me. His remark took me aback, and I wondered if I was really meant to settle here. I had heard about this elder back in Chechnya, but this was the first time I had met him. I would visit him many times at his home in Paterson, New Jersey. At eighty-three, he was a distinguished-looking man with a snow-white beard and a proud way of carrying himself that he could only have learned in the mountains of the Caucasus. Over his couch hung a large painting of a Chechen rider on a white stallion against a backdrop of snowcapped peaks reaching into the clouds. The horseman wore the traditional sheepskin *papakha,* black leather boots, and a black Cherkessk jacket, taken in at the waist, with cartridge

From left to right: My friend Larry Ellis, Chechen elder Hamid Ozbek-Umarov, his daughter, Handan, me with my back turned, and Rachel Denber of Human Rights Watch.

pouches across the chest. From his belt hung a silver-handled *kinjal*. Spread around the room were books, newspapers, and magazines about Chechnya.

Any Chechen in need of help or advice could receive it from Hamid or his daughter, Handan. She was born in Turkey. Although she doesn't speak Chechen, she was raised with our traditions, speaks perfect English, Circassian, and Turkish, and knows the American ways. She was always ready to jump into her car and drive me wherever I needed to go—to New York or Boston.

Hamid's memory was crystal clear, and he liked to tell stories about his life, how he fought in the Soviet army during the Second World War, was taken prisoner by the Germans, and put in a concentration camp. After escaping from the camp, he made his way to Turkey, and from there to the United States, where he has lived for the last forty-seven years. He is as proud to be American as he is to be Chechen. He speaks English, Chechen, Russian, German, and Turkish. Listening to him transported me to another era. For a moment, I forgot where I was.

After my first meeting with Hamid, I couldn't sleep that night. The thought of not returning to Chechnya panicked me. How could I stay in the United States? What would happen to my family? My parents were getting on in age. Who would look after them? I needed to go home to help my family; it was my duty.

To stay or not to stay? The arguments spun in my head. In Chechnya I was a hunted man, but in America, as Sasha pointed out, I was nothing. To practice medicine in the United States, I needed to be licensed. That could take up to ten years. I didn't speak English, and with the present state of my concentration, I sometimes doubted I ever would. How would I support my family? Would Zara and the children be able to join me?

I was steeped in Chechen traditions and wanted my children to grow up in that culture, not like some American children I saw in the supermarkets, disobeying their parents when told to stop running or not to touch the produce. Furthermore, I didn't want my children watching violence and sex on television. In Chechnya, Zara and I had taught the children to hide their heads in a pillow when couples started to kiss in the imported Russian films—films which showed even more nudity and violence than I have seen so far in the United States.

On the other hand, in America my children would be safe. They would learn English and live in freedom. The children would adapt to the West, but Zara and I would work hard to help them maintain their Chechen culture. I could always turn off the television.

What finally convinced me to ask for political asylum at the end of May was a telephone call from my sister Malika. "Your photograph is posted at all the military checkpoints," she said. "The Russians are hunting you down, and you shouldn't return." I consulted Hamid, who again repeated that it was Allah's will that I had come to the United States. "It is your destiny to stay here," he said.

Once I made the decision to stay, I started to worry about getting my family out of Chechnya and to the United States. Soon after I left for America, Nana, Dada, Zara, and the children returned to Alkhan Kala from Ingushetia. Everyone was desperate to get back into their homes even if they were half destroyed. It was still risky, but better than living as refugees. Telephone communications were nonexistent, but Malika would go to Ingushetia to call me periodically. Although she tried to downplay the dangers in Alkhan Kala, I read between her words. After each call, I couldn't sleep. Moreover, I knew from news reports that the towns and villages were under constant attack. The Russians would use any excuse for a *zachistka* in Chechnya. Wearing black masks, the *kontraktniki* kicked down doors, searching for weapons and something to steal. Men continued to disappear off the street. At this time, Ali and Adam's older brothers were living in Moscow, and Hussein and Rita were safe in Ingushetia.

Malika let it slip that the mercenaries even threw Dada off his cot during a search. The children were terrified. Once when a workman came to fix a radiator, two-year-old Markha ran to find the family's passports for him to check. She apparently thought the handyman was a Russian soldier carrying out another *zachistka*.

I consulted Wendy Atrokhov, a lawyer who spoke Russian, and told her I wanted to apply for political asylum for myself and my immediate family. She helped me complete the papers for the Immigration and Naturalization Service. Since I was wanted by the Russian military, I suspected it would be difficult to get permission for my family to leave Russia.

Contemplating my family's plight, I thought, too, about my brother's children, Khava and Adam. They had lived with us for so long at Alkhan Kala that they were like my own. When I left for America, I was supporting a total of thirteen people in our extended family, and Hussein was out of work. On one occasion, he confided to me that if there ever was a chance, he wanted his children to go to America to get an education. This was a painful possibility for him and Rita to contemplate. Alone, by myself in Washington, with no means of support and an uncertain future, I decided to tempt fate and try the impossible: I told Wendy that I wanted political asylum not just for myself and my immediate family. I wanted to bring Khava and Adam over too.

Chapter 22

Heartbreak

M Y WASHINGTON LAWYERS submitted a petition by
mid-July to the Immigration and Naturalization Service, and within two weeks it was granted. I enrolled
in free English classes while continuing to see Dr. Judy every week.
Learning a new language was hard for me. Besides battling depression,
my mind kept circling back to my family in Chechnya.

One night before the end of summer, I received a telephone call
from one of Ali's older brothers. He said that masked soldiers had broken into Raya and Lecha's house in Alkhan Kala and taken Ali away.
They had kept the news from me for several weeks, not wanting to
worry me, and knowing that I couldn't do anything about it even if I
did know. Initially, Ali had stayed behind in Ingushetia when the rest of
the family returned. In Chechnya young men were not safe. At any
time they could be arrested, held for ransom, or sent to a filtration
camp. Ali, however, became homesick. In the fall, the situation in
Alkhan Kala seemed to be stabilizing, and he decided to return home.

It was a sunny August morning around lunchtime when the Russian soldiers came for Ali. He and his father were outside tinkering
with the car. His mother was preparing lunch when six or seven soldiers arrived at the door and demanded to see Ali's documents.

"Are you the one who works in the hospital with your bandit uncle?" one of the *kontraktniki* asked. Ali acknowledged he had helped
out in the hospital. That was enough. The soldiers blindfolded him by

pulling his T-shirt up over his face, exposing his belly. They shoved him into an armored personnel carrier and drove off to a filtration camp. My sister Raya tried to fling herself in front of the armored personnel carrier, begging the soldiers not to take her son away. They pushed her aside.

Many months later, Ali described what happened to him. He said he had no idea where they took him. After the vehicle stopped, they threw him out, kicked him several times in the groin, searched his pockets for money, and confiscated his belt and shoes.

"From under my T-shirt I saw two other boys on the ground," Ali told family members. "Then I heard a Russian soldier yell that they were going to run a tank over us." A voice called out, "Save an ear for me! I collect Chechen ears." At first, the Russians wanted to execute Ali and dump his corpse in a mass grave, but decided it would be better to hold him for ransom. Lecha and Raya eventually discovered where Ali was being held by bribing four young soldiers with several hundred dollars to search the camps.

Ali was held in a pit, twelve feet deep, so cramped he couldn't stretch out. When it rained, the water poured through the metal grate that covered the opening. His only protection was a pair of pants. Every day, sometimes two or three times, soldiers would haul him to the surface for a beating. Because of his blindfold, he never knew where the blows would fall—sometimes in the groin, sometimes about the kidneys, sometimes on the jaw. His captors had names for their tortures. They sat him in the "surgeon chair" (*kreslo khirurga*), shackled his hands behind his back, then hit him with a bottle filled with water. They applied electric shocks to the fingers, ears, lips, and genitals. This was followed by the "manicure" (*manikiura*)—inserting needles under the fingernails.

"There was one FSB officer, always the same one, who liked to burn my body with his cigarette," Ali said. "He removed my blindfold, and he always smiled when he did it."

Once, they forced him to perform the "swallow" (*lastochka*). In this torment, the victim is forced to sit cross-legged with hands shackled behind his back. Then the torso is pushed forward toward the floor. "They pushed down on my back with their knees," Ali recounted. "The pain was excruciating. If they keep this up for forty-five minutes, the blood circulation blocks and the victim dies."

Ali's tormentors also hung him upside down by his legs, demanding to know where his brother Adam was. Ali prayed that Adam had left the country, but you never knew with him because he was traveling back and forth across the borders with his videos. They also interrogated Ali about me, trying to discover how I had eluded them. "I prayed that they would kill me and end the torture. I was one hundred percent sure I would die anyway, so I refused to speak," Ali said. When he passed out, they threw a bucket of cold water on him and shoved him back in the pit.

Ali wasn't sure if he hallucinated in the pit, or whether he saw dreams or visions. "Sometimes I saw my mother coming toward me with food," he said. "Sometimes I would go into our house, and all my relatives were at a big table in the front yard. They had lots of food and were smiling. I trained my mind to have those visions." Finally, after thirty-nine days in the pit, Ali was released.

The first thing Ali did when he reached home was drag himself into the washroom. His mother boiled water on the stove to wash and bathe his wounds. Adam entered the room and closed the door. "I'm so proud of you; you went through all that like a man," he said. "When I talk to you now, I have the impression you are so much older than I am because you learned so much in that hole."

When I was finally told about Ali's arrest, the only details I knew were that he had been taken to a filtration camp and that we had to raise money to get him out. The two oldest of Ali's brothers, who lived in Moscow, rushed to Alkhan Kala to organize his release. A relative, who learned from the FSB that Ali was in the pit, said he was barely alive; so we had to act fast. The price was high: $3,000 to stop the beatings; $10,000 for his release. I sent $2,000 from America, which depleted my meager savings. In addition, the jailers demanded ten guns. Eight were purchased from Russian soldiers—the main source of

Chechen arms during the war—and two were donated by friends of ours. The deal was negotiated between the two brothers and the Russians over elaborate dinners, flowing with vodka, which they demanded and the brothers hated.

The Russians had confiscated his passport and other documents, so he had to go into hiding. He urgently needed medical treatment. His brothers managed to find a doctor to come to the house to treat him, and Malika nursed him. The torture and beatings had damaged his kidneys, broken several ribs, fractured his lower jaw, and temporarily blinded him in one eye. Cigarette burns pitted his stomach, and his skin had turned black from sitting in the water at the bottom of the pit.

ALI'S RELEASE WAS a great relief, though I knew he was still in danger. As a young man of fighting age, he could be rearrested at any time. Never a day went by when I didn't think about my nephews. Late that November, tragedy struck again.

I had been invited to spend the Thanksgiving holiday—my first in the United States—in New England with American friends of mine. Two nights prior to leaving Maryland for Vermont, I had that recurring nightmare of pursuing snakes and hemorrhaging. As always in this bad dream, I slapped on the tourniquet, but still the blood flowed. Each time, I woke up in a cold sweat, my heart pounding. I believe dreams are messages from the unconscious, and had a strong foreboding that something had happened to Ali or Adam. I knew the Russians were hunting for them, particularly for Adam, who continued his freelance work for Reuters.

For months I had been sending Adam messages, urging him to leave Chechnya immediately. I was his uncle and his elder. He should have obeyed me. Human Rights Watch in New York was prepared to sponsor him for a visa to the United States. I dreamed of bringing him to America, where he would be safe and could train as a professional journalist.

"Yes, yes, I have just a few more things to do, and then I will leave," Adam had promised the last time he called me from Ingushetia.

What Adam was doing was making arrangements for Ali to leave Chechnya. Of course, he could not tell me that in a telephone conversation, as all communications were monitored. Rumors circulated that the FSB was unhappy with its share of the ransom for Ali and wanted to kidnap him again. Or maybe the FSB thought that Ali had a "rich" uncle in America who would pay the ransom. Everyone wants a share in the spoils of this unconscionable business: the Federals (Russian troops), the Russian security services, Russian intelligence, and Chechen assassins like Barayev who often do the Russians' dirty business. The stakes are so high that fighting often breaks out between parties.

The day before leaving for Thanksgiving in Vermont, I received a telephone call saying that Adam had been killed and Ali wounded in Alkhan Kala. I can hardly write about what happened, it is so painful.

On the night of the shooting, the two brothers were at a neighbor's house watching TV. They were inseparable, and until then, slept in a different place every night to avoid the Russian security services. However, on this night they made an exception and stayed two nights in one place. Suddenly, three masked thugs burst in, spraying bullets right and left, hitting Ali in the leg and Adam in the stomach and groin. The assassins vanished as swiftly as they appeared. The room was dark, and Ali didn't want to turn on the light. He crawled across the floor, feeling for Adam, who was sprawled near the couch. He felt the blood on Adam, but he was terrified to look at his wounds. He cradled Adam in his arms, the blood soaking into his clothes.

"Keep talking to me. Keep me awake," Adam mumbled to Ali.

When Adam asked for water, Ali refused. "No, there is no way I am going to give you a drink," Ali said. "Don't even think of it." He knew from working with the wounded that a request for water signaled the approach of death.

Neither Ali nor the neighbors were able to stop the bleeding from the femoral artery. There was nowhere near to take Adam immediately.

My hospital was bombed out. Furthermore, the town was under cur-few. Anything that moved was shot at by the Russians. In the end, they loaded Adam in a car and drove to the nearest checkpoint, hoping to get him to the hospital in Urus-Martan. It was too late. By the time they got there, Adam was dead. Ali received treatment for his leg wound.

I was desperate to go back to Chechnya for Adam's funeral. The only thing I could think about was being with Raya and Lecha and the rest of my family. Family and friends tried to dissuade me, saying that I would be killed as soon as I arrived. Others pointed out that I was not free to travel to Russia since the United States had given me political asylum. Ultimately, the only thing I could do was arrange for a Moscow friend of mine to loan me $3,000 to pay for the funeral, and I sent the money to the family to give Adam a decent burial.

It is hard to know who murdered Adam. The killers were masked and spoke Chechen. My family and I suspect Arbi Barayev was in-volved. The thought that had I been there I might have saved Adam tortures me. Maybe I could have stopped the bleeding. To stop the gush of blood from a femoral artery is extremely hard, but I had de-veloped a technique to do this under the primitive conditions war imposes. It would involve amputating the leg high up. But at least he would still be alive.

Chapter 23

Hope and Despair

URING THAT TRAGIC year of 2000, there was one bright spot. In October, Human Rights Watch named me one of the four Human Rights Monitors of the year. Human Rights Monitors are individuals who have spoken out for justice in their countries. My name was included with three others—Abdul Tejan-Cole of Sierra Leone, Rebiya Kadeer of China's Xinjiang Province, Martin Chhotubhai Macwan of India—as well as the National Jordanian Campaign Committee to eliminate so-called crimes of honor. After a week of press conferences, meeting with reporters, human rights groups, and U.N. representatives, Human Rights Watch held a luxurious fund-raising dinner at New York's Museum of Natural History on November 14. After the New York dinner, we monitors flew to Los Angeles for another dinner and more meetings. For me, it was a proud week when I felt I was doing something useful for Chechnya.

Three months later, I moved to Boston for good. I hoped that with all the medical facilities in Boston, I might find a niche, though I knew that without English and some kind of certification I wouldn't be allowed to touch a patient. I realized that America is full of people who have started over. Some friends of mine took me to visit a few of the historical sights. I delighted in Boston's association with the history of the American struggle for independence. Chechnya is not the only country that has struggled for independence, I thought, as I stood on the wooden bridge at Concord where the first shots were fired in April 1775 in America's struggle against the British. By today's standards, England surely would have called George Washington a terrorist.

At first, I worried how the Russian émigré community of Boston, some 50,000 strong, would accept a Chechen, especially at a time of war. I hoped that as Jews and victims of discrimination in Russia, many of these immigrants would be sympathetic, that they hadn't brought the Russian stereotypes of Chechens to the United States with them. A few of them viewed me with suspicion, but most of them welcomed me.

"Are you the Chechen doctor who appeared on television in Moscow?" a Russian woman asked after coming up to me in the Russian bookstore one morning. I told her I was.

"It's that Chechen doctor who treated everyone," she announced loudly to the other shoppers. Soon a crowd of Russian well-wishers surrounded me, asking how I was and what they could do for me. Later, that first Russian woman called me at home, asking what she could do for me. There really was nothing; she was struggling to make her own way in the United States just as I was. But her kindness touched me.

I am always amazed at the power of kindness, like that of Liuba Vartikovski, a Russian-born physician, who is president of a group of Russian-speaking doctors in Boston. Liuba introduced me to her judo coach, Bill Stevens, who worked out at the Tohoku Club in Somerville, Massachusetts. She said that when she first came to this country, judo had helped her maintain sanity. The club was an amazing place with athletes from Europe, South America, and Africa. Although some of us didn't speak English, communication was not a problem.

Some of my friends suggested I find a psychologist in Boston, since Dr. Judy had helped me so much when I was in Washington, but I told myself that if I could survive the war, I could overcome the inexplicable bouts of depression, my lack of concentration, the outbursts of anger. Once again I turned to athletics to help me. Thirteen

years had passed since I had set foot on a tatami mat, and I worried
that the war might have impaired my agility and reflexes. To my surprise, I found that in some ways it may even have improved them. My
balance and control on the mat were as good as ever, even better. All
those times at Russian military checkpoints when the soldiers hurled
insults at me, I had practiced control and patience. Their jibes taught
me to swallow humiliation, which for a Chechen is hard, but during
the war self-control became a survival mechanism; reacting to insults
invited execution.

NINE MONTHS AFTER I had arrived in the United States, I still
hadn't received permission to bring my family here. Finally, the Immigration and Naturalization Service approved my petition. Now the
issue was how to get the family out of Chechnya. Under the 1975
Helsinki Final Act, people have the right to leave their country, travel
abroad, and return to their country of origin or settle elsewhere. An
international organization called the International Office of Migration in Moscow was in charge of processing would-be emigrants.
Once the INS agreed to accept my family, the case was passed to the
International Office of Migration, which then cleared the request
with the Russian security services.

Zara and the children made the thirty-six-hour train trip to Moscow
to await clearance to leave. My sister Raya and Lecha accompanied
them. Since they didn't have Moscow residency papers, they lived with
relatives in the town of Tver, north of Moscow. Friends of our family
wrote letters of support to the U.S. and Russian authorities, urging that
their case be settled. I fretted endlessly. Finally, the International Office
of Migration approved their departure.

This, however, didn't assuage my worry. They could be stopped
at the airport, especially when the border guards saw that they were
going to the United States. To avoid this problem, we bought them
round-trip tickets to Warsaw. "We are going to visit friends, for a
holiday," Zara told Passport Control at the airport in Moscow. Once
in Warsaw, they picked up one-way tickets to the United States

(bought by American friends), which were waiting for them at the airport.

On February 5, 2001, I drove from Boston to Kennedy airport in New York to meet Zara and the children. I was very nervous, not believing that they were really coming. All sorts of scenarios ran through my mind: They could have been pulled off the plane by the FSB; they might have been arrested in Warsaw. The hours ticked by, and finally the Polish jetliner arrived—and on time. First Adam, then Khava, Maryam, and Islam emerged out of customs into the arrival hall. Then came Zara with Markha in her arms. I could hardly believe it. When they ran to embrace me, I saw the strains of war on their faces and knew I had made the right decision to stay in the United States.

Housing a family of seven was a problem. Some friends of mine offered us their house in the small town of Andover, Vermont. We lived there for almost nine months. The house stood at the top of a high hill amid green forests, distant mountains, and cascading streams, reminding me of Chechnya. At first, my friends were nervous about leaving us in such an isolated place. They needn't have worried; no sooner did we arrive than townspeople offered help.

"Your children have to learn English," said Charlene Huyler, a kindergarten teacher, throwing dozens of books across the dining room table. Soon she had the kids singing children's songs. She persuaded us to send Adam, Maryam, and Islam to the elementary school, and Khava to the high school, in nearby Chester. Each weekday morning at 7 A.M., the yellow school bus would drive to the house to pick them up. Dick Andrews, our next-door neighbor who knew some Russian, helped me with English and any problems we encountered. People brought clothes, bicycles, and toys for the children. John Sinclair, a dentist in nearby Springfield, worked free of charge on everyone's teeth, which were in bad shape after the war.

For the first time since I left Chechnya, I began to feel at home. Since we only feel really at home when we entertain, Zara and I invited our new American friends to meals at the house and taught them how to dance the *lesghinka*. Eventually, we found permanent housing in

Zara and me at a reception in Boston, October 2002.

Boston. Before we moved away, Charlene's mother-in-law, Ella, made us two patchwork wall hangings—a Chechen flag and an American flag. We hung the two flags side by side above the couch in our new residence. I never look at them without recalling the kindness of a small town in Vermont, which helped us in our search for peace.

Before we left Vermont for Boston in August 2001, Ali made it to the United States. After Adam's funeral, he had left for Moscow using the domestic passport of a neighbor's dead son. His brothers bribed the train attendant, who hid him in her compartment. In Moscow he stayed in different apartments for over six months, never venturing into the street. Finally, with the help of American human rights organizations, he left for the United States. Zara and I met him at Kennedy airport.

For two months after Ali's arrival, I didn't mention Adam's name. Then one day as we were driving home from a gym, I volunteered that fate was strange. I had planned for Adam to join me in America, but in the end it was Ali who came. Ali finally broke down and cried. He said he felt Adam should be here, not he.

Ali says he often talks to Adam in his mind. "Whatever I do," he says, "I think Adam is beside me. When I am driving alone, my thoughts drift. I ask him how he likes the drive. Adam was always so good to our parents, and I know that I must take his place and help them. That is what he would want me to do."

War changes people, sometimes for the better and sometimes for the worse. Some turn into animals. Others become kinder. Ali matured from a boy to a wise young man who avoids speaking ill of the Russians. "If I did something bad to them, I would be no better than they are. I don't want revenge. I want to be human. I don't want to hate."

Ali credits the kindness of a single Russian soldier nicknamed Kuzmich for helping him survive confinement and torture. One night, Kuzmich came to the edge of the pit where Ali was held. He was a young Russian recruit who worked in military transport. It was dark, so Ali never really saw what he looked like. Soldiers were always coming to look at the prisoners as if they were animals in a zoo.

"What did you do that they put you in the pit?" Kuzmich asked Ali.

"I am a Chechen, that's all."

"But you are a fighter?"

"No, I worked in the hospital with my uncle."

The next night, Ali recalled, Kuzmich came back with condensed milk and hard crackers. "Don't tell anyone," he said, lowering them into the pit. "You may be a bandit, but no one should be put in these conditions."

Kuzmich told Ali he was an orphan and that he had been sent to Chechnya for being drunk on duty. He said he hoped he would survive his tour. Each night from then on, he and Ali talked. One of Kuzmich's best friends had been killed by the Chechens, he said, but he had nothing against Chechens as a people. The night before Kuzmich's tour in Chechnya ended, he sat atop the pit again. "I am worried about what will happen to you when I am not here. No one will give you food or water."

Before he left, Kuzmich brought Ali a large two-liter bottle of water, which Ali hid in the mud at the bottom of the pit. Kuzmich wrote his name and address on a piece of paper; Ali hid it in the cuff of his trouser leg.

"You'll be out of here soon," he said. "I want you to visit me. You will come to my home, and we will eat and drink like normal people."

A FEW MONTHS after my family arrived in the United States, my friend Viktor Tatarkin called me from New York. "The World Judo Championship is taking place in Arizona over the July Fourth weekend. Why don't we participate?" he said.

At first I hesitated. I was thirty-eight years old. I hadn't competed in more than a decade. Some of my friends thought it was madness. I didn't care so much about winning; the idea was to participate. I had dreamed about this since I was a boy sneaking off to Grozny behind Dada's back. "Let's do it," I told Viktor, and I started training.

The championship coincided with a trip to Los Angeles at the invitation of Human Rights Watch. Oleg Takhtarov, a friend of Viktor's who had settled in Los Angeles, made all the arrangements. From Los

When I took first place in the World Cup Sombo Championship in Nice, France, in November 2001, I raised the Chechen flag.

Angeles, we drove to Tucson for the World Judo Championship and then on to Albuquerque for the combined ninth U.S. Sombo and World Championship. The long car ride opened up a whole new landscape—no green, just muted shades of brown and yellow, and huge cactuses. It was unlike anything I had ever seen and quite beautiful. It was also the first time I had seen Native Americans.

I took fourth place in my weight category in the judo competition in Tucson but won the sombo championship in Albuquerque. I fought under the Chechen flag, which made me very proud. By winning the sombo competition, I felt I had overcome my opponents and my own frailties, but I had also overcome those KGB people who had kept me from competing by pulling me off the plane in 1983. My win got a lot of publicity in Russia, causing the poison-pen critics to question why I was allowed to represent Chechnya, still part of Russia from Moscow's point of view. I didn't care. I savored the irony that I had triumphed on American Independence Day.

Of course, I was proud to fight as a Chechen because it was the first time anyone had done that, but now what I really wanted was to represent the United States. America had given my family a safe harbor, and the opportunity for me to take up the sport I loved. It had helped me regain some sanity. To fight on a U.S. team in an international competition would allow me the opportunity to give something back. Everyone told me that was impossible because I wasn't a U.S. citizen.

In June 2002, I went to Shreveport, Louisiana, to defend my title at the World Sombo Championship. Before the matches, I approached Josh Henson, the president of the American Sombo Association. "I want to fight for America," I said, not really thinking it would happen.

He shook his head. "You are not a citizen."

"But I have a social security number; I have a Massachusetts driver's license," I said, pulling them from my wallet. "And I have applied for a permanent residence card."

Josh said he would consult with his colleagues and let me know. He came back twenty minutes later. "The answer is yes," he said. On the weekend of June 22–23, 2002, in Shreveport, I won the world championship in my weight category, successfully defending my title.

Kavkazpress, a Chechen Web site, publicized my victory on the Internet. Winning gave me a tremendous lift.

UNFORTUNATELY, BAD MEMORIES still intrude on the good. I continue to be drawn to news about Chechnya, and most of it is bad. I still click on Kavkaz-Tsentr, a Chechen Web site. Much as I would like to, I cannot break this habit. The news makes me heartsick and angry. Russia tries to pretend the war is over, but every day people are killed, including young Russian soldiers from the thousands of Russian troops still stationed in Chechnya. There is no letup in the suffering of the civilians. Officially, filtration camps no longer exist. Now they are called "places of temporary imprisonment" and are located at some fourteen locations throughout Chechnya where Russian troops are stationed. These so-called temporary prisons are actually large pits, covered by grilles, holding up to thirty men. In addition, smaller pits exist adjacent to Russian checkpoints where prisoners are held until their families pay ransoms. Every time I hear about the death squads that roam the streets at night or about the disappearance of a young Chechen male during a *zachistka*, I am filled with helpless anger and the terrible feeling that our nation is being annihilated.

Instead of winding down, the war took an ominous turn on October 24, 2002, when Chechen fighters took more than 800 people hostage in a Moscow theater. I watched in horror as the tragedy unfolded on television, knowing it could end in deadly reprisals all over Chechnya. Like many other people, I also feared this terrible act of violence would play into the hands of President Putin, who is trying to convince the world that Chechens are all terrorists supported by al-Qaeda.

The second night of the hostage situation, I received a telephone call from my old Russian journalist friend Dima Belovetsky. "We need your help to get the hostages released," he said.

I told Dima I was hesitant about getting involved. It was true that Movsar Barayev, the leader of the hostage takers, came from Alkhan Kala and that I had operated on his mother. Movsar was the nephew of Arbi Barayev, who had threatened to kill me in 1999.

"If I become involved, I will be accused tomorrow of helping terrorists," I told Dima, once I got my thoughts together. "Maybe if I am asked officially, I would try."

Dima said he would get in touch with someone and call me back. At 2 A.M. the next morning, the telephone rang again. It was Dima. "I am passing the phone to Lt. General Vladimir Pronin, chief of the Moscow police."

"Greetings, Khassan," the voice on the other end said. "How are you doing there in America? I saw you several times on the television." After we exchanged greetings, the chief of police told me he needed my help.

"I am willing to try," I said, "but I need a guarantee that no one will accuse me later of consorting with terrorists."

The chief replied, "I give you my word. After all, what we are trying to do is to help people, to do good." He gave me the telephone numbers of the hostage takers in the theater. I hung up and dialed. The police must have been listening in because when there was no reply at first from the hostage takers, a voice broke in: "What's wrong? Aren't they picking up?"

I knew it was unlikely I could say anything that could persuade the hostage takers to release the hostages, but I was willing to try anything to avoid a catastrophe. Movsar might listen to me as his elder, but he was not alone; there were a number of young men and women with dynamite strapped to their waists, desperate individuals who wanted to draw the world's attention to the forgotten war. Unlike my generation, who were educated in Russia and had Russian friends, this younger generation of Chechens has known nothing but death at the hands of Russia.

After dialing several times, a woman answered. I could tell by her voice she was young and very nervous. I told her who I was and said I wanted to talk to Movsar. She left the phone. After several minutes, she returned to say that Movsar couldn't talk to me now, but to call back. Before hanging up, I tried to chat with her a bit. "Why did you do this?" I asked.

"I have nothing to lose," she replied. "I have lost seven people in my family. We are ready for death. The only thing we want is to stop the war."

When I finally reached Movsar, his voice was calm. "You know what is going on in Chechnya," he said. Listening to him, I recalled my own desperation. I remembered how life lost all value when every day I saw absolutely innocent people being killed, maimed, raped, kidnapped, and tortured.

He said that the hostage takers wanted to meet with representatives of an international organization, but that the Russians refused to let them in or allow a press conference. "We gave an interview to NTV, explaining our positions, but it was never broadcast."

"Please let the children go," I said after I realized there was no changing his mind.

"We've released all the children under ten years of age. Here they are saying that kids up to fifteen or sixteen are still children," he said. "In Chechnya, Russians treat children over ten as fighters and kill them."

I went on to suggest he release the foreigners and anyone who was ill. He said they had released people with medical conditions, and he was willing to release all foreigners if their representatives would come and pick them up. "But the Russians refuse to let anyone come for them."

The Russian special forces pumped a sleeping gas into the building, then stormed it. The rescue was botched. All but two of the unconscious hostage takers were executed with a shot to the head. Many of the hostages lost their lives because the Russian doctors, expecting to treat gunshot wounds, received no information about the gas or its antidote. Some weeks after the incident, relatives of mine called to say that several intelligence officials claimed on Moscow television that I should be investigated to discover what ties I have with terrorists!

Watching the victims leave the theater on television, I was more certain than ever that unless there was a political solution to the war, there would be many more such incidents. A few months after the hostage incident in Moscow, a bomb blew up a large building in Grozny housing the pro-Russian Chechen government. I wish the American leadership would take a more active role in moving both sides toward negotiation, but I fear that if Russia supports the United States in the war against terrorism, Washington may turn a blind eye to the continued violation of human rights in Chechnya.

Although news of events in Chechnya and in other war-ravaged places throughout the world continues to trigger bad memories, nightmares, and sleepless nights, I find consolation in the fact that my wife and children are safe. I try to keep good memories of Chechnya alive for our children. They are studying Russian and Chechen during the summer instead of going to camps. Islam says he remembers Dada and Nana and can't wait to show off his English to them. "I remember all the ruins there," he says, "but I want to go back and visit one day." I know Zara misses her family too. But she and I agree that the children should stay here and get an education; then perhaps they can make a contribution to Chechnya. When I see the smiles on their faces, my sense of loss at being in exile and unable to practice surgery recedes. Now that I spend time at home, I am getting to know my children in new and deeper ways. I take pleasure in their progress.

My family of fighters at the Tohoku Judo Club in Somerville, Massachusetts. Left to right: Maryam, Khava, Markha, me, Islam, and Adam.

At peace in 2005. Seated, left to right: Zara, Markha, and me. Back row: Maryam, Khava, American-born Satsita, Adam, and Islam.

Four-year-old Markha hardly knew me when the family first arrived in the United States. In Chechnya, I was always away from home, and she started calling my brother, Hussein, Papa. Now she calls me Papa and often asks me to play with her. She is speaking a mixture of Chechen, Russian, and English. "Hi, sweetie!" she says, demonstrating what she has learned at her Head Start program. Eight-year-old Islam is our intellectual; he speaks English without an accent and is on his third Harry Potter book. Maryam, nine, who arrived in this country so subdued that an American friend of ours voiced concern about her well-being, now talks so much one of her teachers has complained. Adam, ten, is always in good humor, trusting everyone. Khava, who celebrated her sixteenth birthday, is a cherished member of our family and doing well in the local high school.

I ENVY MY children their facility with the English language. Often I ask them to act as my interpreters. My slowness in learning English embarrasses me. I know that without English, I will not enter fully into American society, let alone find a job in medicine. I am making progress, but not as much as I would like. Ever since my concussions during the war, I have had trouble retaining words, especially when my concentration is broken by bad news from Chechnya. When I first arrived in the United States, some people suggested I apply for disability status, but I never wanted to do that. I itch to return to meaningful work. Meanwhile, I work as a volunteer in the radiology department at Newton-Wellesley Hospital in Massachusetts. By now, I have adjusted to the realization that it will be a long time before I can practice as a cosmetic surgeon again, if ever.

When I go to my volunteer job at Newton-Wellesley Hospital, I often remember the nurses and doctors who worked with me in Chechnya. Many were targeted by the Russians after I left. Several left Chechnya and now live in refugee camps in Europe. I want to help them, to send them money, but I haven't the means. So often I feel guilty because people back in Chechnya believe money grows on trees here. Many of them have contacted me, requesting help. They do not understand that I have no influence or money. "Can you send one of those Jeeps?" asked a friend of mine when he called from Moscow. "They are easy to buy in the United States and cheaper than in Moscow."

The son of one Chechen official wrote to me, "Please arrange a medical internship for me in the U.S." I couldn't arrange an internship for myself, let alone someone else.

"You are such a talented surgeon; you must have lots of work," said one of my friends from Moscow. When I told him I didn't have a paying job, the surprise in his voice made me feel like a failure.

★   ★   ★

WHILE LEARNING ENGLISH and writing this book, I also struggle
to understand American customs, many of which are so different from
those in Chechnya that I wonder how many more missteps I will take.
For example, in the beginning I didn't seem able to get to places on
time. I wasn't accustomed to such emphasis on punctuality. "Always be
on time," I was advised. "Call if you're going to be late. Don't drop in on
someone unannounced. Call." Americans arrange business appointments weeks in advance; their vacation, months or years ahead. In
Chechnya, life is so unpredictable that it is impossible to plan ahead.
When we are expecting company, we do not set the table until after the
guests have arrived because we never know how many will actually be
there. We also believe that a guest takes precedence over everything else,
which means that if guests arrive, you stay home to entertain them and
don't go to work. This, as I quickly learned, is not the American way.

When a charitable organization brought two Chechen refugee children to the United States for a summer visit and there was no suitable
place for them to stay, we took them in. "You are crazy," an American
friend of mine scolded me. "It's not fair to Zara, having to look after
seven children."

"You don't understand," I replied. "We are Chechen; it is our duty
to take them in. Zara understands that." I don't think my friend was
convinced.

When I observe how my family is resettling in the United States, I
realize that I am the one with the most difficulties adjusting. Zara has
made American friends, passed her driving test, and was accepted into
a program that will teach her basic office skills. Maybe women and
children are more flexible than men, less wedded to their position in
society. In Chechnya, I had an important job and was widely respected. Here I have no professional status. Like many other immigrants and refugees, I have to start over. But the United States has
been built by generations of people forging new beginnings, as I discovered when one of my friends took me to Ellis Island, New York,
for so many years the main port of entry for people from 122 different countries who came seeking a new life. Historically, people trav-

eled for months, often under terrible conditions, to get here. Most immigrants did not have the kind of support from the U.S. government that my family and I have received. When I saw the haggard faces of men, women, and children in the photographs on the wall of the Ellis Island museum, I marveled at their courage and strength of character and felt a strange sense of solidarity with them. I hope that someday I can make a contribution to this unique country.

Of course, my appreciation of America doesn't mean that I have stopped dreaming of returning to Chechnya. Not being able to bring medical help to my people still grieves me. Once I get on my feet, I would like to start a foundation to bring medical help to Chechnya, especially to the children.

When I was there working as a surgeon during the war, I felt useful. Sometimes I think those terrible times were also some of the happiest moments of my life.

Epilogue

ONE DAY IN the autumn of 2004, I was pushing a patient on a gurney in the hospital where I was working in the transportation department. The woman on the gurney grabbed my hand and said, "You are a nice-looking man. Where are you from?"

"From Chechnya."

"Chechnya?" She seemed aghast. "So why are you killing all those children?" she said.

I felt awful. Before Chechen terrorists attacked the Beslan school in southern Russia, most of the people I encountered at work in the hospital had no idea where Chechnya was. Now the mere mention of "Chechen" revives those terrible images on CNN of the more than three hundred people killed at Beslan, most of them children.

I wanted to tell this woman: please don't judge all Chechens by the barbaric acts of a few madmen. I wished my English were better so I could tell her that those images of bleeding children being carried from the school horrified and angered ordinary Chechens as much as the rest of the world.

Sometimes people also ask if I regretted saving Shamil Basayev's life, as he is believed to have masterminded so many horrible acts of terrorism.

"I am a doctor. I was doing my job. I am not a policeman or a prosecutor," I usually reply.

"But don't you ever wish he had died crossing that minefield?" the questions continue.

"I can't judge that. If he had died on the minefield or on my operating table, it would have been the will of Allah."

I do not pretend to understand the mentality of a terrorist, although I have personally witnessed the despair of people in wartime. A grief-stricken woman, with nothing more to lose, straps on a suicide belt. A man filled with rage hungers for revenge and will stop at nothing. Bloodshed and loss drive people to desperate acts which bring untold sorrow to others—acts that turn the perpetrators into animals.

AS THE SUMMER heat settles over our apartment near Boston, Massachusetts, my thoughts frequently return to my childhood in the mountains. The other night, I dreamed about my ancestral village, Makazhoi. In the dream people had rebuilt the village, and those people who had perished were suddenly alive and well again.

If I close my eyes, I can almost feel the mountain breezes. I am transported to the times when I sat in the back of Dada's truck with

The family I left behind. Seated, left to right: Nana, Dada, Tamara, and Raya; standing, left to right: Razyat, Hussein, and Malika.

Hussein. I see the dirt road winding up, up into the clouds toward Makazhoi, along precipices so steep you can hardly see the bottom, past the zigzagging paths leading to small hamlets behind the ridges. We stop at the overlook before the village. There spread out below is Blue Lake, and in the distance the snowcapped mountains.

These scenes bring me a feeling of peace, connecting me to my roots. One day I hope to take my children to Makazhoi. Even if my village no longer exists, just being in the mountains and seeing the graves of our ancestors will help them understand who they are.

According to a Russian saying, "*Net khuda bez dobra*" (There is no evil without good). It is hard to find anything positive in the sacrifice and suffering of the innocent. Bombs and land mines kill and maim indiscriminately, especially when war is waged amid civilian towns, villages, and farms. Those who survive are changed forever. I know I will never be the same person I was before the wars; I have seen too much violence and death. Still, there is hope. Despite thousands of land mines across the landscape, Chechens are replanting their fields, and women are having babies.

Not a day goes by when I don't think about my family back in Chechnya. Over the past five years when I have been living in the United States, I have lost many friends and relatives. Just weeks ago, I got word that Dada had died of natural causes. I see old men in the hospital sometimes who look like him, and I am filled with guilt that I was not with him to say my last goodbyes, which is an important Chechen tradition.

Earlier my sister Raya's husband, Leche, was murdered when gunmen broke into their house. Malika's husband, too, has been killed. These are everyday murders in Chechnya, where a quarter of the population has perished, thousands of them children.

The thought of not seeing Nana before she dies tortures me. The pressure builds up in my head, and I can't concentrate; I can't sleep. I want to catch the next plane back to Chechnya.

But life goes on. I am adjusting slowly. Exercise helps me dissipate the tension. I have taken up judo and sombo again and to everyone's amazement I have won a number of national and international championships. I am doing what I can, too, to help the wounded children back in Chechnya. I now head up the International Committee for the Children of Chechnya, a nonprofit organization which was started in 1996 by two American friends. We have adopted a school for the deaf in Grozny, sending them classroom supplies and providing teachers with special instruction on how to teach the deaf.

My family in America has grown. On February 4, 2003, Zara gave birth to a little girl. We named her Satsita.

My first thought when the nurse showed me our little girl was that she was born in freedom. She will never have to go through what I and my family went through. In Chechnya, my family and Zara's were happy to have a new grandchild. Malika told me later in a telephone conversation that Hussein goes around telling everyone, "We have our first little American girl." Who knows? She could become the first Chechen-American senator.

NOT LONG AGO, an American friend of mine gave me a snakeskin that he had found in his garden. The skin is paper-thin, translucent, with an unusual pattern of ribs and honeycombing. I took it in both hands so as not to break it. I have never liked snakes since that day in the mountains of Chechnya when a snake slithered over my legs. Even today, snakes still chase me in my dreams, flashing their forked tongues, reaching for my ankles, trying to trip me up. Yet I know snakes also symbolize hope and regeneration because they grow a new skin every year; that's why they wind themselves around the cup of healing—the caduceus—the universal symbol of physicians.

I draped my American snakeskin over the framed portrait of a Japanese athlete whom I revere: Jigoro Kano, the founder of judo, a sport which has done so much to lift my spirits and help me in my new life. I sometimes think about how hard it is for snakes to shuck their old skins. The reptile must anchor itself between sharp rocks, split the skin, and wriggle free. Here in America, far from my homeland, I too am trying to anchor myself and shed one life—reluctantly and with difficulty—for a new one.

Where Are They Now?

Nana continues to live in Alkhan Kala. In spite of poor health, Nana insisted on acquiring two new cows. **Dada** died in 2004.

Hussein and **Rita** also live in Alkhan Kala and help look after Nana. Hussein is out of work. My sister **Razyat** and her husband, **Alikhan,** returned from Kazakhstan to live near Dada and Nana. My oldest sister, **Tamara,** also lives in Alkhan Kala with her husband.

Raya, my sister, lives not far from Nana and looks after her as best she can. Her husband, **Lecha,** made the pilgrimage to Mecca in February 2003; only four months later he was murdered by three unknown masked men.

My sister **Malika** has a job at the Ninth City Hospital in Grozny, which is operating again.

My nephew **Ali** is in Vermont. He has learned English, is training to be a nurse's assistant at Fletcher-Allen Hospital in Burlington, and hopes one day to become a surgeon. Like me, he draws strength from sports. In 2001, he took the world title in his division at the World Tae Kwon Do Federation championship in Toronto, Canada.

Musa Saponov, my cousin who was so helpful to me in Moscow, his wife, and their three children returned to Alkhan Kala and live with his mother, my adopted sister **Larissa.** Musa no longer does business in the Russian capital; he now raises cows, sheep, and chickens.

My farewell to boyhood pals. Front row, left to right: Olkhazur and me; back row, left to right: Khamzat, Ruslan, Bislan, and Hamid.

My schoolteachers: **Tamara Mikhailovna** died of burns in southern Russia when a cauldron of jam she was boiling tipped over on her; **Khava Zhaparovna** is still teaching at Middle School No. 1, which is the only school operating in Alkhan Kala.

My old frends: After medical school, **Musa Salekhov** moved to Kazakhstan and worked as a dentist for a year, then went into business. He didn't return to Chechnya. As for boyhood playmates, **Bislan** and **Lyoma** are out of work; **Khizir** works in Grozny in the Ministry of Housing; **Khamzat** is a businessman in Chelyabinsk; **Bayali** perished when his house burned up as a result of a gas explosion; **Adlan,** my boyhood schoolmate, was murdered when masked men broke into his house.

Khassan Taimaskhanov, who helped tutor me for the Medical Institute, is now living in Belgium as a refugee with his wife and their five children. He is studying to become a construction engineer.

Salman Raduyev, the field commander whose face I reconstructed, was arrested trying to leave Chechnya in 2000, put on trial, and sentenced to life imprisonment. In December 2002, he suffered a hemorrhage in prison and died. My Chechen friends believe the hemorrhage was brought on by beatings he received after refusing to implicate Akhmed Zakayev, President Maskhadov's European representative, as a terrorist.

Shamil Basayev, the Chechen field commander, remains at large in the mountains and continues operations to drive the Russians out of Chechnya.

Musa Muradov, my courageous editor friend, struggles to keep his newspaper, *Groznenskii Rabochii,* alive while working as a correspondent for the Russian newspaper *Kommersant* in Moscow.

Dima Belovetsky, my Russian journalist friend, works in Moscow for the Russian *Literaturnaya Gazeta* and continues his interest in Chechen news.

Malika Umazhova, the woman whose cow Zoyka I treated, went on to become president of the Alkhan Kala local council. She was a much-loved figure in the community. When asked by the Russians to sign affidavits that the cleansing operations were performed peacefully, she refused. On the night of November 29, 2002, armed soldiers entered her house, forced her out to the barn, and killed her in cold blood.

Nuradi Isayev remains in Alkhan Kala, where his personal mission is to care for the dead. When the minefield south of Grozny was finally cleared, he took on the job of interring the remains of the 150 victims who had been lying there since Basayev's retreat at the beginning of February 2000.

Said-Ali Aduyev, the dentist who was always at my side during the second war, lives in Alkhan Kala. He raises livestock.

Addi, my faithful medical volunteer, was killed by unknown persons who broke into his house.

Zina Aduyeva, our volunteer gynecologist during the war, lives in Alkhan Kala and works at my old hospital, which has been repaired thanks to support from the International Committee of the Red Cross.

My nurses **Razyat, Zara, Leila, Zarina, Maryam,** without

whom I could not have functioned, survived the war, but their lives remain hard. Not long ago I received a handwritten letter from Razyat and Zarina. They wrote: "Our whole team wants to know how you are. When we all gather together we always remember those difficult times. Now that things have become a little more settled, we even remember some funny incidents when you taught at us like children. But now that we have grown up and are independent we do not fear you (joke)."

Rumani Idrisova, the nurse at my side through the worst times, now works at Grozny's Fourth City Hospital and trades in the bazaar during her off moments to make ends meet. She lives with her husband and children in the village of Kirovo. After I left, the Russian military authorities arrested her, accused her of working for me and of treating bandits. "She insisted on her rights and stated that if she remained alive she would continue to treat them," Razyat wrote in her letter to me. "In the end, they let her go and threatened her to keep her mouth closed. Now everything is OK with her."

Zaurbek, who fought to keep our hospital generator running, ekes out a living as a private electrician in Alkhan Kala.

Raisa, who struggled so valiantly to keep the floors of our hospital clean, works again at the hospital in Alkhan Kala. **Roza,** who cooked for the hospital, lives at home in Alkhan Kala.

And finally, about **Ruslan Temirkhanov**—the FSB colonel who helped me escape from Chechnya. He was murdered in Ingushetia with his wife. The unidentified killers dumped their bodies in a village cemetery in Chechnya, obviously as a warning to others. Without him, I would not be here. My family would not have found refuge in America. This book would not have been written.

Index

In this index, KB is used for Khassan Baiev.

Achkoi-Martan, 99, 170
Aduyev, Said-Ali, 259–60, 259*f*, 365
Aduyeva, Zina, 251, 365
Aigumov, Vakha, 226, 230, 298, 308
Akhigova, Zara, 259, 365–66
Alexander I, 2
Alexeyevich, Alexei, 275
Alikhan (businessman; husband of Razyat), 223, 363
Alkhan Kala, xvi, 11–12, 41, 44, 67, 84, 93, 96, 136, 137, 148, 159, 230, 301, 302, 304, 313, 351
   attacks on, 112–13, 278–79, 281, 284–85
   Baiev family returning to, 335–36
   bombing of, 263, 266–67, 274, 275
   devastation in, 316
   hospital, xix, 105–7, 108, 110–12, 113, 167, 168, 249–51, 254–55, 256–58, 266, 269, 274, 275–76, 277, 282, 286, 289–90, 292, 294–300, 303, 305–6, 327
   hospital: hit by fire, 284, 285
   hospital: transporting patients from, 278–79
   KB's home in, 101, 121
   KB leaving, 115–16
   KB's return to, 222
   KB's trip to, 177–84
   medical rounds in, 132
   military buildup around, 160–65
   military checkpoint, 243–44
   people in mourning, 223
   people leaving, 251–52
   rebuilding in, 188
   Russian military headquarters, 152
   saving, 160–66
   schools in, 170
   shelling of, 107, 109–10, 167, 226, 260–61, 266–67
   situation in, 337
   women from, 98
   wounded in, 277
Alkhan Kala Middle School No. 1, 26–27
Alkhan Yurt, 181, 198, 274, 275–76
   mullah, 332
   siege of, 261
All-Russian Junior Championship, 43
All-Union Judo Cup, 59
All-Union Junior Championship, 43
Almatova, Razyat, 257, 262, 298, 299, 365–66
Amnesty International, 318, 330
Amputations, xvi–xvii, 91, 167, 242, 298, 300, 307, 317
   Basayev, 297–98
Ancestors, 28–42
Animals, 109–10, 143
   KB treating, 270–73
Armenia, 2, 68
Aslanbekov, Zaurbek, 250, 279–80, 366
Atagi, xxi, 117, 118, 119–20, 142
Atrokhov, Wendy, 336
Azerbaijan, 2, 11, 68, 95, 320
Azhiev, Khamzat, xix–xxi

Babichev, Ivan, 99–100
Babitsky, Andrei, 242
Baghdad, 220

Baiev, Adam (son of Hussein), 223, 242, 315
    in U.S., 346, 354*f*, 355, 355*f*
Baiev, Dada (father of KB), 11–24, 17*f*,
    26–27, 47, 58, 61, 65, 91, 153, 156, 168,
    175, 177, 182, 192, 214, 215, 222, 248,
    308, 321*f*, 354, 360, 360*f*
    advice from, 261
    age-old remedies, 264–65
    and bombing of Grozny, 95
    and case against KB, 227
    on Deportation, 32–35, 37
    failing, 361, 363
    as father, 22–23
    and grandchild Markha, 223, 242
    herbal medicine, 17, 27
    houses, 67
    and Hussein's move, 223
    on independence, 75
    job in Kazakhstan, 43–44
    and KB's escape, 315–16
    and KB's house, 116
    and KB's marriage, 83
    KB's responsibility for, 155, 207
    and KB's wife, 76, 84
    and Koran, 220
    and Makazhoi, 28, 29, 32–35, 38, 39,
        41–42, 359
    prayer *Lak'ad Djaakum*, 179
    refused to take shelter, 108, 109, 110
    returning home, 132, 335, 336
    risked prison, 213
    ritual slaughter of animals, 109–10
    and Russian deserters, 137, 138–39, 141
    on Russians, 82
    and second war, 252, 253–54, 309
    in Second World War, 15–16, 35, 57
    war medals, 16, 17*f*
Baiev, Hussein (brother of KB), 11, 12,
    13–14, 13*f*, 17–18, 19, 20, 21, 22, 26,
    27, 67, 96, 156, 188, 252, 320, 355, 359,
    360*f*, 362, 363
    at Agricultural Institute, 51
    finding Ruslan's corpse, 231
    house, 267
    in Krasnoyarsk, 155
    and Makazhoi, 32, 33, 40, 41, 42
    marriage, 58, 76
    move to Alkhan Kala, 223
    and second war, 242, 277–78, 279, 291,
        315, 336
Baiev, Islam (son of KB), 98, 127, 132, 155,
    197, 207, 315
    in U.S., 346, 354*f*, 355, 355*f*

Baiev, Khassan, 1, 62*f*, 194*f*, 215*f*, 268*f*, 290*f*,
    296*f*, 299*f*, 321*f*, 347*f*
    accused of being traitor, 7, 282
    accused of fraternizing with Russians, 225,
        227, 229
    accused of treating Russians, 280, 281
    American visa, 320
    arrangements to leave Chechnya, 308–10
    athletic training, 19–20, 22, 27, 54, 59, 60,
        61, 95
    becoming a doctor, 27, 43–66
    children, 97, 109, 137, 158, 252, 321–22,
        335, 354–55, 354*f*, 355*f*, 356
    children: move to U.S., 345–46
    criminal case against, 224–30
    consulting psychologist in U.S., 332–33,
        337
    denied visa to England, 205, 211
    depression, 197–200, 206–9, 219, 223, 337,
        344, 361
    early life, 11, 13–15, 17–22, 155–57, 359
    education, 26–27, 43–44
    education: Medical Institute, 47–53, 59–65
    in emergency room, xvi, xvii, xviii, xix,
        xxi
    escape, 313–26
    family concerns, 170
    finding a wife, 67–88
    hard of hearing, 17–18
    injured in missile strike, 119–21
    journal, 274–76
    memory problems, 121, 204, 224, 356
    money matters, 73, 87–88, 91, 191–92
    near-death experience, 120, 126–27
    offer of job in Mecca, 217
    order for arrest of, 313–16
    plans to leave Chechnya, 288, 289, 291
    relationships with girls/classmates, 54–55,
        56–58, 64–65, 66
    residency/internship, 65–66, 78, 79–81, 82,
        85–86
    responsibility to family, 44, 191–92, 207,
        335
    role in family, 26
    salary, 69, 86
    taken for helping Sasha escape, 153–55,
        157–59, 160, 244
    visa to Saudi Arabia, 211–12
    wanted by Russians, 336
Baiev, Khava (daughter of Hussein), 188, 242,
    315, 316, 336
    in U.S., 346, 354*f*, 355–56, 355*f*
Baiev, Larissa (adopted sister), 16, 76, 363

Baiev, Malika (sister of KB), 14, 18*f*, 20,
    22, 23, 93–95, 120, 135, 168, 182,
    183–84, 224, 227, 340, 360*f*, 361,
    362, 363
  apartment for, 73
  and arrangements for KB to leave
    Chechnya, 308, 309
  birth of, 39
  and Chechen counterattack, 170, 171,
    174–75, 176, 177
  and deserters, 137, 140, 141
  education, 27
  employment, 192
  and Hussein's daughter, 188
  about KB staying in U.S., 335, 336
  leaving Alkhan Kala, 109, 113
  and Nana's illness, 320
  nurse at hospital, 90
  in old house, 67
  in parents' house, 137
  return home, 132
  and second war, 242, 252, 253, 267,
    277–78, 279, 291, 300
  and wife for KB, 75–76, 77–78
  and Zara's C-section, 96, 97, 98
Baiev, Markha (daughter of KB), 223, 242,
    315, 336
  in U.S., 346, 354*f*, 355, 355*f*
Baiev, Maryam (daughter of KB), 86–87, 89,
    127, 155, 197, 207, 315
  return home, 132
  in U.S., 346, 354*f*, 355, 355*f*
Baiev, Nana (mother of KB), 12–18, 18*f*, 20,
    22, 23, 27, 34–35, 44, 58, 76, 86, 90,
    96, 105, 113, 116, 135, 161, 168, 243,
    267, 309, 321*f*, 354, 360*f*
  and her animals, 109
  and bombing of Grozny, 95
  and case against KB, 227
  and deserters, 140
  failing health, 361, 363
  after first war, 188
  and Hussein's move, 223
  illness, 320–21
  job, 54
  and KB's depression, 197, 198
  KB's responsibility for, 155, 207
  and KB's wife, 84
  marriage, children, 38–39
  naming KB's son, 98
  in new house, 67
  refused to take shelter, 110
  return home, 132, 335

  and safety of Razyat and Malika, 175, 177,
    182–83
  and second war, 242, 252, 254–55, 260,
    266, 275, 277–78, 279, 291, 300, 315
Baiev, Raya, *see* Tepsurkaev, Raya
Baiev, Razyat (sister of KB), 14, 15*f*, 20, 22,
    109, 135, 168, 309, 360*f*, 363
  birth of, 39
  bride stealing, 23–26
  and Chechen counterattack, 170, 171,
    174–75, 176, 177, 182, 183–84
  and deserters, 140
  education, 27
  employment, 192
  marriage, 223
  in old house, 67
  in parents' house, 137
  return home, 132
  and wife for KB, 77–78
Baiev, Rita (wife of Hussein), 58, 76, 223,
    242, 267, 336, 363
Baiev, Satsita (daughter of KB), 355*f*, 361
Baiev, Tamara (sister of KB), 14, 34, 39, 360*f*,
    363
Baiev, Zara (wife of KB), xxi, 85, 88, 90, 91,
    120, 127, 135, 140, 155, 158, 168, 182,
    197, 227, 318, 320, 321–22, 335, 347*f*
  in Baiev parents' house, 137
  children, 86–87, 89, 96–98, 201, 223, 361,
    362
  and deserters, 137, 141
  going to relatives in Urus–Martan, 109
  KB proposed to, 77–78
  and KB's depression, 198
  and KB's escape, 315
  KB's responsibility to, 207
  move to U.S., 345–46
  return home, 132, 335
  and second war, 242, 252, 254, 309, 316
  in U.S., 347, 354, 355*f*, 357
  wedding, 83–84
Baiev extended family, 336
Baiev family
  in Chechnya, 361
  in Ingushetia, 266, 335, 336, 337
  KB bringing to U.S., 345–47, 357
Baligova, Zarina, 259, 365–66
Baltic republics, 4, 68
Bamut, massacre at, 5, 133
Barayev, Arbi, 226, 227, 235–36, 237, 241,
    242, 244, 276, 285, 341, 351
  in Alkhan Kala, 278, 279
  and death of Adam, 342

Barayev, Arbi (*continued*)
  threatened to execute KB, 279–84, 288, 289
  thugs, 244, 245, 286
Barayev, Movsar, 351–53
Basayev, Shamil, 5, 26, 133–34, 171, 232,
    245, 365
  attack on Dagestan, 6, 246–47
  contender for president, 189
  evacuating Grozny, 293–94
  treated at Alkhan Kala hospital, 295*f*,
    296–98, 309
Baskhanov, Mokhdan, 224, 225–27, 229
Battle of Tours, 220
Ibn Batuta, 217–18
Bayram, 109–10
Belovetsky, Dima, 244–46, 320, 351–52, 365
bin Laden, Osama, 7
Birth defects, 69, 190–91, 223
Bisultanov, Abek, 192, 201, 247–48
Blood/bleeding, xv, xx, xxi, 108, 142, 169,
    181, 196
Blood vendettas, 41–42, 150–51, 158, 235,
    236
Bombs/bombing, 117, 260, 293
  Grozny, 93–96, 98, 100–101
Borovoi, Konstantin, 165
Boston, 330, 343–44, 347, 359
Bouckaert, Peter, 318, 319
Bribery/bribes, xix, 209, 225–26, 248, 253,
    263
Bride stealing, 23–26
Brzezinski, Zbigniew, 330
Budyonnovsk, 5, 134, 171
Burevestnik judo training camp, 44, 45, 46
Burial, xvi, 35, 41, 231–32
Burns, 143, 264
Bush, George W., 7

Capitalism, 81, 86, 201
Caspian Sea, 5, 11, 23, 36, 197
Caucasian Mountains, 1, 11, 272
Cellars, taking shelter in, 108, 260, 277, 288
Center for Multi-Cultural Human Services,
    332
Central Maternity Hospital, 96–97
Chalaeva, Markha, 259*f*, 307
Chapaev, Vakha, 19–20
Chechen field commanders, 293, 294, 298,
    319, 320
Chechen fighters, 101, 107, 108–9, 118, 124,
    135, 144, 163, 164, 263, 268*f*
  blowing up ammonia in Grozny, 260
  defending Alkhan Kala, 113

drove Russians from Grozny, 170–77, 187
escaped from Grozny, 293
in Grozny, 114, 117, 133
KB treated, 160
protecting KB, 228
transporting from hospital, 278–79, 282,
    301–2, 304–5
treated at Alkhan Kala hospital, 283, 294–97
Chechen government, 236, 353
  criminal case against KB, 224–30
Chechen language, 27, 188, 216
Checheno-Ingush Republic, 36, 39–40, 47,
    82
Chechens, 3, 61, 65, 160, 247, 352, 360, 361
  accused of collaboration with Nazis, 16, 36,
    39, 82
  blamed for Moscow bombings, 247–48
  collaboration with Russians, 237
  hostility toward, in Moscow, 78–79, 81–82,
    85, 202–3, 206–7
  Moscow's crackdown on, 247–49
  in New Jersey, 333–35
  postwar malaise, 189–91
  resistance by, 3–4, 6, 30
  return from exile, 15
  in security services, 184
Chechnya, xxi–xxii, 1–7, 32
  attack on, 277, 278
  dream of returning to, 358, 360, 361
  falling behind, 201–2
  fear gripping, 241–42
  free-trade zone, 86
  independence, 2, 4–5, 7, 74–75, 85, 177,
    246, 294, 343
  KB talking about, in U.S., 330–33
  letting world know about, 273–76, 290, 318
  memories of, 354
  news about, 316–17, 351
  political status of, 6, 187
  relations with Russia, 226
  situation in, deteriorating, 89–91
  spirit of, 99
  withdrawal of Russian troops from, 187–88
Checkpoints, 6, 140, 168, 175, 274, 277
  Alkhan Kala, 243–44
  Chechens surrounding, 176
  disappeared, 187
  KB stopped at, xix, 124–27, 128, 132–33,
    152–53, 314, 345
  Kulari, 313
  prisoners held at, 351
Cherkessiya, 242
Chernokozovo filtration camp, 304–5, 318

Chernomyrdin, Viktor, 5, 134, 187
Chernorechye, 123–24, 178, 179
Childbirth, 86, 361–62
Children, 181, 182, 188, 265–66, 353
    birth defects, 69, 190, 223
    burns in, 143
    in Moscow hospital, 203–4, 206
    shell-shocked, 254
    showing respect, 213
Civilians, xxii, 330
    deaths, xxi, 117, 123, 163, 181, 249
    shooting at, 107, 109
    suffering of, 174–75, 177, 351
    victims, 83, 261, 273
Clan (*teip*), 41, 94, 224
Cleanliness, 138, 251
Cobey, James, 327, 328
Committee of Soldiers' Mothers, 114, 139
Communist Party, 4, 53, 64, 68, 213, 315
Competitions, 20, 21, 26, 27, 43, 44, 46,
    49–50, 59–61, 64, 178, 245
    on Soviet team, 53–54
    in U.S., 349–51, 349f
Corpses/bodies, 4, 35, 175, 176–77, 178, 294
    finding, 43, 44
    identified and buried, 113, 114, 123
    paying for return of, 292
    selling to relatives, 242
Cosmetic surgery, 69, 72–73, 86, 91, 192–93
Criminal gangs, 232, 241, 246
Crimes, 83, 188–89, 233–37
Crimes of honor, 343
Culture (Chechen), 2, 27, 85, 188, 335, 361
Culture clash, 361–62

Dagestan, 2, 3, 6, 11, 70, 120, 127, 188, 197
    Basayev attack on, 246–47
    campaign against Islamic extremists, 241
Death, 268–69
    KB escaping, 120, 126–27, 159, 183, 243,
    288, 289
    preparing for, 158–59, 232
    telling patients truth and, 264
Denber, Rachel, 325, 326, 334f
Deportation (the), 12, 15, 27, 32, 33–41, 44,
    74, 177
Deserters, Russian, 136–41
Dinamo Stadium, 265
Divide-and-conquer policy, 3, 82, 246
Doctor, idea to become, 43–66
Doctor, KB's work as, xv, xvi–xvii, 66, 358
    first Russian-Chechen war, 106–7, 108,
    110–12, 113, 117, 121–22, 130, 131,

132, 142–49, 152, 160, 167–70, 174,
    181–82
    in Grozny, 69–73, 132, 142, 167
    post-first war, 187, 190–93, 202–3, 226,
    228
    private practice, 72, 73, 192–93
    second Russian-Chechen war, 244,
    249–51, 256–58, 260, 261–66, 269–73,
    277, 283–84, 289–90, 292, 294–300,
    306–8, 317
    treating patients in their homes, 121–22
    see also Treating all in need
Doctors, xviii, 69, 90, 117, 356
    Alkhan Kala hospital, 256, 258
    from Grozny, 298, 299, 300–301
    killed, 171
    leaving, 91, 100–101
    stayed at First City Emergency Hospital,
    101, 107
Doctors of the World, 106
Doctors Without Borders, 106, 191, 254
Dudayev, Dzhokhar, 5, 6, 74–75, 86, 165–66,
    193
Dudayev, Lecha, 293, 294, 298
Dzhafarev, Vakha, 144–47, 148

Elders, 23, 30–31, 188, 233, 236, 243
    Alkhan Kala, 105, 106, 107, 164
    family, 18, 23, 25
    lists of wounded and dead, 292
Ellis, Larry, 333, 334f
Ellis Island, 357–58
Emergency medicine, 91, 111–12, 142
Emirs, 280, 281, 282, 283
English language
    Baiev children learning, 346, 354, 355, 356
    KB lacked, xvi, 335, 343, 356
    KB learning, 204–5, 206, 337, 357
Ezirkhanov, Malizha, 230, 231, 232, 234–35
Ezirkhanov, Ruslan, 105, 108–9, 161–62,
    163, 164, 165, 316–17, 364f
    death and burial, 230–35

Federals/Federaly, 146, 161, 275, 277, 278,
    284, 291, 317, 341
Filtration camps, 6, 125, 154, 158, 237, 273,
    278, 303, 304–5, 316, 337, 351
    Ali in, 339
    Chernokozovo, 318
First City Emergency Hospital (Grozny), 69,
    73, 90, 132, 173
    doctors at, 101, 107
    KB surgeon at, 91–93, 94, 95–96, 101

Ford, Doug, 319, 332
Fourth City Hospital, 171, 250, 259
Frishberg, Ilya, 78, 85, 202
FSB (Federal Security Bureau), 141, 308, 310,
   314, 317, 325, 339, 341, 346
Funerals, 233–34

Gairbekova, Satsita, 171–72
Ganayev, Sultan, 264
Gangrene, 91, 142, 307
Gantimirov, Bislan, 301, 302, 303, 304–5
Gelayev, Ruslan, 298
Geneva Convention, 111, 332
Georgia, 2, 68
Glasnost, 4, 68
Gorbachev, Mikhail, 4–5, 16, 68, 73
Grachev, Pavel, 6, 100
Great Mosque, 218
Grozny, xvi, 6, 11, 68*f*, 83, 96, 97, 188, 197,
   251, 265, 353
   ammonia blown up in, 260
   after bombardment, 293, 293*f*
   bombing over, 93–96, 98, 100–101, 249
   Chechen counterattack on, 170–77, 187
   Chechen fighters in, 114, 117
   escape from, 167–84
   evacuating, 293–94
   hospitals, 187
   KB doctor in, 69–73, 132
   KB's return to, 66, 67–68
   KB's trip into, 122–29
   militarization of, 89–90
   puppet government in, 133
   rebuilding in, 188
   refugees from, 160
   ruins of, 242
   Russian attack on, 101, 107
   in Russian hands, 132
   Russian soldiers killed in, 277
Grozny All-Russian Junior Championship, 21,
   22
Grozny Nursing School, 27
Gulag Archipelago, The (Solzhenitsyn), 3–4
Gynecology, 51–53

Ibn al-Haytham, 221
Helicopter gunships, 107, 110, 171, 180–81
   firing on Russians, 113–14
   targeting KB's house, 114–15
Helsinki Final Act, 345
Herbal medicine, 17, 27, 265
Hippocrates, 222
Hippocratic Oath, xviii, 7, 47, 64, 90, 263

Hospitality tradition, 22, 136, 137, 183
Hostage taking, 1, 171–72, 351–53
House(s), 121
   Baiev family, 12, 132, 267
House(s), KB, 255
   attacked, 110, 132, 143, 266–67
   commandeered by Russians, 291
   patients in, 113
   struck by missile, 114–16, 116*f*
House of Wisdom, 220
Human rights abuses, 273, 354
Human Rights Monitors, 343
Human rights organizations, 274, 318, 319,
   343, 347
Human Rights Watch, 318, 320, 324, 325,
   330, 340, 343, 349

Idigov, Magomed, 170–71, 172, 174, 183
Idrisova, Rumani, xvii–xviii, xx, xxi, 257,
   259, 259*f*, 263, 266, 273, 283, 284, 297,
   299, 307, 308, 366
Immigration and Naturalization Service, 336,
   337, 345
Independence movements, 68
Ingushetia, 2, 11, 35, 82–83, 99, 139, 140,
   257, 308
   Baiev family in, 266, 335, 336, 337
   getting videotapes to, 309
   KB in, 317, 320
   refugee camps, 98
   seeking refuge in, 252, 253, 254
Institute of Cosmetology, 78, 79–81, 82,
   85–86, 192, 202
International community, 246, 248
International Junior Tournament, 53–54
International law, 106, 125
International Office of Migration, 345
Internet, 220, 221, 351
Ibn Isa, Ali, 221
Isaev, Akhmed, 250, 265
Isaev, Nuradi, 249–50, 257, 258, 261, 265,
   266, 277, 278, 289, 292, 295, 300, 365
Isaev, Vakha, 84, 132, 167–70
Islam, 27, 33, 74, 212, 213, 215
   exploitation of, 235
   five pillars of, 213
   history of, 220–22
Islamic extremists, 1, 241, 246, 331
Isparilov, Hunkar-Pasha, 298
Ivan the Terrible, 2

Journalists, 245, 246, 248–49, 293, 297, 318,
   320

Judo, 2, 19, 21, 43, 49, 59, 124, 245, 344
world championship, 349–50

Kaaba (Stone of Paradise), 218–20, 233
Kabzon Foundation, 203
Kadeer, Rebiya, 343
Kalinin, Mikhail, 40
Kazakhstan, 3, 11, 16, 41, 43–44, 192
deportation to, 33, 34, 38–39
KGB, 68, 80, 81, 141, 150, 350
asking KB to be informant, 59–61
control over sports, 53
Khanbiev, Oumar, 298
Khrushchev, Nikita, 4, 69, 82
Kidnappings, 188, 225, 228, 235, 242–44,
290–92
Moscow's role in, 244–46
Kirghizia, 3
Kizlyar, 146, 193
Kontraktniki, 119, 124–25, 126, 128, 133,
136, 171–72, 336, 337–38
civilians victims of, 261
looting and kidnapping, 242, 290–92
took KB, 285–88
treated by KB, 263
Koran, 73, 83, 84, 98, 158, 199, 200, 207,
212, 217, 220, 232, 281, 294, 298
Chechen traditions and, 213
commands regarding burial, xvi, 231
living by, 282
prayer for the dead, 179
Krasnoyarsk, 44–46, 49, 50, 51, 53, 54, 58,
59, 60, 61, 62, 64, 70, 76, 96, 132, 133,
135, 140, 188, 232, 263
authorities in, 69
Hussein in, 155, 223
KB's trip to, for treatment, 223–24
Krasnoyarsk Medical Institute, 45–46, 47, 49,
65, 66, 222
colleagues at, 62*f*
KB applying to, 47–49
KB student at, 50–53, 54–56, 59–65
Krasnoyarsk Sports Committee, 54
Kremlin, 82, 89, 193, 246, 260
Krivkov, Alexei Alexeyevich, 45–47, 49
Kulari, 278, 279, 284, 291, 303, 313
Kurbanov, Hasilbek, 105, 113, 302, 303, 304,
305, 306, 308

Lak'ad Djaakum (prayer), 179–80
Lasanov, Khamzat, 313
Latvia, 4
Lebed, Aleksandr, 6, 187

Lermontov, Mikhail, 81
Lesghinka, 13–15, 84, 99
"Little Switzerland," 28, 29*f*
Looting, 242, 261, 290–91

McCain, John, 330
Macwan, Martin Chhotubhai, 343
Magomadov, Said-Akhmad, 40–41, 43
Magommadov, Khamzat, 188
Makazhoi, 28–35, 38, 39, 41, 42, 43, 92, 93,
105, 155, 224
KB dreams about, 359
Malik, Abdul, 298
Mansur, Sheikh, 30
Marina (classmate girlfriend of KB), 56–58,
62–63, 64–65, 66
Marriage, 57–58, 76, 83
Martial arts, 2, 19–20
Maskhadov, Aslan, 6, 101, 176, 187, 230, 232,
241
elected president, 189
and kidnappings, 242–43
Maskhadov government, 225
Master of Sport, 49, 61
Mecca, 233
pilgrimage to, 210, 211–22, 223, 253
Medical equipment/supplies, 90, 328
KB's, 69, 73, 91, 106, 144, 167, 192, 248,
306
for the poor, 92
shortage of, 264–65
stockpiling, 242
Medical tents, 254
Medicine, Muslims and advances in, 221–22
Medina, 215
Melikyan, Karina, 317–18, 319, 320, 325
Men (Chechen), 18, 19, 22, 58
and childbirth, 361–62
martial arts, 2
relations with women, 191
Merited Doctor of Russia, 224–30
Mikhailovna, Tamara, 26–27, 364
Mines, 143, 167, 251, 294
Moscow, 61
bomb explosions in, 247, 249
crackdown on Chechens, 247–49
hostility toward Chechens, 78–79, 81–82
KB in, 85–86, 88, 91, 201–10, 319, 320,
322
and kidnappings, 244–46
theater hostages, 1, 351–53
Moscow–Baku highway, 99, 107, 182, 252
Moscow Health Department, 208

Mothers rescuing soldier sons, 135, 139–40
Mountain *shaitany*, 157
Mozdok, 315
Muhammad, 94, 212, 213, 215, 220
"Mukhadjereen" policy, 216
Mullah(s), 83, 84, 98
  KB consulting, regarding depression,
    198–200, 206, 209, 332
Muradov, Musa, 245, 320, 365
Muslim Declaration of Faith, 99
Muslim Empire, 220
Muslims, 73, 82, 84, 212, 294
  burial traditions, 38
  cleanliness, 138
  pilgrimage to Mecca, 211, 213
  racial profiling, 360
  scholars and scientists, 220–22
  traders and travelers, 217
Mutabbakani, Salakh, 215*f*, 216–18, 219–20
Mutabbakani, Zakiya, 216, 217*f*

National Jordanian Campaign Committee, 343
Nazis, 3, 16, 36, 39, 82
Nazran, 140, 252, 314, 318
Newton-Wellesley Hospital, 356
Nicholas I, 2, 3
Ninth City Hospital, 132, 134, 135, 142, 170,
    196, 203, 226, 243, 244, 249
NKVD secret police, 3, 35–36, 37
Nord-Ost Theater (Moscow), 1
North Caucasus, 3, 67, 74, 82, 131, 140, 241
North Ossetia, 82, 89, 315, 323
NTV independent television, 319, 353
Nurses, xvii, xviii, 149, 356
  Alkhan Kala hospital, 251, 256, 258–59, 261
  Atagi regional hospital, 117
  from Grozny, 298, 299, 300–301
  killed, 171, 172
  leaving, 100

Obstetrics, 51–53
Oil, 5, 68, 74
Okawa, Judy, 332–33, 337, 344
Operation Jihad, 170–77, 183, 278, 281
Ophthalmology, 221
Ozbek-Umarov, Hamid, 333–35, 334*f*
Ozbek-Umarov, Handan, 334, 334*f*

Partizansk, 66, 69
Peace agreement, 189
Peace march, 98–99
Peace talks, 134, 146
Pentagon, 7

Perestroika, 68, 73
Peter the Great, 2, 11, 30*f*
Petrov, Sasha, 320
Petrovna, Natasha, 203–5, 206
Physicians for Human Rights, 7, 318, 319,
    326, 330
Pisarenko, Mikhail, 80, 81
Plastic surgery, 65, 78, 142, 143–48, 190–91
Political asylum, 335, 336, 337, 342
Polyglukin, xvii, 147, 168, 242, 307
Poor (the), treating, 92
Post-traumatic stress disorder, 208–9, 361
Presidential elections, 6, 188–89
Presidential Guard, 227–28
Presidential Palace, 90, 127
Press, 319
Press conference, 318
Prisons, temporary, 351
Pronin, Vladimir, 352
Purges, 15, 35
Pushkin, Aleksander, 149
Putin, Vladimir, 6–7, 249, 251, 351

Raduyev, Salman, 146–48, 193–97, 194*f*, 226,
    229, 245, 364–65
  arrest of, 320
Rape, 131, 261, 262–63, 273
Al-Razi, 221
Rebuilding, 6, 187–200, 267
Reconstructive surgery, 69, 71–72, 78, 134
Red Cross, 106, 131, 254
  workers murdered, 6, 188–89
Refugee camps, 254
Refugees, 112, 178, 180
  first war, 106–7
  from Grozny, 160, 181, 293
  second war, 252, 253, 254
  women having babies, 250–51
Reichel, Chris, 333
Reuters, 273, 297, 309, 315, 318, 340
Rituals
  burial, 231–32
  before pilgrimage to Mecca, 212
Russia, 12, 13, 273
  attacks from, 95, 96
  and Chechnya, 2–7, 74, 99, 226, 351
  human rights violations, 330, 354
  relations with U.S., 330–31, 354
Russian-Afghan war, 124
Russian-Chechen wars, xv, xvi, 53
Russian-Chechen wars, first, 5, 6, 105–84
  cease-fire, 133, 134
  eve of, 89–101

Russian-Chechen wars, second, 241–55
  double jeopardy, 277–88
  Moscow theater hostages, 351–53
  need for political solution to, 353–54
  reaching a climax, 256–76
Russian émigré community in Boston, 344
Russian Empire, 11
Russian Federation, 5, 48, 75, 82
Russian military, 163–65, 187, 336
Russian military hospital, 134–35
Russian Ministry of Health, 208, 224, 229
Russian propaganda, 82, 146, 273
Russian Revolution, 5, 12, 15, 68, 216
Russian security services, 184, 187, 242, 246,
  309, 341, 345
  and Moscow bombings, 249
Russian soldiers/troops, xxii, xviii–xix
  advancing into Chechnya, 5, 98, 99–100,
  132
  attack on Grozny, 101, 107
  attacks on villages, 130–31
  buildup around Alkhan Kala, 161–65
  cigarettes for, 123, 133, 152, 153
  KB treating, 118–19, 283–84
  preparing to attack Chechnya, 241–42
  shooting their own men, 113–14
  withdrawal from Chechnya, 187–88
Russians
  and Chechens, 82
  Chechens collaborating with, 237
  driven out of Grozny, 170–77, 187
  in Grozny, 90, 98, 117
  politeness toward, 164–65

Saadi-Qotar, massacre at, 316–17
St. Petersburg, 3, 149, 151
Salekhov, Musa, 44–46, 45*f*, 47, 48, 50, 51,
  53, 364
Samashki, 5, 130–31, 133, 160, 161, 162,
  163, 164, 167, 276
Saponov, Larissa, *see* Baiev, Larissa
Saponov, Musa, 76–77, 78, 79, 79*f*, 80,
  81–82, 84, 87, 91, 201, 211, 363
Sasha (Russian doctor), 143, 147–55, 160,
  165
  condemned to death, 150–52
  KB's decision to save, 152–55, 162, 164
Saudi Arabia, 211–12, 215
Second World War, 3, 12, 15, 46, 57, 69, 107,
  334
  Dada in, 15–16, 35, 57
September 11, 2001, xiv, 7, 360
Shamanov, Vladimir, 261, 263, 275, 315

Shamanov Division, 261
Shamil, Imam, 3, 30–32, 74
Shariat court, 281, 282
Shpigun, Gennadi, 242
Siberia, 3, 66, 133
Snakes, xv, 46, 292, 340, 362
Snipers, 109, 113, 128, 143, 175, 176, 183,
  277, 294
Solzhenitsyn, Aleksandr, 3–4
Sombo, 2, 19, 49–50, 59
  world championship, 350–51
Soviet National Sombo team, 54*f*
Soviet Sports Committee, 48, 53, 59, 60–61
Soviet Union, 4, 43, 48, 53, 61, 62, 315
  atheistic, 220
  athletics in, 49
  ban on speaking Chechen, 216
  collapse of, 2, 15, 141
  medical centers, 69
Sports, 18, 19, 21, 22, 27, 43, 54
  KGB control over, 53
Stalin, Joseph, 3, 16, 19, 33, 35, 39, 40, 86
  divide-and-conquer policy, 3, 82
Stalin era, 69
Sufism, 99
Suleiman, 227–28, 229
Sunni Muslims, 212
Sunzha River, 11, 19, 20, 118, 175, 278, 279,
  284, 293

al-Tabari, 221–22
Tae kwon do, 2, 124
Taimaskhanov, Khassan, 43–44, 48, 78, 364
Takhtarov, Oleg, 349
Tarzan (dog), 93, 110, 115, 121
Tatarkin, Viktor, 349
Tejan-Cole, Abdul, 343
Temirkhanov, Ruslan, 308–10, 313–14, 316,
  366
Tepsurkaev, Adam (son of Raya), 182,
  273–74, 297, 309–10, 313, 315, 317,
  318, 336, 339
  killed, 340–42, 347–48
Tepsurkaev, Ali (son of Raya), 170, 182,
  183, 259, 259*f*, 273, 296*f*, 297, 298,
  309, 336
  arrested, 337–40, 348–49
  release of, 339–40, 341
  in U.S., 347–48, 355*f*, 363
  wounded, 341–42
Tepsurkaev, Lecha (husband of Raya), 24,
  25, 129, 170, 198, 337, 338, 342, 345,
  363

Tepsurkaev, Raya (sister of KB), 14, 34, 77, 115, 136, 170, 273, 337, 338, 342, 345, 360*f*, 363
  birth of, 39
  illness, 66, 67
Terrorism/terrorists, 1, 7, 187, 247, 248, 273, 351, 352, 353
  war against, 354
Tezyat, 233, 234
Torture, 175, 332, 338–39, 340
Traditions (Chechen), 41, 58, 59, 173, 233, 334, 335
  regarding animals, 110
  bride stealing, 23–26
  condolences after a death, 257
  hospitality, 136, 137, 183
  and Koran, 213
  marriage, 77, 78
  strain on, 191
  war and, 96, 150
  regarding women, 85
Treating all in need, xix, xxi, 7, 90–91, 118–19, 125, 126, 135, 263, 276, 282, 283–85, 309
Treating patients in their homes, 121–22, 142
Troitskoye, 252–53, 314, 320
Troshev, Gennadi, 26, 275
Tsarnaeva, Maret, xvi, xvii, xviii, xix, xxi
Tuberculosis, xxi, 189, 254
Turkey, 3, 86, 216

Udugov, Movladi, 189
Umazhova, Malika, 269–73, 275, 365
United States, 220, 252, 273
  hospital conditions in, 327–28
  KB's choice to stay in, 335–36
  KB going to, 319, 322, 323–24
  KB in, xxi, 7, 324–25, 327–36, 337, 340, 343–47, 349–51, 354–58, 359, 360, 361–62
  KB's volunteer work in, 356
  relations with Russia, 354
Urus-Martan, 108, 109, 111, 117, 119, 129, 153, 162, 226, 301
  Baievs return from, 132
  hospital at, 37–38, 112, 115, 121, 142, 146, 149, 168, 169, 182, 187, 300, 303, 304, 342
  radicals' operations in, 241
  Russian passport office in, 140
U.S. embassy (Moscow), 320
Utsieva, Maryam, 259, 365–66

Vartikovski, Liuba, 344
Videotapes, 273–74, 309, 313, 339
Villages, Russian attacks on, 130–31, 133
Vird, 94
Volunteers, 113, 249, 250, 251

Wahhabis, 212–13, 241, 285, 306
War(s), xxi–xxii, 15
  effects on people, 236–37, 348, 360–61
  see also Russian–Chechen wars
Washington, George, 344
Washington Hospital Center, 326, 327–29, 333
Weddings, 83
Wellstone, Paul, 330, 331*f*
Women, 58, 84–85, 212, 269
  demanding KB's release, 304, 305
  having babies, 250–51
  in keeping the peace, 150
  peace march, 98–99
  relations with men, 191
  role in war, 139–40
  saving KB's life, 287–88
World Cup Sombo Championship, 349*f*, 350–51
World Judo Championship, 349–50
World Trade Center, 7
World Youth Championship, 59
Wounded (the), 95, 108
  Alkhan Kala hospital, 111–12, 114, 115, 257–58, 277, 279, 282, 292, 294–95, 303, 306
  Alkhan Kala hospital: transporting, 300–303, 304–5
  from Grozny, 106–7
  treated at KB's home, 113

Yandarbiyev, Zelimkhan, 6, 166, 189
Yandarov, Salman, 226
Yeltsin, Boris, 5, 6, 133, 189, 251
Yenisei River, 44, 45, 46, 64
Yermolov, Alexei, 2, 67, 131
Yesayev, Nozhu, 41
Yusupov, Ruslan, 97, 98

Zachistka, 278, 285, 288, 290, 291, 300, 301, 306, 336, 351
al–Zahrawi, 221
Zakayev, Akhmed, 189, 365
Zavgayev, Doku, 188–89
Zhabirov, Muslim, 206
Zhaparovna, Khava, 26, 364
Zikr, 99, 234